WALTER PATER AND THE BEGINNINGS OF ENGLISH STUDIES

Walter Pater's significance for the institutionalisation of English studies at British universities in the nineteenth century is often overlooked. Addressing the importance of his volume *Appreciations* (1889) in placing English literature in both a national and an international context, this book demonstrates the indebtedness of the English essay to the French tradition and brings together the classic, the Romantic, the English, and the European. With essays on drama, prose, and poetry, from Shakespeare and Browne to Lamb, Coleridge, Wordsworth, and Pater's contemporaries Rossetti and Morris, *Appreciations* exemplifies ideals of aesthetic criticism formulated in Pater's first book, *Studies in the History of the Renaissance* (1873). Subjectivity pervades Pater's essays on the English authors, while bringing out their exceptional qualities in a manner reaching far into twentieth-century criticism. This title is part of the Flip it Open Programme and may also be available Open Access. Check our website Cambridge Core for details.

CHARLES MARTINDALE is Professor of Latin Emeritus at the University of Bristol. He has published over a wide field, with particular emphasis on English–Classics literary relations, theoretical approaches to literature – in particular, reception theory – and Kantian aesthetics and the importance of 'beauty'. He is the author of four books, and editor or co-editor of fourteen collections.

LENE ØSTERMARK-JOHANSEN is Professor of English at the University of Copenhagen. She is the author of *Walter Pater and the Language of Sculpture* (2012) and of *Walter Pater's European Imagination* (2022). She has edited Pater's *Imaginary Portraits* for the Oxford Collected Works of Walter Pater (2019).

ELIZABETH PRETTEJOHN is Professor of History of Art at the University of York. Her recent research centres on relationships between the arts of past and present, explored in *The Modernity of Ancient Sculpture* (2012) and *Modern Painters, Old Masters: The Art of Imitation from the Pre-Raphaelites to the First World War* (2017).

Nineteenth-century literature and culture have proved a rich field for interdisci-plinary studies. Since 1994, books in this series have tracked the intersections and tensions between Victorian literature and the visual arts, politics, gender and sexuality, race, social organisation, economic life, technical innovations, scientific thought – in short, culture in its broadest sense. Many of our books are now classics in a field which since the series' inception has seen powerful engagements with Marxism, feminism, visual studies, post-colonialism, critical race studies, new historicism, new formalism, transnationalism, queer studies, human rights and liberalism, disability studies and global studies. Theoretical challenges and historiographical shifts continue to unsettle scholarship on the nineteenth century in productive ways. New work on the body and the senses, the environment and climate, race and the decolonisation of literary studies, biopolitics and materiality, the animal and the human, the local and the global, politics and form, queerness and gender identities, and intersectional theory is re-animating the field. This series aims to accommodate and promote the most interesting work being undertaken on the frontiers of nineteenth-century literary studies, connecting the field with the urgent critical questions that are being asked today. We seek to publish work from a diverse range of authors, and stand for anti-racism, anti-colonialism and against discrimination in all forms.

A complete list of titles published will be found at the end of the book.

WALTER PATER AND THE BEGINNINGS OF ENGLISH STUDIES

EDITED BY

CHARLES MARTINDALE

University of Bristol

LENE ØSTERMARK-JOHANSEN

University of Copenhagen

ELIZABETH PRETTEJOHN

University of York

CAMBRIDGE
UNIVERSITY PRESS

Shaftesbury Road, Cambridge CB2 8EA, United Kingdom

One Liberty Plaza, 20th Floor, New York, NY 10006, USA

477 Williamstown Road, Port Melbourne, VIC 3207, Australia

314–321, 3rd Floor, Plot 3, Splendor Forum, Jasola District Centre, New Delhi – 110025, India

103 Penang Road, #05-06/07, Visioncrest Commercial, Singapore 238467

Cambridge University Press is part of Cambridge University Press & Assessment,
a department of the University of Cambridge.

We share the University's mission to contribute to society through the pursuit of
education, learning and research at the highest international levels of excellence.

www.cambridge.org
Information on this title: www.cambridge.org/9781108835893

DOI: 10.1017/9781108869447

First published 2023

A catalogue record for this publication is available from the British Library.

Library of Congress Cataloging-in-Publication Data
NAMES: Martindale, Charles, editor. | Prettejohn, Elizabeth, editor. | Østermark-Johansen, Lene,
1963- editor.
TITLE: Walter Pater and the beginnings of English studies / edited by Charles Martindale, Elizabeth
Prettejohn, Lene Østermark-Johansen.
DESCRIPTION: Cambridge ; New York, NY : Cambridge University Press, 2023. | Series: Cambridge
studies in nineteenth-century literature and culture | Includes bibliographical references and index.
IDENTIFIERS: LCCN 2023013986 (print) | LCCN 2023013987 (ebook) | ISBN 9781108835893
(hardback) | ISBN 9781108798921 (paperback) | ISBN 9781108869447 (epub)
SUBJECTS: LCSH: Pater, Walter, 1839-1894–Criticism and interpretation. | Pater, Walter,
1839-1894–Influence. | Criticism–Great Britain–History–19th century.
CLASSIFICATION: LCC PR5137 .W33 2023 (print) | LCC PR5137 (ebook) | DDC 824/.8–dc23/eng/
20230523
LC record available at https://lccn.loc.gov/2023013986
LC ebook record available at https://lccn.loc.gov/2023013987

ISBN 978-1-108-83589-3 Hardback

Contents

v

Figures

Cover image Dante Gabriel Rossetti, *Mariana*, 1870, oil on canvas,
109.8 × 90.5 cm, Aberdeen Art Gallery & Museums.

The cover image relates to two essays by Pater, one on Rossetti himself
(whom Pater described in 1880 as 'the greatest man we have among us, in
point of influence upon poetry, and perhaps painting'), the other on
Shakespeare's *Measure for Measure*. Pater shared the unusual enthusiasm
of the Pre-Raphaelite group for this play, and it is likely that two Pre-
Raphaelite works helped inspire him to write about it: this painting by
Rossetti (which we know was on the easel in Rossetti's studio, where Pater
must have seen it, between 1868 and its delivery in 1870 to William
Graham), and William Holman Hunt's *Claudio and Isabella*, which Pater
had the opportunity to see in 1865, and mentioned in print a year later,
the strong memory of which informs the passage in the essay where he
emphasises the relationship between Claudio and Isabella. He also
highlights the page's song to Mariana, almost certainly under the
abiding impression of the Rossetti. Rossetti is the modern British artist
most important to Pater from the time of his first visits to Rossetti's house
in Cheyne Walk in the late 1860s through to the portrait of Marguerite
de Navarre as Jane Morris in *Gaston de Latour*. We know that Pater had
seen works by Rossetti, with great admiration, from the reference in 'The
School of Giorgione'; indeed Mariana would be of particular relevance,
partly because of the music-making subject and partly because it is very
much in Rossetti's 'Giorgionesque' manner. The other painters who were
particularly significant for Pater – Solomon, Burne-Jones, Legros,
Whistler – were all members of the circle around Rossetti, the imaginative
leader of this whole artistic movement.

Contributors

STEPHEN BANN, CBE, FBA is Emeritus Professor of History of Art at the University of Bristol

SCARLETT BARON is Associate Professor of English at University College London

LUISA CALÈ is Reader in Romantic and Nineteenth-Century Literature and Visual Culture at Birkbeck College, University of London

KENNETH DALEY is Associate Professor of English at Columbia College Chicago

STEFANO EVANGELISTA is Professor of English and Comparative Literature at the University of Oxford and a Fellow of Trinity College

MICHAEL D. HURLEY is Professor of Literature and Theology at the University of Cambridge, and a Fellow and Director of Studies in English at Trinity College

CHARLES W. MAHONEY is Professor of English at the University of Connecticut, Storrs

CHARLES MARTINDALE is Emeritus Professor of Latin at the University of Bristol

STACEY MCDOWELL is Assistant Professor of English and Comparative Literary Studies at the University of Warwick

FERGUS MCGHEE is currently Departmental Lecturer in English at the University of Oxford, and tutor in English at Corpus Christi College

KATHRYN MURPHY is Fellow and Tutor in English at Oriel College, Oxford

LENE ØSTERMARK-JOHANSEN is Professor of English Literature and Art in the Department of English, Germanic and Romance Studies at the University of Copenhagen

ELIZABETH PRETTEJOHN is Professor of History of Art and Head of Department at the University of York

MARCUS WAITHE is Professor of Literature and the Applied Arts in the Faculty of English at the University of Cambridge and a Fellow of Magdalene College

ROSS WILSON is Associate Professor of Criticism in the Faculty of English at the University of Cambridge and a Fellow of Emmanuel College

ALEX WONG is a College Associate Lecturer and Director of Studies for English Literature at St John's College, Cambridge

Preface

In our earlier collection *Pater the Classicist: Classical Scholarship, Reception, and Aestheticism* (Oxford University Press 2017) we sought to direct detailed critical attention to Walter Pater's writings on classical antiquity, including his book on Plato and his essays on Greek sculpture, which have been largely neglected. We aimed to show that Pater made a significant contribution to classical studies and to combat the idea that he has little to teach us today about his objects of study. Although himself a classicist, Pater also wrote widely about English literature, and collected many of his principal essays on the subject in *Appreciations*, first published in 1889. These essays too have not in general been accorded detailed analysis; all our contributors, whatever their differences of view, agree that Pater has novel, interesting, and important things to say about English authors that merit our serious attention. There is currently no systematic treatment of Pater as a student of English literature, despite its importance to him and his enormous sophistication as a literary critic; this volume aims to fill that gap.

For its realisation *Pater the Classicist* required bringing together Paterians and Victorianists with classicists, including classical philosophers and students of ancient art and archaeology, since in general classicists do not read Pater and Paterians are seldom experts in matters classical. For our new project we adopted a similar research methodology, essential in our view in the case of writings which are so wide-ranging, cosmopolitan, and interdisciplinary. We assembled a group of Pater specialists, Victorianists, and broad-minded scholars who specialise in the authors Pater wrote about, and who are sympathetic to reception studies and the view that Pater has much that is significant to tell us about these writers. In July 2018 we held a two-day workshop in Oxford for contributors (generously supported by the University's English Faculty and by the Department of History of Art at York, and ably managed by Alexandra Gushurst-Moore) to establish a clear sense of the scope and aims of the project and habits of intellectual interchange. Three of the participants, Nicholas Halmi, Catherine Maxwell, and Daniel Tyler, have in the event been unable to contribute to the resulting publication, but assisted in its framing. Stefano Evangelista (one of the editors of *Pater the Classicist*) has not only contributed his own chapter, but has advised on the project throughout, in respect of design and scope. At the outset we received excellent and formative advice from James Williams and David Hopkins. We would also like to thank our anonymous readers for their suggestions and Bethany Thomas, our ever-helpful editor at Cambridge University Press.

   The principal writings that deal with English literature treated in this volume are, in the order of their composition (with dates of subsequent publications in brackets), as follows:

1866 'Coleridge's Writings', rewritten as essentially a new essay 'Coleridge' for T. H. Ward's *The English Poets*, 1880, and the two combined for *Appreciations*, 1889 (hereafter *App.*)

1868 'Poems by William Morris', reworked as 'Aesthetic Poetry', *App.*, 1889, deleted from the second edition of 1890, and never thereafter republished

1874 'A Fragment on *Measure for Measure*', revised as 'Measure for Measure', *App.*
      'On Wordsworth', revised as 'Wordsworth', *App.*

1876 'Romanticism', revised as 'Postscript', *App.*

1878 'The Character of the Humourist: Charles Lamb', revised as 'Charles Lamb', *App.*

1883 'Dante Gabriel Rossetti', in Ward's *The English Poets* vol. 4 (second edition), revised in *App.*

1885 'On *Love's Labours Lost*', revised as 'Love's Labours Lost', *App.*

1886 'Sir Thomas Browne', revised in *App.*

1888 'Style', revised in *App.*

1889 'Shakespeare's English Kings', revised in *App.*

There are also some pieces collected in *Essays from 'The Guardian'* (1908; vol. 10 of the New Library Edition), including reviews of a study of Robert Browning; *The Picture of Dorian Gray*; *Robert Elsmere*; and 'Four Books for Students on English Literature', among them Saintsbury's *Specimens of English Prose Style*; together with some uncollected items.

   It is worth stressing that the collection, in this too like *Pater the Classicist*, is not a series of essays on disparate subjects loosely attached to a principal theme, but a single, focused project: a re-examination of Pater as a critic of English literature in the light of the development of English studies and literary criticism during the period. In that sense it might be better regarded as a book with multiple authors than as an essay collection. Because no one scholar would have the necessary expertise or range required for the project, its successful achievement required such multiple authorship. (Of course one result of this is that there are differences of view and of emphasis in different chapters, but we regard this as an enrichment, not a defect.)

This is moreover an excellent moment for writing about Pater since Oxford University Press's fully annotated new Pater edition is bound to raise his profile and increase serious interest in his work; the first volumes have now appeared. Two of its team of editors are contributing to this volume: Kenneth Daley (*Appreciations*) and Lene Østermark-Johansen (*Imaginary Portraits*). There is evidence, from conferences and elsewhere, that younger scholars are increasingly attracted to Pater's writings. There is also a growing interest in the essay as a literary form and in style, including prose style.

The collection, while its primary focus is on Pater's essays on particular English authors, helps to situate those essays in various wider contexts, including developments in literary criticism and scholarship, and the gradual process that established English as a university subject. Pater, far from being a disengaged recluse, constantly engaged, if often in a characteristically covert way, with the views of his Victorian contemporaries, challenging (if only by implication) dominant views on critical and artistic practice, and on matters including religion and morality. The volume relates his work to other Victorian critics, including Arnold, Newman, and Saintsbury. And it offers material for the study of the development of English as a discipline as well as possible paths not taken (the relationship between English and Classics; the development of literary criticism and its styles; English and the literatures of continental Europe). The volume also contains some reflections on the reception of Pater: Pater as an imaginative writer (and thus himself the object of criticism); Pater and the leading anglophone modernists, including Woolf, Joyce, and T. S. Eliot (Pater is a presence in almost all of them, though often occluded); Pater and the deconstructionists (after the High Modernist period Pater falls to a significant extent into disfavour, but there is an extraordinary revival with the Yale critics, including J. Hillis Miller and Harold Bloom).

Quotations from the writings of Pater are cited within the text in abbreviated form (see xv–xvi for a list of abbreviations). Documentation for all references and citations is given in full in the notes to individual chapters. (For books, the place of publication is London unless otherwise specified.) Our volume also contains, at the end, a specially compiled general bibliography on the subject: this provides overall guidance on publications about Pater and English Literature.

Our group of scholar-critics includes established academics who are leading authorities in their field and those who are nearer the beginning of their career. Our volume is designed not only for enthusiasts for Pater but also for anyone interested in 'Eng. Lit.' and the way it is written about, the history of criticism, and the institutional history of English as a discipline and object of study. We hope that our inclusive, outward-facing, broad-minded approach would also have met with the approval of that most cosmopolitan of writers on English literature: Walter Horatio Pater.

Charles Martindale
Lene Østermark-Johansen
Elizabeth Prettejohn
York and Copenhagen, 2022

Abbreviations

Quotations from the writings of Pater (an inveterate reviser of his own works) are taken, unless otherwise explicitly stated, from the edition of *The Renaissance: The 1893 Text* by Donald L. Hill (Berkeley and Los Angeles 1980) and, for the rest, the New Library Edition published by Macmillan in 1910. We also give references for the published volumes of *The Collected Works of Walter Pater*, general eds Lesley Higgins and David Latham (Oxford 2019–), vol. 3 *Imaginary Portraits*, ed. Lene Østermark-Johansen; vol. 4 *Gaston de Latour*, ed. Gerald Monsman; vol. 8, *Classical Studies*, ed. Matthew Potolsky.

The following abbreviations for Pater's works are used throughout:

'AP'	'Aesthetic Poetry', in the first edition of *Appreciations* (1889), 213–27 (thereafter replaced by 'Feuillet's "La Morte"')
App.	*Appreciations: With an Essay on 'Style'* (New Library Edition, vol. 5)
'CW'	'Coleridge's Writings', *Westminster Review* n.s. 29 (January 1866), 106–32
CW	*The Collected Works of Walter Pater* (Oxford)
Essays	*Essays from 'The Guardian'* (vol. 10)
Gast.	*Gaston de Latour: An Unfinished Romance* (vol. 9)
GS	*Greek Studies: A Series of Essays* (vol. 7)
Houghton MS	Walter Pater's manuscripts held in the Houghton Library, Harvard University, bMSEng 1150
IP	*Imaginary Portraits* (vol. 4)

ME	*Marius the Epicurean* (vols 2–3) (In citations from *Marius*, i and ii refer to the two volumes of the novel; chapter numbers are also given.)
MS	*Miscellaneous Studies: A Series of Essays* (vol. 8)
PP	*Plato and Platonism: A Series of Lectures* (vol. 6)
Ren.	*The Renaissance: Studies in Art and Poetry* (Hill edition)

Other abbreviations used in the notes are:

Arnold, *Prose*	Matthew Arnold, *The Complete Prose Works*, ed. R. H. Super, 9 vols (Ann Arbor, MI 1960–73)
Critical Heritage	*Walter Pater: The Critical Heritage*, ed. R. M. Seiler (1980)
Inman (1981)	Billie Andrew Inman, *Walter Pater's Reading: A Bibliography of His Library Borrowings and Literary References, 1858–1873* (New York and London 1981)
Inman (1990)	Billie Andrew Inman, *Walter Pater and His Reading: 1874–1877: With a Bibliography of His Library Borrowings, 1878–1894* (New York and London 1990)
Letters	*Letters of Walter Pater*, ed. Lawrence Evans (Oxford 1970)
Ricks, 'Misquotation'	Christopher Ricks, 'Walter Pater, Matthew Arnold and Misquotation', in *The Force of Poetry* (Cambridge 1984), 392–416

Introduction: Pater and English Literature

Charles Martindale and Elizabeth Prettejohn

In comparison with other Victorian critics, Walter Pater is, we could say, both too well known and barely known at all. 'She is older than the rocks among which she sits'; 'to burn always with this hard, gem-like flame'; 'All art constantly aspires towards the condition of music' – few critics are so instantly recognisable in fragmentary quotation. Oscar Wilde's character Gilbert in 'The Critic as Artist' murmurs phrases from Walter Pater's description of the *Mona Lisa* whenever he visits the Louvre, in antiphony with an unnamed friend; perhaps the implication is that any friend of an aesthete must have the passage by heart. W. B. Yeats divided the same passage into lines of free verse to print it as the first item in *The Oxford Book of Modern Verse* (1936), so that it becomes the initiating text for twentieth-century poetry. No aesthetic mantra is more vulnerable to caricature than the 'hard, gem-like flame' – unless it be the 'condition of music', so often taken simplistically (and anachronistically) as an endorsement of formalism.

Few authors of such obvious historical importance, on the other hand, have so high a proportion of their writings forgotten or neglected. These largely overlooked works include the essays on archaic Greek sculpture, the unfinished novel *Gaston de Latour*, Pater's last book *Plato and Platonism* (significantly taken far more seriously in continental Europe than in Britain), not to mention such distinctly obscure pieces as that small-scale masterpiece, 'Sir Thomas Browne'. Truly close analysis of Pater's writings, complex and subtle and multi-dimensional as they are, tends to be confined to *The Renaissance* in particular and, to a lesser extent, the fiction.

Pater and English Studies

In nineteenth-century Britain, Classics was the premier university humanistic discipline dealing with matters literary. In the twentieth century, as everyone knows, it was replaced in that position by English.[1] Pater, though himself a Classics don at Oxford who published widely on classical topics as well as art history, also wrote extensively about English literature (nine substantial essays on individual writers or works, plus others on literary topics, and a good number of short reviews). Pater collected most of his essays on English authors in *Appreciations* (1889). Although *Appreciations* is a central concern, our book is not just about that volume. Rather it explores the importance of Pater's writings on English literature in the context of literary criticism and educational developments more generally. And it shows how Pater's approach was radically informed by what we might call his 'cosmopolitanism', and why that mattered and still matters – perhaps more so today than ever.

In 1886 the *Pall Mall Gazette* – in connection with the campaign by John Churton Collins to establish a School of English at the University of Oxford – invited a number of leading intellectuals (including Matthew Arnold, William Morris, Max Müller, and Pater), and of the great and the good of the time, to comment on whether it might be desirable for universities to provide systematic instruction in English literature and, if so, in what form. In his response Pater, although in general liberal and progressive in educational matters, like several others sat on the fence, with three main arguments for maintaining the status quo. English as a university subject might kill off Classics (a prediction that indeed in the longer term proved correct); it might encourage lazy intellectual habits; examinations might destroy the students' natural enjoyment of their native literature. However, Pater's response shows his commitment to literary study broadly conceived, though still within the context of Classics (Churton Collins too argued that Classics and English should work closely together, and that classical texts should feature on an English syllabus). While insisting that the study of classical literature has proved 'effective for the maintenance of what is excellent in our own', Pater adds:

> much probably might be done for the expansion and enlivening of classical study itself by a larger infusion into it of those literary interests which modern literature, in particular, has developed; and a closer connection of it, if this be practicable, with the study of great modern works (classical literature and the literature of modern Europe having, in truth, an organic unity); above all, by the maintenance, at its highest possible level, of the purely literary character of those literary exercises in which the classical examination mainly consists.[2]

One should note the insistent repetition of the word 'literary', and ask what precisely Pater might have meant by it in connection with 'the classical examination'. If we look at the papers for classical 'Mods' (Moderations, the first part of *Literae Humaniores*, focused on Greek and Latin literature) for the 1860s through to the 1880s, we find that most of them are devoted to a single author (in addition to literary figures, there are some historians, as well as Plato and Aristotle).[3] In the earlier period there are just passages for translation and brief notes, but later general questions were added, some of them 'literary'. In due course more general papers appear, the first called 'Questions on Language and Literature', and subsequently a 'General Paper' and some topic papers (including 'History of Greek Drama', 'History of Roman Poetry', 'History of Greek Drama with Aristotle's *Poetics*', 'History of Augustan Literature'). There were also papers on philology, prose and verse composition, and the Bible. What one might call literary-critical questions are in the minority; questions tend rather to be about the text, manuscripts, metre, language, dialect, chronology, the life of the author, or factual details relating to the works. Examples of rather more 'literary' questions include these:

What constitutes originality in a poet? Discuss this with reference to Virgil. (1876)

'The Latin poets had all a strong sense of their own personality'. Show how this sense comes out in the various authors and account for the difference between the Greek and Roman writers. (1878)

'There is no morality in Homer' 'There is no chivalry in Virgil' Discuss these statements. (1886, from 'General Paper')

What are the most remarkable points in Sophocles's treatment of female character? (1887)

Poetry, says Milton, 'should be simple, sensuous, impassioned'. Would you regard the poems of Catullus as fulfilling the requirement of this dictum? (1888)

Interestingly there are some questions concerned with reception, or the classical tradition, or general literary issues, including these:

What are the chief points of contrast between the Greek epic and modern poetry? (1873)

Notice any traces of Virgil's influence on the greatest English poets (1886)

Compare classical Roman poetry with that of any modern nation as a vehicle for (1) sentiment (2) description (3) delineation of character (1887)

What fluctuations have there been in the esteem in which Virgil has
been held from his own time down to the present day? Trace causes,
where you can. (1888)

Pater also might well have regarded translation as a literary activity. He
himself as a student at Queen's College 'every day ... translated a page
from some prose writer—Tacitus, Livy, Plato, Aristotle, Goethe, Lessing,
Flaubert or Sainte-Beuve'.[4] He continued the practice into later life, and
included passages of translation (always in prose, even when translating
verse), as elegant as they are accurate, in his publications. We can see this
again as an aspect of his cosmopolitanism.

   The arguments in Oxford around a School of English concerned not
only its desirability but also its character if established, whether the
emphasis should be on language and philology or literary criticism
(famously derided by one opponent, Edward Augustus Freeman, Regius
Professor of Modern History, as 'mere chatter about Shelley'). Churton
Collins, appalled by the amateurish character of the Clark lectures given in
Cambridge in 1884 by Pater's friend and biographer Edmund Gosse,
wanted academic study that was both rigorous and literary, not merely
linguistic.[5] However, the holder of the first Merton Professorship of
English Language and Literature at Oxford (created in 1885, before the
School) was a philologist, Arthur Napier, later Rawlinsonian Professor of
Anglo-Saxon; only from 1904 did Oxford have a Professor of English, Sir
Walter Raleigh, whose primary concern was with literary criticism. Pater,
while always interested in matters philological, would have been unlikely
to favour any version of English that was philological only. In the event
Schools of English were not established in Oxford and Cambridge until
1894 and 1917 respectively. In 1911 Cambridge, after an internal delib-
eration lasting more than thirty years, made a professorial appointment for
'English Literature from the age of Chaucer', intended to 'promote the
study in the University of the subject of English Literature', and to 'treat
this subject on literary and critical rather than on philological and linguistic lines'.[6] In Pater's own day schools already existed in London
(University College appointed a Professor of English in 1828, King's
College in 1830) as well as in Scotland. And in due course Pater's prose
was itself subjected to criticism of an academic kind. For example, in
1933 Vernon Lee, a writer whom Pater knew and admired, and who
herself conducted a form of 'practical criticism' well before its 'invention'
by I. A. Richards, selected a page from *Marius the Epicurean* for the closest
of close reading, in what in effect was an addendum to her previous

publication *The Handling of Words* (1923), a discussion of prose writing from De Quincey to Henry James.[7]

The passionate late-Victorian debate about English Studies and what form it should take if more widely established as a university discipline, along with the various modes of literary enquiry pursued in this period, had an obvious importance for the formation of the subject and how it was taught, and helps, at least to an extent, to account for the shape it takes today. How would an appropriate measure of rigour be assured? How far would English follow the lines long established for Classics (not a few of its first teachers had themselves been trained as classicists, and the first Professor of English at Cambridge was the classical scholar A. W. Verrall)? Would it focus on language and philology or on literature (in practice it rarely managed to do both satisfactorily)? Would it stress history or critical evaluation? Would it help to build a national identity and ensure a supply of national guardians and public servants; or encourage an understanding of Britain's relationship with the other literatures of Europe and the world? Would it pioneer new models for understanding? Would it develop an aesthetic temper, an ability to discriminate; or serve as a secular alternative to religion, a role for literary study envisaged by Matthew Arnold and others? (Pater's own views on Christianity are somewhat elusive, but he was always interested in the content and lifestyle and history and cultural embeddedness of Christianity and not just its 'aesthetics'.[8]) These are questions that are with us still.

Pater's essays on English Literature are better known than his most neglected writings, but they have scarcely received the close attention they merit as accounts of their subject. Collectively this volume's chapters demonstrate the importance of Pater as a major contributor to the serious study of English literature (just as he was with regards to Classics and Art History) and as, in the words of Jerome McGann, 'the strongest as well as the subtlest literary-critical intelligence of the High Victorian period'.[9] While many of the chapters look closely at particular essays or groups of essays, they also collectively cast light on a number of broader issues: how Pater's way of writing about English literature relates to that of others, both at the time and later; the role he plays in the history of criticism and of English studies (histories that are much less closely intertwined in the nineteenth century than subsequently); and what reading Pater on a particular author tells us about reading that author more generally in the context of the author's reception history.

Appreciations, like its predecessor *The Renaissance*, is made up of essays previously published in periodicals, though carefully revised for their new context in book form. And, again like its predecessor, it is not simply a random ad hoc assemblage in the manner of many Victorian collections, but a carefully contrived whole, in which the individual essays speak to each other and for an overall vision of English literature and its history (see Chapter 1). *Appreciations* comprises a series of essays on individual writers, but these are bookended by two pieces of general import: 'Style', which addresses the central question of what constitutes good writing in both prose and verse (see Chapter 6), and 'Postscript', a revised version of an essay originally called 'Romanticism', but which is rather a discussion of two significant literary phenomena, classicism and romanticism, and which takes us into important issues about literary history and periodisation (see Chapter 5). The word 'Romanticism' in its current valence to describe an early nineteenth-century literary movement that we might trace back to the publication of *Lyrical Ballads* in 1798 (followed by a new edition in 1800, with Wordsworth's 'Preface') was a comparatively late import from Germany into the English critical lexicon. One of the first anglophone authors to use the continental category in this way was Thomas Budd Shaw in 1849, who argued that Scott was 'the type, sign, or measure of the first step in literature towards romanticism', and called Byron 'the greatest of the romanticists'.[10] For Pater the word can be applied both to a particular period in English letters and to a general tendency in all periods, whenever there is 'the addition of strangeness to beauty' ('Postscript', *App.*, 246), a tendency that he is at some pains to approve and show as active in his own day. Pater is always interested in history and literary history, though not in the positivistic way demanded by many of his detractors both at the time and subsequently. In response to criticism by Emilia Pattison and others that it was not a responsible history,[11] Pater changed the title of his first collection from *Studies in the History of the Renaissance* to *The Renaissance: Studies in Art and Poetry*. Clearly in so far as they are 'histories', both *The Renaissance* and *Appreciations* are fragmentary histories (though the latter contains extended discussions of works from every post-medieval century except the eighteenth[12]); but it does not follow that Pater was not interested in history and its relation to art and literature. However, in both cases that interest co-exists with 'aesthetic criticism' (as the title *Appreciations* suggests). The 'Preface' to *The Renaissance* offers a succinct but exceptionally lucid account of what Pater means by 'aesthetic criticism', but it also makes apparent that he wishes to offer more general thoughts on the Renaissance as a historical phenomenon and how we might think about it (paragraphs 6–8); in his words, the studies 'touch what I think the chief points in that complex, many-sided movement' (*Ren.*, xxii).

Pater's Critical Project: Aesthetic Criticism

What, then, is Pater's larger critical project, and why should we value it today? Pater's detractors, who include T. S. Eliot and Eliot's admirer Christopher Ricks, typically accuse him of two failings: a tendency to subjectivism amounting at times to solipsism; and an espousal of belletrism, vagueness, and lack of critical rigour. The two charges, in our view, miss their mark and they are linked; the answer to them lies partly in Pater's philosophical commitments, and in particular his careful attention to the implications of philosophical aesthetics, then still a relatively youthful discipline with its origins in eighteenth-century Germany. One purpose of our earlier volume, *Pater the Classicist*, was to combat the view that Pater's essays tell us little or nothing about his objects of study, only about what Ricks calls his 'fugitive noosphere'.[13] Eliot, in 'Hamlet and his Problems', makes a – moderately – effective joke, in his *de haut en bas* critical mode, about the matter. Having reprimanded 'that most dangerous type of critic: the critic with a mind which is naturally of the creative order' for finding in Hamlet 'a vicarious existence for their own artistic realization' and for substituting their Hamlet for Shakespeare's, he concludes the paragraph: 'We should be thankful that Walter Pater did not fix his attention on this play.'[14] (While we may not agree with Coleridge's characterisation of Hamlet, it surely says something significant about the work, and its representation of subjectivity, that so many readers have subsequently in effect declared 'I am Hamlet'.) Even among Pater specialists some are too sympathetic to reading his work primarily as oblique autobiography. In particular, gay and queer studies have contributed a great deal to a more correct and nuanced evaluation of Pater; but there is also danger in concentrating too much on a writer's supposed sexuality in interpreting his or her work – a version surely of the old 'biographical fallacy' (the view that a work of art is best explained in terms of the artist's life and character).

One of the essays in *Appreciations*, 'Charles Lamb', is especially instructive in this regard (see Chapter 12). Here it is particularly clear that there is an unusual degree of identification, even elision, of author and subject. This is partly because of Pater's admiration for Lamb as an essayist, since the essay – along with its fictional equivalent the 'imaginary portrait' – is always Pater's preferred form. But there are also biographical entanglements, not least Lamb's relationship with his sister Mary, close as was Pater's with his sisters, and places they lived. And there is the sense too in the writings of both of the mingling of joy and sorrow, of 'the fear of death intensified by the desire of beauty' ('The Child in the House', *MS*, 189–90; *CW*, iii. 141). In finding out what Lamb is like, Pater is also finding out what he himself is like; just so, when Ben Jonson imitates Martial or Horace, he is discovering himself, but this does not detract from his 'discoveries' about his classical models. In 'Charles Lamb' Pater praises his predecessor, in connection with his work on Shakespeare and his contemporaries, because 'he has the true scholar's way of forgetting himself in his subject' (*App.*, 111), pointing out beauties in his authors that the reader would not have noticed for him- or herself, which can itself be regarded as an oblique form of creation: 'to interpret that charm, to convey it to others—he seeming to himself but to hand on to others, in mere humble ministration, that of which for them he is really the creator—this is the way of his criticism' (112). But later in the essay Pater stresses that 'with him, as with Montaigne, the desire of self-portraiture is, below all more superficial tendencies, the real motive in writing at all—a desire closely connected with that intimacy, that modern subjectivity, which may be called the *Montaignesque* element in literature' (117). This is the 'formula', to use a word of Pater's, for Lamb.[15] This combination – self-effacing scholarship and a desire for self-portraiture, however indirect – might seem a paradox, even a contradiction, but is evidently not so for Pater. That may be explained in part by Kant's equally paradoxical idea of 'subjective universality'. The judgement of taste is both subjective, the response of a subject to the object of attention, but also 'universal', because it 'imputes', without of course necessarily obtaining in practice, the agreement of others, unlike 'the judgement of the agreeable' (I like spinach or the colour green, you don't, but there is nothing to dispute about). That is to say it is communicable, and subject to contention or assent; in that sense it is emphatically not a form of solipsism.[16]

Eliot wrote of Pater: 'Being incapable of sustained reasoning, he could not take philosophy or theology seriously.'[17] However, Pater's account of the job of the 'aesthetic critic', in the ten economical and elegant paragraphs of the 'Preface' to *The Renaissance*, while presented in a style appropriate to the essay, not the treatise (the term he uses for the form employed by Aristotle and alone approved for philosophical enquiry by analytic philosophers), is philosophically rigorous and assigns it three distinct phases. (One might compare the elegant clarity with which Pater summarises the complex arguments of Hegel's *Lectures on Aesthetics* in

'Winckelmann'.) The first two phases of the critical process show Pater's complete understanding of the main characteristics of aesthetic judgement, 'the judgement of taste', as set out by Kant at length in his Third Critique, the *Critique of Judgement*. The 'judgement of taste', which takes the form 'this painting or poem is beautiful', begins with an encounter by the judging subject that is personal and singular. In Kant's words, 'I must present the object immediately to my feeling of pleasure or displeasure, and that, too, without the aid of concepts' (if there were a definite prior concept, the judgement could be made a priori, without the need for the encounter). No prior authority is of any relevance: 'There must be no need of groping about among other people's judgements and getting previous instruction from their delight in or aversion to the same object.' Appeals to even the greatest critic will make no difference:

> If any one reads me his poem, or brings me to a play, which, all said and done, fails to commend itself to my taste, then let him adduce *Batteux* or *Lessing*, or still older and more famous critics of taste, with all the host of rules laid down by them, as a proof of the beauty of his poem; let certain passages particularly displeasing to me accord completely with the rules of beauty, (as set out by these critics and universally recognized): I stop my ears . . .. I take my stand on the ground that my judgement is to be one of taste, and not one of understanding or reason.[18]

Pater gives an account of what this preliminary stage is like, emphasising the point about subjectivity:

> What is this song or picture, this engaging personality presented in life or in a book, to *me*? What effect does it really produce on me? Does it give me pleasure? and if so, what sort or degree of pleasure? How is my nature modified by its presence, and under its influence? The answers to these questions are the original facts with which the aesthetic critic has to do; and, as in the study of light, of morals, of number, *one must realise such primary data for one's self, or not at all.* (*Ren.*, xix–xx; emphasis added)

But there is a second stage for the aesthetic critic. For the Kantian judgement is, as we have seen, also 'universal'; that is to say, it is communicable, although this may lead to contention, not agreement. And in this stage the job of the critic is, in Kant's words, in relation to their judgements, not to provide 'a universally applicable formula [*Formel*]—which is impossible', but 'the illustration, by the analysis of examples, of their mutual subjective finality, the form of which in a given representation has been shown above to constitute the beauty of their object', what Kant calls the 'art' rather than the 'science' of criticism.[19] Pater goes on to give an account of what such an art of criticism might be like, followed by an example, not a 'universal formula' (Kant's *Formel*) but 'the formula which expresses most adequately this or that special manifestation of it' – what, in the case of Wordsworth, he also calls 'the *virtue*, the active principle in Wordsworth's poetry' (xix, xxii):

> And the function of the aesthetic critic is to distinguish, to analyse, and separate from its adjuncts, the virtue by which a picture, a landscape, a fair personality in life or in a book, produces this special impression of beauty or pleasure, to indicate what the source of that impression is, and under what conditions it is experienced. His end is reached when he has disengaged that virtue, and noted it, as a chemist notes some natural element, for himself and others. (xx–xxi)

The use of scientific metaphors here makes clear that the aim is precision and exactitude; there is nothing vague or woolly about such 'impression-ism' – it is not in the least impressionistic (in the ordinary non-technical sense). And one should note the implication about communicability; the chemist disengages the virtue 'for himself *and others*' (emphasis added). Even this second stage is not the end of the matter, as we have already seen. The final paragraphs concern wider issues about the character of the Renaissance as a historical event; and Pater will go on to make transhis-torical connections with later periods too. But the ordering is important. The historicising literary criticism *de nos jours* gets the process back to front, starting with 'history' and from there approaching the individual work. Pater begins at the beginning, with the 'original facts' and the 'primary data' (xx).

It is easy for a modern reader to 'under-read' so to say Pater's writings, because his critical practice is in important respects unlike those with which we have become more familiar; the dominance of the now not-so-new 'New Criticism' may have been challenged during the theory wars, but many of its principal features remain firmly in place. Thus Pater in general does not engage in the kind of 'close reading' of a Christopher Ricks. This is not because he is incapable of it, as a couple of examples from *Appreciations* will show. Of Shakespeare's lines from *Henry V*,

> My cousin Suffolk,
> My soul shall thine keep company to heaven:
> Tarry, sweet soul, for mine, then fly abreast

Pater writes: 'The complete infusion here of the figure into the thought, so vividly realised, that, though birds are not actually mentioned, yet the

sense of their flight, conveyed to us by the single word "abreast," comes to
be more than half of the thought itself:—this, as the expression of exalted
feeling, is an instance of what Coleridge meant by Imagination'
('Coleridge', 88). Or this in the essay on Rossetti:

> For Rossetti, as for Dante, without question on his part, the first condition
> of the poetic way of seeing and presenting things is particularisation. 'Tell
> me now,' he writes for Villon's
>
> > Dictes-moy où, n'en quel pays,
> > Est Flora, la belle Romaine—
> >
> > Tell me now, in what hidden way is
> > Lady Flora the lovely Roman:
>
> —'way,' in which one might actually chance to meet her; the unmistakably
> poetic effect of the couplet in English being dependent on the definiteness
> of that single word (though actually lighted on in the search after a difficult
> double rhyme) for which every one else would have written, like Villon
> himself, a more general one, just equivalent to place or region. (208)

But such moments are comparatively rare (rarer than they are in Ruskin,
say, among Victorian critics).[20] Pater is supposed to have told his students:
'the great thing is to read authors whole; read Plato *whole*; read Kant *whole*;
read Mill *whole*.'[21] Typically an essay by Pater looks at a writer or artist
whole, offering a kind of portrait not imaginary. Often it includes an
element of biography, without falling into the biographical fallacy, but,
more importantly, it treats the text or artwork rather as if it were a person
with whom one has a relationship. When we talk of, say, 'Milton', we
usually mean not quite the individual in his quotidian existence during his
lifetime nor simply the corpus of his works, but something in between;
and it is this in-between space that is very much the space of Pater's
criticism. It is significant that his aesthetic lists contain, in addition to
natural beauty and works of art, 'the face of one's friend' ('Conclusion',
Ren., 189). If a limitation in Pater is the lack of close reading, the
limitation in a critic like Ricks is that a concern with local particularities,
always brilliant if perhaps not always persuasive, can override larger considerations. Ricks's monograph *Milton's Grand Style*, for example, has
innumerable insights into individual lines and passages but is both less
convincing and more conventional on the experience of reading *Paradise
Lost* in its entirety; Ricks's analysis does not show how the local effects he
describes so well contribute to the poem's larger trajectory and thus its
overall greatness. And, as we have seen, Pater's criticism is 'aesthetic', not

hermeneutic. A modern critic characteristically offers an interpretation, and the holy grail is novelty in interpreting, something which confers prestige on the interpreter as well as insight into the text. Pater has much that is new to say about the objects with which he has to do; but novelty is not the aim, rather it is to convey to the reader the 'virtue', the quiddity, of the thing, the particular form of pleasure that it gives, what it is like in an encounter. And, unlike the judgement of taste, most modern criticism is certainly not 'without a concept', and furthermore claims objectivity; New Criticism, for example, is specifically premised on the merits of paradox and irony and verbal complexity, an a priori stance which stands in the way of the catholicity of taste that Pater seeks always to promote:

> He [the aesthetic critic] will remember always that beauty exists in many forms. To him all periods, types, schools of taste, are in themselves equal. ('Preface', *Ren.*, xxi)[22]

Unsurprisingly Pater was not born fully formed as an aesthetic critic like Athena from the head of Zeus. But his progress was remarkably swift. His first published essay 'Coleridge's Writings' appeared in the *Westminster Review* anonymously in 1866 when he was twenty-six. There is a remarkable level of overall continuity about the concerns that were to preoccupy Pater throughout his life, even though there is also a constant process of adjustment, reformulation, and revision. *Plato and Platonism*, almost his last work published in 1893 a year before his death, shares many of those concerns with 'Coleridge's Writings', though he has achieved greater economy, suppleness, subtlety in the handling of them. Already in 1866 we can hear some of the distinctive notes of the mature Paterian voice; there are numerous felicitous formulations, and the essay is chock-full of ideas. Many central preoccupations that will be frequently revisited are there: the need for the historical sense; the emphasis on the relative ('To the modern spirit nothing is or can be rightly known except relatively under conditions' ('CW', 107)); the interest in German philosophy (Kant, Hegel, Schelling, Heine, Schlegel); the character of romanticism (Coleridge's longing for the absolute makes him 'the perfect flower of the romantic type', representing 'that inexhaustible discontent, languor, and home-sickness, the chords of which ring all through our modern literature', 132). But the piece is also somewhat long-winded as well as unusually long for Pater and somewhat sprawling in structure, in that more like a typical Victorian essay on a subject broadly philosophical, without the concentration that later came to characterise his work. And, as with many a brilliant graduate student today, he is rather too keen to display the range of his learning, tell us everything he knows, and parade his sources.

Above all 'Coleridge's Writings' can be described as in part an exercise in 'negative criticism'. For all the 'charm' (107) and interest of his work, Coleridge for Pater was simply mistaken in his insistence on the absolute, in a way that vitiated his poetry as well as his views on art and religion; Pater only quotes once from the poems (109), in that context making clear his preference for Wordsworth. Such negative criticism is something that Pater subsequently largely eschewed. True, he can on occasion be waspish about critics or even, though much less often, artists; and he certainly concedes that among the gold that displays the qualities of Wordsworth's poetry there is also much dross. But in general Pater's aim is to demonstrate the 'virtue' of his objects of study, both in the particular sense of the word in the 'Preface' to *The Renaissance* and in its more general usage. Doubtless this was in part a matter of temperament and of his overall ethical stance (how unlike in this his great rival Ruskin!), but there may also be a philosophical point at issue. In Kant's Third Critique, apart from the reference in the first sentence to 'pleasure or displeasure', the judgement of taste always takes a positive form, perhaps because negative judgements generally operate by putting the object under a concept, and are not therefore in Kant's view properly 'aesthetic'. We might say that, when we do not find an object beautiful, we withhold the judgement rather than making a negative one. Critics such as Dr Johnson often like to list the 'faults' as well as the 'virtues' of writers; however such 'faults' are often part of what makes a work of art distinctive, and thus contribute to the particular form of pleasure that it gives us. Without his awkwardnesses, his emotionalism, his extravagance, would Dickens be Dickens? When Pater revised his essay on Coleridge for *Appreciations* he reduced the element of negativity, partly by judicious cutting but mainly by grafting in most of the introduction to Coleridge as a poet that he had contributed to Ward's *English Poets* (see Chapter 11). The result is not perhaps altogether satisfactory, because the two projects were so different, the one a critique of Coleridge's whole intellectual programme, the other an exercise in describing favourably the 'virtue' of his poetry. However, it does allow Pater to comment with insight on the merits of Coleridge's best poems, which in his view were nearly all written or planned in his *annus mirabilis* in Nether Stowey in 1797–8. Pater likes to end an essay on a positive or upbeat note, and even in 'Coleridge's Writings' he does so, in this case by means of an ingenious double manoeuvre. First, he insists that the

absolute not only fails to accord with modern scientific knowledge but
issues in an inferior morality:

> The relative spirit, by dwelling constantly on the more fugitive conditions
> or circumstances of things, breaking through a thousand rough and brutal
> classifications, and giving elasticity to inflexible principles, begets an intel-
> lectual finesse, of which the ethical result is a delicate and tender justness in
> the criticism of human life. (131–2)

Then he applies the point to Coleridge's own case: judged according to the
absolute, Coleridge is simply a failure, but, if we invoke the relative spirit, he
becomes, as we have seen, 'the perfect flower of the romantic type' and 'with
his passion for the absolute, for something fixed where all is moving, his
faintness, his broken memory, his intellectual disquiet', he 'may still be ranked
among the interpreters of one of the constituent elements of our life' (132).

Published a year after 'Coleridge's Writings', 'Winckelmann' (which in
revised form Pater included in *The Renaissance* in 1873) represents a
formidable advance on its predecessor. It contains some of Pater's finest
writing, and some brilliant insights into the character and importance of
Greek sculpture. It too is a long essay by Paterian standards, and perhaps
outstays its welcome, and it too at times evinces what Pater in 'Style' would
term 'loose accretion' as opposed to 'composition' (*App.*, 24). One year
more, and in 'Poems by William Morris' (1868) Pater has achieved full
mastery in his mode of 'aesthetic criticism', before its definition in the
'Preface' to *The Renaissance*. The style, though now fully and consistently
Pateresque, is rather more highly coloured than some of his later essays,
partly under the influence of Swinburne; the achievement is the pinpoint-
ing of the particular character of the 'pleasurable sensations' we receive
from these poems by Morris, 'this special impression of beauty or pleasure', their 'virtue' (*Ren.*, xx–xxi). And Pater ends with a piece of theoretical writing that he will extract to form the 'Conclusion' of *The Renaissance*
as justification for the aesthetic life. In its original position it serves a
slightly different purpose: the paragraphs have an explicit relevance to a
main concern of the Morris essay, the defence of a poetry of Morris's kind
that reworks material from the past, by way of the preceding passage,
deleted in the later versions, with its dramatic intervention by a hostile,
presumably French critic (someone like Champfleury or Proudhon, supporters of Courbet and modern realism):

> '*Arrière!*' you say, 'here in a tangible form we have the defect of all poetry
> like this. The modern world is in possession of truths; what but a passing
> smile can it have for a kind of poetry which, assuming artistic beauty of

form to be an end in itself, passes by those truths and the living interests which are connected with them, to spend a thousand cares in telling once more these pagan fables as if it had but to choose between a more and a less beautiful shadow?' It is a strange transition from the earthly paradise to the sad-coloured world of abstract philosophy. But let us accept the challenge; let us see what modern philosophy, when it is sincere, really does say about human life and the truth we can attain in it, and the relation of this to the desire of beauty.[23]

Pater thus refutes the view of those critics, whether of his own day or ours – they continue to rule the roost in History of Art, where Pre-Raphaelite and Aesthetic art is still barely respectable – who argue that a modern artist must treat only modern-life subjects.

Form and Style

'Form' was a word of power for Pater, but it is important not to jump to conclusions about what he meant by it. Clearly Pater was not a formalist in the manner of writers on art and literature of the Modernist period, such as Roger Fry (who, at his most extreme, argued that the subject matter of an artwork was of no moment in respect of its aesthetic impact or value) or Clement Greenberg, though Greenberg professed a debt to him.[24] The merest glance at the final paragraph of 'Style' should be enough to clear us of this misapprehension; there 'great' as opposed to 'good' art is charac-terised as 'devoted further to the increase of men's happiness, to the redemption of the oppressed, or the enlargement of our sympathies with each other, or to such presentment of new or old truth about ourselves and our relation to the world as may ennoble and fortify us in our sojourn here' – the examples Pater gives are *The Divine Comedy*, *Paradise Lost*, *Les Misérables*, and *The English Bible* (*App.*, 38). The nearest he comes to formalism of the Modernist kind is when writing about painting in 'The School of Giorgione':

> In its primary aspect, a great picture has no more definite message for us than an accidental play of sunlight and shadow for a few moments on the wall or floor: is itself, in truth, a space of such fallen light, caught as the colours are in an Eastern carpet, but refined upon, and dealt with more subtly and exquisitely than by nature itself.

But, once Pater starts to characterise the 'Giorgionesque' in all its richness, the world with its multiple entanglements comes flooding back in; or, as the next sentence in our passage reads, 'this primary and essential condition fulfilled, we may trace the coming of poetry into painting'

(*Ren.*, 104) – 'primary' here refers to a first stage (as with the 'primary data' of the 'Preface'), and is not a loose synonym for 'most important'. 'Aesthetic criticism' is indeed precisely not a formalist matter, since the subjectivism involved means that we are not in the first instance talking about qualities of the object but about the sensuous and sensual experience of the individual receiver, from the Greek word for perception, sensation, the process of perceiving, *aesthesis*. Pater's most famous piece of art criticism (admittedly rather atypical of him) – the passage on the *Mona Lisa* – is not formalist in any sense whatever.[25]

Pater was well aware that, even for the oldest and seemingly 'primary' writers such as Homer and Plato, there was always a backstory, as he points out in a paragraph that is much beloved of poststructuralist critics:

> The thoughts of Plato, like the language he has to use (we find it so again, in turn, with those predecessors of his, when we pass from him to them) are covered with the traces of previous labour and have had their earlier pro-prietors. If at times we become aware in reading him of certain anticipations of modern knowledge, we are also quite obviously among the relics of an older, a poetic or half-visionary world. It is hardly an exaggeration to say that in Plato, in spite of his wonderful savour of literary freshness, there is nothing absolutely new: or rather, as in many other very original products of human genius, the seemingly new is old also, a palimpsest, a tapestry of which the actual threads have served before, or like the animal frame itself, every particle of which has already lived and died many times over. Nothing but the life-giving principle of cohesion is new; the new perspective, the resultant complexion, the expressiveness which familiar thoughts attain by novel juxtaposition. In other words, the *form* is new. But then, in the creation of philosophical literature, as in all other products of art, *form*, in the full signification of that word, is everything, and the mere matter is nothing. ('Plato and the Doctrine of Motion', *PP*, 7–8)

This passage anticipates twentieth-century theories of intertextuality, as Chapter 7 shows: indeed throughout his career a key part of Pater's project is to suggest that every piece of writing or work of visual art – what we today call textuality – is orientated both ways, backwards and forwards, and thus does not in itself partake of either origination or finality. But what are the implications of the claim that only the form is new? Form, like its antonyms (content, or matter), is a slippery thing.[26] It is perhaps best to treat these terms not as properties 'in' the work of art, but as mental frameworks useful in thinking about it; and certainly critics should not treat the words as having self-evident meaning, as they so often do (particularly when accusing their opponents of formalism). Here Pater may have in mind, as often, analogies from modern science: the world is composed of multiple stuff, chemicals and so forth, that then combine into various forms (human beings, for example). That 'the form is new' does not entail that Plato, or Pater, is a formalist. Pater is also probably thinking of an analogy familiar from German philosophy, in Schiller, for example: the artist in any medium takes unformed matter and shapes it into a work of art, as the potter shapes a pot from raw clay. Indeed, Pater often has Schiller's *Aesthetic Letters* in mind when writing of such things, not least the 22nd letter, where Schiller writes:

> In a truly successful work of art the contents should effect nothing, the form everything; for only through the form is the whole man affected, through the subject matter, by contrast, only one or other of his functions. ... Herein, then, resides the real secret of the master in any art: that he can make his form consume his material ...[27]

One might compare one of Pater's most distinguished pieces of writing, the 'Conclusion' to *The Renaissance*; every idea in it has its parallel in some other text, but there is nothing quite like it in the whole world of letters – only the form is new. It is not Plato, but his enemies the sophists who are the true formalists as valuing form without content:

> With them art began too precipitately, as mere form without matter; a thing of disconnected empiric rules, caught from the mere surface of other people's productions, in congruity with a general method which everywhere ruthlessly severed branch and flower from its natural root—art from one's own vivid sensation or belief. ('Plato and the Sophists', *PP*, 117–18)

Plato is a better philosopher than the sophists because he is a better artist who, like any good artist, uses words with precision to express what is to be expressed; the matter is 'nothing', if it is 'mere' matter that is not formed. Thus, although Pater uses some of the same words (such as 'form' and 'abstract') as the twentieth-century formalists, he does so with a quite different valence; his discussion of the form of a painting (or any other artwork) is never just an opposition between its subject matter and the style of treatment, but something much richer and more complex.

For Pater the aesthetic critic, aesthetic judgement – Kant's 'judgement of taste' – was always a judgement of form and content (on more or less any interpretation of these terms) *together*. And, in common with many other critics, he believed that, in any really distinguished piece of writing or work of art, form and content operated together to produce their effect on the reader or viewer. But he did not make the mistake of further arguing for an essentially 'organicist' account of that relationship. In an acute paragraph on Shakespeare in 'Coleridge' he warns wisely against any such assumption:

> The first suggestion in Shakespeare is that of capacious detail, of a way-wardness that plays with the parts careless of the impression of the whole; what supervenes is the constraining unity of effect, the ineffaceable impression, of Hamlet or Macbeth. His hand moving freely is curved round as if by some law of gravitation from within: an energetic unity or identity makes itself visible amid an abounding variety. This unity or identity Coleridge exaggerates into something like the identity of a natural organism, and the associative act which effected it into something closely akin to the primitive power of nature itself. (*App.*, 79)

(Pater's distinguished contribution to Shakespeare's criticism is insufficiently acknowledged; see Chapter 8.) In this way Pater avoids the romantic idea – found in Schiller as well as Coleridge – that in poetry there is necessarily a profound 'organic' unity between form and content. Much of the intellectual project of the Yale critic Paul de Man was devoted to attacking this view as the kind of aesthetic ideology that evinced ontological bad faith. It is a trap into which, for all his emphasis on form, Pater did not normally fall. Instead he stresses the literary artist's striving towards both 'clearness of idea' and 'clearness of expression': 'The philosophic critic, at least, will value, even in works of imagination, seemingly the most intuitive, the power of the understanding in them, their logical process of construction, the spectacle of a supreme intellectual dexterity which they afford' ('Coleridge', *App.*, 81).

In 'Style' Pater applies the 'condition of music' argument from 'The School of Giorgione' to literary style, including the writing of prose, for him 'the special art of the modern world' (*App.*, 11). Perhaps no sentence of Pater's is quoted more often, indeed often misquoted – there is a world of difference between 'to' and 'towards' – than '*All art constantly aspires towards the condition of music*' (*Ren.*, 106). But the sentence's meaning is frequently misconstrued when taken out of its context. Pater is emphatically not saying that music is superior to other art forms (he repudiates hierarchy of such kinds consistently throughout his writing, and is anyway much less interested in music than he is in art and literature), still less that all art should try to be 'musical', or like music in some unspecified way, or become self-contained with no reference as it were beyond the score. It is rather that what he calls the condition of music or the musical law – the interpenetration of form and content – is the standard (he calls it the 'measure') for judging the quality of any artwork:

> If music be the ideal of all art whatever, precisely because in music it is
> impossible to distinguish the form from the substance or matter, the subject
> from the expression, then, literature, by finding its specific excellence in
> the absolute correspondence of the term to its import, will be but fulfilling
> the condition of all artistic quality in things everywhere, of all good art.
> (*App.*, 37–8)[28]

So long as the principle is observed that supreme excellence in prose resides
in the correspondence of the term to its import, no particular style can be
ruled out: style can be 'reserved or opulent, terse, abundant, musical,
stimulant, academic, so long as each is really characteristic or expressive'
(36). And the same is true of literary content in general; the attempt to set
limits to prose style is 'as useless as the protest that poetry might not touch
prosaic subjects as with Wordsworth, or an abstruse matter as with
Browning, or treat contemporary life nobly as with Tennyson' (6). Such
catholicity, as we have seen, is indeed another fundamental premise of
Paterian criticism. It is all too easy to misunderstand art for art's sake, as
limited to a particular way of writing, and important to remember that
Gautier's example of it is Shakespeare's *Othello* as opposed to Voltaire's
propagandising *Mahomet.*[29] Gautier indeed insists that *l'art pour l'art* is not
form for form's sake. For Pater 'art for art's sake' is rather a matter of the
'disinterested' service of literature shown by its practitioners, something for
him more characteristic of French than of English letters, which does not
preclude 'an enduring moral effect also, in a sort of boundless sympathy'.
Thus of Lamb he writes: 'In the making of prose he realises the principle of
art for its own sake, as completely as Keats in the making of verse' ('Charles
Lamb', *App.*, 109–10).

In 'Style' Pater praises Flaubert for 'the exact apprehension of what was
needed to carry the meaning' (*App.*, 33); and that was always the goal for
his own writings. Critics usually describe Pater's style as though it were a
single thing. It might indeed be better to talk of Paterian styles rather than
style, even in the same work. In the case of *The Renaissance*, for example,
the elegant clarity of the 'Preface' is very different in texture from the more
highly coloured and resonant manner of the 'Conclusion'. At some points
Pater can be briskly informative, at others the quality he finds in
Shakespeare's *Measure for Measure* may correspond to something of his
own, 'that sort of writing which is sometimes described as *suggestive*, and
which by the help of certain subtly calculated hints only, brings into
distinct shape the reader's own half-developed imaginings', a very different
matter from 'writing merely vague and unrealised' (*App.*, 173). At the
beginning of his career Pater had in part modelled his style on that of

Swinburne, including his 'Notes on Designs of the Old Masters at
Florence' (1868), in a form of respectful imitation, most notably in the
essay on Leonardo, something recognised, without annoyance, by Rossetti
and Swinburne in correspondence.[30] In doing so he greatly improved on
his Swinburnian model, with its tendency to formlessness and rhetorical
excess, accretion rather than composition, bringing out the full potential of
this manner through discipline, control, improved structure, and generally
greater economy, what Pater himself might have called *ascêsis*. It was a
style, at times poetic and rhapsodic, that some of Pater's hostile critics
stigmatised as 'epicene'.[31] But thereafter Pater went his own way, and,
while he engaged with the major Victorian critics – including Carlyle,
Newman, Ruskin, Arnold, Saintsbury – and learned from them, as he did
from the classical and modern European authors he read and translated, he
never again practised such direct imitation. The aim was always to convey
what was to be conveyed without remainder: 'Surplusage! he will dread
that, as the runner on his muscles' ('Style', 19): 'The one word for the one
thing, the one thought, amid the multitude of words, terms, that might
just do: the problem of style was there!—the unique word, phrase, sentence, paragraph, essay, or song, absolutely proper to the single mental
presentation or vision within' (29). Pater is an exact thinker, and that is
why he is also an excessively fastidious or finicky writer – a student recalled
him saying that he never published anything unless he had rewritten it
seven times.[32] It is often with something like physical pain that he notes
the 'uneven' or 'unequal' quality of a writer or artist (the ethical connotation seems significant): Botticelli, Wordsworth, Thomas Browne, or
Measure for Measure in explicit contrast to the 'flawless execution of
Romeo and Juliet' (*App.*, 170). Interestingly his own prose often rises to
its best when he is dealing with a writer or artist whose technique he thinks
uneven, as though he is making reparation or healing a wound. So Pater's
literary fastidiousness is no mere belletrism. Rather it is a form of scholarly
ethics: it is the responsibility of scholars to write as well as they think.[33]

When Pater revised 'Romanticism' as the 'Postscript' to *Appreciations*,
he added a final paragraph, newly composed (260–1). Forthright, unusually combative for Pater, it is as much a manifesto as the 'Conclusion' to
The Renaissance, this time on the subject of how to conduct 'the literary
art' in Pater's own day. It rejects any version of revivalism (as Pater had
done long before in the Morris review), insists that modern writing must
be eclectic, given the rich but 'contorted, proportionless accumulation of
our knowledge and experience, our science and history, our hopes and
disillusion', and makes stylistic recommendations ('to write our English

language as the Latins wrote theirs, as the French write, as scholars should write' (260–1)). It ends with these resounding, fighting words:

> To discriminate schools, of art, of literature, is, of course, part of the obvious business of literary criticism: but, in the work of literary production, it is easy to be overmuch preoccupied concerning them. For, in truth, the legitimate contention is, not of one age or school of literary art against another, but of all successive schools alike, against the stupidity which is dead to the substance, and the vulgarity which is dead to form. (261)[34]

Education

From time to time contributors to this volume throw out suggestions about what general conception of English as a discipline Pater's writings might imply, and how they might help us to configure it now (see, for example, Chapter 13). Considering the alarming fall in competence in modern languages in the UK, it is important to be reminded of the transnational Republic of Letters in which writers like Pater formed their practices of reading and writing.[35] This has implications for the ambitious task of rethinking and remaking the discipline today. And certainly one characteristic of English Literature as a developing university subject that Pater would undoubtedly have deplored was its intermittent tendency to what might be called 'Little Englandism', a tendency evident for example in some aspects of the work of the more extreme disciples of F. R. Leavis. Pater of course loved English literature, but he was equally committed to the literatures of Europe, in particular those of France, Germany, and Italy. He was strongly influenced by Montaigne, Sainte-Beuve, Gautier, and Baudelaire. Flaubert is the central presence in 'Style'. The first chapter of *The Renaissance* is entitled 'Two Early French Stories', and in the 'Preface' he, perhaps surprisingly, talks about the Renaissance as beginning and ending in France, not Italy; could this be part of a sustained critical project to unsettle our received ideas about the 'nationality' – or even 'nationalism' – of significant historical movements? He wrote essays on Joachim du Bellay, Ronsard, Pascal, Mérimée, and the contemporary novelist Octave Feuillet (there are also shorter sympathetic reviews of writings by Ferdinand Fabre, Augustin Filon, and the Francophone Swiss writer Henri-Frédéric Amiel). He was a profound student of German philosophy and German scholarship, and the heroes of 'Winckelmann', the representatives of the spirit of the Renaissance in the Enlightenment, are both Winckelmann himself and Goethe. In addition to his studies of the Italian Renaissance he provided an introduction for his friend C. L. Shadwell's translation of Dante's *Purgatorio* (1892).

Overall then Pater was always the cosmopolitan, committed to a general culture; as we saw at the outset, he thought that classical literature and the literatures of modern Europe constituted a unity. In his Introduction to *Purgatorio* – one wonders if perhaps partly to cheer himself up in view of the nationalistic emphasis in much contemporary writing about literature – he uses the word 'cosmopolitan' in describing his own age which he describes as 'sympathetic, eclectic, cosmopolitan, full of curiosity and abounding in the "historic sense"'.[36] Subsequently he praises 'the un-provincial or cosmopolitan air of the *Divina Commedia*' itself;[37] we are reminded of T. S. Eliot's view in 'What is a Classic?' that one of the marks of the classic is an absence of provinciality. In 'Style' a French author is the principal exhibit, and in the 'Postscript' Romanticism is a pan-European phenomenon. Early reviewers of *Appreciations* picked up on the emphasis on France, including the possible French implications of the book's title, and Mrs Oliphant strongly criticised it.[38] In all this Pater was at one with the views of Matthew Arnold, and, like him, might well have preferred a degree in Comparative Literature to one in English. In his inaugural lecture at Oxford in 1857, 'On the Modern Element in Literature', Arnold famously insisted that 'everywhere there is connexion, everywhere there is illustration: no single event, no single literature, is adequately comprehended except in its relation to other events, to other literatures'.[39] In 'The Literary Influence of Academies', he regrets a lack of '*urbanity*', 'a *note of provinciality*', in much English prose that might have been avoided if the country possessed an institution like the French Academy. He starts his essay by quoting as 'exhilarating' an example of exceptionalist boosterism by Macaulay ('It may safely be said that the literature now extant in the English language is of far greater value than all the literature which three hundred years ago was extant in all the languages of the world together'); and ends by excoriating this as 'both vulgar, and, besides being vulgar, retarding'.[40] In 'The Function of Criticism at the Present Time' he writes:

> By the very nature of things, as England is not all the world, much of the best that is known and thought cannot be of English growth, must be foreign; by the nature of things, again, it is just this that we are least likely to know, while English thought is streaming in upon us from all sides, and takes excellent care that we shall not be ignorant of its existence. The English critic of literature, therefore, must dwell much on foreign thought, and with particular heed on any part of it, which, while significant and fruitful in itself, is for any reason specially likely to escape him.[41]

(For the importance of French criticism, not least that of Sainte-Beuve, to Pater, as to Arnold, see Chapter 2.) Accordingly we adopt a prismatic approach to Pater in relation to the dynamic and fluid contours of a nascent discipline that was not yet defined by the exclusion of literature in other languages. Chapter 4 on Pater's 'cosmopolitan criticism' is thus integral to this project as providing the required dialectical angle for thinking about a European take on English. Similarly Pater's art criticism can illuminate his way of reading English and a sense of form and style that defines the workings of literature as a medium in relation to other media (see Chapters 10 and 14 on Blake and Rossetti).

Unlike most other leading Victorian men of letters Pater was himself an educator, a teacher of the young; he seems indeed to have been a conscientious tutor. And perhaps his role as tutor and his fondness for the essay form are related: the undergraduates presented an essay for their tutorials (some essays by Gerard Manley Hopkins written for his Oxford tutors who included Pater survive[42]); and even today the essay remains in many places the prime mode of assessment for a degree in English. Of this at least we can be sure, that Pater would have abhorred the instrumentalist bias currently in vogue throughout today's schools and universities – 'learning outcomes', 'the skills agenda', and the like. One story about him is that in a discussion about educational reform in the Brasenose common-room he expostulated:

> I do not know what your object is. At present the undergraduate is a child of nature; he grows up like a wild rose in a country lane; you want to turn him into a turnip, rob him of all grace, and plant him out in rows.[43]

Pater obviously thought hard about how education should be conducted. 'Emerald Uthwart' and parts of *Plato and Platonism*, for example, show the process in action, with an awareness of both the benefit and the dangers involved; *Marius the Epicurean*, subtitled 'His Sensations and Ideas', is an account of the 'aesthetic education' of a particular young man, in the light of the German tradition of *Bildung*. In his thinking Pater was doubtless influenced by debates in Germany (Schiller, Fichte, Alexander von Humboldt, Schelling) as well as in Britain. Indeed some of his critics found something disagreeably un-English in his overall approach. W. J. Courthope, for example, in an anonymous article 'Modern Culture' published in the *Quarterly Review* in 1874, censured Carlyle, Arnold, John Addington Symonds, and Pater for their espousal of 'self-culture' in accordance with their 'Gospel according to Goethe' and in a manner that undermined manliness, good sense, and patriotism for the

pursuit of 'feverish excitement'. And in 1876 Courthope continued his
attack on Pater and romanticism more generally in his essay 'Wordsworth
and Grey' ('Romanticism' may be in part Pater's response).[44]

Pater's espousal of the essay as a form can also be connected with his
pedagogical goals. His most complete theorisation of the essay occurs in a
discussion that ought to be much better known: the second section of the
chapter on 'The Doctrine of Plato' in *Plato and Platonism* entitled
'*Dialectic*', in connection with the literature of philosophy. This he divides
into 'three distinct literary methods' (174): the poem – 'a matter of
intuition, imaginative, sanguine, often turbid or obscure' (174); the treatise – the invention of Aristotle, 'the proper instrument of dogma' (187),
'with its ambitious array of premiss and conclusion' (175); and the essay.
For the modern period his prime exemplar of the essayist is, as always,
Montaigne (see on this Chapter 3), and the essay is thus associated with
scepticism and the modern relative spirit, 'that characteristic literary type
of our own time' (174). But it is Pater's lifelong concern to complicate this
picture and make the essay a more constant presence in the Western
tradition by tracing its origins back to the dialogues of Plato. Each of
these three methods is 'determined directly by matter, as corresponding to
three essentially different ways in which the human mind relates itself to
truth' (175). Plato's dialectical method involves a 'continuous discourse
with one's self, being, for those who prosecute it with thoroughness, co-
extensive with life itself' (185), and can best be figured as a journey
(179–80). In that dialogue 'many persons, so to speak, will necessarily
take part; so many persons as there are possible contrasts or shades in the
apprehension of some complex subject' (183–4). There can be little doubt
about Pater's own preferences in all this. The final sentence of this whole
section reads like a personal credo (note such key Paterian words as
'culture', 'receptivity', 'faithful scholar', 'philosophic temper'):

> Such condition of suspended judgment indeed, in its more genial develop-
> ment and under felicitous culture, is but the expectation, the receptivity, of
> the faithful scholar, determined not to foreclose what is still a question—the
> 'philosophic temper,' in short, for which a survival of query will be still the
> salt of truth, even in the most absolutely ascertained knowledge. (196)

Contrary to the criticisms made of him by such as Eliot and Ricks, Pater is
always concerned with truth, and the – sometimes unsuspected – obstacles
to it, including particular methods of argumentation (see Chapter 6).[45]
There is a potential 'politics' here too (something generally denied to the
supposedly apolitical Pater).[46] It is certainly possible to prefer Pater's

critical idiom to Eliot's – lordly, dogmatic; Pater's is more *democratic*, dialogic, in his own terms evincing the proper character of the essay. That is due to his commitment to a dialectical form of thinking, a commitment as deeply held as Marx's and from the same proximate source in the recent philosophy of Hegel, although, as we have just seen, in Pater's case it was also a project to retrace it, for his own and his students' benefit, back to the dialogues of Plato. As a result no quotation from Pater is complete without its dialectical counterpart; to quote a single sentence or phrase is not merely to present one half of an argument as though it were the whole, but systematically to suppress the dialectical play of *sic et non*. Pater thus seems to have regarded his job as an academic and educator as being not to inculcate any particular point of view but rather, in his words about Plato and Winckelmann, to help 'form a temper'; and with many tempers formed on Paterian lines – attentive, curious, undogmatic, eager for dialogue with others, always willing to modify their view, suspicious of received opinion, cosmopolitan – our world might be in a rather better place.

Conclusion: A Place for Pater?

It has always been difficult to find a 'place for Pater', to use Eliot's words. What is one to make of an author, whose most famous work, perhaps, is not a great poem or play or novel, but a short essay on Leonardo da Vinci? It may be that Pater is one of those artists that he himself characterised as follows:

> There are a few great painters, like Michelangelo or Leonardo, whose work has become a force in general culture . . .. But, besides those great men, there is a certain number of artists who have a distinct faculty of their own by which they convey to us a peculiar quality of pleasure which we cannot get elsewhere; and these too have their place in general culture, and must be interpreted to it by those who have felt their charm strongly, and are often the object of a special diligence and a consideration wholly affectionate, just because there is not about them the stress of a great name and authority. ('Sandro Botticelli', *Ren.*, 48)

Indeed Botticelli, about whom he wrote those words, has, partly as a result of this very essay, subsequently entered the canon of great artists. And Pater, for those who have come to admire, and even to love, his writings, becomes a highly important part of their mental furniture. On one thing at least Eliot was right: Pater, like his hero Goethe, is 'that most dangerous type of critic: the critic with a mind which is naturally of the creative order'; but that does not mean that he cannot teach us much of value about his objects of study, including a number of key figures in English literature. Himself a relentless critic of disciplinary boundaries, a comparatist of formidable learning, Pater is unusually difficult to pigeonhole. He believes in the fine discriminations of the aesthete but also the capacious interests of the intellectual. Interdisciplinarity, that academic slogan of our time! – he has much to teach us about that too. And if anglophone criticism still has difficulty finding a place for him, perhaps that is because a strong suspicion of the aesthetic persists: 'beauty' is not nearly so embarrassing to even the most radical French intellectual as it is to a British academic. As we have seen, Pater thought one should read authors *whole*. And to read Pater whole is to receive an aesthetic education of very great value, as well as an opportunity to enjoy (dare we say it) the sheer beauty of his prose.

Notes

1 For the history of this process see the works cited in the Bibliography, under 'The Development of English Studies as a University Discipline'. For Churton Collins's campaign, and his attacks on Gosse and Saintsbury, see in particular Alexandra Lawrie, *The Beginnings of University English: Extramural Study, 1885–1910* (2014), ch. 2 (32–55).

2 'English at the Universities. –IV.', *Pall Mall Gazette* (27 November 1886); repr. in *Letters*, 68–9 (69).

3 For supplying us with the material in this paragraph we are indebted to Dr Joanna Parker. Greats papers by contrast were concerned mainly with history and philosophy.

4 Thomas Wright, *The Life of Walter Pater*, 2 vols (1907), i. 194; so too William Sharp, 'Some Personal Reminiscences of Walter Pater', *Atlantic Monthly* 74 (December 1894), repr. in *Walter Pater: A Life Remembered*, ed. R. M. Seiler (Calgary 1997), 78–98 (86).

5 Published as *From Shakespeare to Pope: An Enquiry into the Causes and Phenomena of the Rise of Classical Poetry in England* (Cambridge 1885).

6 Statute E, XXXII, announced in the *Cambridge University Reporter* of November 15, 1910. We owe this information to Dr Alison Wood, to whom we are grateful for much help with this section; see also Alison Wood, 'Secularity and the Uses of Literature: English at Cambridge, 1890–1920', *Modern Language Quarterly*, 75 (2014), 260–77.

7 Vernon Lee, 'The Handling of Words: A Page of Walter Pater', *Life and Letters* 9: 50 (September 1933), 287–310. Though the essay is a bravura performance, the overall view of Pater is rather conventional.

8 Pater's religious views are hard to pin down, and characteristically complex. As a young man he apparently rejected the truth of Christianity altogether, and

religious scepticism clearly remained a constant throughout his life, though he certainly became more sympathetic later, not least to religious observance and ritual. His review of Mrs Humphry Ward's *Robert Elsmere* – perhaps the finest of his shorter reviews – is to our mind particularly revealing of his position by 1888, as well as typically nuanced (*Essays*, 55–70). One suspects that in his comment 'But then there is also a large class of minds which cannot be sure it [the sacred story] is false—minds of very various degrees of conscientiousness and intellectual power, up to the highest' he may be speaking partly of himself. As he puts it, 'It is philosophical, doubtless, and a duty to the intellect to recognize our doubts, to locate them, perhaps to give them practical effect. It may also be a moral duty to do this.' But this is immediately followed in typical Paterian dialectical fashion by a 'But': others 'will think those who are quite sure it [the sacred story] is false unphilosophical through lack of doubt' (67–8). Certainly Pater argues that Mrs Ward is to a degree simplifying a complex issue. We do not think that the mature Pater either replaces Christianity with literature and art in the simple-minded way that Arnold does on occasion, or reduces religious matters to a purely artistic aestheticism (except, perhaps, in the very early essay on Coleridge). But of course for him the aesthetic always involves strenuous intellectual effort and ascesis; he is always a philosophical critic as well as an aesthete in the more vulgar sense. See further Michael D. Hurley, 'Pater and Religion', in *The Cambridge Companion to Pater*, ed. Francis O'Gorman (Cambridge, forthcoming).

9 *Dante Gabriel Rossetti: Collected Poetry and Prose*, ed. Jerome McGann (New Haven 2003), xxii.

10 Thomas Budd Shaw, *Outlines of English Literature* (Philadelphia 1849), 343, 350. We are grateful to Christin Neubauer for this reference. For the use of the words 'romantic' and 'romanticism' and their equivalents in other European languages see Hans Eichner, ed., *'Romantic' and its Cognates: The European History of a Word* (Manchester 1972) – on England see the chapter by George Whalley, 157–262.

11 See *Critical Heritage*, 71–3 (an unsigned review in *Westminster Review* n.s. 43 (1873), 639–41); for the reception of *The Renaissance* more generally, 19–26, 47–112.

12 The eighteenth century, or at any rate the writings of the 'Augustans', was indeed something of a blind spot for Pater; in this respect, if in no other, he was, in a limited sense, a man 'of his time'. But the point must not be exaggerated; consider his interest in Watteau, Winckelmann, Kant, Goethe, Samuel Johnson.

13 Ricks, 'Misquotation', 408. While Ricks's dislike for Pater as a critic and writer is obvious, he is also taking aim at some contemporary critics, presented as the heirs of Pater: Harold Bloom in particular is in his sights (see Stephen Bann's 'Postscript' to this volume). It is unfortunate that this essay, marked by both an obsessive character and a lack of generosity, is one of the best-known discussions of Pater's writings in the current world of 'Eng. Lit'. And it is also unclear what precisely Ricks has proved. He certainly adduces some definite

instances of misquotation, though not all of his examples are convincing (the use of quotation marks in Pater does not always signal an actual quotation). But their frequency is unclear, since Ricks surrounds them with a characteristically coruscating firework display of assaults on Paterian mannerisms and features of style that he dislikes. Victorian critics – Ruskin would be an example – frequently quote from memory, a practice that always runs a significant risk of error. And in the case of authors such as Shakespeare it is unclear whether Ricks has checked the supposed misquotations against editions that Pater is likely to have used. Are misquotations more or less common in Pater than in other writers in his or other periods? (We once checked quotations from Pater's own texts in a scholarly publication we were editing, and found more than 400 mistakes.) Ricks's defence of Arnold's much more cloth-eared habit of mis-quotation seems merely perverse. Helen Law by contrast demonstrates ('Pater's Use of Greek Quotations', *Modern Language Notes* 58 (1943), 575–85) that Pater's citations from Greek texts usually show a high degree of accuracy, as indeed do his translations from various languages, ancient and modern.

14 T. S. Eliot, *The Sacred Wood: Essays on Poetry and Criticism* (1920), 87–94 (87). Pater does in fact refer to *Hamlet* on a number of occasions; it may have been one of his favourite plays.

15 Wright, *Life of Pater*, ii. 151: 'that is Lamb's *formula*'. According to Wright, much of the essay was written in Richard Jackson's library, where Pater was surrounded by Lamb's books and memorabilia (but Jackson's testimony has been doubted).

16 For a brief account of Kant's principal aesthetic views see Charles Martindale, *Latin Poetry and the Judgement of Taste: An Essay in Aesthetics* (Oxford 2005), 8–54.

17 T. S. Eliot, 'The Place of Pater', in *The Eighteen-Eighties: Essays by Fellows of the Royal Society of Literature*, ed. Walter de la Mare (Cambridge 1930), 93–106 (103); the essay was often reprinted as 'Arnold and Pater', its title when first published in *The Bookman* (September 1930). Eliot was of course committed to a particular way of doing philosophy within an Anglo-American tradition. *Pater the Classicist* (ed. Charles Martindale, Stefano Evangelista, and Elizabeth Prettejohn (Oxford 2017)) has, we think, put the question of Pater's competence with respect to ancient philosophy beyond any reasonable doubt (see especially part 4: Philosophy); his profound knowledge of modern German philosophy, including Kant, Schiller, and Hegel, is equally demon-strable. It is ironical that those, such as Richard Jenkyns, who have criticised Pater as having 'no comprehension of abstract thought' (*The Victorians and Ancient Greece* (Oxford 1980), 258) are generally much less expert in matters philosophical than Pater himself. And Pater also has the gift of communicat-ing his findings, fully absorbed within his own intellectual position, in a language, largely free of philosophical jargon, that is both attractive and intelligible to non-philosophers.

18 Immanuel Kant, *The Critique of Judgement*, trans. James Creed Meredith (Oxford 1952), §8, 55; §32, 137; §33, 140.

19 Kant, *Critique of Judgement*, §34, 141–2.

20 The same is true of another of our greatest literary critics, Samuel Johnson. Superficially Pater and Johnson might seem markedly dissimilar, but closer inspection reveals affinities; interestingly Pater drafted an almost completed essay on Johnson, but sadly it is lost. More recent critical modes mean that many practitioners join Pope's category of 'verbal critic' only (*Essay on Criticism*, 261), unable to see the larger picture beyond the ever more intricate – and sometimes self-regarding – detail.

21 A. C. Benson, *Walter Pater* (1906), 194.

22 The critic and teacher George Saintsbury, who ended a varied career as Professor of Rhetoric and English Literature at the University of Edinburgh, describes Pater's critical procedure thus: 'Expose mind and sense to them [poets of various kinds], like the plate of a camera: assist the reception of the impression by cunning lenses of comparison, and history, and hypothesis; shelter it with a cabinet of remembered reading and corroborative imagination; develop it by meditation, and print it off with the light of style' (*A History of English Criticism* (1911), 499). The passage is quoted by James R. Sutherland in 'The English Critic', his inaugural lecture at University College London (1952), an elegant and thoughtful survey of what Sutherland regards as the main and best tradition of English literary criticism from Dryden onwards (16).

23 Anonymous, 'Poems by William Morris', *Westminster Review* n.s. 34 (October 1868), 300–12 (309).

24 'Towards a Newer Laocoon', in *Clement Greenberg: The Collected Essays and Criticism*, vol. i, ed. John O'Brian (Chicago and London 1986), 23–38 (32).

25 Cf. Michael Levey, *The Case of Walter Pater* (1978): 'What Pater is analyzing – where he might superficially seem merely rhapsodizing – with every nuance of punctuation as well as vocabulary, wielding the precision instrument of prose, is the meaning of this image to its creator' (126).

26 For a fuller discussion see Martindale, *Latin Poetry*, ch. 2, 'Content, Form, and Frame' (especially 55–74).

27 Friedrich Schiller, *On the Aesthetic Education of Man in a Series of Letters*, ed. Elizabeth M. Wilkinson and L. A. Willoughby (Oxford 1967), 155–7.

28 It is of course difficult to say what the 'content' of a piece of music is that might be separated from its 'form'. By contrast the 'content' of works of literature can include elements of argument and sentiment that might seem to be divorceable from the 'form' in which they are cast; part of Pater's point is presumably that such a separation is misleading when applied to the greatest verbal art

29 Théophile Gautier, 'Du Beau dans l'art', *Revue des Deux Mondes* 19 (1847), 887–908 (900).

30 Friday [26 November 1869], *The Correspondence of Dante Gabriel Rossetti: The Chelsea Years 1863–1872* (vol. iv of the complete edition of the letters), ed. William E. Fredeman (Cambridge 2004), 324: 'What a remarkable article that is of Pater's on Leonardo! Something of *you* perhaps, but a good deal of himself too to good purpose.'

31 So W. J. Courthope, *Critical Heritage*, 93.
32 See G. Monsman and S. Wright, 'Walter Pater: Style and Text', *South Atlantic Quarterly* 71 (1972), 106–23 (111).
33 For a good account of Pater's style, and indeed his whole critical project, see the introduction to Alex Wong, ed., *Walter Pater: Selected Essays* (Manchester 2018), 9–38 (especially 19–24). For representative recent accounts of his style see Bibliography under 'Form and Style'.
34 If 'the vulgarity which is dead to form' is a reference to conservative criticism which looked only for morally improving content, perhaps 'the stupidity which is dead to the substance' refers to the work of the extreme devotees of the kind of writing we tend today to call 'decadent'? Pater dissociated himself from any such literary 'movement', disliking the term.
35 University teachers of English, while virtually all opposed to Brexit, by their actions have supported part of its concomitant, an ignorance of foreign languages. For example, at the University of York the degree English and Related Literatures used to require the study of another language (including French, German, Italian, Arabic); this requirement has now been dropped. At Bristol there was a degree in English and French, since discontinued. At Oxford English Prelims once had options to study a work in an ancient or modern European language.
36 Introduction to Charles Lancelot Shadwell, *The Purgatory of Dante Alighieri (Purgatorio I-XXVII): An Experiment in Literal Verse Translation* (1892), xv. This passage is quoted at the start of Stefano Evangelista, *Literary Cosmopolitanism in the English Fin de Siècle: Citizens of Nowhere* (Oxford 2021). A striking further example is Pater's praise of Raphael's 'immense cosmopolitan intelligence' ('Raphael', *MS*, 58). For Pater's European orientation generally see Lene Østermark-Johansen, *Walter Pater's European Imagination* (Oxford 2022), and the Bibliography under 'Pater and European Literature'.
37 Shadwell, *Purgatory*, xxvi.
38 *Critical Heritage*, 214–19 (unsigned review, *Blackwell's Magazine* 147 (1890), 140–5) and for the reception of *Appreciations* generally 29–33, 194–241. For comments on the possible French inflection of the title see *Critical Heritage*, 201 (Arthur Symons); 211 (C. L. Graves); 220 (Lionel Johnson). But Pater may be thinking rather of the Latin derivation, from *appretio* ('put a price on') and *pretium* (so Oscar Wilde, *Critical Heritage*, 233).
39 Arnold, *Prose*, i. 20–21. See too Warren Anderson, 'Matthew Arnold and the Grounds of Comparatism', *Comparative Literary Studies* 8 (1971), 287–302, which cites a letter of Arnold's from 1848: 'How plain it is now, though an attention to the comparative literatures for the last fifty years might have instructed anyone of it, that England is in a certain sense *far behind* the Continent' (288). Anderson notes how reviewers in the major British periodicals regularly combine deeply rooted ignorance with superficiality (297). It is this insularity that Pater, like Arnold, writes to combat.

40 Arnold, *Prose*, iii. 244, 245, 232, 257. In 'The Study of Poetry', which was written as the introduction to T. H. Ward's *The English Poets*, he is careful to remind the reader that 'the stream of English poetry' is 'only one of the several streams that make the mighty river of poetry' (Arnold, *Prose*, ix. 161). Ward, married to Arnold's niece, the novelist Mrs Humphry Ward, both of them close friends of Pater, explains that this multi-volume work was designed to fill a gap, 'that of an anthology which may adequately represent the vast and varied field of English Poetry'. Pater's contributions to this project, on Coleridge and Rossetti, show his interest in the idea of literary history, but one conducted on Arnoldian, not exceptionalist or nationalistic, principles. See also the essay on Rossetti, Chapter 14, in this volume.

41 Arnold, *Prose*, iii. 282–3.

42 See *The Collected Works of Gerard Manley Hopkins, vol. 4: Oxford Essays and Notes*, ed. Lesley Higgins (Oxford 2006); the introduction includes a useful account of Classics (then, as now, called *Literae Humaniores*) as taught in Oxford at Balliol in the 1860s, including the content of examinations (72–85).

43 Wright, *Life of Pater*, ii. 119.

44 See Inman (1990), 107–9, 219–20.

45 'Style', *App.*, 10: 'Truth! there can be no merit, no craft at all, without that. And further, all beauty is in the long run only *fineness* of truth'; 34: 'In the highest as in the lowliest literature, then, the one indispensable beauty is, after all, truth:—truth to bare fact in the latter, as to some personal sense of fact, diverted somewhat from men's ordinary sense of it, in the former; truth there as accuracy, truth here as expression ....'

46 There seems sometimes to be an assumption that Pater was in some sense 'conservative'. It is true that he rarely comments directly on contemporary politics. But his early essays were published in radical or progressive journals (*Westminster Review* and *Fortnightly Review*), and as a young man he was described as a Liberal in politics (see Wright, *Life of Pater*, i. 215). He may have grown more conservative in later life, but there is no clear evidence for this; his hostility to all forms of cruelty (including to children and animals) certainly remained undiminished.

General

Introduction to Part I

The first part of this book looks at Pater's contribution to English studies and literary criticism within a number of broader contexts. Kenneth Daley provides initial orientation for the reader. He compares Pater's *Appreciations* with the writings of other critics in the period, stressing how the volume asserts the centrality of the 'romantic' tradition in English literature, and contributes influentially to late nineteenth-century literary historiography and the tradition of the English critical essay. *Appreciations* may not have enjoyed the *succès de scandale* of *The Renaissance*, but it was widely disseminated and admired, with six editions and thirteen other reprintings up to 1927.

Pater pioneered a new literary form which he called the 'imaginary portrait', a hybrid of fiction and essay, which had a considerable influence, first on Oscar Wilde and Vernon Lee, and then on the Modernist generation, and which can be read as literary or artistic criticism in another mode. Lene Østermark-Johansen focusses on two such portraits with an English setting and on the nature of the 'Englishness' involved: the unfinished fragment 'An English Poet' written in the late 1870s but not published until 1931; and the short manuscript fragment for Pater's proposed third novel entitled 'Thistle' (late 1880s). In their concern with *Bildung*, with the coming-into-being of the poet or aesthete, and the growth of the imagination, these exhibit Pater as a late-flourishing romantic, while also closely tracking Sainte-Beuve's *portraits littéraires*, and so giving the stories a European dimension.

Pater devoted much of his career as a writer to the essay form (and its fictional equivalent, the imaginary portrait). Along with the dialogues of Plato, Montaigne's *Essais*, which, perhaps surprisingly, Pater seems to have read, not in the original French, but in Charles Cotton's elegant seventeenth-century translation, were always, for him, especially exemplary for the mode. In his view the essay suited 'the relative spirit' so characteristic of modernity: sceptical, informal, undogmatic, provisional

('*Que sais-je?*'), committed to suspended judgement, multi-faceted, fluctuant and diverse, above all revealing of personality. Furthermore, in *Gaston de Latour* Pater brings Montaigne to life, introducing him, as Fergus McGhee argues, not only as a philosopher and self-inquirer, but as a 'lover of style', anticipating Harold Bloom's characterisation of the *Essays* as a vast work of literary criticism.

In parallel with the establishment of English as an academic subject, Pater's lifetime coincided with the institutionalisation of Modern Languages as an independent field of enquiry within British universities; in 1886 – the year of the *Pall Mall Gazette* survey on English at Oxford – H. M. Posnett's *Comparative Literature*, the foundational document in English for comparative literary studies, was published. Stefano Evangelista shows how Pater's writings on English literature, like those of Matthew Arnold, favoured cosmopolitan and comparative approaches that rejected the increasingly widespread Victorian practice of appropriating English literature for the promotion of a nationalist ideology. Evangelista pays particular attention to Pater's late lecture (1890) on the French writer Prosper Mérimée, which he was invited to deliver as part of the Taylor Lectures alongside European figures such as Stéphane Mallarmé and Paul Bourget, and which were later collected, after Pater's death, in a volume entitled *Studies in European Literature* (1900).

To conclude *Appreciations*, Pater repurposed his essay of 1876 'Romanticism' (a telling title for an essay that actually deals with the opposition between romanticism and classicism). The new title, 'Postscript', as Ross Wilson observes, reminds us that for Pater there is never, except contingently, a last word, and of his commitment to the provisional and to second thoughts, and a never-ending process of revision, refinement, and reformulation. Wilson explores the complexities in Pater's account about aesthetic and historical categorisation, and about the way that periodisation can act as a straitjacket inhibiting proper understanding and appreciation; on this reading the essay becomes a key text for a crucial ongoing debate in literary study.

This first part concludes with two very different takes on Pater's somewhat controversial essay 'Style', an essay that over the years has been both highly praised and roundly disparaged. Michael Hurley contrasts Pater's views with those of three influential contemporaries, Arnold, Saintsbury, and Newman. He also insists that Pater's version of art for art's sake has been widely misunderstood by those who ignore his emphasis on 'truth'; for this reason, he sees the eloquent final paragraph of 'Style' as entirely at one with Pater's larger vision. Scarlett Baron, by contrast, finds here an inconsistent return to literary orthodoxy on Pater's part, but she also highlights the way that other aspects of his style and aesthetics, which he explores in 'Style' through his reading of Flaubert, position him on the threshold of Modernism, and explain his influence on authors such as Joyce and Woolf. Pater's practice of citation, which has aroused some criticism, can be seen more profitably as an anticipation of twentieth-century accounts of intertextuality from Joyce to Kristeva and the practice of 'second-hand writing' (to coin a phrase from Antoine Compagnon's *La seconde main*).

CHAPTER I

'Of the true family of Montaigne': Appreciations and the Essay Tradition in English Literature

Kenneth Daley

> When I first had the privilege—and I count it a very high one—of meeting Mr Walter Pater, he said to me, smiling, 'Why do you always write poetry? Why do you not write prose? Prose is so much more difficult'.[1]

The conscious apprehension of aesthetic value in nonfictional prose first emerged in English literature with Romantic prose writers such as Coleridge and De Quincey. Walter Pater represents the apogee of this critical development; he was the first to proclaim the prose essay the characteristic literary genre of his day, and to insist explicitly on its status as fine art, the province of the aesthetic critic. Despite the monumental achievements of the prose essay in Victorian literature, the great practitioners of the form made no significant claims for its aesthetic value. Even late in the century, nonfiction prose, like the novel, had not yet achieved fully respectable status, a function of its ubiquitous presence in the periodical press and popular culture, its cross-disciplinary purposes, and its connection with the occasional nature of the review, among other reasons. It was left to Pater not only to proclaim the essay a literary genre, but also to confirm its aesthetic possibilities. 'And prose thus asserting itself as the special and privileged artistic faculty of the present day', Pater declares in 'Style', 'will be, however critics may try to narrow its scope, as varied in its excellence as humanity itself reflecting on the facts of its latest experience—an instrument of many stops, meditative, observant, descriptive, eloquent, analytic, plaintive, fervid' (*App.*, 11).[2] Pater refers to no fewer than seventy nonfiction prose writers in *Appreciations*, projecting a wide and deep command of the prose tradition, from ancient to modern, across disciplines and national boundaries. The groupings in the opening paragraph of 'Style', and of *Appreciations* as a whole, establish the range, yoking together prose writers from across time and space as representative of specific aesthetic qualities – Livy, the great ancient Roman historian, with Carlyle, the modern Scottish historian (the 'picturesque'); Cicero, Livy's older Roman contemporary and crucial figure in the development of Latin prose, with John Henry Newman (the 'musical'); Plato with Jules Michelet, the French republican historian, and Sir Thomas Browne (the 'mystical and intimate'). If the attribution of aesthetic effect is at times somewhat enigmatic (with Francis Bacon, for instance, prose is 'found to be a coloured thing'), the point is in the emphatic discrimination of the aesthetic impression (*App.*, 6).

Appreciations: With an Essay on Style (1889, 2nd edition revised 1890) represents a culmination, collecting all of the essays on English literary subjects Pater regularly published in roughly two-year intervals following *Studies in the History of the Renaissance* (1873), as well as significant portions of his first published essay, on Coleridge's philosophical and religious thought (1866), and the early 'Poems by William Morris' (1868). Other than short reviews of Oscar Wilde's *The Picture of Dorian Gray* (1891) and Edmund Gosse's book of poems, *On Viol and Flute* (1890), the eclectic publications of the final years of his life do not include any further treatment of English literature.[3] Despite covering more than two decades of criticism for a range of periodicals, the volume coheres both structurally and thematically. While the book does not offer a comprehensive treatment of literary history, in the manner, for example of Hippolyte Taine's four-volume *History of English Literature* (1863–4), or, in the other direction, George Saintsbury's *Short History of French Literature* (1882), it nevertheless represents a significant contribution to late nineteenth-century literary historiography, and, in particular, the delineation of the English literary essay tradition. In its organisation and treatment of subjects, Pater's book asserts the centrality of romanticism in English literature, and develops a historical schema and characterisation of the English essay in conscious opposition to the prevailing historical narrative, most prominently articulated by Matthew Arnold, that regards eighteenth-century prose as the apogee of the English achievement in that mode, the consummation of an English Attic prose style derived from French neoclassicism and antique models. Against this narrative, Pater sets a modern, romantic tradition of English prose derived from Montaigne, and inaugurated by English writers of the late sixteenth and seventeenth centuries. This alternative genealogy of English essayists, 'of the true family of Montaigne', as Pater suggests in the essay on Charles Lamb (116), epitomises the central romantic impulse of English literature, 'that modern subjectivity' (117) which Pater traces in *Appreciations* from Shakespeare to Morris and Rossetti. As I will show, Pater's treatment of the English

romantic literary tradition and the development of English prose constitutes a pointed response to the late-Victorian recuperation of Augustan
and neoclassical literature undertaken by critic-scholars such as Leslie
Stephen, George Saintsbury, and W. J. Courthope, and associated with
the rise of English studies and the campaign for the institutionalisation of
English at Oxford and Cambridge.

By the time of *Appreciations*, English authors regularly issued compila-
tions of previously published material. As early as 1859, John Stuart Mill
introduced his two-volume collection of essays, *Dissertations and
Discussions: Political, Philosophical, and Historical, Reprinted Chiefly from
the Edinburgh and Westminster Reviews*, with the observation that the
'republication in a more durable form, of papers originally contributed
to periodicals, has grown into so common a practice as scarcely to need an
apology' (iii). Mill probably has in mind the self-effacing prefaces of
Thomas Babington Macaulay (*Critical and Historical Essays*, 3 vols,
1843) or Francis Jeffrey (*Contributions to the Edinburgh Review*, 4 vols,
1844), who, embracing the same humility topos, blames the republication
of his work on the insistence of the *Review*'s publishers. In contrast,
Thomas Carlyle's four-volume *Critical and Miscellaneous Essays* appeared
in 1838–9 without apology. Behind Carlyle, we have the example of
William Hazlitt, and, in a different vein, Charles Lamb. Thomas De
Quincey was not to publish his four-volume collection, *Selections Grave
and Gay: From Writings Published and Unpublished*, until 1853–4, but by
the second half of the century, as Mill's note indicates, the practice became
ubiquitous. '[A]lmost every author had one or more such collections',
according to Gertrude Himmelfarb.[4] Major examples prior to
Appreciations include Arnold's *Essays in Criticism* (1865, 1888),
Newman's *Historical Sketches* (1872), Pater's own *Studies in the History of
the Renaissance* (1873), and A. C. Swinburne's *Essays and Studies* (1875).
Between 1870 and 1881, T. H. Huxley published three separate collections. In the last decades of the century and into the next, the preternaturally prolific George Saintsbury published a new collection of essays
seemingly every other year.

If *Appreciations* perhaps does not possess the cultural significance of
Pater's *Studies in the History of the Renaissance*, nor that book's sustained
intensity, it nevertheless stands as a more intricately designed and unified
collection of previously published essays than the majority of its Victorian
counterparts. Central to *Appreciations* is Pater's desire to assimilate the
principles and achievements of the romantic tradition into the mainstream
history of English literature, an effort shared by Carlyle, Mill, Ruskin,

Arnold, Swinburne, but never in such sustained and cohesive a fashion. Over the previous twenty plus years of his career, Pater had established his use of the term, 'romantic', given explicit definition in the essay 'Romanticism' (1876), as 'an ever-present, an enduring principle in the artistic temperament', discernible across historical time and national boundaries.[5] Repurposed as the 'Postscript' to *Appreciations*, the 'Romanticism' essay eventually exerted a profound influence on subsequent Anglo-American literary historiography and scholarship, affirming the classical-romantic distinction, in the words of George Whalley, as 'both new and axiomatic for the polarity of all literature',[6] while also contributing substantially to the establishment of the term 'Romantic' to define and delineate English literature of the early nineteenth century.[7] Most significantly, Pater is the first English writer to defend the concept of romanticism against its conservative Victorian critics. Pater's Renaissance was an explicitly romantic movement, ranging from the medieval France of Abelard and Heloïse through sixteenth-century Italy into the eighteenth-century Germany of Winckelmann and Goethe. For Pater, Renaissance artists and art work are replete with the qualities he repeatedly associates with the romantic spirit: individualism, strangeness, curiosity, rebelliousness, antinomianism, sympathy. *Appreciations* extends Pater's transhistorical and transnational treatment of the 'romantic spirit', tracing it throughout the history of English literature, in close relation to its manifestation in the modern French and German literary traditions.

The volume's delineation of the English romantic tradition begins *in medias res* with the portraits of Wordsworth, Coleridge, and Lamb; moves backwards in time through the 'genuinely romantic' (156) prose literature of the seventeenth century, exemplified by Sir Thomas Browne, and settles and centres in Shakespeare, the quintessential 'humourist', a term Pater uses throughout the volume to denote English counterparts to Montaigne. In the book's final sequence, Pater leaps forward to his present day and the late romanticism of Morris and Rossetti, establishing the modern-day 'aesthetic poetry' as a highly self-conscious manifestation of the English romantic impetus, an 'afterthought' of the 'romantic school' ('AP', 214). The title of the essay, 'Aesthetic Poetry' (a revised version of the essay of 1868 on Morris), makes explicit the link between the work of the contemporary poets and Pater's own 'aesthetic criticism', first defined in the 'Preface' to *Studies in the History of the Renaissance*.

Two of the final three pieces that Pater composed, 'Sir Thomas Browne' (1886) and 'Style' (1888), combine with the earlier essays on Coleridge (1866) and Lamb (1878) to bring the subject of prose to the forefront.

In its defence of prose as the quintessential modern literary form, the opening 'Style' stands as a significant counterpoint to Arnold's 'The Study of Poetry', with its defence of poetry's high purpose and 'destiny' in the modern world, and which Arnold placed as the opening essay in his *Essays in Criticism: Second Series*, published only a year before *Appreciations*.[8] Indeed, as a literary form, prose is given at least equal footing, in Pater's volume, with poetry and Shakespeare's plays. The first edition of *Appreciations* combines essays on prose (three), poetry (three), and drama (three), with 'Coleridge' standing as a hybrid text, a composite of Pater's earlier essays on the philosopher-poet's prose and poetry, and the concluding theoretical 'Postscript', too, focused primarily on prose texts. 'Style' represents, as well, a major contribution to the vibrant late-Victorian theoretical discourse on prose style, which includes, among essays published prior to Pater's, John Dennis's 'Style in Literature' (1885) and Robert Louis Stevenson's 'On Style in Literature: Its Technical Elements' (1885). Most directly, 'Style' responds in a number of significant ways to George Saintsbury's 'English Prose Style' (1886), which served as the introduction to his anthology, *Specimens of English Prose Style: From Malory to Macaulay* (1886), and which Pater reviewed in *The Guardian* as part of his omnibus 'Four Books for Students of English Literature' (1886).[9] With 'Style', together with the portraits of English prose writers, *Appreciations* stands as the most significant and most influential account of nonfictional prose as an art form of the Victorian age.

***

Pater's opening manoeuvre in *Appreciations* to establish prose as a 'fine art' is to dismantle the conventional hierarchy between poetry and prose. Those 'who have dwelt most emphatically on the distinction … have been tempted to limit the proper functions of prose too narrowly.… Critical efforts to limit art *a priori* … are always liable to be discredited by the facts of artistic production' ('Style', 5–6). This position is consistent with the mainstream of romantic poetics and its opposition, for instance, to the extreme conventions and strict rules of eighteenth-century French neoclassicism. Pater has in mind Wordsworth's famous attack, in the 'Preface' to *Lyrical Ballads* (1800), on Thomas Gray's alleged attempt 'to widen the space of separation betwixt Prose and Metrical composition'.[10] Both Wordsworth and De Quincey are presented as romantic theorists advancing the far more vital distinction between 'imaginative and unimaginative' composition (7). Pater takes interpretive liberties with his

implied characterisation of De Quincey's categories, 'literature of knowledge' and 'literature of power', but deftly reworks them into his own terms:
the achieved distinction between 'literature of fact' and the 'literature of
imaginative fact' clears the ground for the discussion of prose style to
follow, and establishes the artist's representation of fact 'as connected with
soul, of a specific personality' as the very condition of literary art, in poetry
or prose (10).[11]

As a representative neoclassical adversary, Pater singles out John
Dryden, the great early Augustan, who 'with the characteristic instinct of
his age, loved to emphasise the distinction between poetry and prose' (7).
Yet, almost nowhere in Dryden does one find him taking up the distinc-
tion, let alone defending it. His only direct treatment is brief, from the
'Preface' to *The State of Innocence* (1674) and the discussion on '*Poetique
License*', the 'speaking things in Verse which are beyond the severity of
Prose', characterised by tropes and figures, 'both which are of a much
larger extent, and more forcibly to be us'd in Verse than Prose';[12] and from
the 'Preface' to *Fables: Ancient and Modern* (1700): 'Prose allows more
Liberty of Thought, and the Expression is more easie, when unconfin'd by
Numbers.'[13] Pater is probably thinking too of the distinctions Dryden
draws, in both the 'Epistle Dedicatory of the *Rival Ladies*' (1664) and *An
Essay of Dramatic Poesy* (1668), between rhymed and blank verse, the
'sound', 'sweetness' and resulting 'advantage' of rhyme absent in blank
verse, which he likens to prose.[14] But Pater's claim is vastly overstated.
Remarkable too is the condescending tone with which Pater represents
Dryden. The writer's 'protest' against any 'confusion' between poetry and
prose comes 'with somewhat diminished effect from one whose poetry was
so prosaic' (7), Pater comments, if not derisively, at least with an irony less
oblique than is customary:

> In truth, his sense of prosaic excellence affected his verse rather than his
> prose, which is not only fervid, richly figured, poetic, as we say, but vitiated,
> all unconsciously, by many a scanning line. Setting up correctness, that
> humble merit of prose, as the central literary excellence, he is really a less
> correct writer than he may seem, still with an imperfect mastery of the
> relative pronoun. (7)

There is not, perhaps, a more patronising moment in Pater's oeuvre than
the dig at Dryden's 'imperfect mastery of the relative pronoun'. Certainly,
this unusual confrontation with Dryden, at the very opening of the
volume, signifies the polemical nature of Pater's treatment of the essay
tradition in English literature. For his real adversaries are not the Augustan

writers themselves, but rather critics of his own day, most prominently Matthew Arnold and George Saintsbury, who regard Dryden as the founder, and the eighteenth century as the standard, of distinguished modern English prose.

Pater's familiar catholicity of taste seemingly does not extend to eighteenth-century English literature, an age, we might say, he regards as classical in tendency to a fault. In this, Pater's attitudes are largely consistent with the predominant mid-Victorian literary-critical reception of the period, exemplified in the rhetoric of Carlyle and Arnold. Eighteenth-century writing, they claim, is deficient in lyric impulse, imagination, and sincerity, while it is excessive in reason, artifice, and wit – 'that unreal and transitory mirth', as Pater defines 'wit' in the essay on Charles Lamb, 'which is as the crackling of thorns under the pot', as opposed to the 'humour' characteristic of Lamb and predominant in the literature of the nineteenth century, 'the laughter which blends with tears and even with the sublimities of the imagination, and which, in its most exquisite motives, is one with pity' (105).[15] From the early essay on Morris, Pater paints the neoclassicism of the eighteenth century as 'outworn' and 'severed … from the genuine motives of ancient art' ('AP', 214). In 'Romanticism', Pater deems Pope the representative poet of 'too little curiosity', 'in common with the age of literature to which he belonged': 'there is always a certain insipidity in the effect of his work, exquisite as it is' ('Postscript', *App.*, 247). A later reference to Pope and Dryden, from Pater's review of Arthur Symons's *Nights and Days* (1889), borders on satire, impatient of the fetishised 'correctness' of style and 'academical proprieties' Pater consistently associates with Dryden (246), while acknowledging in a more positive, yet still attenuated fashion, Pope's poetic achievement: 'for a poet after Dryden, nothing was left but correctness, and thereupon the genius of Pope became correct, with a correctness which made him profoundly original'.[16]

Yet, although Pater contributes to the portrait of the age as colourless and correct, he rejects critics' concomitant (and influential) characterisation of it as the great age of English prose. Instead, in *Appreciations* he constructs a powerful alternative narrative of the development of the English essay tradition. Again, the chief undercurrent is a reaction against Arnold.[17] In 'The Study of Poetry' (1880), Arnold famously declares Dryden 'the puissant and glorious founder', and Pope 'the splendid high priest, of our age of prose and reason'; '[t]hough they may write in verse … Dryden and Pope are not classics of our poetry, they are classics of our prose'.[18] With Dryden, Arnold proclaims, 'at last we have the true English prose, a prose such as we would all gladly use if we only knew how'.[19] As he had maintained in the 'The Literary Influence of Academies' (1864), Arnold believed that 'the true prose is Attic prose',[20] 'prose of the centre',[21] index of 'correctness' (in information, judgment, taste), the realisation of an evolutionary 'stage in culture' beyond the 'provincial'.[22] Arnold employs the ancient Western (and hence orientalist) distinction in style between the Attic and Asiatic; '*Asiatic* prose' in the English literary tradition, as exemplified in the Anglican sermons of Jeremy Taylor, Arnold deems 'extravagant', 'barbarously rich and overloaded', marred by the persistent 'note of provinciality ... the want of simplicity, the want of measure'.[23] In 1864, Arnold had not yet identified the eighteenth century as the golden age of a new English prose, but merely the period of 'our provincial and second-rate literature'. By the time of the 'Preface' to his popular selected edition of Samuel Johnson's *Lives of the Poets* (1878), however, Arnold had come to regard the eighteenth century as 'a period of literary and intellectual movement' representing the 'passage' of the English nation 'to a type of thought and expression modern, European, and which on the whole is ours at the present day, from a type antiquated, peculiar, and which is ours no longer'.[24] Arnold uses the 'Preface' to construct a literary-historical narrative in which the Restoration initiates a decisive break from the prose style of the past, marked by 'length and involvement',[25] in favour of a cleaner, more athletic prose, derived from French models, characterised by 'qualities of regularity, uniformity, precision, balance',[26] and responsive to the conditions of modern life. The achievement in eighteenth-century prose Arnold regards as both resulting from and encouraging the period's deficiency in 'poetical instincts' and 'mistaken poetical practice'.[27] 'The glory of English literature is in poetry, and in poetry the strength of the eighteenth century does not lie', Arnold intones, yet the age 'accomplished for us an immense literary progress, and its very shortcomings in poetry were an instrument to that progress, and served it'.[28] With the 'ten-syllable couplet' as its 'ruling form', the 'poetry of the century was a perpetual school of the qualities requisite for a good prose',[29] Arnold explains, in a comment that prefigures Pater's characterisation of the 'prosaic' quality of Dryden's poetry. As Arnold more memorably articulates the matter, in 'The Study of Poetry', 'it was impossible that a fit prose should establish itself amongst us without some touch of frost to the imaginative life of the soul'.[30]

***

Appreciations appeared during the most volatile years in the campaign for the institutionalisation of English in British universities, led with maniacal energy and determination by the London Extension lecturer, John Churton Collins. From 1886 to 1891, the publication year of Collins's manifesto, *The Study of English Literature: A Plea for its Recognition and Organization at the Universities*, the subject inspired something of a national conversation, both within and beyond the peculiar political dynamics of Oxford and Cambridge. In his only explicit contribution to the heated debates, the brief comment published in November 1886 as part of the series 'English at the Universities' in the *Pall Mall Gazette*, Pater provides a more reserved endorsement than the majority of respondents to Collins's questionnaire, reflecting his position as Classics don at Oxford, as well as his relatively new status as a successful English novelist (*Marius the Epicurean* was published only one year earlier, in 1885). But Pater's reticence was surely inspired too by the figure of Collins himself, a staunch critic of Pater's own style and mode of subjective literary criticism. Only a year earlier, Collins had published in the *Quarterly Review* a long, scathing review of John Addington Symonds's *Shakspere's [sic] Predecessors in the English Drama* (1884),[31] using the occasion to launch an attack on the Aesthetic Movement and aesthetic criticism (although Collins does not use the term). Collins anoints Swinburne the 'leader and founder'[32] of a 'morbid'[33] school of literary criticism, characterised by arrogant displays of imagination and emotion, exaggerated eroticism, and unruly prose.[34] With Swinburne and his followers, Collins complains, style functions as means of obfuscation and index of affectation: 'With them the art of expression is ... the art of simulating originality and eloquence.'[35] Symonds's work is 'deformed with the offensive jargon' and 'metaphorical extravagance' of 'his master' Swinburne (337).[36]

Collins's polemic closely resembles the rhetoric of W. J. Courthope and the conservative critics of the *Quarterly* from the previous decade. Members of this 'minority tradition' in Victorian criticism, conspicuous as well in periodicals such as *Fraser's Magazine* and the *Edinburgh Review*, sought 'to reassert a broadly Augustan conception of the nature and function of literature', and to promote 'a wider movement towards classicism in literature'.[37] They waged a sustained attack on the 'modern romantic school',[38] which they regarded as promoting unhealthy tendencies in contemporary literature – excessive subjectivism, obscure subject matter, indefinite thought, and a perverse preoccupation with style. Yet the primary focus of their efforts was the state of contemporary English poetry as manifest, for example, in Browning, Rossetti, and especially Swinburne (all poets championed by Pater). Collins shifts the focus explicitly to prose and literary criticism:

> In former times this style ... though ridiculous and pernicious ... was not
> without a certain propriety. In our time it has invaded criticism where it is
> simply intolerable.[39]

Although Collins never mentions Pater by name, he is unavoidably associated with the substance and language of the attack; the thought and
diction of the following passage reads almost like a parody of both the
'Preface' and 'Conclusion' to *The Renaissance*, and anticipates, humour-
lessly, the wit of Wilde in 'The Critic as Artist':

> The mind dwells not on the objects themselves, but what is accidentally
> recalled or accidentally suggested by them, and nothing is but what is not.
> Criticism is with him neither a process of analysis nor a process of inter-
> pretation, but simple fiction. What seem to be Mr. Swinburne's convictions
> are merely his temporary impressions.[40]

Appreciations engages the contemporary arguments concerning English
studies and the rehabilitation of eighteenth-century neoclassical literature.
Both movements were characterised to a significant degree by anti-
romantic sensibilities and a hostility towards the 'impressionist' criticism
of Pater and the aesthetic fashions of the 1870s. By the 1880s, the
'minority tradition' in Victorian criticism had blossomed into a full-scale
'Queen Anne' revival.[41] By 1880, Arnold had already observed that 'the
authority of Wordsworth and Coleridge does not weigh much with the
young generation, and there are many signs to show that the eighteenth
century and its judgments are coming into favor again'.[42] Scholarship
focusing on eighteenth-century literature proliferates at the end of the
century and into the next with books of literary history, biographies,
editions, and articles in the periodical press. Almost half of the original
English Men of Letters series, edited by John Morley, are of Augustan and
neoclassical writers, beginning with Leslie Stephen's *Samuel Johnson*
(1878), and in general the largely conservative, so-called bookmen are
partial to the period. Courthope, named Oxford Professor of English
Poetry in 1895, was involved throughout the decade with a new, definitive
edition of Alexander Pope, using the platform to excoriate contemporary
literary values, and to resume his attacks on romantic individualism and
nineteenth-century poetic language from the essays of the mid-1870s.
Collins's own collection, *Essays and Studies* (1895), which includes the
Symonds review, focuses on the Augustans, including a long opening essay
on Dryden (1878), as exemplars of literary and critical standards, and as
'protest against the mischievous tendencies of the New School of

Criticism, a school as inimical to good taste and good sense as it is to morals and decency'.[43]

***

Saintsbury, appointed to the Chair of Rhetoric and English Literature at Edinburgh in 1895, is another of the eighteenth-century enthusiasts, contributing *John Dryden* (1881) for the English Men of Letters, and re-editing the text of Sir Walter Scott's 18-volume edition of Dryden (1882). A more complex figure than either Collins or Courthope, Saintsbury was himself something of an impressionistic critic, and a consistent admirer of Pater, praising his writing as early as 1875, culminating in what remains one of the most sympathetic, discerning analyses of Pater's prose style in *A History of English Prose Rhythm* (1912).[44] Yet Saintsbury clearly regards the developments of English prose in his own time as a momentous falling away from the standards of form and style achieved in the earlier century. 'English Prose Style' hews closely to Arnold's historical narrative, with Dryden the chief representative of the Restoration reform of English prose, completed by the writers of the Queen Anne school – Swift, Addison, and Steele. Before 'the period itself had ceased English prose as an instrument may be said to have been perfected'.[45] Beginning with the reign of George IV (1820), prose style becomes increasingly 'disarranged',[46] giving rise to a 'literary antinomianism',[47] characterised by a 'laboured and ornate manner'[48] and a confusion of the 'distinct aims'[49] of the prose writer and poet, 'faults' discernible in both 'French naturalism and English aestheticism'.[50]

Pater regarded Saintsbury's essay as a provocation. Scholars have long recognised that the argument of Pater's review of Saintsbury's *Specimens* (1886) prefigures 'Style'.[51] Pater deems the prose style of Dryden and the eighteenth century as merely one stylistic possibility among many, generating a 'specific and unique beauty' (*Essays*, 5), following from its 'strictly prosaic merit' and 'conformity, before all other aims, to laws of a structure primarily reasonable' (6). The claim for neoclassical prose as manifestation of 'true law' (Arnold), the fulfilment of prose style's 'obvious requirements' (Saintsbury), Pater regards as 'savouring . . . of the arbitrary psychology of the last century, and with it the prejudice that there can be but one only beauty of prose style' ('Style', *App.*, 8). In a footnote Pater added to the *Appreciations* version of 'Style', he describes Saintsbury's anthology as tracing 'the tradition of that severer beauty' of English prose, 'of which this admirable scholar of our literature is known to be a lover' (12). Dryden is Saintsbury's 'favourite',

Pater writes in the *Guardian* review, the 'first master of the sort of prose he prefers' (*Essays*, 7, 4). Pater's description of the period's anti-idealist orientation, its absence of speculative and religious instincts, echoes Arnold's characterisation of the imaginative limitations of the age, its 'touch of frost' and disregard of the 'deeper powers of mind and soul'.[52] The 'reaction' of Dryden and his followers 'against the exuberance and irregularity' of Elizabethan prose, Pater asserts, 'was effective only because an age had come—the age of a negative, or agnostic philosophy—in which men's minds must needs be limited to the superficialities of things, with a kind of narrowness amounting to a positive gift' (*Essays*, 9). Arnold's 'age of prose' yields, for Pater, nothing 'fit' nor 'true', but rather a style narrow, regulated, codified. The prose style of Richard Steele, whom Pater regards as the most personal and 'impulsive' (11) of the neoclassical school, a 'pioneer of an everybody's literature' who nevertheless 'had his subjectivities' (10), 'is regular because the matter he deals with is the somewhat uncontentious, even, limited soul, of an age not imaginative, and unambitious in its speculative flight' (12).[53]

Three months before the appearance of 'Style', Pater published his own most explicit definition of the essay, pronouncing the genre the 'characteristic' literary form of his day. Paradoxically, Pater conveys this important critical statement within the fourth chapter of the serialised, ultimately unfinished, novel *Gaston de Latour*, 'Peach Blossom and Wine' (published in *Macmillan's Magazine*, September 1888), an example of his insistent crossing of generic boundaries, a central strategy of *Marius* and the *Imaginary Portraits*. The subject is Michel de Montaigne. Pater's narrator deems the author of *Les Essais* the 'inventor' of the form: 'the essay in its seemingly modest aim, its really large and venturous possibilities—is indicative of his peculiar function with regard to that age, as in truth the commencement of our own'.[54] For Montaigne, as for Pater,

> the essay came into use at what was really the invention of the relative or 'modern spirit' in the Renaissance of the sixteenth century.... It supplies precisely the literary form necessary to a mind for which truth itself is but a possibility, realizable not as general and open conclusion but rather as elusive effect of a particular experience—to a mind which, noting faithfully those random lights which meet it by the way, must needs content itself with suspense of judgment at the end of the intellectual journey, to the very last asking *Que sais-je?*[55]

In Pater's view, the essay embodies the relativity of knowledge and individualism that constitute the defining features of the modern romantic spirit as he repeatedly describes it.[56]

Thus, *Appreciations* inscribes a Montaignian tradition of the essay in English literary history, a literary-historical narrative derived in part from the work of the English Romantic prose writers, but unique in the Victorian criticism of English prose, and in deliberate opposition to the prevailing Arnoldian vision of the English essay and its development. Beginning with Sir Thomas Browne, who represents for Pater the early modern English reception and assimilation of Montaigne, Pater presents an English tradition of the essay as 'self-portraiture' ('Charles Lamb', *App.*, 119), idiosyncratic and stylistically heterogeneous. Towards the end of the seventeenth century, that tradition is interrupted and 'reformed', bringing to fruition, what Pater calls in Browne, 'the tradition of a classical clearness in English literature' (125), one with its own early modern antecedents (Pater singles out Hugh Latimer and Sir Thomas More). With Charles Lamb and other prose writers of the Romantic period (Hazlitt, Hunt), the Montaignian tradition is revived, taking the shape of what has come to be known as the 'romantic familiar essay', a tradition carried on by Pater himself, whose critical work one might regard as a defamiliarisation of the familiar essay as practised by an earlier nineteenth-century generation of literary 'men of taste'.

The magisterial opening paragraph of 'Sir Thomas Browne', an essay first published only three months after the *Guardian* review of Saintsbury's anthology, deftly articulates the contours of the development of the English essay, as well as its relation to the traditions of France and Germany. Pater introduces Browne as a culmination of that early English prose before the advent of neoclassical correctness represented by Dryden and Locke. The development of English prose follows the pattern established in France. Montaigne, the founder of the essay as a literary form decidedly unprofessional, informal, even confidential, addressed to a 'friendly reader', is displaced by the classical ethos of the French Academy and 'the school of Malherbe', as Pater had called French neoclassicism in 'Joachim du Bellay' (*Ren.*, 132). Dryden will lead the derivative classical reforms of the Augustan age, displacing the Montaignesque prose literature of early modern England. Like Montaigne, Pater insists, who gives his reader 'so much ... of the "subjective," ... of the singularities of personal character', Browne affords the reader a picture of the vision within, 'a matter ... "bred"' wholly, '"amongst the weeds and tares" of his own brain' (125). Pater acknowledges the Arnoldian critique of the extravagance and persistent note of provinciality that characterises early modern English prose, its 'unevenness ... in thought and style', 'lack of design', and 'lack of authority' (125). It is all 'so oddly mixed', Pater observes, demonstrating 'how much he [Browne], and the sort of literature he represents, really stood in need of *technique*' (126). But for such 'faults' (125), abundant 'recompense' (see, for a full discussion, Chapter 9). Sincerity, such a serious and important word in Pater's lexicon, always signifying profound artistic achievement, is more easily and transparently expressed in an earlier intellectual culture, one yet to embrace correctness, technique, professional training: 'in their absolute sincerity, not only do these authors clearly exhibit themselves ... but, even more than mere professionally instructed writers, they belong to, and reflect, the age they lived in' (127).

I close with another crucial interlocutor for Pater's *Appreciations*: W. J. Courthope, who gives his most concerted late-century critique of English romantic values in *The Liberal Movement in English Literature* (1885), a collection of essays previously published in the *National Review*. The book extends the mid-century Tory polemic, setting the 'conservatism' of the eighteenth century against the 'Romantic movement' of the nineteenth, and its liberal ethos, which he deplores. With *Appreciations*, the long-standing debate between Courthope and Pater takes the form of competing book-length treatments of English romanticism. Read next to each other, Pater's antinomian vision of ethics and justice starkly counters Courthope's assertion of 'ancestral *law*' as the defining virtue of conservatism and the eighteenth century.[57] It is in the concluding section of the essay on Shakespeare's *Measure for Measure* that Pater expresses most powerfully that 'idea of justice', cultivated by aesthetic experience and the relative spirit, 'beyond the limits of any acknowledged law' (183). But it equally informs his treatment of Wordsworth's poems as teaching the 'art of ... contemplation' (62), 'being' rather than 'doing', a protest against the machine-like conception of means and ends in practical, argumentative discourse. Above all, it is the character of the essay and the essayist, Pater suggests, amid the increasing moral and intellectual complexities of the late nineteenth century, that is most capable of conveying 'true justice' as 'in its essence a finer knowledge through love' (183). *Appreciations* represents a major contribution to the centuries-long conversation about the 'essay' as genre, a mode characterised by its heterogeneity and empathetic imagination, sympathy conveyed through sensibility, and subjectivity embedded in style – all privileged Paterian terms aligned with 'romanticism' and the 'romantic spirit'.

Notes

1 Oscar Wilde, review of *Appreciations*, 'Mr. Pater's Last Volume', *The Speaker* (22 March 1890), 319–20, repr. in *Critical Heritage*, 232.
2 For discussions of Pater's central role in the nineteenth-century apprehension of the prose essay as art form, see George Levine and William Madden, 'Introduction', in *The Art of Victorian Prose*, ed. George Levine and William

Madden (New York 1968), vii–xxi; and Travis R. Merritt, 'Taste, Opinion, and Theory in the Rise of Victorian Prose Stylism', ibid., 3–38.

3 Less than a year before *Appreciations* appeared, Pater published, in both the *Athenaeum* (26 January 1889), 109–10 and the *Guardian* (27 February 1889), 317–18, unsigned omnibus reviews of new editions of Wordsworth's work. His brief unsigned review of the French-born Mark André Raffalovich's book of poems, *It Is Thyself* (1889), appeared in *The Pall Mall Gazette* (15 April 1889), 3. Three other review essays published in the *Guardian* prior to *Appreciations* complete the total of Pater's published work on English literary subjects. They include 'Four Books for Students of English Literature' (17 February 1886), 246–7; a review of Arthur Symons's *An Introduction to the Study of Browning* (9 November 1887), 1709–10; and a review of Mary (Mrs Humphry) Ward's *Robert Elsmere* (28 March 1888), 468–9. Houghton MS 13, entitled 'English Literature', includes a sketch of an essay detailing a scheme of English literary history, from the medieval to the modern; summary notes for the project, including parallels to the visual arts; and detailed commentary on Chaucer and Shakespeare. This work is probably related to the manuscript material on Thomas Hobbes, Houghton MS 18. The manuscripts also include an essay-in-progress on Newman, 'The Writings of Cardinal Newman' (Houghton MS 12), as well as other occasional comments on English authors and texts. In addition, we know from May Ottley of the essay-in-progress on Samuel Johnson that was among Pater's papers at his death, and now presumably lost.

4 'Introduction', *The Spirit of the Age: Victorian Essays*, ed. Gertrude Himmelfarb (New Haven 2007), 27.

5 *Macmillan's Magazine* 35 (November 1876), 64–70 (64).

6 The Schlegels' famous classical-romantic distinction, although well known in England (particularly after the 1813 publication in English of Madame de Staël's *D'Allemagne*), never inspired the fierce debates that it did in Germany, France, Italy, and Spain. Pater's essay is, to that date, the most significant treatment of the term 'romanticism' in England. See George Whalley, 'England/Romantic—Romanticism', in *'Romantic' and Its Cognates: The European History of a Word*, ed. Hans Eichner (Toronto 1972), 157–262, for the most substantial history of the term's development in England. Coleridge, De Quincey, Hazlitt, Scott, Henry Crabb Robinson, and Thomas Campbell are among writers earlier in the century who take up the Schlegels' distinction, but without establishing it for serious critical consideration. See also Herbert Weisinger, 'English Treatment of the Classical–Romantic Problem', *Modern Language Quarterly* 7 (1946), 477–88; René Wellek, 'The Concept of "Romanticism" in Literary History. I. The Term "Romantic" and Its Derivatives', *Comparative Literature* 1 (1949), 1–23; and David Perkins, *Is Literary History Possible?* (Baltimore 1992), 85–120.

7 The French critic and historian Hippolyte Taine, in his five-volume *Histoire de la littérature anglaise* (1863–9; English trans. 1872), is apparently the first to refer to the 'English Romantic school', and the Romantic poets of the early

nineteenth century, although Wellek identifies a few mid-century handbooks of English literature that use the term with reference to English writers, including David Macbeth Moir's *Sketches of the Poetical Literature of the Past Half Century* (1852): 'The further spread and establishment of the term for English literature of the early nineteenth century is probably due to Alois Brandl's *Coleridge und die romantische Schule in England* ['Coleridge and the Romantic School in England' (1886)], translated by Lady Eastlake (1887), and to the vogue of Pater's discussion of "Romanticism" in *Appreciations*' (Wellek, 'The Concept of "Romanticism"', 16).

8 Laurel Brake makes this point in *Subjugated Knowledges: Journalism, Gender and Literature in the Nineteenth Century* (New York 1994), 63–82. See also Brake, 'Aesthetics in the Affray: Walter Pater's *Appreciations, with an Essay on Style*', in *The Politics of Pleasure: Aesthetics and Cultural Theory*, ed. Stephen Regan (Buckingham 1992), 59–86. Pater, of course, first knew Arnold's essay as the general introduction to T. Humphry Ward's anthology, *The English Poets* (1880, 1883), to which Pater contributed his essays on Coleridge (1880) and Rossetti (1883).

9 See Billie Andrew Inman, 'Reaction to Saintsbury in Pater's Formulation of Ideas on Prose Style', *Nineteenth-Century Prose* 24 (1997), 108–26, and John Coates, 'Controversial Aspects of Pater's "Style"', *Papers on Language & Literature* 40 (2004), 384–411. Inman observes that Pater's review of Saintsbury's anthology 'is the first of four closely-linked discussions' on prose style, including 'Sir Thomas Browne' (1886); 'Peach Blossom and Wine' (1888), a chapter of *Gaston de Latour*; and 'Style' (1888).

10 *Lyrical Ballads, and Other Poems, 1797–1800*, ed. James Butler and Karen Green (Ithaca 1992), 749.

11 De Quincey first formulates his distinction in 'Letters to a Young Man whose Education has been Neglected' (1823), and then, significantly revised, in 'The Poetry of Pope' (1848), later reprinted as the opening essay in his collection *Leaders in Literature, With a Notice of Traditional Errors Affecting Them* (Edinburgh 1863). For an account of Pater's manipulation of De Quincey's terms, see Inman, 'Reaction to Saintsbury', 125, n. 88.

12 *The Works of John Dryden*, ed. E. N. Hooker, H. T. Swedenberg Jr., et al., 20 vols (Berkeley), xii, ed. Vinton A. Dearing (1994), 96.

13 *The Works of John Dryden*, vii, ed. Dearing (2002), 43.

14 'An Essay of Dramatick Poesie', ed. Samuel H. Monk, A. E. Wallace Maurer and Vinton A. Dearing (1971), 71.

15 Recent scholarship has complicated the conventional account of the Victorian reception of the eighteenth century. See especially *The Victorians and the Eighteenth Century: Reassessing the Tradition*, ed. Francis O'Gorman and Katherine Turner (Aldershot 2004), and B. W. Young, *The Victorian Eighteenth Century: An Intellectual History* (Oxford 2007). See also Linda C. Dowling, 'The Aesthetes and the Eighteenth Century', *Victorian Studies* 20 (1977), 357–77.

16 'A Poet With Something to Say', *Pall Mall Gazette* 49 (23 March 1889).

17 The Preface to *The Renaissance* (1873) begins by countering Arnold's suggestion that the critic's task is 'To see the object as in itself it really is' (*Ren.*, xix).
18 Arnold, *Prose*, ix. 180–1.
19 Arnold, *Prose*, iii. 179.
20 Arnold, *Prose*, iii. 247.
21 Arnold, *Prose*, iii. 246.
22 See John Campbell Major, 'Matthew Arnold and Attic Prose Style', *PMLA* 59
   (1944), 1086–1103.
23 Arnold, *Prose*, iii. 247.
24 Arnold, *Prose*, viii. 312.
25 Arnold, *Prose*, viii. 314.
26 Arnold, *Prose*, viii. 317.
27 Arnold, *Prose*, viii. 318.
28 Arnold, *Prose*, viii. 316.
29 Arnold, *Prose*, viii. 317.
30 Arnold, *Prose*, ix. 180.
31 [John Churton Collins], '*Shakspere's Predecessors in the English Drama*',
   Quarterly Review 161 (October 1885), 330–81.
32 Collins, '*Shakspere's Predecessors*', 335.
33 Collins, '*Shakspere's Predecessors*', 334.
34 Collins's attack rehearses many of the arguments made against Swinburne,
   D. G. Rossetti, and others by 'Thomas Maitland' [Robert Buchanan], 'The
   Fleshly School of Poetry', *Contemporary Review* 18 (October 1871), 334–50.
35 Collins, '*Shakspere's Predecessors*', 334.
36 Collins, '*Shakspere's Predecessors*', 337.
37 See R. V. Johnson, 'Pater and the Victorian Anti-Romantics', *Essays in Criticism*
   4 (1954), 42; I take the term 'minority tradition' from R. G. Cox, 'Victorian
   Criticism of Poetry: The Minority Tradition', *Scrutiny* 18 (1951), 2–17.
38 [W. J. Courthope], 'Wordsworth and Gray', *Quarterly Review* 141
   (1876), 107.
39 Collins, '*Shakspere's Predecessors*', 335.
40 Collins, '*Shakspere's Predecessors*', 335–6.
41 Perhaps first coined by Grant Allen in comments on R. L. Stevenson's *Travels
   with a Donkey in the Cévennes*: 'Mr. Stevenson's manner may be regarded as
   one among the many products of the Queen Anne revival. His writing is a
   phase of that reaction which is everywhere making itself felt against the
   formless solidity of the age in which we live' (*Fortnightly Review* 32 (1879),
   154). See Oscar Maurer, Jr., 'Pope and the Victorians', *Studies in English* 24
   (1944), 211–38.
42 Arnold, *Prose*, ix. 178.
43 *Essays and Studies* (1895), viii.
44 Saintsbury's theory of 'English Prose Style' represents a radical embrace of
   form at the expense of meaning, earning even a mild rebuke from Pater
   himself: 'If there be a weakness in Mr. Saintsbury's view, it is perhaps in a
   tendency to regard style a little too independently of matter' (*Essays*, 15).

45 Saintsbury, 'English Prose Style', in *Specimens of English Prose Style* (1886), xxii.
46 Saintsbury, 'English Prose Style', xvi.
47 Saintsbury, 'English Prose Style', xxxii.
48 Saintsbury, 'English Prose Style', xxxvii.
49 Saintsbury, 'English Prose Style', xvi.
50 Saintsbury, 'English Prose Style', xviii.
51 In addition to Inman, 'Reactions to Saintsbury', and Coates 'Controversial Aspects of Pater's "Style"', see A. J. Farmer, *Walter Pater as a Critic of English Literature: A Study of 'Appreciations'* (1931; repr. Folcroft, PA 1969), 107; Germain d'Hangest, *Walter Pater, Études Anglaises*, 2 vols (Paris 1961), ii. 373, n. 55; David De Laura, *Hebrew and Hellene in Victorian England* (Austin 1969), 329.
52 'Thomas Gray', in Arnold, *Prose*, ix. 200.
53 In notes for an essay on English literature (Houghton MS 13) Pater describes the eighteenth century in similar terms, as the 'age of nihilism', which, 'on the whole, represents culture. Berkeley, Pope, &c. turn to mere manners, accidents', as opposed to the 'idealism' and '\rel[igio]n/' of the 'age of hyp[otheses]' which Pater associates with the late sixteenth and seventeenth centuries.
54 *Macmillan's Magazine* 58 (September 1888), 393–400 (397).
55 'Peach Blossom and Wine', 396–7. Pater deleted the passage on Montaigne's modernity from the manuscript version of the completed chapters, and it does not appear in the text of the novel printed by Shadwell. Pater repurposed the passage, revised and slightly expanded, in 'The Doctrine of Plato' in *Plato and Platonism* (1893). See also *CW*, iv. 215–16.
56 On Pater's definition and theory of the essay, see Stefano Evangelista, 'Things Said by the Way: Walter Pater and the Essay', in *On Essays: Montaigne to the Present*, ed. Thomas Karshan and Kathryn Murphy (Oxford 2020), 241–57. Evangelista emphasises Pater's relation to the nineteenth-century European tradition of the essay, specifically German romantic criticism and French aesthetic prose. See also Wolfgang Iser, *Walter Pater: The Aesthetic Moment*, trans. David Henry Wilson (Cambridge 1987), 17–19.
57 W. J. Courthope, *The Liberal Movement in English Literature* (1885). The 'nature of English Conservatism, religious, political, and literary, in the eighteenth century' presupposes 'that all spiritual, political, and artistic development must proceed in conformity with an ancestral *law*' (43–4); for Anglican divines, it is the authority of 'Christian law' (48); in politics, the law of 'inheritance' (52); in poetry, 'correctness', as exemplified by Pope, 'obedience to the *laws* of imaginative thought, . . . justice of poetical conception'.

CHAPTER 2

Unravelling Pater's English Poet: The Imaginary Portrait as Criticism

Lene Østermark-Johansen

The adjective 'English' begins to figure in the titles of Walter Pater's essays and reviews in the 1880s: 'The English School of Painting', 'Four Books for Students of English Literature', 'English at the Universities', 'Shakespeare's English Kings'.[1] Pater's unfinished portrait, published posthumously under the title 'An English Poet',[2] probably in part derives from this period, when his two contributions (Coleridge and Rossetti) to T. H. Ward's *The English Poets: Selections* also appeared. This emphasis on 'English' might suggest an increasing concern with art and literature at a national level, yet Pater was still acutely aware of the European influence on English culture. When, in the autumn of 1886, the *Pall Mall Gazette*, then under the editorship of W. T. Stead, selected Pater as one of the contributors to the lengthy debate about the introduction of English as a university subject, the choice fell on an author whose publications reflected his profound concern with English literature. Although an Oxford classicist, Pater's publications on Greek subjects were by 1886 limited to mythological essays on Dionysus, Demeter and Persephone, and three essays on Greek sculpture. His public engagement with English literature, on the other hand, with essays on two of Shakespeare plays, on Browne, Wordsworth, Coleridge, Lamb, Morris, D. G. Rossetti, and on Romanticism as a European phenomenon, marked him out as an authority on sixteenth- and nineteenth-century English literature, a likely supporter of Stead and John Churton Collins's campaign for the establishing of schools of English. Yet Pater's hesitations and reservations on the matter were audible throughout his contribution: pointing out the 'organic unity' of classical and modern European literature, he was wary that any examination in a literary discipline would result in the fading of the '"fine flower" of English poetry, or Latin oratory, or Greek art', as 'Intelligent Englishmen' naturally resorted 'for a liberal pleasure to their own literature'.[3]

Pater undoubtedly counted himself among such Englishmen enjoying English literature as 'truant reading' (*ME*, i. 54, ch. 4), that which you read for pleasure when you are really supposed to be reading something else. His floral imagery suggested aesthetic sensitivity and delight; in his fiction his protagonist with the flowery name, Florian Deleal, emerged in a modern allegory reminiscent of John Bunyan's *Pilgrim's Progress* as an aesthete in the making, perceptive of the beauty of the red hawthorn and associated with the wallflower, linking him to the house in which he was once a child. His Wordsworthian English poet, drawn to the rose and the honeysuckle, fully aware of the fragrance of words, encountered a wealth of wild marigold, yellow horned poppies, lavender, and dwarf-rose the moment he set foot on French soil, suggestive of the wealth of French literature awaiting him. And Gaston, having read Pierre de Ronsard's poetry – such as the famous 'To Cassandra' ('Mignonne, allons voir si la rose') in which youth, flower, and femininity merge – sought out the retired leader of the Pléiade, now turned gardening prior,[4] while realising that even beautiful blossoms might be Baudelairean flowers of evil.

In the late 1870s and throughout the 1880s Pater developed the form of the imaginary portrait as a mode of literary criticism, merging fiction, (auto)biography, and travel writing into a genre which enabled him to write creatively in dialogue with English and French literature. The freedom he enjoyed once he embraced the short portrait of some 7,000 to 8,000 words, often based on a rough biographical outline of a young talented male protagonist, opened up a plethora of generic and intertextual possibilities for the study of literature in a self-reflexive mode in which he could imitate or comment on the literature and criticism of both the past and the present. In choosing the term 'portrait', he was inviting a dialogue with Charles Augustin Sainte-Beuve who between 1827 and 1846 had published some 150 literary essays under the heading *Portraits: Critiques et portraits* (1839), *Portraits des femmes* (1844), *Portraits littéraires* (1844), and *Portraits contemporains* (1846). An ardent reader of Sainte-Beuve, Pater was repeatedly borrowing his works and acquiring his volumes for his private book collection.[5] Most of the French subjects for Pater's essays had been treated by Sainte-Beuve: Ronsard, du Bellay, Montaigne, Marguerite de Navarre, Pascal, Flaubert, and Mérimée. Sainte-Beuve's works blended biography with criticism, but also grew out of his own early toying with poetry and fiction. For Pater the liberty permitted by the imaginary portrait released the more playful and poetic parts of his intellect, although, interestingly, his name appeared on the title pages of both *Marius the Epicurean* (1885) and the *Imaginary Portraits* (1887) as 'Walter Pater, M.A./Fellow of Brasenose College, Oxford'. The portraits might be imaginary, but they were still published by an academic with a college affiliation at one of England's two leading universities.

The cross-pollination between Pater's literary essays and his portraits is profound; often he was working on essays, reviews, and portraits at the same time, and certain clusters of closely connected pieces of criticism and fiction were the result.[6] Places, ideas, motifs, and atmospheres recur, yet treated in radically different ways. The large holdings of Pater's unfinished manuscripts in the Houghton Library suggest that many of Pater's texts had lengthy gestation periods: begun, left to simmer, sometimes for years, and then taken up again much later.[7] Developments in Pater's handwriting, references to the books he was borrowing in the Oxford libraries, or cross-references to some of Pater's other texts provide clues to his lengthy composition process which, at the time of his death, was well known.[8] Yet the dating of the manuscripts remains problematic, full of uncertainties and loose conjectures.[9] The core texts for examination in this chapter are three such fragments, all revealing Pater's strong interest in English literature in the mid-1880s: one long and one short manuscript fragment, and one posthumously published fragment of which there is no known manuscript in existence. One is an essay or lecture on English literature;[10] the second a rough plot outline for a long imaginary portrait, entitled 'Thistle' (thus in keeping with the floral imagery), set in England in the second decade of the nineteenth century ('STC. Keats, Shelley, Wordsworth, Byron, are around.'[11]); the third is the polished fragment of just over 5,000 words published in 1931 under the title 'Imaginary Portraits 2: An English Poet'.[12] There is inconsistency with respect to the title; the heading of the 1931 text is 'Imaginary Portraits 2: An English Poet', while the title which precedes Pater's narrative reads 'The English Poet.' Irrespective of whether Pater desired the definite or the indefinite article, the text is the only one of his portraits which foregrounds national identity. All three fragments reflect Pater's concern with the impact of the reading of English literature on the individual, at the same time as they view English literature in a European perspective. They contextualise his contribution to the *Pall Mall Gazette* debate, even if his response turned out not to be quite as supportive as the editor might have hoped.

The three texts invite us to consider the individual as part of a zeitgeist: the harmony of Chaucer's writings as emblematic of the undivided medieval church,[13] the post-revolutionary protagonist Thistle as a Romantic precursor of John Henry Newman,[14] and the nameless English poet as a mid-Victorian cosmopolitan writer, of Anglo-French descent, brought up in Cumberland on Renaissance and Romantic poetry, and ready to embrace his European heritage when the text finishes abruptly mid-sentence. William Hazlitt's *The Spirit of the Age: Or, Contemporary Portraits* (1825) had used character sketches of real writers and philosophers to paint a portrait of his own era (he did, after all, have an artistic background as a portrait painter); by contrast, Pater's imaginary portraits were concerned with Newman's Romantic ancestors or an anonymous nineteenth-century poet whose fondness for hard, artificially crafted verses might remind the reader of Théophile Gautier's *Émaux et camées* (1852–72). The zeitgeist left its imprint on great and small alike; in his 'Preface' to *The Renaissance* Pater made his aesthetic critic ask, 'In whom did the stir, the genius, the sentiment of the period find itself? where was the receptacle of its refinement, its elevation, its taste?' (*Ren.*, xxi). Quoting from Sainte-Beuve's definition of a humanist (from one of his essays on Joachim du Bellay), Pater envisioned his aesthetic critic:

> Let us allow ourselves to imagine what it was like to be a friend of Racine or Fénelon, a M. de Tréville, a M. de Valincour, one of those well-bred people who did not aim at being authors, but who confined themselves to reading, to knowing beautiful things at first hand, and to nourishing themselves on these things as discriminating amateurs, as accomplished humanists. For one was humanist then, something almost no longer permitted today. (*Ren.*, xxi)[15]

Sainte-Beuve's humanists and Pater's 'intelligent Englishmen' are 'truant readers', whose discerning tastes rest on their extensive reading, equipping them for their own aesthetic criticism. Pater quotes William Blake's 'genius is always above its age', but his imaginary portraits are less concerned with the outstanding individual than with the less remarkable people who surround them. Where many of his essays revolve around the life and activities of the individual genius, in the portraits the focus is on the minor spirits in their orbits. At the very beginning of the long manuscript subsequently entitled 'English Literature', Pater outlines two different types of contemporary criticism:

> Perhaps the most interesting form of criticism, a form of crit/m <wh. has been> brought to gt. perfection in our own {time} day, is that wh. aims at the def/n of what is most personal & intimate in a writer or a bk. after what may be called the psychological method. Quite the opposite sort of crit/m. {however} the crit/m wh. aims at a ph/y of lit. at the [space for word] {allegation reference ascription} of the individual writer or bk. the special quality {lit. phenomenon} into to some general phase of evolution is another char/tic growth of the present day.[16]

His imaginary portraits develop the first type of criticism, as they focus on intimate personality, while 'English Literature' outlines a series of evolutionary phases, like Ward's *English Poets*, beginning with Chaucer and ending with the nineteenth century. The manuscript, probably begun in the mid-1870s when Pater borrowed Hippolyte Taine's *Histoire de la littérature anglaise* (1863) and the medieval volume of the Catholic John Lingard's *The History of England: From the First Invasion to the Accession of Henry VIII* (1819),[17] was probably worked on again in the late autumn of 1885 when he returned to Taine and Lingard.[18] By then it appears as a lecture ('I wish to dwell for a few minutes on a general/n'),[19] and the first-person pronoun is repeated in a way uncharacteristic of Pater's written work. In Pater's sparse correspondence there is no reference to such a lecture but inevitably one wonders what kind of audience Pater had in mind and whether the lecture was ever delivered. The piece reworks a series of clearly outlined periods in English literature (because Pater needed to work them out for himself or because he was attempting to be peda-gogical?), which in some respects seem uncharacteristically dogmatic:

The Ph/y of Eng. poetry; imag. lit.

Its writers, products, dev/t, considered, traced on an int/l scheme. Hence its novelty—certain int/l cond/ns determining it—& its groups. Affords a scheme for placing every writer.

1. The age of the harmony of the mind with itself & society—the unity of rel. belief & hope, with thought; of culture with rel/ n—Cheerful Eng/ d. 15th c.
2. That breaks up at the Ren . & the Ref/n. A vaguely sceptical, yet hopeful period, charact/d by Mont. generally, by Shak. in Engl. This developes into 3 and 4. 16th c.
3. The age of hyp. —Pl/ic, or otherwise—reconstruction—Hooker & Angric/sm—Ideal love in Sidney{—17th c}—Art for art .
4. The age of nihilism—as 3, on the whole, represents rel/n; so this, on the whole, represents culture. Berkeley. Pope, &. c. turn to mere manners, accidents. 18th c.
5. Reconstruction—3 based on 4—harmony of re/n & cult. still future— but tendencies there too observable—Coleridge, Wordsworth, Tennyson. 19th c.[20]

As Pater's heading informs us, this is a systematic philosophy of English poetry, of imaginative literature, rooted in Lingard's view of the Reformation as the great schism bringing religious and philosophical

division into Western literature. From Chaucer's 'cheerful' England to the
scepticism of Montaigne and Shakespeare and the nihilism of the eighteenth century, the drive is towards a nineteenth-century reconstruction,
a return to the harmony of religion and culture which had existed in the
medieval period. Pater stresses the international scheme in his headnote
(where 'international' would seem to be familiar enough for abbrevia-
tion), and elsewhere sees Chaucer in the context of Dante and Petrarch.
For Pater English literature begins with Chaucer; a large part of the
manuscript revolves around Chaucer with notes about his life and
individual Canterbury tales. By comparison, William Morris, in his
contribution to the *Pall Mall Gazette* debate, had voiced concern that
most teachers of the discipline would trace a national literature back only
to Shakespeare, whereas, in fact, the relatively recently discovered
Beowulf ought to be the originating point of English literature.[21] The
internationalism Pater sought from the initial stages of English literature
was Greek, Italian, and French, rather than rooted in myths of the
barbaric North.

For his four-volume *The English Poets* (1880) T. H. Ward had selected
Chaucer as his point of departure. In his introductory essay to the
anthology, Matthew Arnold, tracing 'the stream of English poetry' to its
'historic origins', connected Chaucer with early French poetry, while
presenting him as 'the father of our splendid English poetry', since 'he is
our "well of English undefiled," because by the lovely charm of his
diction, the lovely charm of his movement, he makes an epoch and founds
a tradition'.[22] Spenser, Shakespeare, Milton, and Keats were all indebted
to Chaucer's 'liquid diction' and 'fluid movement', in Arnold's view, and
although admitting that Chaucer's language posed a difficulty, he concluded that 'He will be read, as time goes on, far more generally than he is
read now'.[23] Whatever the exact date(s) of Pater's 'English Literature'
manuscript, his general outline of the philosophy of English poetry has
significant overlaps with Ward's, something which is hardly surprising,
given the close friendship between the Paters and the Wards, and Ward's
affiliation to Pater's Oxford college. If one looks across Pater's writings for
references to Chaucer, the medieval writer becomes almost as plastic as
Pater's concept of the Renaissance; he could write of love between men in
a Greek context in 'The Knight's Tale', introduced in the second edition of
The Renaissance (1877; *Ren.*, 7). Elsewhere Chaucer's characteristic ani-
mation or expression of life was detected in the Marbles of Aegina, as Pater
concluded his essay of 1880:

> In this monument of Greek chivalry, pensive and visionary as it may seem, those old Greek knights live with a truth like that of Homer or Chaucer. In a sort of stiff grace, combined with a sense of things bright or sorrowful directly felt, the Aeginetan workman is as it were the Chaucer of Greek sculpture. (*GS*, 268; *CW*, viii. 154)

By pointing out the qualities found in the crudeness of the Aegina figures Pater was acknowledging them on an equal footing with the relatively recent appreciation of Chaucer's verse, thus taking canonical sculpture and literature one step further back than the classical period and the Renaissance. In the 'English Literature' lecture, Chaucer's monolithic unity was compared to the great Gothic cathedrals: 'he stands complete, of one piece, like one of the just finished ^contemporary^ Gothic cathedrals, in wh. the creatures of an alien sp/t figure only as gargoyles, caricatures, just permitted as exceptions'.[24] When in 1888 Pater's sixteenth-century Gaston glanced at the pilgrims outside the cathedral at Chartres, this is what he found:

> A motley host, only needing their Chaucer to figure as a looking-glass of life, type against type, they brought with them, on the one hand, the very presence and perfume of Paris, the centre of courtly propriety and fashion; on the other hand, with faces which seemed to belong to another age, curiosities of existence from remote provinces of France, or Europe, from distant, half-fabulous lands, remoter still. (*Gast.* 43; *CW*, iv. 57)

The allusion to Chaucer's pilgrims in a narrative set during the French religious wars marks him out as part of the old-world order in a modern world undergoing rapid change. Like Chaucer's pilgrims, Gaston's 'motley host' came from 'every shires ende',[25] from all walks of life; the *Canterbury Tales* might well be regarded as a series of character studies or imaginary portraits. Not only was Chaucer the father of English literature, but he was also the father of the genre which Pater himself would develop as a hybrid form between fiction and criticism in his search for the individual behind the type, the ordinary man or woman rather than the unique genius.

The full extent of Pater's lecture on English literature will probably never be known, unless a more finished manuscript or a printed text surfaces one day. From the outline in the Houghton manuscript we can see that he also intended sections on Shakespeare, Bacon, and Hobbes; indeed, the fragments on Hobbes in the same collection may well be part

of the English literature manuscript.[26] Pater's interest in the study of
English literature in the mid-1870s probably sprang from his essay on
Wordsworth (1874) and the early essays on Shakespeare ('A Fragment on
Measure for Measure' (1874) and 'On *Love's Labours Lost*' (1878)), at a time
when he also stood for the Oxford Professorship of Poetry (1877) and
began the writing of his first imaginary portraits. The literary ambitions
which made him put his name forward for the post, recently occupied by
Matthew Arnold (1857–67) and Francis Hastings Doyle (1867–77), suggest that he did not see himself solely as a classicist with an added interest
in the visual arts. What made him abandon the piece on English literature,
we do not know, nor what made him return to it with renewed interest in
Chaucer. Pointing out the Greek aspects of Chaucer, Pater made him a
missing link between a classical Continental tradition and an emerging
national school of English literature, thus stressing the 'organic unity'
which he pointed out in his contribution to the *Pall Mall Gazette*.[27]

In the mid-1880s, as he returned to his reading of Taine and Lingard,
he plotted an ambitious trilogy of novels. *Marius the Epicurean*, described
by himself as an imaginary portrait,[28] had appeared to great acclaim early
in 1885; by January 1886 he was writing to an American admirer that

> 'Marius' is designed to be the first of a kind of trilogy, or triplet, of works of
> a similar character; dealing with the same problems, under altered historical
> conditions. The period of the second of the series would be at the end of the
> 16th century, and the place France: of the third, the time, probably the end
> of the last century—and the scene, England.[29]

The second novel became the unfinished *Gaston de Latour*, serialised in
Macmillan's Magazine in the autumn of 1888 and published as a fragmentary novel posthumously in volume form in 1896, edited by Pater's friend
and literary executor Charles Lancelot Shadwell. As for the third of Pater's
projected long imaginary portraits, the 'Thistle' manuscript may provide
us with a brief outline of the intended historical setting and a few lines
about the central character, enigmatically named 'Thistle'. We are left
guessing why Pater selected this upright, spiky, solitary, but colourful,
flower, emblem of Scotland and Lorraine, as the name for his protagonist.
'Thistle' is an unusual choice – less poetically evocative than Florian
Deleal – for a young sensitive man given to a fondness for things medieval.
Notice how Pater, in his notes to himself, embeds his character in a literary
ambience, internationally and nationally, before he zooms in on some of
the personal characteristics of his protagonist 'after what may be called the
psychological method':

Thistle.

The beginning of this cent. in Eng/d.
Rousseau & Voltaire, have been.
Kant, has been—opening a double way.
The Fr. Rev/n has been.
STC. Keats, Shelley, Wordsworth, Byron, are around.
He finds, defines, realises, something diff/t from all those
forces—a something rep/d best by Newman—of whom in a way, &
amid quite other cond/s, outward & inward, he is an anticipation.

<In S> Ts much interested, preoccupied, with, Morte d'Arthur—
Especially the episode of The Grail.
An Obermann, & c., with the cure.
The most beautiful parts of England—Oxford—[30]

Peering over Pater's shoulder in the early stages of the creative process
allows us to observe the ways in which he thought of periods with clear
reference to major moments, movements, and figures in European philosophy and literature. Probably only relatively few of the French, German, or
English writers and philosophers would have figured explicitly in his
imaginary portrait of a young man, who, coming after centuries of divi-
sions between culture and religion, would become an anticipation of
Newman. An imaginary Coleridge, Shelley, Wordsworth, or, indeed,
Newman might have been intended as the counterpart to the walk-on
parts of Lucian, Marcus Aurelius, Ronsard, and Montaigne in the two
previous novels. We can only regret that Pater did not live to create such
fictional counterparts to the writers on whom he had written critical essays.
Pater's vision of the healing powers of Romantic literature in the long
nineteenth century, with Newman as a central figure (Newman having
himself, in his article 'The state of religious parties' (1839), argued for the
inclusion of the Oxford Movement as part of Romanticism), paved a way
for a return to the unity of Chaucer's time. His Thistle is a neo-medieval
seeker, fascinated by the quest for the Holy Grail, harking back to the
Christian European myths of Anglo-French Romance. In many ways
Pater's initial outline for his third novel supplements the evolutionary
sketch of English literature from his fragmentary lecture with a view of
the nineteenth century as a new period of reconstruction and reconciliation, not unlike the Renaissance reconciliation of paganism and
Christianity.

The thistle as an emblem of Pater's own era emerges as one potential
reading of another of his notes to himself in the 'Thistle' manuscript, in
which he speaks of its 'perfect flower', of 'the <u>permanent</u> tendency,

strength, truth of the 19th c.'[31] Interesting words from the man who previously had argued for the need to 'grasp at any exquisite passion, or any contribution to knowledge that seems by a lifted horizon to set the spirit free for a moment', while 'all melts under our feet' (*Ren.*, 189). If anything, the thistle is long-lived, strong and forthright in its physical appearance, a hardy plant, and a powerful symbol, combining beauty and strength in its own peculiar way. The spiritual awakening experienced by Pater's protagonist points towards Newman's emphasis on soul and imagination in both education and religious experience, an issue further explored in 'Style' (1888), as discussed in Chapter 6. It might well be argued that Newman is a constant presence in Pater's note, with links to the Houghton manuscripts 'Art and religion' and 'The Writings of Cardinal Newman',[32] pointing towards the celebration of the perfection of Newman's style and his *Idea of a University* (1873) in 'Style' (*App.*, 18):

> In a sense he anticipates the 19th c.—finely, & anticipating it
> gives it at its best—first & last, meeting—its perfect
> flower—as if in memory—What he needs is a larger-soul[']d
> life than his own—the working-out of the spiritualities of what
> then, is. In this way, might be indicated, the permanent
> tendency, strength, truth of the 19th c. He conceives it, as it
> is, in idea.[33]

What Pater's own idea of a university might have been is left to speculation. Solitary and shared reading and conversations with senior writers form the most important components of the education of his protagonists, in the long as well as the short imaginary portraits. His English poet is rounded by a formative reading of English literature, a childhood in Cumberland, and the imprint on his soul of a romantic landscape and the ghost of Wordsworth. A catalogue comprising Hawthorne, Ruskin, Carlyle, Arnold, Coleridge, Clare, and Browning is expanded with Browne, Webster, Chapman, and Shakespeare, giving us a sense of a canonical education in which verses are linked with European topography, from Valhalla and the Alps to the Roman Campagna and the coast of France. Just as Pater had been concerned with the growth of Florian's aesthetic awareness, so, in 'An English Poet', he was keen to trace the origins of the poetic spirit and the interplay between reading, perceiving, and creating. Pater's own literary beginnings as a poet may run as an autobiografictional undercurrent; he had tried his hand at poetry before turning to prose in the 1860s.[34] Pater marks out the awakening of the poet's imaginative and critical faculties, together with a sense of literary topography which connects books with places. His protagonist's Englishness resides in a merging of ancestry and the notion of 'mother tongue' which gives him an affinity with the English language, despite his Anglo-French origin, born of an English mother and a French father in Normandy:

> What was strange was that, although half of foreign birth, he had come to be so sensitive of the resources of the English language, its rich expressiveness, its variety of cadence (the language of "   ")[35] with all the variety of that soft modulation at which foreigners with an ear wonder and admire. Expression, it may be verbal expression, holds of what may be called the feminine element and tradition in things, and is one of those elemental capacities which the child takes for the most part from its mother.
>
> And such inheritance of an instinctive capacity for utterance he, the boy, had developed among the racy sources of fully male English speech among the Cumberland mountains, and among people to whom a great English poet attributed a natural superiority in the use of words.[36]
>
> And so it happened that while he hardly felt at all the impress of that same rich temperance in English scenery and English character, the English tongue had revealed itself to him as a living spirit of mysterious strength and sweetness and he had elected to be an artist in that. (*CW*, iii. 151–2)

The text has fourteen occurrences of 'English', several of which cluster in the passages above. Pater invited the reader's contemplation of the interrelationship between language and literature as something arising out of an interplay between landscape, spirit of place, and national character. Keen to tie his English poet to the European Continent, not merely by means of his gene pool, Pater singled out the French red honeysuckle blossoming in Cumberland (a counterpart to Florian's red hawthorn) as the fragrant flower which triggered the poet's imagination, in curious conjunction with a flowery metal screen wrought in Germany. The flower, even of English literature, has European roots and tendrils, we must infer. When in the last pages of the unfinished narrative the poet returns to Normandy and experiences a personal and poetic awakening, North is replaced with South and the poet's aesthetic sense aroused, undoubtedly with the intention of setting his Englishness into relief by a European experience. We shall presumably never know what conclusion Pater intended for his fragmented narrative, or whether he ever wrote one.

'An English Poet' is in every respect a romantic text. Not only does it deal with the coming into being of a young orphaned poet, whom tuberculosis has singled out as its victim; it also deals with the impact of

nature and literature on the individual. It is an important foundational
text, elucidating Pater's experiment with fiction as criticism in dialogue
with Sainte-Beuve and his English admirer Matthew Arnold within the
genre of the literary portrait. Arnold, one of the chief promoters of Sainte-
Beuve to an English audience, had visited and corresponded with him, and
written extensively about him.[37] Sainte-Beuve frequently traced the poets'
family origins, together with their education. Interested in the first signs of
poetic talent, in the moment when genius came into its own, he observed:
'If you understand the poet at this critical moment, if you unravel the node
to which everything will be connected from that moment on, if you find
what you might call the key to this mysterious link made half of iron and
half of diamonds joining his second, radiant, dazzling, and solemn existence to his first, obscure, repressed, and solitary one (the memory of
which he would more than once like to swallow up), then one could say of
you that you thoroughly possess and know your poet.'[38] Pater's concern
with the English poet's family, upbringing, and education gives us the very
same focus. The images of iron and stone recall Pater's evocation of the
way the poet works with language and matches form to matter. Our
narrator has the longer view; he knows the young man will turn into a
poet before we see it happening in the narrative in a way similar to Sainte-
Beuve's well-informed critic.

    Pater may have intended his English poet as a counterpart to Sainte-
Beuve's *Vie, poésies et pensées de Joseph Delorme* (1829), an early study of a
fragile medical student and poet who dies an early death (whether of
tuberculosis or of a weak heart remains uncertain) and leaves his poems
(also written by Sainte-Beuve) to posterity. The text appeared anonymously, as an edited heterogeneous text, comprising prose and poetry,
explanatory narrative, and extracts from the young man's journal, followed
by some of his verses. The life explains the poetry, just as the poetry
explains the life in a circular movement. From the first we know that we
will be witnessing the confessions of a romantic young man: 'The friend
whose works we now publish was torn from us very young, some five
months ago. A few hours before dying, he left into our care a journal into
which are confined the main circumstances of his life and some pieces of
poetry which are nearly all devoted to the expression of his personal
grief.'[39] Arnold, in his essay on Sainte-Beuve written for the *Encyclopedia
Britannica* (1886), described Joseph Delorme as 'not the Werther of
romance, but a Werther in the shape of a Jacobin and medical student,
the only Werther whom Sainte-Beuve by his own practical experience
really knew'. He drew the reader's attention to Sainte-Beuve's English

background: his mother was half-English, and he was brought up in Boulogne-sur-mer in a geographical location similar to that of Pater's English poet. Arnold quoted Sainte-Beuve's admiration for English poetry: praising the English for having 'a poetical literature far superior to ours, and, above all, sounder, more full', with Wordsworth as a supreme example of a great untranslatable modern poet, Sainte-Beuve advised his friend to go to the fountainhead for poetry and learn English.[40] Sainte-Beuve's awareness of the interdependence between language and literature, of language as that which gives poetry its national specificity, reminds us of Pater's English poet: rhythm and rhyme reside in language, and with Sainte-Beuve's allusion to Wordsworth, and to the interrelationship between landscape, language, and demotic verse,[41] Pater's English poet becomes solidly rooted in a contemporary Anglo-French context. His unfinished portrait engaged with the English poet who for most of his life grappled with the growth of the poetic mind, with the leading French critic and experimenter with the literary portrait – a man who like Pater himself had turned from poetry to critical prose – and with the Oxford Professor of Poetry, who mastered both poetry and prose, and served as a go-between of the English and French literary worlds. With such an ambitious merging of *Bildung*, criticism, and life-writing with the poetry of place, it is perhaps little wonder that Pater never finished the manuscript sufficiently to publish it.

The allusions to the visual arts in Sainte-Beuve's portraits indicate a degree of self-awareness, as his criticism hovers teasingly between the objective and the subjective. His elaborate narrative frames serve to alert us to the fact that the portrait is self-consciously poised halfway between two worlds. In choosing the term 'portrait' and by employing many of the Sainte-Beuveian devices, Pater acknowledged his indebtedness to the French writer and his merging of criticism and life-writing with a touch of fiction and self-reflection. Sainte-Beuve often let his subjects speak, allowing their own texts to form the core of his portraits. The function of the critic becomes partly a framing device, introducing the subject's own words by means of a biographical narrative, sometimes preceded by the critic's own meta-reflective thoughts on his task. In 'An English Poet', the life is foregrounded at the expense of the works, as is often the case with biographies of poets, even in so-called literary biographies.[42] Pater's English poet has been silenced; the omniscient narrator may give us access to his thoughts and sensations through descriptive passages which sometimes blend the poet's experiences with those of the narrator himself by means of pronouns such as 'one' and 'you'. The poet's direct voice is never heard. One might well argue that, with his long lyrical landscape descriptions and his chronicling of the poet's mother's sentiments and her son's inner growth, Pater's narrator is far more poetic than his poet. The poetic tendrils that we never see fully explored in the poet's own verses unfold themselves beautifully in the framing device in which the voice of a sensitive and perceptive persona draws our attention to the attractive Anglo-French subject.

Pater's view of Romanticism as the most important artistic and literary movement of the nineteenth century, paving the way for a return to a new European cultural revival, may well have served to challenge too narrow ideas of patriotism. The essays which frame *Appreciations* – 'Style' (1888) and 'Romanticism' (1876) – are Anglo-French and essentially European in their approach, alerting our attention to the international context in which the English writers who constitute the core of his book lived, thought, and worked. Pater's accentuated use of the adjective 'English' inevitably makes us question the peculiarity of the national as opposed to the international: what made the poet English was the language in which he worked rather than a narrowly patriotic approach to literature. The '"fine flower" of English poetry, or Latin oratory, or Greek art' needed an international environment in order to reach its finest bloom. Pater's characteristically cautious contribution to the *Pall Mall Gazette* debate may have surprised the editor but was fully consistent with the major argument which would structure his *Appreciations* some three years later.

Notes

1 See nos. 35, 39, 44, and 64 in Samuel Wright, *A Bibliography of the Writings of Walter H. Pater* (New York 1975).

2 'Imaginary Portraits 2: An English Poet', *Fortnightly Review* 129 (1931), 433–48.

3 'English at the Universities. –IV.', *Pall Mall Gazette* (27 November 1886), 1–2 (1).

4 Ronsard had retired from the public world to become Prior of the Monastery of Saint Cosme near Tours in 1565. In *Gaston de Latour* the protagonist encounters the French poet, in Pater's description the spitting image of Charles Baudelaire, busily engaged in cultivating the monastic garden. See Patricia Clements, *Baudelaire and the English Tradition* (Princeton 1985), 86–96.

5 See Inman (1981), 109, 192, 215, 219. Pater's own collection contained the *Portraits contemporains* and fifteen volumes of the *Causeries du lundi* (ibid., 336–8).

6 Consider the grouping of 'The Child in the House' (1878) and 'The Character of the Humourist: Charles Lamb' (1878); 'Amiel's Journal: The Journal Intime of Henri-Frédéric Amiel' (1886), 'Sebastian van Storck' (1886), and 'Sir Thomas Browne' (1886); 'Denys l'Auxerrois' (1886) and 'The Bacchanals of Euripides' (1878/89); 'Lacedaemon' (1892) and 'Emerald Uthwart' (1892).

7 See Sharon Bassett, 'Dating the Pater Manuscripts at the Houghton Library (bMSEng 1150)', *Pater Newsletter* 25 (1990), 2–8.

8 See Edmund Gosse, 'Walter Pater: A Portrait', *Contemporary Review* 66 (1894), 795–810 (806–7).

9 There can be little doubt of the vast number of challenges for the editor of the forthcoming volume 10 of the Oxford *Collected Works of Walter Pater*, which, for the first time ever, will publish the entire body of Pater's manuscripts.

10 'English Literature', Houghton MS 13.

11 'Thistle', Houghton MS 31, fol. 3 recto.

12 The last pages may have been lost in the 1920s when the Ottley family, copyright holders of Pater's writings after Hester Pater's death in 1922, attempted to place the manuscript with a publisher. 'An English Poet' was referred to as being 'quite complete' by Canon Ottley in a letter to George Macmillan sent on 11 January 1924, but the text which eventually saw publication, edited by the Canon's wife May Ottley, is cut off abruptly. The manuscript itself appears to have been lost, which is unfortunate, as May Ottley confesses to having tampered with the text. See her 'Prefatory note to 'An English Poet', 435, and B. A. Inman, 'Tracing the Pater Legacy, Part II: Posthumous Sales, Manuscripts and Copyrights', *Pater Newsletter* 32 (1995), 3–8 (4).

13 'English Literature', fol. 6 recto.

14 'Thistle', fol. 3 recto.

15 Sainte-Beuve translated in Donald Hill's explanatory note, *Ren.*, 298–9.

16 'English Literature', fol. 1 recto, kindly transcribed by Lesley Higgins.

17 Inman (1990), 4, 156.

18 Inman (1990), 159, 464.

19 'English Literature', fol. 21 recto.

20 'English Literature', fol. 17 recto.

21 William Morris, 'English at the Universities', *Pall Mall Gazette* (1 November 1886), 1–2.

22 Matthew Arnold, 'Introduction', in *The English Poets: Selections*, ed. T. H. Ward, 4 vols (1880), i. xvii–xlvii (xvii, xxiv, xxxii).

23 Arnold, 'Introduction', xxx.

24 'English Literature', fol. 6 recto.

25 Chaucer, 'General Prologue' to the *Canterbury Tales*, 15.

26 Houghton MS 18.

27 Chaucer's cosmopolitanism has been confirmed in Marion Turner, *Chaucer: A European Life* (Princeton 2019).

28 See letter to Vernon Lee of 22 July 1883 in which he refers to *Marius* as 'an Imaginary Portrait of a peculiar type of mind in the time of Marcus Aurelius' (*Letters*, 79).

29 Letter to Carl Wilhelm Ernst, 28 January 1886 (*Letters*, 96).

30 'Thistle', fol. 3 recto.

31 'Thistle', fol. 7 recto.

32 Houghton MS 11 and 12. Bassett, 'Dating the Pater Manuscripts', 4–5, points out (together with William Shuter and Lawrence Evans) that those two essays most likely derive from early to mid-1880s.

33 'Thistle', fol. 7 recto.

34 See Wright, *Bibliography*, 138–56, largely based on details given in Thomas Wright, *The Life of Walter Pater*, 2 vols (1907).

35 This is one of Pater's celebrated manuscript 'blank spaces'.

36 Wordsworth, born in Cumberland, had famously defined the poet as 'a man speaking to men' in the Preface to the *Lyrical Ballads* (1880).

37 See Arnold Whitridge, 'Arnold and Sainte-Beuve', *PMLA* 53 (1938), 303–13; R. H. Super, 'Documents in the Matthew Arnold–Sainte-Beuve Relationship', *Modern Philology* 60 (1963), 206–10. For Pater's dialogue with French literature, see John Conlon, *Walter Pater and the French Tradition* (Lewisburg, PA 1982).

38 From Sainte-Beuve, 'Pierre Corneille'. Quoted from and translated in Ann Jefferson, *Biography and the Question of Literature in France* (Oxford 2007), 130.

39 English translation mine. 'L'ami dont nous publions en ce moment les oeuvres nous a été enlevé bien jeune, il y a environ cinq mois. Peu d'heures avant de mourir, il a légué à nos soins un journal où sont consignées les principales circonstances de sa vie, et quelques pièces de vers consacrées presque toutes à l'expression de douleurs individuelles.' (C. A. Sainte-Beuve, 'Vie, poésies et pensées de Joseph Delorme', in *Poésies complètes de Sainte-Beuve* (Paris 1840), 5–22 (5).)

40 'Sainte-Beuve', in Arnold, *Prose*, xi. 106–19 (113).

41 For a discussion of 'An English Poet' in the context of Wordsworthian 'spots of time', sculpture, and language, see Lene Østermark-Johansen, *Walter Pater and the Language of Sculpture* (Farnham 2011), 278–90.

42 See ch. 1, 'The Voice of the Biographer', in Paula R. Backscheider, *Reflections on Biography* (Oxford 2001).

CHAPTER 3

Pater's Montaigne and the Selfish Reader

Fergus McGhee

I am glad that one living scholar is self-centred & will be true to himself though none ever were before; who, as Montaigne says, 'puts his ear close by himself, & holds his breath, & listens'

Ralph Waldo Emerson[1]

'A book, like a person', suggests the narrator of *Marius the Epicurean*, 'has its fortunes with one; is lucky or unlucky in the precise moment of its falling in our way' (*ME*, i. 93, ch. 6). In the autumn of 1877, advertisements began to appear for a new English edition of Montaigne's *Essais*.[2] Fresh from a tour of France, his mind still grazing on 'stained glass, old tapestries, and new wildflowers', Pater was thirty-eight years old – the very age at which 'this quietly enthusiastic reader', as he would later call Montaigne, withdrew from public office to begin a life of literary adventure in his book-jammed tower (*Gast.*, 89, ch. 4; *CW*, iv. 83).[3] Pater had reasons to feel similarly disposed. As the controversy kindled by *The Renaissance* in 1873 once again fanned into flame, it seemed to put a decisive end to his remaining Oxford ambitions. Renewed attacks in the press coincided with the publication in book form of W. H. Mallock's *The New Republic* (successfully serialised the previous year), with its caricature of Pater as the whimsical and fleshly 'Mr Rose'. In March, he withdrew from the race to become Oxford's next Professor of Poetry, but the student press continued to give him a thrashing, and in May, Macmillan published the second edition of *The Renaissance*, stripped of its controversial 'Conclusion' at Pater's own request.[4] The nature of the attacks on Pater in this period bear a remarkable resemblance to the fraught reception of Montaigne's *Essays*, arraigned down the centuries for their egotism, scepticism, and sensuality.

Patricia Clements has observed that, after *The Renaissance*, Pater's work was largely 'tailored as explanation and justification'; but rather than viewing this process as a bashful retreat from youthful indiscretion, it might better be understood as a witness to the tenacity of his convictions.[5] Montaigne's essays, I want to suggest, played a vital role in helping Pater to articulate a renewed defence of his critical enterprise. The character of this enterprise is adumbrated by Mallock in the suggestion that Mr Rose has but two interests: 'self-indulgence and art'.[6] Mr Rose, one might say, indulges himself in art and makes an art of self-indulgence. I propose to take this criticism seriously, as I believe Pater did, and to examine both halves of this far from ill-chosen term of abuse in connection with Pater's portrayal of Montaigne. If Pater fashions Montaigne as an exemplary reader, he does so not in spite of, but *because* of his being – as William Hazlitt warmly described him – a 'most magnanimous and undisguised egotist'.[7]

Pater borrowed the first volume of Charles Cotton's seventeenth-century translation of the *Essays* from Brasenose College library in October 1877, and later acquired his own copy of the revamped version of Cotton published that November, edited by William Carew Hazlitt (grandson of the famous essayist).[8] Hazlitt's edition sought to take advantage of the French variorum edition published in Paris in 1854, gently pruning Cotton's translation of redundancies and paraphrases, and restoring passages omitted by Cotton's eighteenth-century editors on the grounds of delicacy.[9] Though it may have lacked the exuberance of John Florio's Elizabethan translation, Cotton's version was rightly regarded as more accurate and scholarly, and still more so in the light of Hazlitt's emendations. A landmark essay on Montaigne by Henry Crabb Robinson (1820), for example, praised Cotton for reproducing 'the quaintness, liveliness, and simplicity, of the author's style, with great felicity and effect'.[10] As the century wore on, 'Cotton's Montaigne' began to attain the status of a classic of *English* literature, hallowed by the love of Byron, Hazlitt, Emerson, and Arnold (Cotton was, after all, a vigorous poet in his own right).[11] This context may partly explain why Pater did not choose to read Montaigne in the original, uniquely among the French writers on whom he wrote. At least, there is no evidence he did so, and every one of Pater's quotations from the *Essays* is drawn from Hazlitt's Cotton.

Pater's own three-volume copy of this edition now resides at Brasenose, and like his volume of Flaubert's *Trois Contes* (also published in 1877), its margins bristle with ticks and scores in pencil.[12] Though none of Pater's other extant books are marked in this way, Edmund Gosse makes tantalising mention of a 'curiously marked copy of *Mademoiselle de Maupin* belonging to Pater' in 1885.[13] Moreover, the documented chains of provenance of the Montaigne and Flaubert volumes are substantially distinct, reducing the possibility that the annotations can be attributed to subsequent owners.[14] It is tempting to speculate, therefore, that the markings are Pater's own, but in the absence of further evidence this surmise remains impossible to prove. If such evidence were ever forthcoming, it would suggest just how much Montaigne meant to Pater; but we need no archival proof of that – it is written all through Pater's later work.

To Eat of All the Trees

Indulge: 'To give free course to one's inclination or liking', suggests the *OED*.[15] In his review of *The Renaissance*, Sidney Colvin had worried that Pater's 'Conclusion' would lead to 'general indulgence', and when the second edition appeared the admonitions grew still more excitable: 'Pater-paganism', it was warned, with its gospel of 'promiscuous indulgence', would unleash 'the worst passions and most carnal inclinations of humanity'.[16] The fear that Pater had provided an intellectual licence for unrestrained sensual gratification was central to criticism of his work through the 1870s. Pater was accused of leading young men 'miserably astray' by teaching them to abandon all 'self-restraint'; of being like a highly cultivated Renaissance prince who besmirched his honour with 'license foul'; of providing an insidious 'sanction' for 'casting to the winds ... all exterior systems of morals or religion which can restrain a man against his will'.[17] So widely had Pater's influence penetrated, agonised one writer in the reliably illiberal student press, that in certain public schools 'many subjects are daily discussed, which should never be discussed at all and many others treated as open questions which in sober earnest, are no more open questions than the facts of our own existences'.[18] As Pater's rival for the Chair of Poetry, W. J. Courthope, suggested in a vituperative article of 1876, the 'general point at issue' in Pater's reception was 'the right of the imagination to unlimited liberty'. Accordingly, accusations of 'scepticism and sensuality' went hand in hand.[19]

I quote these assaults in quantity because they sow the seeds of Pater's portrayal of Montaigne as one who provided 'a theoretic justification, a sanction' for the liberty of thought and sensation which Pater associated with the Renaissance and, by extension, 'modernity' (*Gast.*, 83, ch. 4; *CW*, iv. 80).[20] In Pater's unfinished novel *Gaston de Latour* (the first five chapters of which, including the ones on Montaigne, were published in *Macmillan's Magazine* in 1888[21]), the impressionable young hero's arrival at the Château de Montaigne emblematises the wider historical moment when humanity 'was called, through a full knowledge of the past, to enjoy the present with an unrestricted expansion of its own capacities' (82–3, *CW*, iv. 80). The crucial 'justification' for this emancipating ethic, argues Pater, 'was furnished by the Essays of Montaigne' (83; *CW*, iv, 80). In making this claim, Pater granted Montaigne a much more significant role as a moral philosopher than he had usually been accorded in Britain, where he was regarded as a congenially empirical thinker hopelessly compromised by his 'carelessness' and inconsistency, his lack of intellectual 'refinement'.[22] As with so many of the portraits in *The Renaissance*, then, Pater's account of Montaigne is highly revisionist: not only does he give Montaigne pride of place among Renaissance philosophers, he refutes the charge that his thinking lacked refinement by invoking 'the spectacle of that keen-edged intelligence, dividing evidence so finely, like some exquisite steel instrument with impeccable sufficiency' (104, ch. 5; *CW*, iv. 91).

But if Montaigne's mind was not held in especially high esteem in Victorian intellectual culture, he was nonetheless widely respected for his benevolent heart: Montaigne was the 'apostle of toleration', a voice of sanity and moderation who loathed all forms of cruelty and persecution.[23] Pater endorsed this view of Montaigne as a 'singularly humane and sensitive spirit' (88, ch. 4; *CW*, iv. 83), going so far as to call him 'the solitary conscience of the age' (114, ch. 5; *CW*, iv. 96). And yet he also insinuated a 'strange ambiguousness in the result of his lengthy inquiries', which threw some doubt on the effects, if not the motives, of his singular moral temper (114; *CW*, iv. 96). The scene of Ulysses approaching the palace of Circe, illustrated by the tapestry in Montaigne's study, becomes a symbol for this lingering anxiety in the novel. 'Was Circe's castle here?' Gaston wonders; if she 'could turn men into swine, could she also release them again?' (90, ch. 4; *CW*, iv. 83). When, therefore, the narrator notes Montaigne's stress on 'Man's kinship to the animal, the material' (112, ch. 5; *CW*, iv. 95) – 'the earthy side of existence' (108; *CW*, iv. 93) – these homely observations come haunted by the ghost of Homer's enchantress. And just as Circe's song 'makes one forget everything beside' (*CW*, iv. 138, ch. 9), Montaigne's 'magnetic' conversation (87, ch. 4; *CW*, iv. 82) insulates Gaston against the 'reverberation of actual events around him', and still more of 'great events in preparation', like the terrible massacre of St Bartholomew's Day (115, ch. 5; *CW*, iv. 97). In Paris, Gaston reflects that he may have learned Montaigne's lesson too well, or perhaps that he had taken one side of it too much to heart. Following 'with only too entire a mobility the *experience* of the hour', he finds himself 'more than he could have thought possible the toy of external accident' (124, ch. 6; *CW*, iv. 103). Unleavened by judgement, Pater implies, such mobility may wither into helplessness; and experience, which might have been 'water to bathe and swim in' (as he puts it in his preternaturally eloquent early essay on William Morris) may leave us 'washed out beyond the bar in a sea at ebb'.[24]

This glimmer of Montaigne as a potentially threatening, even Mephistophelean, presence had played almost no part in his English reception hitherto, but was a key aspect of his reception in France, notably in the writings of Pascal and his nineteenth-century chronicler, Sainte-Beuve. In an extraordinary passage of *Port-Royal* (1842), which Pater was reading at Brasenose in 1868, Sainte-Beuve compares Montaigne to 'a cunning demon, a cursed enchanter' who takes his victims by the hand, draws them into his sceptical labyrinth, and tells them to trust to his lamp alone, before snuffing it out with a chuckle.[25] For Sainte-Beuve at this period (he later modified his view substantially) Montaigne was a playful figure who may have meant little harm but who wreaked havoc through the godless radicals inspired by his writings, like Rousseau and Bayle.[26] The pleasant-seeming roots of 'paganism' planted by Montaigne had grown into a Dantesque abode of suicides: a 'thick, dark, and poisonous forest ... fatal to Werther and to all dreamers who fall asleep in its shade'.[27]

The parallels with Pater's reception are striking: 'Could you indeed have known the dangers into which you were likely to lead minds weaker than your own,' his colleague John Wordsworth wrote to him, 'you would, I believe, have paused.'[28] Pater's was 'the voice of the charmer', leading unsuspecting young men to their doom.[29] In 1877, an article on him observed that 'The cultured College Tutor ... wields a potent influence over his pupils', and Pater himself was to use the loaded Oxford term 'tutor' to describe the role Montaigne occupied in relation to Gaston (*CW*, iv. 166, ch. 11).[30] Indeed, Pater repeatedly invoked Montaigne to parry contemporary criticism of his own supposed debaucheries, first by exposing the hypocrisy of such indictments and secondly by demonstrating the tact and acuity of Montaigne's famous fleshliness.

As early as *Marius the Epicurean* (1885), Pater had contended that, like the '"aesthetic" philosophy' of the Cyrenaics, the 'kindly and temperate wisdom of Montaigne', though it be 'refining, or tonic even, in the case of those strong and in health', was 'as Pascal says ... "pernicious for those who have any natural tendency to impiety or vice"' (*ME*, i. 149, 150, ch. 9). This exculpation reappears in *Gaston*, which quotes Montaigne's own plea to this effect: 'In truth,' the narrator admits, Montaigne 'led the way to the immodesty of French literature', but he 'had his defence, a sort of defence, ready.—"I know very well that few will quarrel with the licence of my writings, who have not more to quarrel with in the licence of their own thoughts"' (*Gast.*, 112, ch. 5; *CW*, iv. 95). Pater's late essay, 'Pascal', turns the tables on Montaigne's great antagonist by applying the same principle. For Pascal might equally be credited with 'a somewhat Satanic intimacy with the ways, the cruel ways, the weakness, *lâcheté*, of the human heart', writes Pater; 'so that, as he says of Montaigne, himself too might be a pernicious study for those who have a native tendency to corruption' (*MS*, 85).[31] Montaigne had been habitually rebuked in the nineteenth century for his 'love ... of coarseness and obscenity', his 'indecency', his 'unabashed and deliberate filthiness'.[32] But the fact that Montaigne was 'not revolted' by such subjects, Pater argues, should not blind us to his keenly discriminating sensibility (*Gast.*, 112, ch. 5; *CW*, iv. 95). 'Delicacy there was, certainly', he suggests, '—a wonderful fineness of sensation' (111; *CW*, iv. 94). Pater pieces together a *cento* of quotations in support of this provocative reading, citing Montaigne's intense sensitivity to particular scents and climes, his ear for the breeze that forebodes the storm, and his desire for wine served in the clearest of glasses, 'that the eye might taste too' (112; *CW*, iv. 95). Pater's Montaigne, then, is not (or not merely) a bantering bawd but a scrupulous aesthete. And nowhere does he apply his discernment more scrupulously, and more passionately, than in his appreciation of literature.

Lively Oracles

When the poet Ronsard commends Montaigne to Gaston, it is not as a philosopher, an analyst of human behaviour, or a delightful raconteur, but as a student of style: 'Monsieur Michel could tell him much of the great ones—of the Greek and Latin masters of style. Let his study be in them!' (69, ch. 3; *CW*, iv. 71). In Montaigne's tower, Gaston finds 'quaintly labelled drawers' filled with 'Notes of expressive facts, of words also worthy of note (for he was a lover of style)' (86, ch. 4; *CW*, iv. 81). This makes Montaigne sound not unlike the subject of Pater's 'An English Poet', who has 'a savour before all things of the style—how things were said—of manner' (*CW*, iii. 151). Given that Pater composed this essay around 1878, just as he was devouring the *Essays*, it is perhaps no coincidence that Pater there defines style as 'those elements of taste or of literary production which, because they are so delicately and individually apprehended and are yet so real, resemble physical sensations' (151). For this is how Montaigne describes the language that makes the greatest impression on him: the 'sinewy' style of his Gascon countrymen, or the 'sharp' style of Seneca's Latin, which 'pricks and makes us start'.[33] Language, in this way, may evoke what one of Pater's most influential critical heirs, Bernard Berenson, called 'tactile values': weaving a Pateresque chaplet of nouns, Berenson describes how the work of art may 'appeal to one's senses, nerves, muscles, viscera'.[34] Cognition is not eschewed in favour of frissons that are merely skin-deep, but continually proved on the pulse, so that (as *Marius* suggests) 'one's whole nature' is mobilised as 'one complex medium of reception' (*ME*, i. 143, ch. 8).

An extraordinary gift of receptivity is what Gaston finds in Montaigne, a profound interest in his own responsiveness to the world that is the very opposite of solipsistic: 'openness—that all was wide open, searched through by light and warmth and air from the soil' – as with the house, so with its master (*Gast.*, 84, ch. 4; *CW*, iv. 80). Pater's celebration of the breezy openness of Montaigne's abode, and by extension his writings, defiantly revises the French historian Michelet's crotchety characterisation of the *Essays*, in his monumental *Histoire de France* (1833–67), as 'this airless *bookshop*' ('cette *librairie* calfeutrée').[35] That Pater should champion the vitality of Montaigne's romance with literature is entirely apt, since as Denis Donoghue notes (with a coolness somewhat mysterious in a professional literary critic), 'Such thinking as Pater did, he did by commenting on the work of other writers'.[36] In *The Renaissance*, Pater had lovingly quoted Goethe's remark about Winckelmann's writings: 'they are a life, a living thing, designed for those who are alive' ('Winckelmann', *Ren.*, 155), and in *Gaston* he makes the same suggestion about Montaigne's *Essays*: they 'were themselves a life' (83, ch. 4; *CW*, iv. 80).

This is no casual hyperbole: for Montaigne himself, Pater writes, the activity of reading, 'which with others was often but an affectation, seducing them from the highest to a lower degree of reality, from men and women to their mere shadows in old books, had been for him nothing less than personal contact' (97, ch. 5; *CW*, iv. 88). Mallock's *New Republic* made much comic ado about people throwing their 'souls and sympathies' into 'the happier art-ages of the past', lampooning those quixotic creatures for whom 'Borgia is a more familiar name than Bismarck'.[37] Pater calls Montaigne as his witness against this parochialism of the present: for if '"we have no hold even on things present but by imagination", as he loved to observe,—then, how much more potent, steadier, larger, the imaginative substance of the world of Alexander and Socrates, of Virgil and Cæsar, than that of an age, which seemed to him, living in the midst of it, respectable mainly by its docility' (98, ch. 5; *CW*, iv. 88). Seen in this context, the well-worn criticism of Pater's fictional method – that Gaston 'seems almost to be reading about himself and the age in which he lived' – self-combusts.[38] In Pater's account, reading is not a bloodless imitation of reality, but one of the most powerful, intimate, and sensuous ways we have of experiencing it. In his unpublished essay 'The Aesthetic Life' (probably begun around 1877), Pater wrote lyrically of 'that large life wh[ich] he looks in the face, ponders like a strange book';[39] as though reading were a way not of shirking reality, or facing it down, but of squaring up to it in all its breadth and mysteriousness.

Montaigne's scepticism is both cause and effect of his many-mingled engagement with literature: whereas in *Marius* the satirist Lucian's scepticism is said to have 'surrounded him ... with "a rampart," through which he himself never broke, nor permitted any thing or person to break upon him' (*ME*, ii. 143, ch. 24), Montaigne's was 'the proper intellectual equivalent to the infinite possibilities of things' (*Gast.*, 104, ch. 5; *CW*, iv. 91). Not things in general merely, but *particular* things. For 'it is "things" after all which direct him', as Erich Auerbach would later say of Montaigne: 'he moves among them, he lives in them; it is in things that he can always be found, for, with his very open eyes and his very impressionable mind, he stands in the midst of the world'.[40] 'Montaigne was constantly, gratefully, announcing his contact', Pater marvels, 'in life, in books, with undeniable power and greatness, with forces full of beauty in their vigour' (95, ch. 5; *CW*, iv. 87). Pater's account of Montaigne's pre-eminent impressionability builds upon Matthew Arnold's observation, in *On Translating Homer* (1861), that the critic of poetry should have 'the most free, flexible, and elastic spirit imaginable', ever aspiring towards 'the *undulating and diverse* being of Montaigne'.[41] But Pater also controverts Arnold by insisting that, for Montaigne, 'the essential dialogue was that of the mind with itself' – the very malaise with which Arnold thought modern literature was afflicted (85, ch. 4; *CW*, iv. 81). Such '*inward converse*', Pater suggested, was not in the least hidebound, let alone 'morbid' and 'monotonous' (as Arnold had claimed), because it 'throve best' with 'some outward stimulus', like 'some text shot from a book', for example (85, ch. 4; *CW*, iv. 81).[42]

Pater quotes Montaigne's testimony that books were ever 'at his elbow to test and be tested' (88; *CW*, iv. 82), alluding to the literary form which he credited Montaigne with inventing: the essay, cognate with 'assay', 'A trial, testing'.[43] The quotation nicely suggests the reciprocal nature of Montaigne's relationship to literature, which both bombards him with impressions and calls forth his own best powers in response. In *Marius*,

Pater had compared Marcus Aurelius in his *Meditations* to 'the modern essayist', whose desire is 'to make the most of every experience that might come' (*ME*, ii. 47, ch. 18), while in his essay on Lamb he associated 'true essay-writing' with 'the dexterous availing oneself of accident and circumstance, in the prosecution of deeper lines of observation' (*App.*, 118). Pater's portrayal of Montaigne glances back at these earlier formulations of the essayist's double existence as pursuer and pursued. Pater pictures Montaigne 'shrewdly economising the opportunities of the present hour' (*Gast.*, 104, ch. 5; *CW*, iv. 91), sifting experience with a bright expectancy: 'That "free and roving thing," the human soul,—what might it not have found out for itself, in a world so wide?' (113; *CW*, iv. 96).

This Montaigne is indeed 'the studious man' (84, ch. 4; *CW*, iv. 81), but his 'studies' are of a very particular kind, for which Pater celebrates the essay as the ideal medium. In a passage which he later plucked from *Gaston* for his lectures on Plato, Pater identifies this medium as 'that characteristic literary type of our own time, a time so rich and various in special apprehensions of truth, so tentative and dubious in its sense of their *ensemble*, and issues' ('The Doctrine of Plato', *PP*, 174).[44] These two aspects of the essay's identity are related to its ambiguous location 'midway' between two earlier historic forms of philosophical thought, the poem and the treatise (174). As Pater notes, Montaigne rejoiced in prose that shone with 'the lustre, vigour and boldness . . . of poetry' (*Gast.*, 101, ch. 5; *CW*, iv. 90), and in Pater's essay on 'Style' he too would insist that poetry was no unwelcome 'intruder' in prose (*App.*, 6). As an instrument of literary criticism, the essay is at once keenly investigative like the treatise, while at the same time willing to risk lyricism in virtue of the peculiarly evocative character of its objects of investigation. Just as Montaigne did with the moral and historical curiosities he loved to recount, the essay is always insisting that experience is 'not to be resolved into anything less surprising than itself' (*Gast.*, 95, ch. 5; *CW*, iv. 87). Its distinctive mission is the pursuit of truth, 'not as general conclusion, but rather as the elusive effect of a particular personal experience' (*PP*, 175).[45]

Spontaneous Me

Montaigne's essays, Pater affirms, are an account of 'how things affected him, what they really *were* to him, Michael, much more than man' (*Gast.*, 105, ch. 5; *CW*, iv. 92), echoing the demand which *The Renaissance* makes of every encounter: 'What is this . . . to *me?*' ('Preface', *Ren.*, xix–xx). 'Every one has heard of Montaigne's egotism', observed R. W. Church in

1857, and Pater does not shrink from the charge: 'beyond and above all the various interests upon which the philosopher's mind was for ever afloat,' the narrator of *Gaston* reflects, 'there was one subject always in prominence—himself' (105, ch. 5; *CW*, iv. 92).[46] Pater's sentence glows with ironic lustre, for he himself had been unceasingly accused of just this: 'Selfishness', 'self-worship', 'self-centred thought'.[47] Christopher Ricks is the most accomplished recent critic to have picked up this baton (or bludgeon): 'criticism, like creation for him', he laments, 'is not a loss of self, joyful or otherwise, but ... a matter of never finding yourself at an end'.[48] Selfishness, however, comes in many guises. There is the selfishness of self-conceit – 'the egotism which vulgarises most of us', as Pater deplores it in 'Emerald Uthwart' (*MS*, 225; *CW*, iii. 188) – but there is also the stealthier selfishness of self-effacement. There is a curiously Nietzschean moment in Pater's essay on Wordsworth where he alludes to the pursuit of 'mean, or intensely selfish ends' like those 'of Grandet, or Javert' (*App.*, 60). As if selfishness might keep company, not with indulgence, but with meanness: the wretched austerity of Balzac's miser, or the sinister sobriety of Hugo's police inspector, with his 'life of privation, isolation, self-denial'.[49] By contrast, Montaigne takes an 'undissembled' interest in the quality of his own various and volatile awareness of the world (*Gast.*, 105, ch. 5; *CW*, iv. 92). Like Socrates, not the least of his virtues is '[t]o make men interested in themselves' ('Plato and the Sophists', *PP*, 120).[50]

From Pater's very first mention of Montaigne in the essay on du Bellay, he had associated him with 'something individual, inventive, unique, the impress there of the writer's own temper and personality' (*Ren.*, 137), and in the essay on Lamb he dubbed such subjectivity 'the *Montaignesque* element in literature' (*App.*, 117). In these circumstances, it might even be said that 'egotism is true modesty', as John Henry Newman had outrageously proposed in his much-discussed *Grammar of Assent* (1870). The honest religious inquirer, Newman wrote, 'brings together his reasons, and relies on them, because they are his own, and this is his primary evidence'.[51] Three years later, Pater would make the parallel insistence that in the realm of aesthetic experience, 'one must realise such primary data for one's self, or not at all' ('Preface', *Ren.*, xx). Though Newman's seeker is convinced that others will agree with him if they themselves 'inquired fairly', or will only 'listen to him', he is at the same time clear that 'he cannot lay down the law'.[52] Montaigne makes a still humbler and more hospitable claim, as Pater observes: 'I never see all of anything' (and 'neither do they who so largely promise to show it to others', he roundly adds (*Gast.*, 103, ch. 5; *CW*, iv. 91)). For this reason Montaigne can maintain that 'a competent reader often discovers in other men's writings other perfections than the author himself either intended or perceived, a richer sense and more quaint expression'.[53] This, of course, is a notorious trademark of Pater's own critical practice, whether it be his perception of a vein of 'sweetness' in Michelangelo or a kind of sceptical indifference in the expression of Botticelli's Madonnas – insights which baffled critics pledged to hair-shirt historicism.[54]

The Montaignesque critic, attracted by 'some new light' he finds in one in a hundred of the faces belonging to the work under contemplation, will in turn leave much to the 'willing intelligence' of the reader (103; *CW*, iv. 91). Such writing, then, participates in a virtuous spiral: 'dependent to so great a degree on external converse for the best fruit of his own thought', as Pater observes of Montaigne, 'he was also an efficient evocator of the thought of another—himself an original spirit more than tolerating the originality of others,—which brought it into play' (86–7; *CW*, iv. 82). In this spirit of curiosity and respect, Pater goes on, Montaigne 'would welcome one's very self, undistressed by, while fully observant of, its difference from his own' (87; *CW*, iv. 82). Not only, perhaps, because he wants to see the object from a different angle, but because he values new ways in which he might differ from himself.

Writing, then, if it touches us at all, bids for an interest that is vitally personal, not because it can be threaded through the needles of our existing interests and commitments but precisely to the extent that it prises open those needles' eyes. 'For if men are so diverse', remarks Montaigne, 'not less disparate are the many men who keep discordant company within each one of us'; hence, Pater comments, 'the variancy of the individual in regard to himself' (93, ch. 5; *CW*, iv. 86). The theme is recognisably Paterian: consider the 'strange, perpetual, weaving and unweaving of ourselves' insisted upon by the 'Conclusion' (*Ren.*, 188), or Emerald Uthwart's 'vagrant self' (*MS*, 207; *CW*, iii. 180), or the 'elusive inscrutable mistakeable self' evoked in 'The History of Philosophy'.[55] But Montaigne inflects it for him with a bracing sense of possibility missing from these elegiac intimations, and he does so by uniting it to Pater's passion for surprise: 'even on this ultimate ground of judgement', notes the narrator of *Gaston*, 'what undulancy, complexity, surprises!' (*Gast.*, 106, ch. 5; *CW*, iv. 92). 'The more I frequent myself ... the less do I understand myself', Pater quotes, and the words have the air of a boast, not a concession (107; *CW*, iv. 92–3). Montaigne's sense of the self as inchoate and anticipatory – a fount of 'miraculous surprises' – suggests that we reimagine self-indulgence as a kind of sociable self-experiment (89, ch. 4; *CW*, iv. 83).

Aesthetic experience may be richly and ineluctably personal, but it is not ineffably private nor jealously proprietary. What's more, if the self is perpetually at stake in such encounters, then it is never something already given, nor has it need of any anxious defence. The antithesis of blocked sympathies and cloying consumption, the selfish reader so conceived comes close to fulfilling one of Pater's earliest and most hopeful intuitions: that 'the choice life of the human spirit is always under mixed lights, and in mixed situations; when it is not too sure of itself, is still expectant, girt up to leap forward to the promise'.[56]

Notes

1　Ralph Waldo Emerson to Thomas Carlyle, 14 May 1834, in *The Selected Letters of Ralph Waldo Emerson*, ed. Joel Myerson (New York 1999), 130.

2　See, for example, *Academy* 283 (6 October 1877), ix.

3　Pater to Edmund Gosse (10 September 1877), in *Letters*, 26.

4　See the notice of Pater's withdrawal in *Oxford and Cambridge Undergraduate's Journal* no. 233 (15 March 1877), 305.

5　Patricia Clements, *Baudelaire and the English Tradition* (Princeton 1985), 81.

6　W. H. Mallock, *The New Republic*, 2 vols (1877), i. 24.

7　William Hazlitt, 'On the Tatler' (1815), in *The Selected Writings of William Hazlitt*, vol. 2, ed. Duncan Wu (1998), 10−13 (10).

8　Inman (1981), 404.

9　See 'Preface', *The Essays of Montaigne*, ed. William Carew Hazlitt, 3 vols (1877), i. v−viii. This edition was based on the earlier edition (1842) of Hazlitt's father.

10　'Montaigne's Essays', *Retrospective Review* 2 (1820), 209−27 (227). Jane Campbell identifies the author in *The Retrospective Review (1820−1828) and the Revival of Seventeenth-Century Poetry* (Waterloo 1974), 59.

11　Richard I. Kirkland Jr., 'Byron's Reading of Montaigne: A Leigh Hunt Letter', *Keats-Shelley Journal* 30 (1981), 47−51; Hazlitt, 'On the Tatler'; Emerson, 'Montaigne, or the Skeptic', in *Representative Men* (1850), *The Collected Works of Ralph Waldo Emerson*, vol. iv, ed. Wallace E. Williams and Douglas Emory Wilson (Cambridge 1987), 83−106; Matthew Arnold to Arthur Hugh Clough, 1 May 1853, in *The Letters of Matthew Arnold*, ed. Cecil Y. Lang, 6 vols (Charlottesville 1996−2001), i. 263.

12　Oxford, Brasenose Library, Sparrow 53, 54, 55; the Flaubert is Oxford, Brasenose Library, Sparrow 145.

13　Edmund Gosse to Ellen Gosse, 1 November 1885, Cambridge, University Library, MS Add 7020.2.

14　Both were donated to Brasenose by John Sparrow. *Trois Contes* passed by bequest to Clara Pater, then Hester Pater, May Ottley, and Constance Mary Ottley, who sold it to John Sparrow in 1972. The provenance of the

Montaigne volumes, which bear Pater's signature, is hazy: the endpapers bear the name G. W. Young (probably Geoffrey Winthrop Young, 1876—1958) as well as a price of £6 / 6s, suggesting they were sold (or offered for sale) at some point before 1971. It is unknown when they entered Sparrow's possession or from whom he acquired them.

15 'indulge, *v.*', *OED Online*, sense I.1b.

16 Sidney Colvin, 'Studies in the History of the Renaissance', *Pall Mall Gazette* (1 March 1873), repr. in *Critical Heritage*, 47—54 (54); 'Muscular Christianity', *Oxford and Cambridge Undergraduate's Journal* no. 240 (31 May 1877), 450—2 (451).

17 J. F. Mackarness, 'A Charge Delivered to the Diocese of Oxford' (1875), repr. in *Critical Heritage*, 94—7 (96); W. W. Capes, sermon quoted in *Oxford Undergraduate's Journal* no. 149 (27 November 1873), 98—9 (98); 'Paganism', *Oxford and Cambridge Undergraduate's Journal* no. 236 (3 May 1877), 370.

18 'Paganism', 370.

19 W. J. Courthope, 'Wordsworth and Gray', unsigned review of Alexander Grosart (ed.), *The Prose Works of William Wordsworth*, *Quarterly Review* 141 (January 1876), 104–36 (134, 136).

20 Cf. the Preface to *The Renaissance* on 'the breaking down of those limits which the religious system of the middle age imposed on the heart and the imagination' (*Ren.*, xxii–xxiii). *Plato and Platonism* declares that Montaigne 'does but commence the modern world' (*PP*, 194).

21 The chapters on Montaigne are (IV) 'Peach-Blossom and Wine' and (V) 'Suspended Judgment'.

22 See for example Henry Hallam, *Introduction to the Literature of Europe*, 4 vols (1837—9), ii. 169—77 and Dugald Stewart, 'Dissertation, exhibiting a General View of the Progress of Metaphysical, Ethical, and Political Philosophy, since the Revival of Letters in Europe' (1815—21), in *The Works of Dugald Stewart*, 7 vols (Cambridge 1829), vi. 91—8. The charge of 'carelessness' is Hallam's (ii. 169), lack of 'refinement' Stewart's (vi. 94).

23 Alexander Smith, 'An Essay on an Old Essayist—Montaigne', *Good Words for 1862*, ed. Norman Macleod (1862), 362—6 (366); see also W. E. H. Lecky, *History of the Rise and Influence of the Spirit of Rationalism in Europe*, 2 vols (New York 1866), ii. 63. An important exception to this view in England was Bayle St John, Montaigne's first biographer (in any language), who held the triumph of his conciliatory politics responsible for 'the adjournment of Liberalism for exactly two centuries'. See *Montaigne the Essayist: A Biography*, 2 vols (1858), i. 80.

24 'Poems by William Morris', *Westminster Review* 34 (October 1868), 300—12 (309, 311).

25 See Inman (1981), 192—3; C.-A. Sainte-Beuve, *Port-Royal*, III, vol. 2 (Paris 1867), 441.

26 See Donald M. Frame, 'Influence of Montaigne's Thought: Sainte-Beuve', in *Montaigne in France 1812—1852* (New York 1940), 140—84.

27 Sainte-Beuve, *Port-Royal*, III, 405.

28 John Wordsworth to Pater, 17 March 1873, repr. in *Critical Heritage*, 62.

29 'Paganism', 370.

30 'Æstheticism', *Oxford and Cambridge Undergraduate's Journal* no. 235 (26 April 1877), 350–1.

31 The direct reference to Montaigne's French could be seen as evidence of Pater's engagement with the original text, but he could equally have picked it up second-hand from Sainte-Beuve's criticism, e.g. *Causeries du Lundi*, 3rd ed., 15 vols (Paris 1857–62), iv. 90. This is the edition Pater owned; see Inman (1981), 338.

32 Thomas Carlyle, 'Montaigne', in *The Edinburgh Encylopædia*, ed. David Brewster, 18 vols (Edinburgh, 1820), xiv. 675–9 (658); Hallam, *Introduction*, 176; R. W. Church, 'The Essays of Montaigne', in *Oxford Essays, contributed by Members of the University: 1857* (1857), 239–82 (245).

33 Montaigne, 'Of Presumption', *Essays*, ii. 418; 'Of Physiognomy', *Essays*, iii. 342.

34 Bernard Berenson, *Aesthetics and History* (New York 1948), 69, 67.

35 Jules Michelet, *Histoire de France*, 17 vols (Paris 1852–67), x. 401. Pater borrowed this particular volume from Brasenose in 1868 (see Inman (1981), 166).

36 Denis Donoghue, *Walter Pater: Lover of Strange Souls* (New York 1995), 97.

37 Mallock, *New Republic*, ii. 118, 119.

38 Gerald Monsman, 'Critical Introduction', *CW*, iv. 12.

39 'The Aesthetic Life', Houghton MS 39.

40 Erich Auerbach, *Mimesis: The Representation of Reality in Western Literature*, trans. Willard R. Trask (Princeton 1953), 294.

41 Arnold, *Prose*, i. 174.

42 Matthew Arnold, 'Preface to First Edition of *Poems* (1853)', Arnold, *Prose*, i. 1–15 (3).

43 *OED*, 'essay, *n.*', sense I.1a.

44 For the original version of the passage intended for *Gaston de Latour*, see *CW*, iv. 215–16.

45 Cf. *CW*, iv. 215–16.

46 Church, 'Montaigne', 251.

47 'Paganism', 370; W. J. Courthope, 'Modern Culture', *Quarterly Review* 137 (October 1874), 389–415 (412); Capes, sermon, 98.

48 Ricks, 'Misquotation', 415.

49 Victor Hugo, *Les Misérables*, trans. Lascelles Wraxall, 3 vols (1862), i. 145, 146.

50 Compare Montaigne's famous remark, 'If the world find fault that I speak too much of myself, I find fault that they do not so much as think of themselves' ('Of Repentance', *Essays*, iii. 23).

51 John Henry Newman, *An Essay in Aid of a Grammar of Assent* (1870), 379.

52 Newman, *Essay*, 379, 380, 381, 380.

53 Montaigne, 'Various Events from the Same Counsel', in *Essays*, i. 142.

54 See Colvin, 'Studies', 51—2; Margaret Oliphant, unsigned review of *The Renaissance*, *Blackwood's Magazine* 114 (November 1873), repr. in *Critical Heritage*, 85—91 (88—9).
55 Houghton MS 3, fol. 23 verso.
56 'Poems by William Morris', 307.

CHAPTER 4

Studies in European Literature: Pater's Cosmopolitan Criticism

Stefano Evangelista

Pater lived at a time of mounting nationalism. In the closing decades of the nineteenth century, in Britain as all over Europe, the study of literature became increasingly bound up with questions of national identity, both in educational institutions and in the public sphere at large. At the same time, however, this period also witnessed the birth of comparative literature as an independent branch of literary enquiry and numerous practical and theoretical attempts to inject new life into Goethe's idea of *Weltliteratur*. Registering this schism between nationalist and cosmopolitan approaches to literary studies, Pater championed a cosmopolitan method that was informed by a polyglot mentality and celebrated the diversity of European literatures and cultures. Rejecting nationalist agendas, he practised criticism as an art of dialogue and exchange that transported readers beyond the narrow moral and cultural horizon of the nation. His intervention in this charged field was neither totalising nor systematic, but it was powerful nonetheless: true to the principles of aesthetic criticism that he laid down in the 'Preface' to *The Renaissance*, he was weary of abstract methodological discussions, preferring instead to express his theories through critical practice, for instance by focusing on figures that exemplified his own cosmopolitan interests.

Several Oxford figures intervened in the public debate on literature and national identity. In 'The Function of Criticism at the Present Time' (1864), for instance, Matthew Arnold was passionate about the fundamental role of literary criticism in shaping the intellectual life, and consequently the character, of the nation; in his view, by not taking criticism seriously, the English revealed an inferiority to the French and the Germans – an inferiority that could only be remedied by improving the quality of periodicals and educational curricula. With a nod back to Goethe's *Weltliteratur*, Arnold urged English literary critics to concentrate only on 'the best that is known and thought in the world'.[1] This necessarily meant reading extensively in foreign literatures and leaving undistinguished domestic products to one side, since Arnold made no bones about his low opinion of much contemporary English literature and his impatience with the bad habit of inflating the merit of English authors on patriotic or chauvinistic grounds. Because of this double argument about the need to institutionalise criticism and, at the same time, to study English literature in an international perspective, Arnold's essay has been seen as marking an important stage both in the rise of English as an academic subject and in setting a comparative agenda for literary studies.[2] Indeed, his often-cited plea that criticism should regard 'Europe as being, for intellectual and spiritual purposes, one great confederation' implies that a study of literature unbound by parochial loyalties and national interests fostered a desirable internationalism – or, in other words, that criticism paved the way for the 'spiritual' unity of Europe.[3] Max Müller was even more explicit about the urgent spiritual mission of literature at a time when 'national partisanship threatens to darken all wise counsel and to extinguish all human sympathies'.[4] Müller was the first Oxford Professor of Comparative Philology, a discipline that prepared the ground for comparative literary studies as we understand and practise them today. Speaking as the first President of the newly formed English Goethe Society and again inspired by Goethe's *Weltliteratur*, he urged that cosmopolitan reading habits and a greater respect for the diversity of the world's literatures would not only improve public culture in England but also encourage peaceful relations between the nations of Europe.

Müller's inaugural lecture to the English Goethe Society took place in May 1886, and it was circulated in periodical form later that year. It therefore coincided in the public sphere with the debate in the *Pall Mall Gazette* on a possible School of English at Oxford initiated by John Churton Collins, in which Müller was among those invited to contribute. That same year also saw the publication of the Irish philologist Hutcheson Macauley Posnett's *Comparative Literature*, the first book to make a sustained case in English for comparative literary studies as an academic discipline.[5] This historical convergence should encourage us to see the public debate on English at Oxford, ostensibly a controversy between English and Classics, as bleeding into the politically charged question of national identity and national feeling in literary studies. The question that was being discussed in the *Pall Mall* was not only whether English should be approached through the prism of literature or philology, and where it should fit within existing disciplinary structures, in Oxford and elsewhere. It was also about the role of literary studies in the increasingly tense field of international literary relations outlined by Arnold and Müller. Should the study of English literature aim to cement national sentiment and bolster Englishness at home and internationally? Or should it be conceived in a way that encouraged dialogue and connection with foreign forms and ideas? In other words, should studying English serve a national or a cosmopolitan idea of culture?

Pater's intervention in the *Pall Mall Gazette* touched on these questions in a characteristically oblique way when he argued that classical study would be expanded and enlivened by 'a closer connection ... with the study of great modern works (classical literature and the literature of modern Europe having, in truth, an organic unity)'.[6] Pater followed Arnold, who had spoken of 'a knowledge of Greek, Roman, and Eastern antiquity' as 'the proper outfit' for the members of his European 'great confederation', and who reiterated his opposition to separating Classics, English, and modern European languages in his own response to the *Pall Mall Gazette* survey.[7] Arnold used Classics to dismiss patriotism and nationalist sentiment as belonging to what he calls 'those alien practical considerations' that had no place in his definition of criticism.[8] Read in this context, Pater's defence of Classics over English must therefore also be seen as a rejection of the nationalist mentality in which the rise of English in universities found itself implicated. This chapter examines Pater's positioning vis-à-vis English studies by shifting the focus to another discipline that was struggling for academic recognition in those years: Modern Languages. Pater's commitment to the study of modern languages at Oxford and in his literary criticism more broadly comes together in his late essay on the French writer Prosper Mérimée – a relatively under-studied work that sheds light on Pater's subtle undermining of cultural nationalism. With its nod to the evolutionary method of Müller's comparative philology, Pater's image of the 'organic unity' of classical and modern European literatures sees the natural place of English within a broader economy of world-literary exchanges that transcends national borders.

The Taylor Institution and the Taylor Lectures

First, it will be useful to explore the institutional background out of which the Mérimée essay came into being. In nineteenth-century Oxford, the debate on the establishment of a School of English ran parallel with an equally embittered controversy over the creation of a new School of Modern Languages. An account published in 1929 by the historian Charles Firth – Regius Professor of Modern History and a controversial figure within Oxford – charts the struggle for recognition fought by Modern Languages. Firth explains that the turning point in the fortune of foreign languages at Oxford came with the establishment of the Taylor Institution, which was explicitly conceived mid-century as a foundation dedicated to European languages.[9] The Taylorian was to have its own library and support its own educational activities, notably through the appointment of a new Professor of Modern European Languages. In 1848, the first person to hold this post was the polyglot Swiss-born Indologist Francis Henry Trithen, who gave lectures on the language and literature of Russia.[10] Then, in 1854 the position went to Max Müller, who dominated the life and reputation of the Taylorian for the whole second half of the century. Müller, who would achieve global fame for his studies of comparative mythology, was an extremely prestigious appointment, but his expertise was in philology rather than in literature. In recognition of this, in 1868 the university created for him a bespoke Professorship of Comparative Philology that remained attached to the Taylorian and effectively caused the Professorship of Modern European Languages to lapse. Like English, therefore, and replicating a dynamic that also operated within Classics, the early development of Modern Languages as an academic discipline within Oxford was caught in an opposition between philology and literary scholarship. Those who favoured the latter felt that provision for the teaching of modern European literatures was disappointingly poor – a perception that was endorsed by a University commission appointed in 1877, which found that the available modern language teaching was mostly restricted to grammar. The commission's report resulted in a protracted discussion about the establishment of a School of Modern Languages, with numerous pamphlets being issued for and against, prior to the eventual defeat by Congregation (the sovereign body of the University) in 1887.

In the absence of a dedicated Professorship, the Curators of the Taylorian tried to fill the gap by inviting distinguished foreign scholars to offer ad hoc lecture courses. The first person to receive the prestigious commission in 1871 was the French critic Hippolyte Taine, who had come to prominence with his *Histoire de la littérature anglaise* (1863), where he pioneered a philosophical-scientific approach to literature based on the three key variables of 'race, surroundings, and epoch'.[11] Taine's presence in Oxford was a concrete sign that the University was starting to heed Arnold's appeal to import modern European criticism (Taine was also awarded an honorary doctorate when he was there). Most importantly, the circumstances shed light on the workings of the Taylorian not only as an academic institution but also as a social and intellectual space. Despite the fact that his visit was constantly overshadowed by the distressing news coming from France, where Paris was falling to the Germans at the culmination of the Franco-Prussian war, Taine enjoyed a busy social life in Oxford, which he depicted in his detailed letters to his wife.[12] He had many conversations with Max Müller, who acted as his professional host, and was introduced to several of the University's literary personalities, including, besides the ubiquitous Benjamin Jowett, Arnold, Swinburne, and Emilia Pattison (later Lady Dilke). His lectures took place in French (not uncontroversially, according to Müller), and he noted that his audience always comprised a majority of women.[13] In other words, well before the official establishment of Modern Languages as an academic discipline within Oxford, which would not take place until 1905, the Taylorian was able to create and support a network of those interested in modern European languages and literatures that cut across faculties and colleges, that involved prominent literary figures, and that crucially included women as well as men.

In his Oxford letters Taine does not mention meeting Pater, who in 1871 was still making his first forays into periodical publishing and was therefore unlikely to have been introduced to the French critic as one of the university's literary personalities. We do know, however, from his borrowing records that Pater made extensive use of the Taylorian library over the years.[14] And we should understand this close relationship with the Taylorian not simply as showing that Pater was a solitary reader of European literature and criticism, which formed the core of the Taylor's collections, but that he belonged to the cosmopolitan Oxford set encountered by Taine for which the Taylorian now provided a gathering point. Over the years, as Pater's published works, deeply informed as they were by the Taylorian holdings, projected the cosmopolitan mission of the Institution in the public sphere, Pater participated in the discursive construction of a symbolic space within Oxford for the critical study of modern European languages. While Max Müller embodied the philological side of the project of comparatism at Oxford, Pater belonged to its literary side.

Pater's collaboration was formally recognised by the Curators of the Taylor Institution when they invited him to participate in their second major initiative to promote the cause of Modern Languages at Oxford and on the national stage: in 1889, they launched a series of annual lectures on a subject related to the topic of 'foreign literature' for which they commissioned an impressive list of international speakers. The inaugural lecture was given by Edward Dowden, the first chair of English literature at Trinity College Dublin. Dowden was not only a distinguished literary scholar (he was a specialist on Shakespeare) and biographer (he wrote a widely noted life of Shelley), but he was also an advocate of Goethe's ideal of world literature.[15] In fact, two years previously Dowden had succeeded Max Müller in the presidency of the English Goethe Society. In Oxford, Dowden lectured on 'Literary Criticism in France', a topic that linked back to Taine's visit almost twenty years earlier. The second invited speaker was Pater, who delivered a lecture on Prosper Mérimée on 17 November 1890.

The choice of Pater as the first Oxford figure to be included in the Taylor lectures is significant. It honours the public contribution to the knowledge of European literature that he had made not only in his criticism but, as Lene Østermark-Johansen has shown, also in his fiction.[16] At the same time, this prestigious commission helps us to put into focus Pater's reputation within the university, where the Brasenose Classics don was clearly perceived as an outstanding critic of foreign literatures and an intellectual ally of those who fought the cause of modern European languages. Indeed, surveying the first series of Taylor lectures, which were delivered between 1889 and 1900, what stands out is that Pater is the only Oxford speaker alongside the now obscure Henry Butler Clarke, who taught Spanish at the Taylorian Institution and gave his lecture on the subject of Spanish picaresque novels in 1898. The others comprised Professors of English Literature in other universities (Dowden, C. H. Herford, W. P. Ker) as well as distinguished historians and literary critics (Horatio Brown, William Michael Rossetti, T. W. Rolleston) who all shared interests in European literature and culture that went beyond their narrow disciplinary fields. The series also included three important French speakers who, like Taine, delivered their lectures in their native language: the leading Hispanist Alfred Morel-Fatio, and the star contributors Stéphane Mallarmé and Paul Bourget, who lectured respectively on the topic of music and literature, and on Gustave Flaubert. Taken together, this heterogeneous group, which in the course of ten years covered the major languages of Western Europe (French, German, Spanish, and Italian), embodied the cosmopolitan mission of the study of modern languages as the Taylorian conceived it.

It is possible to get a clearer sense of the mission and pitch of the Taylor lectures by turning again to Pater's predecessor, Edward Dowden. In *New Studies in Literature* (1895), where he later collected the text of the Taylor lecture together with various addresses to the English Goethe Society and other essays, Dowden gave a very cautious assessment of the conflict between national and cosmopolitan points of view. He conceded that literature must always retain the mark of the 'profound differences' between the nations caused by their use of different languages, and he portrayed a self-conscious cosmopolitanism in literature as a sign of decline;[17] but he also stressed literature and criticism's need to be hospitable to foreign ideas, praising Carlyle's ability to be simultaneously a citizen of Scotland and Weimar, and chastising the nationalist sentiment that accompanied the contemporary Irish literary revival.[18] When it came to studying English at university, Dowden explained that he wanted his students to 'conceive the history of English literature as part of a larger movement': if he could have his way, their university education would start with a historical map of European literature that would encourage them to draw international connections between authors and gain a broader understanding of the transnational evolution of genres and literary movements.[19] He pleaded for a comparative or, as he called it, 'philosophical' approach to literary studies that went beyond narrow national concerns:

> lifting his eyes and looking abroad, the student of English literature will perceive that there are groups of writings not arbitrarily formed and larger than can be comprehended within any age or even within the history of any nation. ... That is to say, the investigator who has examined a piece of literature simply in order to know what it is, and who inquiring then how it came to be what it is, has studied first the genius of an individual author and next the genius of a particular period to which that author belongs, is now compelled to take a wider view; and seeking to know whether there be not certain principles common to all literature and derived from the general mind of humanity, he passes from the biographical and the historical to the philosophical study of literature.[20]

By choosing to speak about French criticism in front of his Oxford audience, the English Professor made a deliberate gesture: it was his way of performing the ideal of literary comparatism and the critique of cultural nationalism articulated here. The Taylor lectures created a prestigious stage on which the complex relationship between English and Modern Languages was entangled and unravelled, and in which the type of cosmopolitan criticism outlined by Dowden was publicly advocated.

Mérimée and European Literature

If the essay on Mérimée still remains among Pater's least discussed works, this is mostly due to its publication history: shortly after giving it as a lecture in Oxford, Pater delivered it again at the London Institution, where its metropolitan audience included Oscar Wilde and Michael Field (Katharine Bradley and Edith Cooper). 'Prosper Mérimée' was then promptly printed in the *Fortnightly Review*, but it was never issued in book form during the author's lifetime. After Pater's death, his literary executor Charles Lancelot Shadwell included it in *Miscellaneous Studies* (1895), the volume where he assembled the remaining uncollected pieces of Pater's corpus admittedly without a 'unifying principle'.[21] As a result, 'Prosper Mérimée', which is arguably one of the most accomplished of Pater's late works, has always existed in a vacuum. In fact, however, the natural 'home' of this seemingly eccentric essay was, in the first instance, the Taylorian Institution and, later, the bilingual volume *Studies in European Literature* (1900), which collected the first series of Taylor lectures with the intent to 'contribute to further the study of foreign letters beyond as well as in the University'.[22] *Studies in European Literature* provides us with a context to retrace the shared intellectual endeavour to which Pater's essay on Mérimée belongs. Disparate though they are in terms of topics and approaches, its contributions sketch out a highly selective and partial but nonetheless organic notion of European literature as a 'confederation' of sorts, to go back to Matthew Arnold's terms. They embody a vision of *Weltliteratur*, understood as writing that has a significance beyond the nation in which it was produced, from the perspective of cosmopolitan English and French critics. Conscious of entering a distinctive intellectual community, the authors occasionally echo each other. Bourget's essay, for instance, delivered as a lecture in 1897, starts with a tribute to Pater, whom he had met on a previous visit to Oxford. The French author compared Pater as 'scrupuleux ouvrier de style' ('scrupulous craftsman of style') to the subject of his lecture: Flaubert – perhaps as a way to pay a posthumous homage to the Oxford don who had left a powerful critical portrait of Flaubert in the essay on 'Style'.[23]

'Prosper Mérimée' shows substantive elements of continuity with 'Style': both essays are about nineteenth-century French writers who, after their deaths, acquired a notable and slightly sensational profile as letter writers. Mérimée's *Lettres à une inconnue* (1873), which Pater cites, was the record of the notoriously reserved author's romantic exchange with an anonymous correspondent said to be an aristocratic English woman. In the years preceding Pater's lecture the *Lettres* had gone into several English editions and, in fact, Pater's publisher Macmillan had just issued a book that purported to be the missing half of the correspondence: *An Author's Love: Being the Unpublished Letters of Prosper Mérimée's 'Inconnue'* (1889) pretended to be the mysterious literary lady's replies to the French author's letters but was in fact the work of the American writer Elizabeth Balch.[24] Pater's interest in Mérimée may well have been triggered by the renewed public curiosity aroused by the letters. In any case, there were several aspects of the French author's work that would have persuaded Pater to make him the subject of his lecture. Mérimée's double profile as writer and as inspector of French historical monuments meant that his literary writings engage with material culture, preservation, and survival in a manner that resonated heavily with Pater's own interests. In particular, Mérimée's famous short story 'La Venus d'Ille' (1837), in which a recently unearthed ancient statue of Venus comes back to life, provided one of the urtexts for Pater's uncanny rendition of classical myth in the imaginary portraits. More generally, as he made very clear in the essay, Pater admired Mérimée as a stylist and a literary aesthete, although he also expressed certain reservations about what he perceived as Mérimée's coldness and reserve, and what he calls his 'contemptuous grace'.[25] If John J. Conlon is right in seeing a strong element of kinship and self-recognition in Pater's portrait of Mérimée, it is even more striking that he did not shy away from stressing Mérimée's quest for 'a kind of artificial stimulus' in art (*Studies in European Literature*, 44; *MS*, 27), as well as an obsessive quality and propensity for aestheticised violence – a set of characteristics that Pater arguably also shared and that his turn-of-the-century audience might have recognised as 'decadent'.[26] Indeed, by labelling Mérimée as 'the unconscious parent of much we may think of dubious significance in later French literature' (47; *MS*, 31), Pater built a bridge between Mérimée and the contemporary trends that Arthur Symons would shortly examine in 'The Decadent Movement in Literature' (1893), where Symons would name Pater himself as a leading English voice of literary decadence.

Above all, however, Pater wants to give a full and nuanced portrayal of Mérimée's cosmopolitanism – a concept that he does not name explicitly but that clearly shapes his understanding of Mérimée's literary significance. Pater's Mérimée is therefore first and foremost a 'man of the world' (33; *MS*, 14) by which Pater means that he had the qualities of eloquence and social polish, worldliness and 'infallible self-possession' (33; *MS*, 14) that made him a successful public figure. The real hallmark of Mérimée's social cosmopolitanism was his irony – a detached attitude to the world that also informed his literary work and that, to follow Pater's own habit of projecting into a later decadent sensibility, anticipates the blasé attitude that Baudelaire saw as the emblem of dandyism and cosmopolitan self-fashioning.[27] Mérimée's worldliness took the form of a relentless intellectual curiosity about the world in all its variety, and found an outlet in travel, international friendships, and a wide reading in foreign literatures. The French author's heightened receptivity to foreign ideas, combined with the ability to reconfigure them across space and languages, meant that his literary achievement as characterised by Pater rested chiefly on his talent for translation and mediation – a talent that comes to the fore in his handling of Russian literature. Pater compares Mérimée's discovery of Russia to the laying open of a new quarry of an ancient marble that had long been thought exhausted: the French writer, 'like a veritable son of the old pagan Renaissance', seems to find in the 'youthful Russia' of the mid-nineteenth century the survival of certain characteristics of old Roman civilisation that had otherwise been obliterated from the belated cultures of Western Europe (36; *MS*, 17). Pater is right in stressing that Mérimée played a pioneering role at a time in which the knowledge of Russian language and culture was extremely rare in the West, and when, even within Russia, the educated classes used French as the chief medium of communication. There is something of the visionary quality that Pater had attributed to Winckelmann's quest for ancient Greece in the way in which Mérimée penetrates this alien world in order to reveal the concealed greatness of Russian literature in a series of groundbreaking French translations of works by Pushkin, Gogol, and Turgenev among others.[28]

The references to Russian literature would have resonated with the cosmopolitan literary crowd in the Taylorian (as we have seen, the first Professor of European Languages at Oxford was a Russianist), as well as with Pater's early readers, because Britain was then experiencing a vogue for Russian novels that had come from France. In an influential essay on Tolstoy (1887), Matthew Arnold encouraged English readers to admire the ethical realism of '*Anna Karénine*' (which, in the absence of an English translation, he was reading in French), as an alternative to the lubricity and '*petrified feeling*' that he associated with French naturalism and Flaubert – an author that, as we have seen, Pater held as a model of good style.[29] The image of Russian literature that Pater shows his audience through Mérimée, while also mediated by way of France, is different both from the version of realism that appealed to Arnold and from the philosophical/political Russia that would take hold of English readers in the 1890s. It is an earlier and more exotic Russia captured by Pater's orientalising comparison of Mérimée's style to 'some harshly dyed oriental carpet from the sumptuous floor of the Kremlin, on which blood had fallen' (37; *MS*, 18). It is a romantic Russia identified with Pushkin – or 'Pouchkine' (44; *MS*, 27) as Pater writes, following Arnold's francophone spellings – which

Mérimée introduced to France and more broadly to readers in Western
Europe through translation (Pater refers to Mérimée's translation of
Pushkin's novella 'The Shot') but that he also filtered through his own
fiction – the famous short story 'Carmen' (1845), which Pater also
discusses, was based on Pushkin's poem *The Gypsies* (1842), which
Mérimée rendered into French. By drawing attention to the Russophile
current of Mérimée's work, Pater undoes the dichotomy created by Arnold
between realist/vitalist Russia and naturalist/decadent France. Instead, he
unravels a thread that goes from the origins of modern Russian literature to
those fictions of 'dubious significance' that mark out the literature of the
fin de siècle, in Britain as well as France.

   If we turn back to the Taylorian Institution and the Oxford School of
Modern Languages, we can start to see that Mérimée could be presented as
an excellent advocate of why the study of foreign languages and literatures
was a matter of profound importance. In the centre of an international
network that connected Russia, France, Spain, and Britain, but that also
reached back to classical antiquity, Pater's Mérimée exemplified a way of
practising literature and criticism that was based on acts of reception,
transition, and cultural contamination rather than on the quest for a
national identity. Indeed, the vexed question of nationality in literature
became an explicit concern in later Taylor lectures. In 1892, the poet and
Lessing scholar Thomas William Rolleston put it succinctly in these terms:
'Literature is universally regarded as being something peculiarly national.
How far does the actual history of literature justify this view?'[30] Chief
among those who argued for the close bond between literature and the
nation was none other than former Taylor guest lecturer Hippolyte Taine:
his famous mantra of 'race, surrounding, and epoch' propounded in the
Histoire de la littérature anglaise implied that individual authors and their
works could only be properly understood through the prisms of national
history and national character – the variables embraced by his ambiguous
term 'race'. A corollary of this theory was that literary criticism became a
vehicle to prove, essentialise, or even magnify the differences between
nations, potentially feeding into nationalist thought.

   In the inaugural Taylor lecture that preceded Pater's by a year, Dowden
had spoken against the French critic. He argued that Taine's criticism
overlooked both the agency of the individual writer and what he called 'the
universal mind of humanity', which can be glossed as literature's ability to
transcend boundaries and, by so doing, connect rather than separate
nations.[31] This is the same spiritual power that Goethe ascribed to
Weltliteratur. Believing that a work of literature ought not to be reduced

to 'a document in the history and the psychology of a people', Dowden found fault with a fundamental premise of Taine's theory of literature – his problematic slippage between the concepts of 'race' and nation: 'There is no pure, homogeneous race in existence, or at least none exists which has become a nation, none which has founded a civilized state, and produced a literature and art. Nor is it true, as M. Taine assumes, that the intellectual characteristics of a people persist unchanged from generation to generation.'[32] In his essay on Mérimée, Pater also demonstrates a critical stance towards Taine, who is a hidden presence in the text as Pater borrows from Taine's own portrait of Mérimée in his preface to *Lettres à une inconnue* (1873).[33] Rather than presenting the author and his works as the mirror of a French national identity, Pater sees them as the site of crossings and transitions: Mérimée is delineated against the backdrop of a cultural geography of Europe that stretches from Moscow to Seville by way of the Balkans and France. The same is also true of Pater's indirect account of Russian literature, whose evolution and reception are pointedly divorced from the growth into self-consciousness of the Russian nation.

The study of translation is integral to this de-nationalised model of criticism. Pater, as we have seen, emphasises the porousness between Mérimée's work of translation and his 'original' writings, refusing to see translation as a derivative or purely ancillary form of literature. This enlarged concept of translation embraces a range of different practices, such as imitation and creative translation, building a bridge between philology and literature that resonates with Pater's description of the writer as a scholar of language in 'Style'. Particularly characteristic of Mérimée, however, is the genre of pseudotranslation: his debut work *Le Théâtre de Clara Gazul* (1825) purported, in Pater's description, 'to be from a rare Spanish original, the work of a nun, who, under tame, conventual reading, had felt the touch of mundane, of physical passions; had become a dramatic poet, and herself a powerful actress' (46; *MS*, 29–30). The slightly later *La Guzla* (1827) – Pater mistakenly inverts the chronology – presented itself as a translation of popular verse collected by the author in the course of extensive travels through Dalmatia, Bosnia, Croatia, and Herzegovina. In the former Mérimée created not only a fictive author, Clara Gazul, but also a fictive translator, Joseph L'Estrange, adding layer on layer of mystification; he even had a portrait of himself painted as Clara, draped under a mantilla, which he included in presentation copies for some of his friends.[34] In the latter he described himself as an Italian, the son of a Morlach woman from Spalatro [*sic*], who had recently become a naturalised French citizen and had decided to write his translations in

French despite his non-native command of the language.[35] The fact that
La Guzla was partly translated into Russian by none other than Pushkin,
who believed the work authentic and included it in his *Song of the Western
Slavs*, creates a felicitous short-circuiting between the two writers' identities
as poets and translators. For Pater, these works exemplify Mérimée's taste
for masks and deception – a taste that was cleverly mirrored in the recent
An Author's Love, mentioned earlier, in which the American Elizabeth
Balch had masqueraded as Mérimée's 'inconnue', inventing the mysterious
lady's replies to the French author's letters. Balch's work was also a
pseudotranslation, complete with a learned preface full of critical quotations. Pater shows that this network of mystification is also part of
Mérimée's literary cosmopolitanism, which collapses different forms of
identity, exposing the practice of reifying the foreign and the exotic and,
at the same time, subverting the ideal of authenticity that was crucial to
ethnocentric and national models of literary criticism.

Conclusion

The essay on Mérimée should be read within a corpus of late essays on
foreign literatures that also comprises 'Style' and Pater's introduction to
Shadwell's translation of Dante's *Purgatorio* (1892). The latter – a bilingual
volume – is, in fact, another testimony to Pater's involvement in an
intellectual community in Oxford that actively promoted foreign languages and literature. Across these late works Pater engages with fundamental questions related to cosmopolitan literary practices, such as
translation and how to understand the universality of world literature –
this is the substance of the argument on 'the soul of humanity' in the
closing of 'Style' (*App.*, 38). In the introduction to the *Purgatorio*, Pater
also explicitly deploys the concept of cosmopolitanism in relation to
literature and criticism. He argues that Dante's work spoke directly to a
cosmopolitan orientation that was characteristic of the 'genius' of the
nineteenth century, which he defined as a 'minute sense of the external
world and its beauties' coupled with a demand for 'a largeness of spirit in
its application to life'.[36]
    Assessing the parallel struggle for recognition fought by English and
Modern Languages at Oxford, Charles Firth noted that 'there was
throughout a working alliance between the group who studied English
and the groups who studied other European tongues'.[37] Occurring as they
did within a short time lapse, Pater's contribution to the *Pall Mall Gazette*
and his Taylor lecture show that he had a foot in both camps: in this

crucial phase of the history of academic specialisation, he played a medi-
ating role within Oxford but also on the national stage, largely by resisting
the pressures of the modern culture of specialisation. His criticism of both
English and European literatures, as much as his writings on classical
cultures and art history, manifest his unwillingness to abide by the new
institutional and disciplinary boundaries that were being erected in the
world of academia. Pater's literary criticism did not embrace the new
advancements in the comparative method, like Müller's, and it generally
shied away from making systematic statements of the type we find in
Arnold's and Dowden's, but it was nonetheless firmly committed to what
we now recognise as a comparative path. His interest in points of contact
between cultures and in how ideas and forms travel across borders reveals
his opposition to the nationalist project attached to English studies and to
sectarianism in literary studies more generally.

Notes

1 Arnold, *Prose*, iii. 284.
2 See Alan Bacon, *The Nineteenth-Century History of English Studies* (Aldershot
   1998), 10; and Joseph Th. Leerssen, *Comparative Literature in Britain:
   National Identities, Transnational Dynamics 1800–2000* (Cambridge 2019),
   55 ff.
3 Arnold, *Prose*, iii. 284.
4 Max Müller, 'Goethe and Carlyle', *Contemporary Review* 49 (1886), 772–93
   (772). Müller's address was published in the first volume of the *Publications of
   the English Goethe Society* and then reprinted in the *Contemporary Review*.
5 On Posnett's place in the histories of comparative literature and world
   literature, see David Damrosch, 'The Rebirth of a Discipline: The Global
   Origins of Comparative Studies', *Comparative Critical Studies* 3 (2006),
   99–112; and Angus Nicholls, 'The "Goethean" Discourses on *Weltliteratur*
   and the Origins of Comparative Literature: The Cases of Hugo Meltzl and
   Hutcheson Macaulay Posnett', *Seminar: A Journal of Germanic Studies* 54
   (2018), 167–94.
6 'English at the Universities. – IV.', *Pall Mall Gazette* (27 November 1886),
   1–2 (1).
7 Arnold, *Prose*, iii. 284; and 'English at the Universities. – IX.', *Pall Mall
   Gazette* (7 January 1887), 1–2.
8 Arnold, *Prose*, iii. 284.
9 Charles Firth, *Modern Languages at Oxford, 1724–1929* (Oxford and London
   1929). The historical information in this paragraph comes from Firth. Firth's
   inaugural lecture as Regius Chair of Modern History at Oxford, *A Plea for the
   Historical Teaching of History* (1904), attacked the system for teaching history
   within the university, causing a controversy; see Ivan Roots, 'Firth, Sir Charles

Harding', *Oxford Dictionary of National Biography* https://doi.org/10.1093/ref:odnb/33137 (accessed 5 November 2021).

10 Gerald Stone, *Slavonic Studies at Oxford: A Brief History* www.mod-langs.ox.ac.uk/sites/www.mod-langs.ox.ac.uk/files/slavonic_studies.pdf, 9 (accessed 5 March 2022).

11 H. A. Taine, *History of English Literature*, trans. Henri Van Laun, 4 vols (1883), i. 17. Taine was followed by the German Klaus Groth in 1872 and the Italian Angelo de Gubernatis in 1878 (Firth, *Modern Languages*, 46).

12 Hippolyte Taine, *H. Taine: sa vie et sa correspondence*, 4 vols (Paris 1902–7), iii. 126–54 (1905).

13 On 5 June 1871, Taine wrote to his wife that '[l]es dames sont toujours en majorité'; Taine, *sa vie et sa correspondence*, iii. 148 ('Women always make up the majority'). On Müller's remarks on the internal opposition to Taine lecturing in French, see Firth, *Modern Languages*, 44.

14 The crucial critical resource here is Inman (1990).

15 See, for instance, Edward Dowden, 'The Interpretation of Literature', in *Transcripts and Studies* (1888), 237–68 (257).

16 Lene Østermark-Johansen, *Walter Pater's European Imagination* (Oxford and New York 2022), especially ch. 3.

17 Edward Dowden, 'Introduction', in *New Studies in Literature* (1895), 1–32 (14, 16).

18 Dowden, 'Introduction', 16, 19.

19 Edward Dowden, 'The Teaching of English Literature', in *New Studies*, 419–51 (421).

20 Dowden, 'Teaching', 450–1. It is worth noting that Dowden's opposition to nationalism brought him in conflict with the Irish literary revival.

21 Charles Lancelot Shadwell, 'Preface', in Pater, *MS*, 1.

22 *Studies in European Literature* (Oxford 1900), n. p. The statement of intent comes from the brief preface by the Curators of the Taylor Institution who put together the collection. The full contents list is as follows: Edward Dowden, 'Literary Criticism in France'; Walter H. Pater, 'Prosper Mérimée'; W. M. Rossetti, 'Leopardi'; F. [*sic*] W. Rolleston, 'Lessing and Modern German Literature'; Stéphane Mallarmé, 'La Musique et les Lettres'; Alfred Morel-Fatio, 'L'Espagne du Don Quijote'; H. R. F. Brown, 'Paolo Sarpi'; Paul Bourget, 'Gustave Flaubert'; C. H. Herford, 'Goethe's Italian Journey'; Henry Butler Clarke, 'The Spanish Rogue-Story (Novela de Pícaros)'; W. P. Ker, 'Boccaccio'.

23 Paul Bourget, 'Gustave Flaubert', in *Studies in European Literature*, 253–74 (254).

24 [Elizabeth Balch], *An Author's Love: Being the Unpublished Letters of Prosper Mérimée's 'Inconnue'*, 2 vols (1889).

25 Pater, 'Prosper Mérimée', in *Studies in European Literature*, 31–53 (34; *MS*, 14); subsequent references to the Mérimée essay will be made in the main body of the text; they will give page numbers both for *Studies in European Literature* and for the Library Edition.

26 Cf. John J. Conlon, *Walter Pater and the French Tradition* (Lewisburg, PA 1982), 143–4.

27 Charles Baudelaire, 'The Painter of Modern Life', in *The Painter of Modern Life and Other Essays*, trans. Jonathan Mayne (New York 1986), 1–40 (9).

28 For a useful overview, see M. Xavier Darcos, 'Mérimée slavophile', *Revue des « Amis de Tourgueniev »* 2004 at https://academiesciencesmoralesetpolitiques.fr/wp-content/uploads/2018/07/merimee_slavophile.pdf (accessed July 2021).

29 Matthew Arnold, 'Count Leo Tolstoi', *Fortnightly Review* 42 (December 1887), 783–99 (791).

30 F. [*sic*] W. Rolleston, 'Lessing and Modern German Literature', in *Studies in European Literature*, 93–130 (97). Rolleston went on to discuss the relationship between literature and patriotism in Germany, and the influence of Lessing on English and European literature.

31 Dowden, 'Literary Criticism in France', in *Studies in European Literature*, 1–29 (23).

32 Dowden, 'Literary Criticism in France', 26, 27.

33 For Pater's borrowings of Taine's *Histoire de la littérature anglaise* from the Taylorian Library, see Inman (1990), x, 3–4, 464. Pater's use of biographical anecdote in particular relies on Taine, whom Pater may have read either in the original or as quoted in English editions of the letters; cf. Hippolyte Taine, 'Prosper Mérimée', in *Lettres à une inconnue*, 2 vols (Paris, 1874), i. i–xxxv.

34 Daniel Gerould, 'Playwright as a Woman: Prosper Mérimée and "The Theatre of Clara Gazul"', *PAJ: A Journal of Performance and Art* 30 (2008), 120–8 (121).

35 [Mérimée], 'Preface' to *La Guzla, ou Choix de poésies illyriques, recueillies dans la Dalmatie, la Bosnie, la Croatie et l'Herzegovine* (Paris 1827), viii.

36 Pater, 'Introduction', in *The Purgatory of Dante Alighieri: An Experiment in Literal Verse Translation*, trans. C. L. Shadwell (London and New York 1892), xii–xxviii (xxiii).

37 Firth, *Modern Languages*, 55.

CHAPTER 5

The 'Postscript'

Ross Wilson

Appreciations, as is well known, gathers a number of essays that Pater had already published. The 'Postscript' both is and, in some notable respects, is not the reissue of an essay already published elsewhere. It is, because Pater had published 'Romanticism' in *Macmillan's Magazine* in 1876 and the 'Postscript' substantially reprises this text. However, there are significant changes – both omissions and additions – as well. (It is striking, incidentally, that in his positive review of *Appreciations* for the *Glasgow Herald*, William Sharp identifies the essay on 'Aesthetic Poetry', replaced in subsequent editions, and the 'Postscript' as 'two suggestive new papers'; both, in fact, had been published in earlier versions before.[1]) In the 'Postscript', for instance, the references to Whitman and Baudelaire that are present in 'Romanticism' are excised and, lest these excisions suggest that Pater was backing away from controversy in the process of revision, a polemical final paragraph is added. At least as significant as these particular emendations is, however, the change of title itself, from 'Romanticism' to 'Postscript'. It is worth noting here that 'Romanticism' was already a significant title, since the essay in fact addresses romanticism *and classicism*, and the dialectical relation between the two. It is tempting to speculate that 'Romanticism' designates what was for Pater the dominant artistic tendency, or the one with which his sympathies reside, or that which stands, in 1876, most in need of defence. The question of Pater's estimation of romanticism is, needless to say, central to this chapter. But the point to emphasise here is that 'Romanticism' is not the title granted this essay (even allowing for the revisions Pater made to it) in *Appreciations*. Indeed, the focus on Pater as a gifted essayist, which has gained considerable impetus from the recent resurgence of interest in the essay as form, runs the risk of deflecting from the fact that much of his work took different forms: there is the novel, of course, and the 'imaginary portrait', but also the lecture and the review, neither of which are straightforwardly subsumable under the omnivorous category of the essay. 'Romanticism' does not appear in *Appreciations* as a merely retitled essay, then, but rather as a text cast in a new and distinctive form: postscripts, that is, are a particular kind of paratext, one that marks the threshold through which the reader makes their exit from the reading of a text at the end of which they have arrived. As such, the relation of a postscript to the texts – the script – it comes after is one not simply of addition, but of reflection and commentary. Given the concern of Pater's *Appreciations* 'Postscript' with questions of before, after, and what exceeds the demarcations of before and after in the course of literary history, this placement and designation is especially noteworthy; its placement at the end – or, even, after the end – of the volume provokes a heightened consciousness of the reader's situation as they finish their reading of *Appreciations* and are thus poised to go on to other reading or, indeed, to other kinds of activity altogether on which reading (and the reading of *Appreciations* in particular) may be hoped to have some bearing. It is the consciousness of this situation that issues in Pater's addition of a final paragraph to the 'Postscript' of which there is no trace in 'Romanticism'. I consider this important addition in more detail at the conclusion to this chapter.

The 'Postscript', therefore, occupies a peculiar place in relation to the other essays in *Appreciations* and, indeed, in relation to its own forebear in print, namely, the *Macmillan's* 'Romanticism'. The peculiarities of the 'Postscript', its marginal (by which I do not at all mean insignificant or unrelated) status with respect to the other essays in *Appreciations*, are detectable in its content as well as in the form by which Pater designates it. A chapter addressing Pater's conception of the relation between classicism and romanticism in a collection on Pater and English studies, for instance, needs to confront the fact that Pater's sense of romanticism (and of classicism as well, for that matter) does not seem especially English. This is by no means a problem for contemporary readers of Pater, for whom Pater's cosmopolitan conception of literary tradition is cause for admiration, although it was a problem, as we shall see, for some of Pater's contemporaries; and it is also the case, of course, that other essays in *Appreciations*, most notably the essay on 'Style', take their bearings from literary traditions from beyond English shores. The point to emphasise here, though, is that any Paterian conception of 'English studies' must be provisional, capacious, and internally differentiated. To be sure, after the opening essay on 'Style' – which, like the 'Postscript', both titularly eschews the focus on one authorship and is marked as paratextual with relation to the other texts in *Appreciations: With an Essay on Style* – the first three essays of *Appreciations* deal with Wordsworth, Coleridge, and

Lamb – all English. In the 'Postscript' itself, Pater adduces Scott as a lover of 'strange adventure' which he 'sought . . . in the Middle Age', as well as Emily Brontë, 'a more really characteristic fruit' borne by 'the spirit of romanticism', the chief characters of whose *Wuthering Heights* are 'figures so passionate, yet woven on a background of delicately beautiful, moorland scenery' (*App.*, 242). As noted above, in the *Macmillan's* essay, Pater had also cited Whitman as an example of the extremity of curiosity into which romanticism may sometimes run, although this example was excised from the 'Postscript'.[2] Yet it is not just Scott's Scottishness nor Whitman's Americanness, nor even Pater's reminder that Brontë belonged to a distinctly non-metropolitan 'Yorkshire village', that foster the sense that Pater's romanticism may be more than English. It is in France, we are told, that 'the romantic movement . . . bore its most characteristic fruits', a point he emphasises again slightly later: 'But neither Germany, with its Goethe and Tieck, nor England, with its Byron and Scott, is nearly so representative of the romantic temper as France, with Murger, and Gautier, and Victor Hugo. It is in French literature that its most characteristic expression is to be found' (*App.*, 243, 249).

What is it that motivates Pater's turn to, and defence of, French romanticism – or, specifically, romanticism as French? The volume's Frenchness was certainly remarked by its original reviewers. Arthur Symons, for instance, noted that 'Appreciations' is 'a word occurring very often in the essays, and used, evidently, in the sense of the French *appréciation*, a weighing, a valuing, more even than in the general English sense of valuing highly'.[3] Symons's 'more even' subtly complicates the suggestion that the French mode of appreciation simply entails a refusal to value, an abdication of praise, and hints in its ampliative reach that 'a weighing, a valuing' involves, in fact, a more capacious and expansive method than merely making a dash for the heights. Symons goes on to extol Pater's 'sympathy' – a term, this time, with Greek roots and many European cousins – noting in particular 'a remarkable breadth and catholicity' discernible, especially, in the essay on 'Style' and the 'Postscript', which Symons, notably, takes together.[4]

Needless to say, not all contemporary readers of *Appreciations* were quite so appreciative of Pater's debts to France. Like Symons, C.L. Graves noticed the linguistic origins of the book's title, although for Graves, however, 'the effort to acclimatise a Gallicism smacks of affectation' (the Germanic 'smacks' is aptly pugnacious);[5] and Mrs Oliphant complained of the 'Postscript' in particular that '[i]t is rather terrible to meet with this old classical and romantic business in the discussion of English literature.

We have had, Heaven knows, enough of it in French to bewilder anyone's brain', before she went on to protest more generally 'against a foreign model which is altogether out of the question as affording any rule for us'.[6] The national exceptionalism in the fields of language and literature – and, by implication, in life in general, to which language and literature give expression – expressed in response to Pater was precisely what Pater had himself been responding to, both in the 'Romanticism' essay and in the placement of a version of this text as the 'Postscript' to his *appréciations* of English texts. 'Romanticism', that is, had responded to a series of decided accounts of modern romantic literature by, above all, W.J. Courthope and John Ruskin. In his account of this context for Pater's essay, Kenneth Daley has emphasised in particular the importance of Ruskin's lecture on 'Franchise', one of the lectures in the latter's *Val d'Arno* series that, Daley suggests, Pater is likely to have heard in Oxford in 1873. I will turn to 'Franchise' in a moment, but first it is worth briefly examining the place of France in Courthope's interventions in the romanticism debate in two essays of the mid-1870s. 'Though much behind the French in polish and critical perception,' Courthope concedes, without caring much for what is conceded, 'England has produced a literature more vigorous and original than her neighbour.' The distinction between the merely perceptive French and the productive English is the keynote of Courthope's interventions in this debate, and he goes on to insist that 'all great poetry stimulates to action'. With grim inevitability, English heroes of wars with the French are Courthope's favourite exemplars of the stimulating power of poetry:

> Marlborough avowed that he knew no history but what he learnt from Shakespeare. And what a depth of meaning lies in the pathetic anecdote of Wolfe, who, as he was being rowed towards the Heights of Abraham, repeated Gray's 'Elegy' to his companions, exclaiming at the conclusion that he would rather have been the author of the poem than be the victor in the approaching battle![7]

Instead of being a victorious British general, Wolfe would rather have written a poem: hardly the emphatic proof of poetry's stimulation to action Courthope imagines. Yet needless to say, Wolfe turned out in fact to be the victor on the Heights of Abraham, and this favourite anecdote was again in Courthope's mind when he remarks in a later essay on 'Wordsworth and Gray' that Gray's 'Elegy' 'appeals immediately, and will continue to appeal, to the heart of every Englishman, so long as the care of public liberty and love of the soil maintain their hold in this country'.

'We feel,' he goes on to say, 'that it is in every way fitting that the author of the "Elegy" should have been the favourite of Wolfe and the countryman of Chatham.'[8] This may appear like so much anti-French patriotic bloviation (because it is), but there is also a serious point at issue here. Courthope's qualification of liberty as '*public* liberty' (emphasis added) is of considerable significance to the arguments that both he and Ruskin advanced against contemporary romanticism. In defending Gray against Wordsworth's depreciation of him, that is, Courthope emphasised that '[t]he real question at issue between the two poets concerns the liberty of the imagination'.[9] Whereas 'Wordsworth and the romanticists' take the liberty of the imagination to be 'absolutely paramount', Gray admits restrictions on imaginative freedom, above all concerning what subjects are (allegedly) appropriate for imaginative treatment, in order to allow to the imagination the greatest degree of '*just* liberty'.[10]

This qualified understanding of liberty is given more historically nuanced expression in Ruskin's 'Franchise'. One gets the sense from Courthope that France as such, and for all time, is the problem, whereas that is far from the case for Ruskin. It is *modern* France – and, indeed, *modern* England – that are at fault:

> France is everlastingly, by birth, name, and nature, the country of the Franks, or free persons; and the first source of European frankness, or franchise. The Latin for franchise is libertas. But the modern or Cockney-English word, liberty,—Mr. John Stuart Mill's,—is not the equivalent of libertas; and the modern or Cockney-French word liberté,—M. Victor Hugo's,—is not the equivalent of franchise.[11]

Anticipating the qualified versions of liberty on which Courthope would insist ('public liberty', '*just* liberty'), Ruskin argues that franchise is governed by law. In this, Frank and Greek are at one, though the laws by which they are governed are nevertheless distinct: that of France is 'the law of love, *restraining* anger', and of Greece, 'the law of justice, and *enforcing* anger' (117). The law of the Franks is one of generosity and boundless munificence; that of the Greeks, judgement and discrimination. Or, alternatively, the law of the Franks is romantic, that of the Greeks, classical (121). It is in invoking these terms that Ruskin shows his hand: 'there is no appeal' from the authority of the classics, whereas 'however brilliant or lovely', the romantic 'remains imperfect, and without authority' (122). Romantic works do have, for Ruskin, the advantage over classical ones, first, that even where they are not fully understood, they give delight, and, second, that they 'fulfil to you, in sight and presence, what the Greek could only teach by signs' (122). These are indeed virtues of romanticism, but for Ruskin, modern French romantic writing – exemplified above all by Victor Hugo – suffers both by its difference from Diana Vernon, the character he advances as the embodiment of a dignified romanticism in Scott's *Rob Roy*, and by its similarity with Mill's liberalism. Ruskin ends his lecture on 'Franchise' with a curt disparagement of contemporary French culture: 'And what Diana Vernon is to a French ballerine [*sic*] dancing the Cancan, the "libertas" of Chartres and Westminster is to the "liberty" of M. Victor Hugo and Mr. John Stuart Mill' (126).

It is in response to these characterisations of romanticism – and of France, modernity, and the political valorisation of liberty with which they are inextricably bound up – that Pater wrote 'Romanticism'. His placement of a revised version of that essay after the end of *Appreciations*, moreover, retrospectively casts the entire volume as a riposte to a narrow conception of English culture and insufficiently nuanced conception of the interweaving tendencies of literary history on the ground of English literature itself. First, Pater senses that the compliment Ruskin pays to romanticism in contrast to classicism – that its works give delight even where they are not understood – is back-handed. He seeks to repay it by ascribing a particular affect to classical works:

> beneath all changes of habits and beliefs, our love of that mere abstract proportion—of music—which what is classical in literature possesses, still maintains itself in the best of us, and what pleased our grandparents may at least tranquillise us. The 'classic' comes to us out of the cool and quiet of other times, as the measure of what a long experience has shown will at least never displease us. (*App.*, 245)

The diminuendo here from pleasure, to tranquillisation, to the failure to displease not only makes the point that the mode of reception of classical works goes beyond the manly, no-nonsense faculty of the understanding, but also that their dissociation from feeling may have more to do with the fact that they have simply faded. But it is in defending recent French romantic writing that Pater's response to Ruskin and Courthope is most marked. Having emphasised that romanticism and classicism 'are tendencies really at work at all times in art' and having described how the history of art is thus a perennial balancing act between these tendencies, 'with the balance sometimes a little on one side, sometimes a little on the other', Pater details how romanticism demands 'strangeness' before allowing its 'passionate care for beauty' to be fulfilled (247). It is Hugo who is the chief exemplar of this pattern of strangeness first, then beauty:

> [Romanticism's] eager, excited spirit will have strength, the grotesque, first
> of all—the trees shrieking as you tear off the leaves; for Jean Valjean, the
> long years of convict life; for Redgauntlet, the quicksands of Solway Moss;
> then, incorporate with this strangeness, and intensified by restraint, as
> much sweetness, as much beauty, as is compatible with that. *Énergique,
> frais, et dispos*—these, according to Sainte-Beuve, are the characteristics of a
> genuine classic—*les ouvrage anciens ne sont pas classiques parce qu'ils sont
> vieux, mais parce qu'ils sont énergiques, frais, et dispos*. Energy, freshness,
> intelligent and masterly disposition:—these are characteristics of Victor
> Hugo when his alchemy is complete, in certain figures, like Marius and
> Cosette, in certain scenes, like that in the opening of *Les Travailleurs de la
> Mer*, where Déruchette writes the name of *Gilliatt* in the snow, on
> Christmas morning; but always there is a certain note of strangeness
> discernible there, as well. (248)

The use of the Ruskinian term 'grotesque', incidentally, warrants attention, since just a few sentences earlier Pater had described 'the grotesque in
art' as the result of 'a great overbalance of curiosity'; he then goes on to
suggest that 'a trace of distortion, of the grotesque, may perhaps linger, as
an additional element of expression' (247), before, in the above passage,
taking the 'grotesque' as a synonym for that 'strangeness' that is the very
condition – not the excess – of romanticism. Grotesquery is thus stripped
of its mischievous connotations in order to prepare the way for the defence
of Hugo. In contrast both to the activist, indeed, bellicose tradition of
English writing advanced by Courthope and to Ruskin's derision of
contemporary French writing typified by Hugo, Pater, in Stefano
Evangelista's words, is articulating 'a definition and defence of a rich
cosmopolitan Romanticism that he sees as a unifying cultural force in
nineteenth-century Europe'.[12] Pater, then, defends romantic writing in its
modern and French forms against Courthope's ultimately anglophile
denunciations and Ruskin's preference for a past world of Gothic franchise. Implicit in this defence, as Daley has noted, is also a sympathy with
the liberalism adumbrated by Mill.[13]

Two objections may be raised at this point, and both have to do with
the place of romanticism in Pater's conception of the history of art and
literature. First, in the above passage, in which he adduces three examples
from Victor Hugo, it is in fact with Sainte-Beuve's definition of 'a genuine
classic', and not with the romantic work, that Pater is concerned. Second,
Evangelista's ascription of a view of romanticism as 'a unifying force in
nineteenth-century Europe' to Pater may be taken to suggest that Pater
views romanticism as belonging to, or, at least, characterising a particular

historical epoch. In response to the first of these objections, it should be noted that it is a major part of Pater's purpose in the 'Postscript' to undermine the sense that classic and romantic are merely opposed: it is not a matter of assigning work *either* to classicism *or* to romanticism. As Wolfgang Iser and others have emphasised, Pater historicises the relation between classic and romantic – rendering them 'contingent powers', rather than normative concepts – but not (and this is where a response to the second objection raised above is pertinent) in order to affix classic and romantic to particular periods.[14] So even where Pater admits that 'in a limited sense' the romantic spirit 'may be said to be a product of special epochs' (*App.*, 250), or that, for instance, '[t]he last century was pre-eminently a classical age, an age in which, for art and literature, the element of a comely order was in the ascendant', the admission is, precisely, limited, and the opposite tendency (classic or romantic) is never simply dormant. 'Yet,' he remarks, in a qualifying gesture typical of his criticism, 'it is in the heart of this century [that is, the eighteenth], of Goldsmith and Stothard, of Watteau and the *Siècle de Louis XIV.*—in one of its central, if not most characteristic figures, in Rousseau—that the modern or French romanticism really originates' (251). It is also typical of Pater's writing that the parenthesis, as well as the repetition of 'in's and 'of's, should have the effect of shifting the ground of his description so that a wider focus is obtained. What is it that Rousseau is meant to be 'most characteristic' of? The eighteenth century? Romanticism? The fact that the answer is 'both' is telling.

In thus acknowledging the characteristics of epochs only within certain bounds, Pater accords individual temperament considerable significance – and indeed, the cultivation of a particular kind of temper, rather than the instilling of identifiable points of view, is a keynote throughout his writing. This accordance of significance to individual temperament was cast as typical of romanticism by T.E. Hulme in his 'Romanticism and Classicism', collected by Herbert Read in the volume he titled *Speculations*, partly in implicit response, no doubt, to Pater's *Appreciations* and Wilde's *Intentions*. Though Hulme nowhere names Pater explicitly, 'Romanticism and Classicism' is thoroughly informed by its reaction against Pater, not least in Hulme's insistence that 'no one, in a matter of judgment of beauty, can take a detached standpoint . . . . Just as physically you are not born that abstract entity, man, but the child of particular parents, so you are in matters of literary judgment'. This reflection on the pre-determined nature of literary judgement is extended to literary creation when Hulme avers (there is a lot of averring in

'Romanticism and Classicism') that 'many acts which we habitually label free are in reality automatic. It is quite possible for a man to write a book almost automatically'.[15] Hulme's stress on the restricted and conditioned nature of both literary judgement and creation is itself, of course, predicated on a classicalist precept: 'The classical poet never forgets this finiteness, this limit of man.'[16]

In defiance of such a view as Hulme would go on to adumbrate, Pater focuses not only on the fact that figures such as Rousseau and William Blake (someone whose theory and practice of composition was inimical to the automisation of creation) are difficult to situate straightforwardly in their times, but on the fact that their singularity is also, in fact, a profound expression of their times in the fullness of their complexity and in contrast to subsequent simplification of them. It is not that Pater advocates the simple overflowing of limits in the manner Hulme associates with romanticism (as per his famous definition: 'It is like pouring a pot of treacle over the dinner table. Romanticism, then, and this is the best definition I can give of it, is spilt religion'[17]), rather, any given historical epoch is the product or, better, forcefield of countervailing tendencies. 'William Blake, a type of so much which breaks through what are conventionally thought the influences of that century,' writes Pater, 'is still a noticeable phenomenon in it, and the reaction in favour of naturalism in poetry begins in that century, early' (*App.*, 257). The ironically belated qualification ('early') in that sentence is a deft touch of Pater's, apt to forestall any attempt to respond to his argument merely by shifting period boundaries: Rousseau and Blake are products of the later eighteenth century, such a response would go, and so we do not have to shift by much our dates for the end of classicism and beginning of romanticism. But Pater eschews the easy option of splitting the difference in this way: the tendencies of romanticism and classicism are not merely opposed, but rather depend upon one another and are thus operative throughout the history of art.

I discussed earlier Pater's defence of French romanticism but it is worth briefly considering at this point a significant German source – one, unlike Goethe, Heine, and others, that is not actually acknowledged in his 'Postscript' – namely, G.W.F. Hegel. In his *Aesthetics*, which Pater knew well, Hegel was himself the author of a consideration of the historical relation between symbolic, classic, and romantic forms of art that cannot simply be mapped on to specifiable historical epochs. Yet it is in fact Hegel's conception of historical process more broadly that is germane to the characterisation of the historical relation between classicism and romanticism in Pater's 'Postscript'. As Anthony Ward shows in his account of Pater's thinking, Benjamin Jowett, one of Pater's most influential Oxford contemporaries, developed what would turn out to be an influential summary of Hegel's historical understanding:

> he views all the forms of sense and knowledge as stages of thought which have always existed implicitly and unconsciously, and to which the mind of the world, gradually disengaged from sense, has become awakened. The present has been the past—the succession in time of human ideas is also the eternal 'now'.[18]

While there are holes one could pick in this as an account of Hegel (Jowett's evocation of 'the eternal "now"' is vulnerable to the critique of sense-certainty Hegel develops in *Phenomenology of Spirit*), the Hegelian sense of the continuity of the past in the present and of the perpetual outworking of spirit in history clearly influenced Pater's insistence that 'Romanticism, then, although it has its epochs, is in its essential characteristics rather a spirit which shows itself at all times, in various degrees, in individual workmen and their work, and the amount of which criticism has to estimate in them taken one by one, than the peculiarity of a time or a school' (*App.*, 256–7). Moreover, Pater's sense that romanticism departs from classicism, but also 'retain[s] the flavour of what was admirably done in past generations, in the classics' (256), clearly owes something to Hegel's conception of *Aufhebung*, usually translated as 'sublation', according to which one concept or force is both superseded and retained in a subsequent form – although, as a number of commentators have emphasised, Pater does not subscribe to the kind of determinable teleology that *Aufhebung* is sometimes thought to subserve in Hegel's work.[19]

Yet despite his emphasis on the relative historical ubiquity, as it were, of both classical and romantic tendencies, Pater's propensity for reverting to the eighteenth century as an instance of a classical epoch (even in order to complicate such an account) and, likewise, of exemplifying romanticism by recent works may nevertheless create the impression that classicism belongs to the past and romanticism to the present. And insofar as it stands for rebellion against fixed standards, then romanticism would seem to appear secondary. But as soon as we have granted the validity of that appearance, we must acknowledge that, insofar as it stands for the imposition of standards on excess, classicism would also seem to need to follow, rather than lead. In order to focus this question of the priority of classicism or romanticism, and, particularly, of Pater's subtle treatment of it, it is worth paying slightly closer attention to an idiosyncrasy in his handling of a particular, although otherwise unremarkable, term. Early in the

'Postscript' Pater describes 'the opposition between the classicists and the romanticists—between the adherents, in the culture of beauty, of the principles of liberty, and authority, respectively—of strength, and order or what the Greeks call κοσμιότης' (*App.*, 244). Returning to the same opposition slightly later, he makes the point in a similar way:

> But, however falsely those two tendencies may be opposed by critics, or exaggerated by artists themselves, they are tendencies really at work at all times in art, moulding it, with the balance sometimes a little on one side, sometimes a little on the other, generating, respectively, as the balance inclines on this side or that, two principles, two traditions, in art, and in literature so far as it partakes of the spirit of art. (247)

If we take 'respectively' to mean '[c]onsidered individually or in turn, *and in the order mentioned*' (*OED*, 'respectively', adv., sense 3; emphasis added), then these are both unusual uses of the word, which reveal something important about the way that Pater handles the relation between romanticism and classicism. The mismatch between terms and what they 'respectively' entail is, indeed, crucial to the at once historicising but not periodising understanding of the relation between classic and romantic that Pater is seeking to articulate. His use of 'respectively' is a 'tiny modification of the expected', which are frequent in Pater and arise from his 'constant recourse to the secondary', his 'act of aftering, reappraising'.[20]

While such an 'act of aftering, reappraising' may be generally discernible in Pater's works – and I agree with Angela Leighton's implication that it is one of Pater's strengths, however much it has often been misjudged as a weakness – it is specifically germane to the 'Postscript', which as I emphasised above is at once a revision of an earlier essay, a backward glance on the essays in *Appreciations* after which it comes, and an intimation of what might come now, after the end. Reappraisal, to borrow Leighton's terms, is not the avoidance of appraisal and modification of the expected is not the disappointment of hopes but the transformation of convention, established order, and precedent. These reflections on Pater's affinity with second thoughts are naturally germane to this consideration of the 'Postscript' and perhaps especially to the ending of the 'Postscript', since this is the site of Pater's most significant revision to 'Romanticism' and the moment in the text where he at once conclusively and prospectively points beyond his own discussion to the task of literary and cultural criticism. To be sure, prior to the addition of what is in effect a kind of coda to the 'Postscript' – recourse not so much to the secondary, then, but even the tertiary – Pater had considered, in a section of 'Romanticism' reprised in the 'Postscript', the consequences of romanticism for those looking to the future. Attempting, again, to account for the 'appeal' of 'the works of French romanticism' to those who are 'weary of the present, but yearning for the spectacle of beauty and strength', Pater acknowledged that there is 'a certain distortion' in the works of Gautier and Hugo, though such distortion is, paradoxically, 'always combined with perfect literary execution', and mounts, via 'grim humour' and 'ghastly comedy' (*App.*, 253), to 'a genuine pathos' (254). He sets out the reason for this as follows:

> for the habit of noting and distinguishing one's own most intimate passages of sentiment makes one sympathetic, begetting, as it must, the power of entering, by all sorts of finer ways, into the intimate recesses of other minds; so that pity is another quality of romanticism, both Victor Hugo and Gautier being great lovers of animals, and charming writers about them, and Murger being unrivalled in the pathos of his *Scènes de la Vie de Jeunesse*. Penetrating so finely into all situations which appeal to pity, above all, into the special or exceptional phases of such feeling, the romantic humour is not afraid of the quaintness or singularity of its circumstances or expression, pity, indeed, being of the essence of humour; so that Victor Hugo does but turn his romanticism into practice, in his hunger and thirst after practical *Justice* !—a justice which shall no longer wrong children, or animals, for instance, by ignoring in a stupid, mere breadth of view, minute facts about them. (254)

The argument is not so much for the temperance of justice by mercy, though that is in the background, but is aimed instead at justifying a dissatisfaction with the merely formal administration of justice understood as the maintenance and application of established standards. Romanticism's regard for 'quaintness or singularity', for what lies beyond the purview of precedent, for what, indeed, is systematically excluded from consideration, is necessary to the functioning of any justice worthy of the name. Though it may be alleged that the 'practice' into which Hugo turns his romanticism is not action itself, but rather 'his hunger and thirst after practical *Justice* !', and hence that his practice is a thirst for practice, Pater can hardly be convicted of avoiding the articulation of a positive ethics that inheres in the just treatment of conventionally ignored beings with whom readers of Murger, Hugo, and, now, Pater share the world.

Where Pater's attempt to derive an ethics of justice from Murger and Hugo depends fundamentally on knowledge – on, that is, ceasing to ignore 'minute facts' about downtrodden and neglected occupants of the world – the newly written coda to the 'Postscript' begins by emphasising the need for the organisation of what we already know. This, strikingly, may appear to give expression to a distinctly classical emphasis on order – 'For the literary art, at all events, the problem just now is, to induce order upon the contorted, proportionless accumulation of our knowledge and experience' (*App.*, 260) – though it is perhaps also worth noting its affinity with Percy Shelley's assertion, made as near to the beginning of the nineteenth century as Pater stood to its end, that '[w]e have more moral, political and historical wisdom, than we know how to reduce into practise; we have more scientific and œconomical knowledge than can be accommodated to the just distribution of the produce which it multiplies'.[21] Pater's concern in *Appreciations* may appear literarily inward – not just in its concern with literary writers but in its cultivation of a particular literary style for criticism of them. And the 'Postscript', in its treatment of the relation between presiding subdivisions of literature, may appear particularly so. But its concern is, in fact, with the relation of artistic practice to 'knowledge and experience', which, as the reflections on Murger and Hugo demonstrate, ought to serve as the foundations of justice. 'Romanticism' had ended with a fairly tepid, if unimpeachable summary of the essay's argument: 'But explain the terms as we will, in application to particular epochs, there are these two elements always recognisable; united in perfect art, in Sophocles, in Dante, in the highest work of Goethe, though not always absolutely balanced there; and these two elements may be not inappropriately termed the classical and romantic tendencies.'[22] But it is here, at the end of *Appreciations* as the volume necessarily begins to give way to what is beyond it, that Pater looks determinedly outside literature to that which it may affect, to what it may 'induce order upon'. 'For, in truth,' Pater concludes the 'Postscript' and so *Appreciations* as a whole, 'the legitimate contention is, not of one age or school of literary art against another, but of all successive schools alike, against the stupidity which is dead to the substance, and the vulgarity which is dead to form' (261). Stupidity and vulgarity are not offences against taste, merely, but against justice, and it is the calling of all literary art to contend against them.

Notes

1 William Sharp, unsigned review, *Glasgow Herald* (28 November 1889), 9; repr. in *Critical Heritage*, 195–8 (196).
2 'Romanticism', *Macmillan's Magazine* 35 (November 1876), 64–70 (66).
3 Symons, unsigned review, *Athenaeum* (14 December 1889), 813–14; repr. in *Critical Heritage*, 201–4 (201).

4 Symons, unsigned review, 203.

5 Graves, unsigned review, *Spectator* (21 December 1889), 887–8; repr. in *Critical Heritage*, 209–14 (211).

6 Mrs Oliphant, unsigned review, *Blackwoods Magazine* 147 (1890), 140–5; repr. in *Critical Heritage*, 214–19 (218).

7 [W.J. Courthope], 'Modern Culture', *Quarterly Review* 137 (October 1874), 389–415 (403–4).

8 [W.J. Courthope], 'Wordsworth and Gray', *Quarterly Review* 141 (January 1876), 104–36 (110–13).

9 Courthope, 'Wordsworth and Gray', 128.

10 Courthope, 'Wordsworth and Gray' 128 (Courthope's emphasis).

11 Ruskin, Lecture VIII: 'Franchise', *Val d'Arno* (delivered 1873, first publ. 1874), in *The Works of John Ruskin*, ed. E.T. Cook and Alexander Wedderburn, 39 vols (1903–12), xxiii (1906), 116. Further references to this lecture are given in parentheses in the text.

12 Stefano Evangelista, 'Rome and the Romantic Heritage in Walter Pater's *Marius the Epicurean*' in *Romans and Romantics*, ed. Timothy Saunders and others (Oxford 2012), 305–26 (310).

13 Kenneth Daley, *The Rescue of Romanticism: Walter Pater and John Ruskin* (Columbus, OH 2001), 129. On Mill's and Pater's liberalisms, see David Russell, *Tact: Aesthetic Liberalism and the Essay Form in Nineteenth-Century Britain* (Princeton, NJ 2018), especially 113 and 117–19.

14 Wolfgang Iser, *Walter Pater: Die Autonomie des Ästhetischen* (Tübingen 1960), 93.

15 T.E. Hulme, 'Romanticism and Classicism', in *Speculations: Essays on Humanism and the Philosophy of Art*, ed. Herbert Read (1924; repr. 1971), 111–40 (123).

16 Hulme, 'Romanticism and Classicism', 120.

17 Hulme, 'Romanticism and Classicism', 118.

18 Benjamin Jowett, introduction to *The Sophist*, in *The Dialogues of Plato*, 3rd edn, 5 vols (Oxford 1892), iv. 405; see Anthony Ward, *Walter Pater: The Idea in Nature* (1966), ch. 3 ('Hegel').

19 See, for example, Giles Whiteley, *Aestheticism and the Philosophy of Death: Walter Pater and Post-Hegelianism* (2010), especially 151–2.

20 Angela Leighton, 'Walter Pater's Dream Rhythms', in *Thinking Through Style: Non-Fiction Prose of the Long Nineteenth Century*, ed. Michael D. Hurley and Marcus Waithe (Oxford 2018), 217–29 (219).

21 Shelley, 'A Defence of Poetry' (written 1821; published 1840), in *Shelley's Poetry and Prose*, 2nd edn, ed. Donald H. Reiman and Neil Fraistat (New York 2002), 509–35 (530).

22 Pater, 'Romanticism', 70.

CHAPTER 6

Form, Matter, and Metaphysics in Walter Pater's Essay on 'Style'

Michael D. Hurley

'Style' is a comparatively rare instance of Pater's direct theorising; more often, his views emerge implicitly, incidentally, through the critical evaluation of specific artists and their works. Even by the standards of his other overtly theoretical interventions, 'Style' stands out, for the breadth and importance of its subject, and for its capstone prominence within 'one of the two most influential volumes of literary criticism the nineteenth century produced'[1] – as the first entry in *Appreciations*, and the only one to make it into the volume's subtitle: '*With an Essay on Style*'. Correspondingly, scholars have often turned to 'Style' as if it were the author's manifesto or *summa* on the subject, being 'in the nature of a personal statement',[2] as 'a crystallizing and rationalizing of his theories and habits as a writer'.[3] Yet the essay tends to disappoint precisely on these terms. If 'Style' is the key to Pater's aesthetic principles, most readers have found the lock jammed.

Oscar Wilde described 'Style' as 'the most interesting, and certainly the least successful' of the essays within *Appreciations*: 'most interesting because it is the work of one who speaks with the high authority that comes from the noble realisation of things nobly conceived'; 'least successful, because the subject is too abstract', and a 'true artist like Mr Pater' is 'most felicitous when he deals with the concrete'.[4] Denis Donoghue, a century later, revived the chiastic snappiness of Wilde's judgement in his estimation of 'Style' as Pater's 'best known but not his best essay',[5] with the corollary complaint that, while Pater is '[a]pparently concerned with style', he 'doesn't quote so much as a line of verse or a sentence of prose to illustrate his argument'.[6]

Wilde and Donoghue raise important questions, but exaggerate and simplify. On the one hand, Pater clearly wrote essays that are better known than 'Style' ('Leonardo', 'Giorgione', his 'Preface' and 'Conclusion' to *The Renaissance*, are obvious examples). On the other hand, it is far from self-evident what constitutes 'interest' and 'success' in Pater's (or any essayist's) account of style, and the relation of these things to 'abstraction'. Abstraction tends to leave subjects unanchored, diffusing thoughts into thin air – that is true. And theorists have found the conceptual category of style in particular to be 'famously indefinable and elusive',[7] such that individual texts tend to become eclipsed within the generalised activity of theorising itself.[8] Which is no doubt why 'literary theory has never tended to bother much with style anyway', to the extent that it has been asked whether literary theory (as against literary criticism) might even be 'definable by its relative indifference to style'.[9] But Pater was not a literary critic who sometimes dabbled in theory. He instead combined and so confounded these separate disciplinary approaches. While he had a high degree of sensitivity to individual aesthetic objects, he was also a scholar of classical philosophy, and his 'high authority' ranged between these modes, even within single essays. Artistic and literary subjects inform but also provide the occasion for his broader philosophical thinking.

It is at once unsurprising and instructive, then, to notice that 'Style's theorising itself grew out of a study of particularity: from his review of 'The Life and Letters of Gustave Flaubert'. Within weeks of its publication in the *Pall Mall Gazette* on 25 August 1888, Pater set to rewriting, teasing out certain universal stylistic principles that he found exemplified in Flaubert's repertoire. 2584 words swelled to 8625, and more significantly, he changed its scope. By the time 'Style' appeared (first in December of the same year for *Fortnightly Review*, and then in the subsequent year within *Appreciations*), Flaubert continued to loom large, but he was no longer the object of study; he had become 'our French guide'. The essay was no longer about a writer but about writing. Or more accurately, it had become an essay of theoretical principles informed by particularised example.

The Flaubert review begins by escorting the reader, with brisk economy, through concentrically nested degrees of generality towards ever-increasing particularity, within a single sentence: 'Prose as a fine art, of which French literature provides a continuous illustration, had in Gustave Flaubert a follower, unique in the decisiveness of his conception of that art, and the disinterestedness of his service to it.'[10] 'Style' reverses that explicatory direction, beginning instead by expanding even the category he had previously taken as the outer ring of generalisation. 'Prose as a fine art' is not, within 'Style', the first step towards specifying a literary tradition on the way to a specific writer within that tradition; it is the first step towards opening up the genre of prose itself. Prose style is not to be seen in clean contrast to poetry; that would be to 'limit the proper functions of prose too narrowly' (*App.*, 5). While recognising the heuristic value of generic differences – it would be 'the stupidest of losses to confuse things which right reason has put asunder', including 'the distinction between poetry and prose' – Pater warns against the procrustean temptation 'to limit art *a priori*, by anticipations regarding the natural incapacity of the material which this or that artists works' (5).

To opine on what is possible in writing, where his essays more typically explore actual artistic achievements, marks a significant shift. But 'Style' is, on closer inspection, still all about specificity. Pater has not simply swapped his microscope for a telescope. Flaubert's voice continues to be heard in the essay, through ample quotation, and the animating principle of the essay's argument – appearing from the very first paragraph – is that artworks cannot be evaluated by normative standards, because they are 'liable to be discredited by the facts of artistic production' (6). 'Appreciation' only makes sense in relation to actual artworks that inevitably proliferate beyond whatever prior categories we seek to explain them.

Insofar as Pater is pursuing an 'abstract' argument, therefore, his argument is waged against the conceit of abstraction itself. What he said of 'beauty' some sixteen years earlier in his 'Preface' to *The Renaissance* holds here too, for how he defines 'style', as something to be understood and 'appreciated': 'not in the most abstract but in the most concrete terms possible, to find, not its universal formula, but the formula which expresses most adequately this or that special manifestation of it, is the aim of the true student of aesthetics' (*Ren.*, xix). 'Style' is, by extension, about writing's potential multifariousness; it is a retort to 'the prejudice that there can be but one only beauty of prose style' (*App.*, 8). A breathless list of divergent examples drives home the point, and the fact that the list has an off-the-cuff carelessness about it, rather than being systematic or exhaustive, is part of the point too, about the unruly fecundity of artistic richness that refuses neat taxonomies:

> while prose is actually found to be a coloured thing with Bacon, picturesque with Livy and Carlyle, musical with Cicero and Newman, mystical and intimate with Plato and Michelet and Sir Thomas Browne, exalted or florid, it may be, with Milton and Taylor, it will be useless to protest that it can be nothing at all, except something very tamely and narrowly confined to mainly practical ends—a kind of 'good round-hand;' as useless as the protest that poetry might not touch prosaic subjects as with Wordsworth, or an abstruse matter as with Browning, or treat contemporary life nobly as with Tennyson. (6)

More than an argument for stylistic diversity within poetry and prose – 'as there are many beauties of poetry so the beauties of prose are many, and it is the business of criticism to estimate them as such' (6) – Pater advances the pluralistic possibility that these separate genres may overlap. Following Wordsworth and De Quincey, Pater suggests that while distinctions between poetry and prose may be formal (the presence or absence of, say, metre or rhyme), there is another and more salient difference to be observed that transcends generic categories; namely, between 'imaginative and unimaginative writing' (7). Poetry may possess 'hard, logical, and quasi-prosaic excellences'; prose may likewise exhibit 'the imaginative power' conventionally associated with poetry – and quite properly so, not as something 'out of place and a kind of vagrant intruder' (6).

As it gathers momentum this line of argument appears to be directed against Dryden, who is derided for failing even to live up to his own narrow prescriptions: 'Setting up correctness, that humble merit of prose, as the central literary excellence, he is really a less correct writer than he may seem, still with an imperfect mastery of the relative pronoun' (7). There is something deliciously waspish in the litotes of 'imperfect mastery', but something rather unjust as well, given the signal potency of his sentences that Gerard Manley Hopkins (among others) admired as 'the naked thew and sinew of the English language'.[11] But Dryden is a red herring. Pater is in fact troubled by another figure altogether, one from his own age. Unnamed except by way of an innocuous footnote, it is the influential contemporary literary scholar and critic George Saintsbury who is, as John Coates puts it, 'the silent adversary in "Style"'.[12]

Pater's straining to make space for diverse, avant-garde and as-yet-unimagined prose styles is a riposte to the narrow and calcified standards promoted by Saintsbury in his valorisation of the historical moment of the 'Queen Anne men' (Addison, Steel, and Arbuthnot) as the apogee of tact, order, and lucid proportion. Pater does not at all object to these traits; he questions only the assumption that English prose style is necessarily best when it expresses itself in this way. That is why he is keen to defend, for instance, the possibility of 'unexpectedness' in writing, not as a requisite but as a possible virtue; disruption and disjunction may have their fit place too.

Having thus loosened up the generic expectations around poetry versus prose, Pater takes one audacious step further. From the possibility that the 'imaginative power' traditionally associated with poetry may find legitimate expression in 'imaginative prose', he moves to the proposition that prose may, at the moment of his writing, possess an even higher authority and power than poetry, as 'the special and opportune art of the modern world' (11). Differently from Hegel's pronouncements on art and the modern world (to which he may or may not be responding), Pater provides his hieratic-sounding claim with a technical rationale, on two levels: prose has greater expressive range, as 'an instrument of many stops, meditative, observant, descriptive, eloquent, analytic, plaintive, fervid'; it can also more properly capture the everyday experience of life, through its 'all-pervading naturalism, a curiosity about everything whatever as it really is, involving a certain humility of attitude, cognate to what must, after all, be the less ambitious form of literature' (11). Such claims must be read against Pater's recurring accent on modernity: the putative specialness of prose style relates to its timeliness. He is not expressing a private view, nor an ahistorical view: he is making an intervention in a debate in 'the present day' about the role and nature of prose in 'the modern world', as part of the rise of English studies as a discipline.

Pater's review of Flaubert had appeared anonymously. But rewritten, retitled, and bearing his name, 'Style' was a way of planting a philosophical flag in the ground. Saintsbury had not by that time been appointed to the Regius Chair of English at Edinburgh that would make him 'the nearest thing to Critic Laureate',[13] but he was already a highly influential figure whose 'contemporary standing must be set in the context of the emergence of English studies in the universities'.[14] '"Style" gains in force and significance', Coates rightly observes, 'if one sees it as a defense of what Pater valued and tried to practice in writing against the formidable and authoritative pronouncements of a dominant figure in the rise of English studies'.[15]

Two years before 'Style', Pater had reviewed Saintsbury's *Specimens of English Prose Style* for the *Guardian*, in which, within an otherwise admiring appraisal, he offers an instructive cavil: 'If there be a weakness in Mr Saintsbury's view, it is perhaps a tendency to regard style a little too independently of matter' (*Essays*, 15). His subjunctive qualifications ('If there be', 'perhaps') together with his generous modifications ('a tendency', 'a little too') read more like politeness than the provisionality they profess. Pater's urbane manner – by turns polite, circumspect, oblique, and ironic – characteristically disguises the incisiveness and boldness of his interventions, but it is clear from the wider corpus of his writings, and indeed their wider cultural context, that he is here expressing a fundamental difference of principle. Coates skewers Saintsbury's prescriptivism on writing as 'the prose equivalent of dressing for dinner',[16] and for Pater, the stakes of style evidently extend beyond some outmoded or bourgeois etiquette of 'good taste'. But how far? To answer this question it is helpful to consider another unnamed interlocutor against whose influential pronouncements 'Style' is also tacitly addressed.

***

Along with *Appreciations*, the other 'one of the two most influential volumes of literary criticism the nineteenth century produced' was Matthew Arnold's *Essays in Criticism*. Scholars have (like T. S. Eliot) sometimes stressed the continuities between Pater and Arnold.[17] But there are salient differences between their literary-critical stances too, as the respective titles of their most famous collections immediately announce. Whereas 'Criticism' comes loaded with the presumption of fixed objective criteria, 'Appreciations' insinuates mutable and varied impressionism, by an approach that is sympathetic and celebratory rather than stringently judgemental.

Laurel Brake has pressed this distinction, emphasising the extent to which Pater opposed Arnold's foundational assumptions about literature and principles for literary criticism as a discipline. Noting their rivalrous public dialogue conducted over many years, Brake interprets 'Style', together with Pater's essay on romanticism (which between them begin and end *Appreciations*), as an indirect but deliberate attack on Arnold's convictions on the comparative inferiority of Romanticism as a movement and on the superiority of poetry as a genre.[18] Arnold's literary-critical bearings were taken from a classical tradition where Pater, though by scholarly formation an accomplished classicist himself, inhabits and seeks to defend the verbal milieu of his moment, and never more trenchantly than in 'Style' – which, as noted, actually elevates prose above poetry, as 'the special art of the modern world'.

Between Saintsbury and Arnold, what's special in Pater's account of the specialness of 'style' begins to emerge by contradistinction. By whatever degree he felt Saintsbury to be in thrall to form, as if it might be entirely self-sufficient, he felt the opposite about Arnold, whose confident formulation of literary-critical judgement on 'the best that has been known and thought' edged towards presenting the 'best' of literature as determined by 'matter' over 'form' – as if the 'best' were a kind of sedimented knowledge existing separately from the style that breathes it into verbal life. Evaluating Pater against Saintsbury and Arnold in this way opens up the knotty conundrums of his gnomic formulations, but it also risks exaggeration.

Because Arnold did himself recognise the limitations of didactic literature, in which matter entirely subordinates form; and because Saintsbury did not, either, view form entirely independently from matter: he viewed matter as entirely dependent on form.

For Saintsbury, 'any subject may be deprived of its repulsiveness by the treatment of it', but that is not to say that the 'subject' of literature is merely the excuse for formal virtuosity.[19] He understood moreover that matter and form, and their interrelations, depend, in turn, on the human world from which they spring. 'Form without matter, art without life, are', Saintsbury says, 'inconceivable':[20]

> That literature can be absolutely isolated is, of course, not to be thought of; nothing human can be absolutely isolated from the general conditions of humanity, and from the other functions and operations thereof. But in that comparative isolation and separation which Aristotle meant by his caution against confusion of kinds, I do thoroughly believe.[21]

While it is right, then, to emphasise the fact that at the time Pater wrote 'Style', Saintsbury was 'widely applauded and about to dominate academic English', it is too much to say that his dominance assumed the absolute position of 'rejecting moral criteria' but endorsing instead 'an overt literary hedonism'.[22] Although critics continue to read Saintsbury as one who advocated an 'extreme interpretation of "art for art's sake"', which meant 'style over subject', where 'manner was everything',[23] his position was not in fact so stark. The 'isolation' he imagines of form from matter is, as he says (and as I have elsewhere sought to demonstrate) avowedly 'comparative'.[24] It remains valuable to suggest that Pater wished 'to guard the subtle and discriminating aestheticism he had tried to formulate from being tainted by association with its popular, clumsy variants' advanced by Saintsbury, or indeed Wilde or Swinburne.[25] But to gloss 'subtlety' as the defining difference between Pater and his aestheticist peers misses something important. Where Pater comes to in 'Style' is not so much a greater *refinement* of art for art's sake as it is a radical *reimagining* of that movement's metaphysical presuppositions, as suggested by the ways Pater finds himself at odds with Arnold too. Arnold's emphasis on 'matter' certainly seems to go beyond Pater, while likewise heeding Aristotle's 'caution against confusion of kinds'; but the matter of 'matter' is yet more complicated.

Arnold is forceful on 'the indispensable mechanical part' of writing as well as on 'soul and matter' ('an artisan's readiness' is not of itself enough, and neither is mere 'spirituality and feeling'),[26] and he diagnosed his own century as underpowered in the latter ('the English poetry of the first quarter of this century, with plenty of energy, plenty of creative force, did not know enough').[27] This judgement recoils onto his own creative writing too, vividly suggested by the tart response he gave to Clough's admiration for one of his poems. 'I am glad you like the Gipsy Scholar—but what does it do for you?' Arnold asks, before impatiently answering himself, in a way that underscores his essential commitment to 'soul and matter': 'Homer *animates*—Shakespeare *animates*—in its poor way I think Sohrab and Rustum *animates*—the Gipsy Scholar at best awakens a pleasing melancholy.' A merely satisfying experience of reading, Arnold explains, is 'not what we want': for literature to 'animate' is to 'ennoble' readers – 'not merely to add zest to their melancholy or grace to their dreams'.[28] 'People do not understand what a temptation there is', Arnold confessed to his sister, 'if you cannot bear anything not very good, to transfer your operations to a region where form is everything':

> Perfection of a certain kind may there be attained, or at least approached, without knocking yourself to pieces, but to attain or approach perfection in the region of thought and feeling, and to unite this with a perfection of form, demands not merely an effect and a labour, but an actual tearing of oneself to pieces.[29]

Arnold here recognises the aestheticist temptation to which Pater had seemingly succumbed in some of his earlier accounts of art, before 'Style'. In distancing himself from unchecked aestheticism, Pater is not seeking to moderate or clarify his earlier position by more fully accommodating 'matter' – more than Saintsbury, that is to say, if still rather less than Arnold. 'Style' is not an attempted *tertium quid* between these Scylla and Charybdis of English studies. It offers more than a tweak of emphasis. Pater is proposing something different in kind. Surprising – even shocking – though it is to read from the one-time author of the 'golden book of aestheticism', he is proposing that 'great' (as opposed to 'good') art requires more than aesthetic achievement, and more even than an Arnoldian affective ambition of ennobling: he contends that it must also be true. That is how 'Style' ends, and that is what most readers and critics and scholars have in the end found most difficult to accept about it.

So difficult indeed that the final paragraph of 'Style' is often said to be dishonest, a 'defensive' attempt, as J. P. Ward and others have argued, to separate himself from the association of aestheticism with amorality and corruption.[30] Pater's gestures to truth are, by this reasoning, nothing more than a concessionary grace note to his insistence on perfect 'form' – a pragmatic move that, Harold Bloom complains, leads him to 'falsify his vision'.[31] René Wellek offers a similarly impugning swipe, calling it a 'recantation at the expense of a unified, coherent view of art'.[32] While the chorus of such disapproval has been extensive, little effort has been made to take Pater's supposed falsification and recantation seriously, to examine how exactly, within his own style, he turns away from the open licence of aestheticism towards the apparent conservatism of cosmic piety.

Pater argues that the value of style is radically contingent. It is not to be estimated as a standalone aesthetic achievement, but expressive – more or less successfully – of articulate content, as the 'adaptation of words to their matter' (*App.*, 35). And: 'In the highest as in the lowliest literature' – here is the controversial kicker – 'the one indispensable beauty is, after all, truth' (34). That seems bluntly clear. But quite what he means by 'truth' requires some unpacking. His governing distinction between 'imaginative and unimaginative writing' with which he leads in 'Style' is later parsed in somewhat enigmatic terms as the difference between language that trades in 'mere fact' (9, 10) or 'bare fact' (10, 34) and 'the writer's sense of fact' (8, 9, 10, 34) or 'soul-fact' (11). Whereas the 'lowliest' literature has an obligation to the former kind, the 'highest' serves the latter, which he glosses, with more poetry than pellucidity, as 'that finest and most intimate form of truth, the *vraie vérité*' (34).

The primary burden of his essay, climaxing in its final paragraph, is to make sense of this axiom: that style aspires to beauty, through multifarious forms, and that beauty is ultimately *convertible* (to use the technical language of philosophical-theology) with 'truth'. While the scientist sticks to objective transcription, the literary artist modifies, not by forsaking or distorting truth, but by interpreting it. The result is not the abandonment of facts for feelings, but what he calls 'the representation of such fact as connected with soul, of a specific personality, in its preferences, its volition and power' (10). The reflexive turn here is by no means total; Pater is not advocating sheer subjectivity. He presses hard on the need for writers to possess a scholar's learning and sensibility so as to respect and exploit the expressive resources of language and literary history, and this works by paradoxical synergy: such 'restraints' beget a 'liberty' in the act of verbal creation with the genius and peculiar 'colouring' of the writer's 'own spirit' (15).

How might this faith in the truth-content of art, so defined, be reconciled with Pater's other writings that have flown under the banner of aestheticism, notably his 'Conclusion' to *The Renaissance*, proclaiming 'art for its own sake'? Is 'faith' – trenching as it does into the religious lexicon – even the right word for what's driving the turn towards 'truth' in 'Style'? In his essay on Rossetti also collected within *Appreciations*, Pater sets his face against 'mere tricks of manner' that force readerly attention in favour of what he calls 'the quality of sincerity' (*App.*, 206). But the 'truth' to which 'Style' tilts is towards an even higher ideal that implies an objective as well as personal value, of the sort advocated by one final, unnamed influence on Pater's understanding and practice of style.

***

John Henry Newman was, David J. DeLaura has shown, of 'decisive importance' for, and 'quite explicitly at the center' of, the writing of 'Style'.[33] Whereas the argument of 'Style' might helpfully be read as a reply to Arnold and Saintsbury, Newman's influence is felt as a positive endorsement of his ideas: on the interpenetrating relationship between 'style' and 'matter' (which Newman advances in his essay on 'Literature' and later elaborated in the second half of *The Idea of a University*), and on the language of 'soul-fact' and 'soul in style'. Newman looms also as 'a supreme practitioner of the sort of "style" Pater most admired'.[34]

To cast Newman as a dominant shaping influence is not to short-circuit to the conclusion that Pater was in fact a crypto-Catholic whose late essay aims to ratify the Christian theology of the co-inherence of truth and beauty. 'Newman's claims upon Pater's attention were multiple and persistent',[35] especially towards the end of this life, when he came to write 'Style'; but they did not extend to anything like a formal or thoroughgoing religious conversion. A nuanced estimation is required. In recent years, critics (such as Coates) have urged differences between Pater and his contemporaries likewise caught up in the movement of aestheticism – yet Pater continues to be widely read as an eremite of art. The idea that his distinctiveness as an 'aestheticist' thinker might include an affront to the foundational premise of art for art's sake remains a heresy within Pater studies.

Turning, however, to the text of 'Style' itself, we may find – in a passage from the middle of the essay rather less picked over than its controversial final paragraph – a decisive clue to Pater's convictions on the criteria for 'great art'. Surpassing Arnold's vision of artistic 'perfection' as an achievable ambition of perfect 'form' that may only, in the works of genius, reach perfect union with 'matter', Pater lingers on the possibility that works of genius express and exert an influence beyond the formalist triumph of uniting form with matter. The 'adaptation of words to their matter' is, for

Pater, an essential condition for good art; but great art opens up a further horizon unimagined by Arnold:

> Different classes of persons, at different times, make, of course, very various demands upon literature. Still, scholars, I suppose, and not only scholars, but all disinterested lovers of books, will always look to it, as to all other fine art, for a refuge, a sort of cloistral refuge, from a certain vulgarity in the actual world. A perfect poem like *Lycidas*, a perfect fiction like *Esmond*, the perfect handling of a theory like Newman's *Idea of a University*, has for them something of the uses of a religious 'retreat.' (17–18)

'Perfection' does not inhere within matter or form, nor merely in the union of these things. While Pater maintained a studied agnosticism when it came to organised religion, his account of artistic beauty here offers more than the 'retreat' from the world that it promises; it opens up also the possibility of redeeming that world. Pater's vision of the artist and the appreciator of art is, by this implicitly metaphysical logic, less like a hermit and more like a monk. To recognise the force of this fortuity we must not skip too quickly to paraphrase. Pater's comments on style here, as throughout the essay, must be read with due attention to their own styling. Newman, in an inspired phrase, once defined style as 'a thinking out into language',[36] and that dynamic and developing and indirect mode is exactly how Pater teases us in this passage, as he explores the 'uses' of the 'fine art' he commends.

For the 'form' of Pater's sentences does not form their 'matter' once and for all. His is, as Angela Leighton deftly describes it, a 're-forming' style.[37] Self-corrections do not delete the prior commitments but recalibrate them, dialectically. Each clause of self-revision marks a movement from provisionality towards a more precise, depurated formulation, whether or not a final, definitive formulation is ever reached. That is the nub of another common complaint against Pater, of course. While readers have always swooned over his verbal felicities (Wilde, quoted earlier, calls *Appreciations* 'an exquisite collection of exquisite essays, of delicately wrought works of art'),[38] when it comes to unpicking the precise meaning of his phrasings, he has attracted his fair share of deprecators too. 'Again and again, one has to re-read a sentence in order to make quite sure of its meaning', complained one contemporary reviewer of *Appreciations*, who quotes only from the essay on 'Style' to make his case, followed by this blustering appeal: 'Now, frankly, reader, have you more than a faint glimmer of the meaning of this wounded snake of a sentence?'[39] Nor has Pater shrugged off this charge in the century since: modern critics have likewise called his method 'desultory', or 'convoluted'.[40]

Even scholars like Leighton who commend Pater's style concede that his sentences sometimes fail to ripen into a thesis. Writing on how the 'very tenuousness' of Pater's suspended syntax and restlessly postmodifying propositions and lapidary but unruly lists (which promise but ultimately refuse definitive illustration and explanation) 'rarely add up to a creed', Leighton suggests that the fugitive imponderability of Pater's style may not in the end be a regrettable weakness but 'the source of his power'.[41] His 'dream rhythms, those pausing secondary and tertiary phrases, those vanishing tricks of his lists', might prompt and allow us to rethink the word 'thinking' itself.[42]

Or as Theodor Adorno would have it, there may be untapped epistemological possibilities attendant on forms of expression in which 'thought does not advance in a single direction', but 'methodically unmethodically'; that is, by an essayistic mode that 'does not strive for closed, deductive or inductive, construction', but which instead rebels against the limitations of thinking imposed by the scientist spirit. The possibility Adorno adumbrates is for a form of truth-telling 'more dynamic than traditional thought' and so more adequate to construing the complex human experience of modernity.[43] Adorno's account of modernity is not identical to Pater's, but they both felt the exceptionalism of their respective moments, in terms of what one of Pater's coevals, Elizabeth Barrett Browning, identified as the entangled challenge of meeting the 'present day' as a writer: 'we want new *forms*, as well as thoughts', she protested, on the understanding – urgently shared by Pater and Adorno – that new thoughts may not be thinkable without new forms to think them.[44]

Pater's passage on literary 'perfection' may be richly approached with that kind of provocation in mind: for the ways its demands of us, as the nonplussed reviewer complained, 'to make quite sure of its meaning', by 're-reading'. Qualifying the vague, vernacular senses of the words he uses, 'refuge' and 'retreat' worry self-consciously towards a different weighting that might look slight in its adjectival adjustment but on which hangs nothing less than everything: 'cloistral' and 'religious' change the domain in which 'truth' is to be understood, from the mundane to the metaphysical.

Reading Pater in this way, for his dynamic and dialectical revisings, is no speculative ingenuity: 'Style' itself provides the warrant, explicitly and at length. Pater spells out the virtue of providing readers with the 'challenge' of a 'continuous effort on their part, to be rewarded by securer and more intimate grasp of the author's sense' (17). That 'sense' may never reach the status of a fixed, stable statement. He does not posit a direct equation between his views and those associated with the Christian religion. The 'refuge' of art is an analogy that is at once self-conscious and self-consciously loose in its analogical suggestion: it is a *sort of* cloistral refuge. Likewise, literary perfection has – we note the fractional measure – *something* of the uses of a religious retreat. Such calibrations do not imply unclarity. Asymptotically aligned though they may be with the theological tradition to which they refer, approaching without quite reaching a definitive creedal conviction, there is nonetheless *something*, some *sort of* alignment. To argue otherwise, or to argue for its insincerity, is to presume bad faith within an epistemological context that presumes faith to be in earnest.

While Pater continues to be read as if he does not believe his own conclusions in 'Style', for readers who have learnt to catch the *essaying* cadences of constellating self-correction, his position is neither obscure nor inconsistent. Mining the subtextual literary-theoretical politics between Saintsbury and Arnold helps us to trace Pater's commitments away from the autotelic tendencies of the former and the over-determining moralism of the latter. Which in turn, remembering Newman, sets up the paradoxical possibility that looks – both as verb and noun – to 'perfect' style as a solace that might ultimately atone for the vulgarity of the world from which it offers retreat and refuge.

Notes

1 William E. Buckler, *Walter Pater: The Critic as Artist of Ideas* (New York 1987), 107.
2 Edmund Chandler, *Pater on Style: An Examination of the Essay on 'Style' and the Textual History of 'Marius the Epicurean'* (Copenhagen 1958), 10.
3 Gerald Monsman, *Walter Pater* (1977), 148.
4 Oscar Wilde, unsigned review, *Speaker* (22 March 1890), 319–20, repr. in *Critical Heritage*, 232–7 (234).
5 Denis Donoghue, *Walter Pater: Lover of Strange Souls* (New York 1995), 222.
6 Donoghue, *Walter Pater*, 224.
7 *Style in Theory: Between Literature and Philosophy*, ed. I. Callus, J. Corby, and G. Lauri-Lucente (2013), 1.
8 See Michael D. Hurley, 'Style', in *The Cambridge Companion to Prose*, ed. Daniel Tyler (Cambridge 2021), ch. 7.
9 *Style in Theory*, 3.

10 *Pall Mall Gazette* (25 August 1888), 1–2.

11 *The Collected Works of Gerard Manley Hopkins, Vol. 2: Correspondence 1882–1889*, ed. R. K. R. Thornton and Catherine Phillips (Oxford 2013), 906.

12 John Coates, 'Controversial Aspects of Pater's "Style"', *Papers on Language and Literature* 40 (2004), 384–411 (394). See also Franklin E. Court, *Pater and His Early Critics* (Victoria, B.C. 1980), ch. 2.

13 John Gross, *The Rise and Fall of the Man of Letters*, 2nd edn (Harmondsworth 1973), 159.

14 Coates, 'Controversial Aspects', 394.

15 Coates, 'Controversial Aspects', 410.

16 Coates, 'Controversial Aspects', 402.

17 T. S. Eliot, 'Arnold and Pater', *Bookman* 72 (1930), 1–7.

18 Laurel Brake, 'The Discourses of Journalism: "Arnold and Pater" Again – and Wilde', in *Pater in the 1990s*, ed. Laurel Brake and Ian Small (Greensboro, NC 1991), 43–61.

19 George Saintsbury, *A History of the French Novel: To the Close of the 19th Century*, 2 vols (1917–1919), ii. 70–1.

20 George Saintsbury, *A Scrap Book* (1922), 115–17.

21 George Saintsbury, *A History of Criticism and Literary Taste in Europe, from the Earliest Texts to the Present Day*, 3rd edn (New York and Edinburgh 1908), iii. vi.

22 Coates, 'Controversial Aspects', 398.

23 Court, *Pater and His Early Critics*, 43.

24 See Michael D. Hurley, 'George Saintsbury's History of English Prosody', *Essays in Criticism* 60 (2010), 336–60.

25 Coates, 'Controversial Aspects', 398.

26 Preface to *Poetical Works*, 1853, in Arnold, *Prose*, i. 1–15 (15).

27 'The Function of Criticism at the Present Time', in Arnold, *Prose*, iii. 258–90 (262).

28 Letter to Arthur Hugh Clough, November 1853, in *Matthew Arnold: The Critical Heritage*, vol. 2 *The Poetry*, ed. Carl Dawson (1995), 123.

29 *Letters of Matthew Arnold*, ed. George W. E. Russell (1901), 2 vols, i. 84.

30 J. P. Ward, 'An Anxiety of No Influence: Walter Pater on William Wordsworth', in Brake and Small, *Pater in the 1990s*, 63–75 (73).

31 Harold Bloom, ed. *Selected Writings of Walter Pater* (New York 1974), 175.

32 René Wellek, *A History of Modern Criticism, 1750–1950*, vol. iv (New Haven 1965), 395.

33 David DeLaura, *Hebrew and Hellene in Victorian England* (Austin, TX 1969), 329, 330.

34 DeLaura, *Hebrew and Hellene*, 331.

35 DeLaura, *Hebrew and Hellene*, 339.

36 John Henry Newman, *The Idea of a University* (1907), 276.

37 Angela Leighton, *On Form: Poetry, Aestheticism, and the Legacy of a Word* (Oxford 2007), 93.

38 *Critical Heritage*, 233.

39 Unsigned review, *Pall Mall Gazette* (10 December 1889), 3; repr. in *Critical Heritage*, 200.

40 Donoghue, *Walter Pater*, 222; Ward, 'An Anxiety of No Influence', 73.

41 Angela Leighton, 'Walter Pater's Dream Rhythms', in *Thinking Through Style: Non-Fiction Prose of the Long Nineteenth Century*, ed. Michael D. Hurley and Marcus Waithe (Oxford 2018), 217–29 (224).

42 Leighton, 'Dream Rhythms', 229.

43 Theodor Adorno, 'The Essay as Form', trans. Bob Hullot-Kentor and Frederic Will, *New German Critique* 32 (1984), 161, 158, 170.

44 *The Brownings' Correspondence*, vol. 10, ed. Philip Kelley and Scott Lewis (Winfield, KS 1995), x. 135.

CHAPTER 7

Walter Pater, Second-Hand Stylist

Scarlett Baron

Walter Pater, Oxford scholar, classicist, lover of the art of the Renaissance and other periods, author of 'imaginary portraits' and 'appreciations', might seem to belong in a different universe from that which presided over the emergence of intertextual theory in the intellectually and politically effervescent Paris of the mid to late 1960s. While his name is virtually synonymous with the idea of subjective aesthetic response, the notion of intertextuality, first named and honed at the hands of Julia Kristeva, Roland Barthes, and Michel Foucault, is, by contrast, tightly intertwined with the idea of authorial impersonality. Yet these realms and modes of style and thought are not as dichotomous as they may initially appear, however starkly distinct their critical languages. Over the decades since his death, Pater's works have given rise to considerable comment regarding his use of source material. As such, his extensively 'second-hand' writing – to use a term suggested by Antoine Compagnon's history of quotation – begs for consideration alongside the writings of those prose modernists such as Flaubert and Joyce, whose extreme citational practices paved the way for the emergence of intertextual theory.[1] While such a comparison opens up the possibility of a neutral – descriptive rather than judgemental – assessment of Pater's sometimes surprising treatment of his sources, it also highlights the nature and scale of the difference between his compositional methods and those of these later practitioners of the second-hand.

'Style' is a salient case to examine in this context. The opening essay of *Appreciations* (1889), first published in the *Fortnightly Review* in 1888, is a piece which not only engages with Flaubert – whom the coiners of intertextuality placed at the origin of a new kind of citationality – but does so in ways which are both markedly intertextual and highly curious.[2] Indeed, Pater's ostensible alignment with Flaubert in the piece rests upon a number of compositional peculiarities and argumentative tensions.[3] On the one hand, Pater makes distinctly odd use of Flaubert's correspondence in quotation and shrouds in silence the name of an important source of knowledge about him; on the other, he glosses over significant points of difference between their conceptions of writing.

The fact of Pater's dependence on source material for information and inspiration is well established. As Billie Andrew Inman puts it, 'he turned to the writings of others for substance and fire', or, as Robert MacFarlane remarks, for Pater 'creation was never a primary act but only a response to or renovation of pre-existing matter'.[4] Among many identified instances of Pater's practice of appropriating and modifying other authors' words, his treatment of Flaubert in 'Style' stands out as 'particularly noteworthy'.[5] In 1914, Samuel C. Chew, Jr. led the way in an article devoted to 'Pater's use and misuse of citations from various authors'.[6] Chew lists among Pater's persistent habits 'the separation of passages joined in the original, the junction of passages far distant in the original, unnoted omissions, and, in some cases, mistranslations'.[7] In support of these claims, he provides numerous instances of acts of textual 'tamper[ing]', all carried out 'with no indication of the liberties taken with the text' of another.[8] At the heart of Chew's demonstration sits the revelation of Pater's handling of Flaubert's letters in 'Style'. Having checked Pater's Flaubertian quotations against the text of the first volume of the newly published Flaubert *Correspondance* (which Pater reviewed for the *Pall Mall Gazette* three months before 'Style' was first published), Chew finds the result 'really astonishing':

> Pater pieces together sentences, and even clauses, that, in the French, are many pages apart. Moreover, he says that several of them are addressed to 'Madame X.' (*i.e.*, Louise Colet) that are in reality addressed to other correspondents.[9]

In the course of his detailed analysis of these quotations, Chew itemises the components of 'an astonishing amalgam' consisting of sentences drawn from several letters to two different recipients and derived, in reverse order, from five different sections of the book.[10] Though Chew's amazement is clear, John J. Conlon, writing several decades later, calls this 'conflation of excerpts' a 'classic case of [Paterian] mis-representation'.[11]

As well as silently altering the verbal contents and addressees of Flaubert's letters, Pater withholds the name of the author of the preface to the *Lettres de Gustave Flaubert à George Sand*, which had appeared in 1884, and on which he relies for his portrait.[12] Variously referred to as 'a sympathetic commentator', 'our French guide', and 'Flaubert's commentator', the mystery source is none other than Pater's famous if rather scandalous contemporary Guy de Maupassant ('Style', *App.*, 29, 36).[13] If Pater's *bricolage* with Flaubert's letters is relatively well known, his anonymisation of Maupassant has received little attention.[14] In an essay so invested in scholarship (the writer, Pater declares, is a 'scholar writing for the scholarly'), such choices raise compositional and ethical questions (17). To what end does Pater produce such misrepresentations and partial representations, and with what consequences?

Flaubert makes his first appearance in 'Style' as the author of *Madame Bovary*, which Pater praises as 'a composition utterly unadorned', without 'removable decoration' (19). As such, it represents the realisation of Pater's ideal of stylistic '[s]elf-restraint'. '[A] skilful economy of means, *ascêsis*', he writes, 'that too has a beauty of its own' (17). What matters in style, 'as Flaubert was aware', is to banish '[t]he otiose, the facile, surplusage' in favour of 'conscious artistic structure' (23, 21, 24).

The central section of the essay, starting a few pages later, draws on Maupassant to sketch its portrait of 'the martyr of literary style' (27). In his prefatory *étude* to the Flaubert-Sand correspondence, Maupassant recalls that 'a single passion, the love of letters, filled his life to his last day. He loved it furiously, absolutely, uniquely'.[15] Pater, following suit, refers to Flaubert's 'leading passion' for literature – one to which 'a living person could be no rival', and one which assumed a quasi-religious place in Flaubert's life (28). While Maupassant mentions the sanctity of Flaubert's writing instruments ('as sacred to him as objects of worship to a priest'), Pater depicts his art as a 'cloistral refuge' (18).[16]

Maupassant also provides the basis for Pater's emphasis on scholarship and revision, referring to Flaubert as an 'insatiable reader' and 'indefatigable researcher', and repeatedly wondering at his 'formidable', 'superhuman', 'beloved', and 'excruciating' labour.[17] It is not surprising that Pater should have felt drawn to such descriptions. He too was an author whose work was 'always the result of much patient and unseen labour' and, as such, 'a travail and an agony'.[18] ('Style' was, fittingly enough given its celebration of literary graft, an especially demanding piece of work.[19] 'Pater once told me', wrote Arthur Symons, 'that the most laborious task he ever set himself to accomplish was his essay on Style'.[20])

For Flaubert, 'the problem of style' entailed a thrilling and tormenting quest for '[t]he one word for the one thing, the one thought, amid the multitude of words, terms, that might just do' (*App.*, 29). Here, Pater paraphrases an assertion by Maupassant which he has in fact already given in translation just above. Flaubert, states Pater's anonymised 'French guide', was '[p]ossessed of an absolute belief that there exists but one way of expressing one thing, one word to call it by, one adjective to qualify, one verb to animate it' (29).[21]

This obsession with the selection of the 'unique and just expression' is linked by both Maupassant and Pater to Flaubert's conviction that 'the style therefore had to be, as it were, impersonal'.[22] Pater quotes Maupassant's account of Flaubert's theory of style:

> Styles (says Flaubert's commentator), *Styles*, as so many peculiar moulds, each of which bears the mark of a particular writer, who is to pour into it the whole content of his ideas, were no part of his theory. What he believed in was *Style*: that is to say, a certain absolute and unique manner of expressing a thing, in all its intensity and colour. For him, the *form* was the work itself. [23] (36–7)

It is in the attempt to reconcile Flaubert's commitment to impersonality with his own contrary investment in subjectivity that Pater finds himself stating that 'If the style be the man ... it will be in a real sense "impersonal"' (38). Though presented as paraphrase, this rewriting is framed with signs of hesitancy – the opening conditional 'If', the distancing quotation marks around 'impersonal'. And for good reason, for Pater's formulation completely alters Maupassant's meaning, proclaiming as it does that a work's impersonality is, in a rich paradox, a factor of the personality of its style. This idea that 'the style is the man' (thrice repeated in 'Style') encapsulates precisely the common view Flaubert opposed (35, 36, 37). As Maupassant explains:

> By 'style' we generally mean the particular way each writer sets out his thinking: thus the style would be different depending on the man, flashy or sober, abundant or concise, according to temperament. Gustave Flaubert held that the personality of the author should disappear into the originality of the book; that the originality of the book must not derive from the singularity of its style.[24]

By contrast, 'Style' accords a defining primacy to an author's subjective apprehension. True art, affirms Pater, consists not in the mere transcription of fact but in the rendition of an author's 'sense of it, his peculiar intuition of a world' (8). '[F]ine art', he continues, is such in proportion to its success in communicating the author's 'vision within', in delineating 'a specific personality' (10). Pater's conception of style, as it emerges here and elsewhere, is, to a significant extent, circular: both the matter of art and the style deployed to convey it are 'the man'.[25] Pater's ostensible alignment with Flaubert, then, conceals a stark discrepancy.

For Max Saunders, the apparent espousal in 'Style' of an impersonal aesthetic positions Pater at the source of modernism:

aestheticism's style-worship turns the autobiographic into the impersonal. ... Modernism's negation of personality begins here, as does its advocacy of stylistic and technical self-consciousness.[26]

Yet such a reading neglects to register the contortions involved in Pater's attempt to telescope the subjective and the objective. Far from advocating the prose equivalent of the 'elocutionary disappearance of the poet' evoked by Mallarmé in 'Crise de Vers' (1897) or the 'depersonalization' advocated by T. S. Eliot in 'Tradition and the Individual Talent' (1919), Pater's essay presents style as, in Ian Fletcher's phrase, 'a total responsive gesture of the whole personality'.[27] The incompatibility of impersonality with Pater's enduring partiality for subjectivity is indicated by the change of mind discernible in his review of the second volume of Flaubert's letters, published the following year.[28] There he states that

> Impersonality in art, the literary ideal of Gustave Flaubert, is perhaps no more possible than realism. The artist *will* be felt; his subjectivity must and will colour the incidents, as his very bodily eye *selects* the aspects of things.[29]

In other words, the style *is* the man, and it *cannot* be impersonal. This revision would seem to testify to Pater's realisation that his argument about impersonality in 'Style' was, as Conlon puts it, 'an aberration from the personal note in literature and art he consistently admired and found so exciting and praiseworthy in the Romanticism of any age'.[30]

These shifting formulations do not exhaust Pater's fascination with the 'im/personality' dyad (to use Saunders' contraction).[31] His essay on Mérimée, published two years after 'Style', suggests a way in which the pair might be reconciled.[32] Mérimée's 'superb self-effacement, his impersonality', argues Pater, is 'itself but an effective personal trait' (*MS*, 37). Thus is impersonality redeemed as a litmus test revealing the lineaments of the very authorial personality it is intended to conceal.

Why, then, to return to our overarching enquiry, does Pater obscure Maupassant's contribution to his portrait (while acknowledging his recourse to *a* source), and what, more generally, are we to make of Pater's extensive and at least partly covert practice of the second-hand? While his copying-and-pasting of Flaubert's letters may conceivably have been motivated by the wish to set out his notion of style 'with a skilful economy of means', the withholding of the name of a well-known contemporary – and a fortiori that of a man of letters like himself – is perplexing (*App.*, 17). The case is not unique. As Inman notes, 'Pater's errors and omissions in regard to proper names are baffling'.[33] Any explanation is necessarily conjectural, but one plausible hypothesis is that

Pater was impelled by a reluctance to risk arousing disapproval: '[h]e had', as Inman states, 'learned to engage in controversy indirectly', and 'would occasionally omit an author's name or omit some suggestive details to avoid being thought decadent'.[34] Such a theory would fit the facts of Maupassant's reputation in England in the 1880s.

'Style' was written at a time when Maupassant was beginning to receive increased attention in the English periodical press. As George Worth chronicles, he 'emerged into the literary world in the 1880s under the dual sponsorship of Zola and Flaubert'.[35] Maupassant was then a far more controversial figure than Flaubert. While the connection to Flaubert worked to Pater's benefit – the trial of *Madame Bovary* lay more than three decades in the past and his death in 1880 had further dimmed memories of his alleged 'offenses against morality and religion' – the connection to Zola and the naturalists was detrimental to his standing.[36] An anonymous essayist writing in 1892, for example, described the naturalists as counting 'among the most dangerous enemies that France has nourished in her bosom', bemoaning their irredeemable 'brutality' and 'putrescence'.[37] It was, Worth observes, extremely common for critics to oppose form and matter in their discussions of Maupassant in this period, castigating him for what they deemed to be his salacious subjects on the one hand, and praising him for his exceptional prose style on the other.[38] (The perceived mismatch, if Pater reflected on it, might have made Maupassant seem a less than ideal expositor of Flaubert's theory of style, prescribing as it does a perfect accommodation of form and matter.) George Saintsbury, for instance, deplored Maupassant's obsession with sex ('He can write on nothing else'), but also called him 'a man of genius' and 'the most really gifted writer, both in prose and verse, that has happened in France in more than twenty years'.[39] Henry James published a long and influential piece on Maupassant, also in the *Fortnightly Review*, two months later. Referring to Flaubert as Maupassant's 'great initiator', he took aim at the unremitting crudeness of his subject-matter while simultaneously dubbing him 'a master of his art' and 'a writer with whom it is impossible not to reckon'.[40] James' and others' references to Maupassant as Flaubert's disciple make it clear that Pater's choice to cite his French guide under cover of anonymity comes at the cost of establishing the special authority of his source – one based on a close personal relationship and years of a 'long and hard apprenticeship of letters' undergone at Flaubert's hands.[41] But maybe the price seemed worth paying to avoid association with an author by whom so many were powerfully repelled.

If wariness of controversy or fear of being classed a decadent prompted the erasure of Maupassant's name from 'Style', it may also explain Pater's disalignment from Flaubert in the essay's closing peroration. The central Flaubert-focused section of 'Style' manages to convey strong admiration in spite of its contradictions. The final paragraph, however, introduces a new conundrum for the reader by effecting a sharp turn away from Flaubertian principles (as indeed from views expressed elsewhere in Pater's oeuvre).[42] Just pages earlier, 'the martyr of literary style' had been quoted railing against the idea that art should have a 'moral end', or any end other than the creation of 'the beautiful' (29). But Pater's epilogue distances itself from this 'art for art's sake' position by training its sights on the definition of 'great' rather than merely 'good' art (38). Where Flaubert's dedication to style over matter was so absolute as to engender his fantasy of 'a book about nothing ... sustained only by the inner force of its style', Pater's conclusion stresses the importance of subject matter, and indeed right-thinking causes, to the production of 'great' art.[43] 'Great art', writes Pater', will be distinguished by its 'dignity of interests', 'its compass, its variety, its alliance to great ends, or the depth of the note of revolt, or the largeness of hope in it'. If it 'be devoted further to the increase of men's happiness, to the redemption of the oppressed, or the enlargement of our sympathies with each other, or to such presentment of new or old truth about ourselves and our relation to the world as may ennoble and fortify us in our sojourn here, or immediately, as with Dante, to the glory of God' or if 'it has something of the soul of humanity in it', it will also be great art (38). The vague and tautological nature of these criteria (as encapsulated by the gnomic assertion that 'great art' must be allied to 'great ends') is striking. But the listing is sufficiently flavoured with Christian language ('redemption', 'ennoble', 'fortify', 'our sojourn here', 'the glory of God', 'the soul of humanity') to suggest a thoroughly orthodox understanding of the purpose of 'great art'. Such a stance would have been anathema to Flaubert, as Pater cannot but have known – not least because it would also have been anathema to other versions of himself.[44] As René Wellek observes:

> There could not be a fuller and more explicit revocation of [his] earlier aestheticism. It is a recantation at the expense of any unified, coherent view of art. It ... introduces a double standard of judgment or shifts the burden of criticism to the subject matter. Pater ends in a dichotomy destructive of his own insights into the nature of art.[45]

Pater's attitudes to his sources, whether they be considered through the prism of his misquotations or failures of acknowledgement, have aroused ambivalence in even firm admirers. Chew, ultimately a defender of Pater's borrowings, acknowledges the discomfort caused by misquotations which verge on the 'dishonest'. '[H]as the critic a right to do this?'[46] he asks, at the close of his catalogue of such discoveries. Conlon, as was mentioned above, refers to Pater's inexactitudes and omissions as 'misrepresentations'. About the collage of Flaubert's letters in 'Style' specifically, he comments that:

> This is clearly the sort of editorial and authorial practice we would find unacceptable in contemporary research. . . . Such a modern response would be entirely appropriate in the exposition of shoddy scholarship since we have . . . both explicit and implicit expectations of those who engage in academic discourse and of their work.[47]

Inman, meanwhile, acknowledges '[t]he liberties that Pater took with his sources' and the 'evasive strategy' he sometimes deployed 'as a defense against misinterpretation and criticism'.[48] Others are less ambivalent. Christopher Ricks impugns Pater's 'inappropriate appropriatingness' and 'play[ing] loose' with other authors' words, deploring a 'faith to one's meaning' which comes at the cost of 'faithlessness to another's meaning'.[49]

For champions of Pater, the answer to the problems raised by his less than scrupulous handling of second-hand language is to take him on his own terms – the terms, set out in 'Style' and elsewhere, which make the artist himself the matter of his art, and make of criticism 'a form of creative self-portraiture'.[50] The solution, in other words, involves an adjustment of the reader's 'horizon of expectations', to use Jauss' phrase.[51] Thus, for Chew, 'when we find him transposing, omitting, re-arranging, mis-ascribing, and in a few cases even apparently substituting his own for somebody else's ideas, there is needed but a generous interpretation of what Pater conceived to be the function of criticism, namely, that it has in it something of the creative art'.[52] For Conlon, Pater's procedures should be understood as intentional aspects of a project to 'make a high art of misrepresentation'.[53] And for Inman, too, the problem is fundamentally generic:

> he was introducing a new type of criticism that required a special type of reading . . . *aesthetic criticism* . . . the aesthetic critic does not approach a work of art as a critic, but as a lover, an amateur, a complete humanist, yielding himself to the influence of the work.[54]

As much is suggested, of course, by the title of *Appreciations*.

It is also relevant to recall that twentieth- and twenty-first-century notions of critical writing are misplaced in the apprehension of a piece written at the contested dawn of English Studies. The institutionalisation of literary criticism to which Pater objected (wary of literature being turned into a 'long, pedantic, mechanical discipline'[55]), and the concomitant regimentation of the essay form over subsequent decades, have fostered expectations of punctilious quotation and formal citation which were, as Inman has explored, not then as entrenched as they have since become.

How, finally, does Pater's practice of second-hand writing compare with that of modernists whose reputation is in large part founded on their deployment of a form of sustained intertextuality designed to facilitate the apprehension of literature as a realm governed by repetition? First, it is important to note that a valuation of the second-hand had been underway for some time when Pater set to work on 'Style'. As MacFarlane has shown, 'from the late 1850s onwards, unoriginality – understood as inventive reuse of the words of others – came increasingly to be seen as an authentic form of creativity'. At the *fin-de-siècle*, 'the idea of literary originality *ex nihilo* came under greater pressure than ever before', with authors such as Pater, Wilde, and Lionel Johnson placing 'great emphasis upon the concept of stylish reuse'.[56] Indeed, there is evidence that Pater himself regarded second-handness as a defining feature of all writing. In 'Style', he makes reference to the ineluctable secondariness of the literary artist's relationship to language itself: 'the material in which he works', he avers, 'is no more a creation of his own than the sculptor's marble' (12). The scholar-artist, in other words, operates within the realm of the *déjà*, working with inherited linguistic materials, meticulously chiselling them to meet particular needs. In *Plato and Platonism* (1893), Pater goes considerably further, articulating a strikingly post-structuralist conception of literary originality as intertextuality:

> in Plato, in spite of his wonderful savour of literary freshness, there is nothing absolutely new: or rather, as in many other very original products of human genius, the seemingly new is old also, a palimpsest, a tapestry of which the actual threads have served before .... Nothing but the life-giving principle of cohesion is new; the new perspective, the resultant complexion, the expressiveness which familiar thoughts attain by novel juxtaposition. In other words, the *form* is new. (*PP*, 8)

Pater's assertion that 'there is nothing absolutely new' in Plato, as well as his metaphors of the 'palimpsest' and 'tapestry of which the actual threads have served before' are remarkably aligned with statements which have become emblematic of intertextual theory. Gérard Genette, for instance, entitled his study of 'second-degree' literature *Palimpsestes*. Sarah Dillon, too, following Genette, seizes on the image of the palimpsest as a figure for intertextuality. Barthes invokes a textile metaphor in referring to texts as 'tissue[s] of quotation'.[57] With this in mind, Pater's handling of sources can be viewed less as the sign of suspect dependence and more as a self-conscious embrace of what he, like Barthes, recognised as 'the truth of writing, [that] the writer can only imitate a gesture that is always anterior, never original'.[58] Viewed in such light, Pater, too, can be cast as a forerunner to twentieth-century theory. As indeed he has been: in 1976, Hillis Miller wrote of him as 'a precursor of what is most vital in contemporary criticism'.[59]

If Flaubert, in association with whose name the notion of intertextuality emerged, can be celebrated as being, in André Topia's words, 'among the first to have deliberately blurred the hierarchy between the original text and the secondary text', should Pater be eligible for similar appreciation?[60] Intertextual theory's founding axiom that 'any text is a mosaic of quotations' is relevant to Pater's case in that it has the power to parry any imputation of plagiarism or overdependence by declaring 'absorption and transformation' to be a universal law of writing.[61] Certainly, Paterians have used the term to give a neutral assessment of the density of appropriated words and ideas in his works. Pater's 'attitudes toward sources and techniques of using them', comments Inman, 'created in his works a profound intertextuality that is essential to his remarkable style'.[62]

That being granted, major differences obtain between Pater's intertextual writing and that of the most radically intertextual modernists. The most fundamental relates to the nature of the intention underpinning these authors' deployment of the second-hand. Intertextuality, in Pater's case, appears to have been incidental rather than programmatic – a means to the end of aesthetic criticism or self-portraiture (whichever one takes to have been his aim). His objective was not to highlight the fact of second-handedness as a constitutive feature of all writing, but to *style* his borrowings in service of his own ends. By contrast, Flaubert's and Joyce's final works, *Bouvard and Pécuchet*, the *Dictionary of Received Ideas*, and *Finnegans Wake*, were assembled through the mobilisation of extremely extensive systems of intra- and intertextual writing, as these authors' enormous manuscript archives testify.[63] In these works, intertextuality becomes an end as well as a means: a compositional principle in and of itself. They were, to reprise Topia's adverbial emphasis, *deliberately* designed to cultivate the reader's sense of language and literature as realms of the *déjà*. This insight is proclaimed in the title of Flaubert's *Dictionary of Received Ideas*; narratively literalised in Bouvard and Pécuchet's decision to devote the remainder of their lives to the manual copying-out of books; and self-referentially inscribed in *Finnegans Wake*'s mentions of 'piously forged palimpsests', 'pelagiarist pens', 'borrowed plumes', and 'quashed quota-toes'.[64] By contrast, Pater, though a 'scissors and paste man' (to use words Joyce once used to describe himself), and one fully aware of the part played by repetition in language and literature, appears to have been a far more discreet, if not secretive, practitioner of the second-hand, even by the standards of his own day.[65] '[M]uch fin-de-siècle writing', writes MacFarlane, 'was more open about its borrowings, appropriations, and renewals than any preceding literary period of the century.'[66] Against such a background, 'Style' stands out for its silent alterations and at best only partial openness about its sources.

Another difference, touched upon above, pertains to the idea of imper-sonality. Where '[s]ubjectivity – the self – is ... the beginning, the end, and the persisting basis in all Pater's writings', Joyce and Flaubert picture the author as an invisible author-god.[67] Intertextual theory was shaped by this modernist intertwining of extensive citationality and authorial imper-sonality – defined, from the outset, as antithetical to ideas of authorial and readerly subjectivity. As Kristeva points out in the essay in which the concept was first named, '[t]he notion of intertextuality replaces that of intersubjectivity'.[68] And as Barthes puts it in 'The Death of the Author', '[w]riting is that neutral, composite, oblique space where our subject slips away, the negative where all identity is lost'.[69]

To these discrepancies of purpose and aesthetic disposition can be added discrepancies of scale. The sheer feats of endurance involved in the deployment of Flaubert's and Joyce's intertexualities are arresting. Flaubert claimed to have read 15,000 books in preparation for the writing of *Bouvard et Pécuchet*; 3,848 pages of notes survive to testify to this labour. Joyce amassed 25,000 pages of manuscript material – many of them filled with reading notes – over the seventeen-year-long genesis of *Finnegans Wake*.[70] Though Flaubertian critics have wondered whether Flaubert 'falsif[ies] the character of what he quotes', the distortions and decontextua-lisations Joyce wrought on his borrowings are both far more obvious (altering the very make-up of words as his portmanteaus do) and far more numerous – so numerous, indeed, as to have prompted speculation that every single word in the *Wake* may be traceable to a source.[71] Moreover, the effects of Pater's derivations on the one hand, and Flaubert's and Joyce's on the other, are sharply distinct, for reasons relating to genre. Whatever the relative freedom of nineteenth-century essayists to gloss over their debts and 'misrepresentations', and whatever Pater's ambition to 'dissolve the critical and creative acts into one another', expectations of careful quotation and faithful translation are nonetheless greater in the reading of discursive prose than in the encounter with that fastest-evolving and 'most fluid of genres', the novel; greater, too, in the experience of a personal, recognisable style than in the immersion in the kind of impersonal, unstyled textuality produced by Joyce in *Finnegans Wake*.[72]

If the extremity of such writing methods paved the way for the emergence of intertextual theory, that theory has in turn given rise to new ways of experiencing literary texts – ways driven not by censoriousness but by a neutral acceptance of the second-handness of all writing. If Pater's silences about his sources suggest a high degree of caution (about courting controversy and owning up to his debts and manipulations), it is also possible to see the idiosyncrasy of his approach as a sign of the poise of one 'bold enough to think himself an artist to whom interfering rules of the antiquarian or the scholar did not apply'.[73] In that disposition, at least, he and his modernist successors are aligned. '[A] brilliant original who did not originate',[74] he had the confidence to know that *styling* the second-hand was art enough.

Note

1 Antoine Compagnon, *La seconde main ou le travail de la citation* (Paris 1979). This genealogy of intertextuality is set out in Scarlett Baron, '*Strandentwining Cable': Joyce, Flaubert, and Intertextuality* (Oxford 2012).

2 Walter Pater, 'Style', *Fortnightly Review* 44 (December 1888), 728–43. Roland Barthes makes *Bouvard and Pécuchet* the signal example of intertextuality in 'The Death of the Author': 'The text is a tissue of quotations drawn from the innumerable centres of culture. Similar to Bouvard and Pécuchet, those eternal copyists ... the writer can only imitate a gesture that is always anterior, never original' (Roland Barthes, 'The Death of the Author' [1967], in *Image Music Text*, ed. and trans. Stephen Heath (1977), 142–8 (146)). Michel Foucault refers to *The Temptation of Saint Anthony* as 'the first work' to enter into an 'essential relationship to books': 'it opens a literary space wholly dependent on the network formed by the books of the past' ('Fantasia of the Library' [1967], in *Michel Foucault: Language, Counter-Memory, Practice: Selected Essays and Interviews*, trans. Donald F. Bouchard and Sherry Simon, ed. Donald F. Bouchard (Ithaca, NY 1977), 86–109 (92, 91)).

3 A. C. Benson goes so far as to call it 'the summary of Pater's artistic creed' and even 'perhaps the only direct and personal revelation of his theory of art' (*Walter Pater* [1906] (1921), 151).

4 Inman (1981), ix.; Robert MacFarlane, *Original Copy: Plagiarism and Originality in Nineteenth-Century Literature* (Oxford and New York 2007), 179–80.

5 John J. Conlon, 'Walter Pater and the Art of Misrepresentation', *Annals of Scholarship* 7 (1990), 165–79 (172).

6 Samuel C. Chew, Jr., 'Pater's Quotations', *Nation* 99 (1 October 1914), 404–5.

7 Chew, 'Pater's Quotations', 404.

8 Chew, 'Pater's Quotations', 404.

9 Chew, 'Pater's Quotations', 405; [Walter Pater], 'The Life and Letters of Gustave Flaubert', *Pall Mall Gazette* (25 August 1888). John Coates and Samuel Wright, among others, regard 'Style' as in part an expansion of Pater's review of Flaubert's letters: John Coates, 'Controversial Aspects of Pater's "Style"', *Papers on Language and Literature* 40 (2004), 384–411 (384); Samuel Wright, *A Bibliography of the Writings of Walter H. Pater* (New York 1975), 31–2.

10 Chew, 'Pater's Quotations', 405.

11 Conlon, 'Art of Misrepresentation', 173–4.

12 *Lettres de Gustave Flaubert à George Sand, précédées d'une étude par Guy de Maupassant* (Paris 1884). Pater's first review of Flaubert's letters mentions (and misdates) this tome (to 1885), without however naming the author of the introduction (Pater, 'Life and Letters of Gustave Flaubert', 52). Pater probably drew on the introduction to the *Correspondance* penned by Flaubert's niece, Caroline de Commanville, who, however, is not even credited in the peculiarly anonymous way reserved for Maupassant: 'Souvenirs Intimes', *Correspondance de Gustave Flaubert*, Première Série (1830–50) (Paris 1887).

13 Conlon identifies Maupassant as Pater's source in *Walter Pater and the French Tradition* (Lewisburg, PA 1982), 120, 123, 125, 134n5.

14 Like 'intertextuality', 'bricolage' entered literary-critical terminology in the 1960s. The term was first used by Claude Lévi-Strauss in relation to mythical thought in *The Savage Mind* ([1962] (Chicago, IL 1966), 11). Denis Donoghue, though intent on arguing that 'Style' is 'desultory work', seems not to know of its debts to Maupassant, of whom no mention is made in the relevant chapter of *Walter Pater: Lover of Strange Souls* (New York 1995), 222–9.

15 Maupassant, 'Gustave Flaubert', in *Lettres de Gustave Flaubert à George Sand*, lxviii. All translations from the French are my own.

16 Maupassant, 'Gustave Flaubert', lxxviii. Commanville remembers her uncle as an art 'fanatic': 'he had taken art for his god' (Commanville, 'Souvenirs Intimes', 10). That Pater would have identified with such descriptions is suggested by Benson's recollection that 'There is always something holy, even priestly, about Pater's attitude to art' (Benson, *Walter Pater*, 212).

17 Maupassant, 'Gustave Flaubert', liii, lxv, lxi, lxiii.

18 Benson, *Walter Pater*, 211; Edmund Gosse, 'Walter Pater: A Portrait', *Contemporary Review* 66 (December 1894), 795–810 (806).

19 Marcus Waithe, '"Strenuous Minds": Walter Pater and the Labour of Aestheticism', in *The Labour of Literature in Britain and France, 1830–1910: Authorial Work Ethics*, ed. Marcus Waithe and Claire White (2018), 152.

20 Arthur Symons, *A Study of Walter Pater* (1932), 61.

21 Maupassant, 'Gustave Flaubert', lxii.

22 Maupassant, 'Gustave Flaubert', lxi.

23 See Maupassant, 'Gustave Flaubert', lxi.

24 Maupassant, 'Gustave Flaubert', lxi.

25 As Pater states in *The Renaissance*, 'the genius of which Botticelli is the type usurps the data before it as the exponent of ideas, moods, visions of its own' (*Ren.*, 42).

26 Max Saunders, *Self Impression: Life-Writing, Autobiografiction, and the Forms of Modern Literature* (Oxford 2010), 60.

27 Stéphane Mallarmé, *Œuvres complètes*, ed. Bertrand Marchal (Paris 2003), ii. 211; T. S. Eliot, 'Tradition and the Individual Talent' [1919], in *Selected Essays* [1932], 3rd edn (1963), 17; Ian Fletcher, *Walter Pater* (1959), 31.

28 'The focus of all Pater's writing is personality', argues J. Hillis Miller ('Walter Pater: A Partial Portrait', *Daedalus* 105 (1976), 97–113 (100)).

29 'Correspondance de Gustave Flaubert', *Athenaeum* (3 August 1889), repr. in Walter Pater, *Uncollected Essays* (Portland, ME 1903), 101–14 (108).

30 Conlon, *Walter Pater and the French Tradition*, 129.

31 See Saunders, 'Im/personality: The Imaginary Portraits of Walter Pater', in *Self Impression*, 29–50.

32 Walter Pater, 'Prosper Mérimée', *Fortnightly Review* 48 (December 1890), repr. in *Studies in European Literature, being the Taylorian Lectures 1889–1899* (Oxford 1900), 31–53 (52).

33 Inman (1981), xxii.

34 Inman (1990), xlix, and Billie Andrew Inman, 'How Walter Pater Might Have Countered Charges That He Misused Sources: A Dialogue between Graduate Student Walter Pater and Professor Samantha Marks at Great State University, U.S.A., in 2003, with an Addendum', *Nineteenth-Century Prose* 35 (2008), 173.

35 George John Worth, 'Maupassant in England', PhD thesis, University of Illinois, 1954, 4.

36 Worth, 'Maupassant in England', 79.

37 'The French Decadence', *Quarterly Review* 74 (April 1892), 504 (quoted in Worth, 'Maupassant in England', 116).

38 Worth, 'Maupassant in England', 113.

39 George Saintsbury, 'The Present State of the Novel. II', *Fortnightly Review* 43 (January 1888), 112–23 (117, 122, 116).

40 Henry James, 'Guy de Maupassant', *Fortnightly Review* 43 (March 1888), 364–86 (379, 385).

41 Arthur Symons, 'Guy de Maupassant', *Athenaeum* (15 July 1893), 97.

42 Maupassant states that Flaubert was deeply opposed to moral didacticism in literature: 'Les romanciers ... n'ont pas mission pour moraliser, ni pour flageller, ni pour enseigner.' ('Novelists ... have no mission to moralise, or flagellate, or educate.') ('Gustave Flaubert', xiv).

43 Flaubert to Louise Colet, 16 January 1852, in Gustave Flaubert, *Correspondance*, ed. Jean Bruneau (Paris 1973–2007), vol. 2 (1980), 31.

44 In *Plato and Platonism*, for example, Pater argues that 'in the creation of philosophical literature, as in all other products of art, *form*, in the full signification of that word, is everything, and the mere matter is nothing' (8).

45 René Wellek, 'Walter Pater's Literary Theory and Criticism', *Victorian Studies* 1 (1957), 29–46 (43).

46 Chew, 'Pater's Quotations', 404–5.

47 Conlon, 'Art of Misrepresentation', 174.

48 Inman (1990), xxxviii.

49 Ricks, 'Misquotation', 406, 408, 403.

50 Gerald Monsman, *Walter Pater's Art of Autobiography* (New Haven and London), 14.

51 Hans Robert Jauss, 'Theory of Genres and Medieval Literature', repr. in *Modern Genre Theory*, ed. David Duff (2000), 127–47 (143).

52 Chew, 'Pater's Quotations', 405.

53 Conlon, 'Art of Misrepresentation', 167.

54 Inman (1981), xxvi.

55 Walter Pater, 'English at the Universities. – IV.', *Pall Mall Gazette* (27 November 1886), 1–2 (1).

56 MacFarlane, *Original Copy*, 8, 162–3.

57 Gérard Genette, *Palimpsestes: La littérature du second degré* (Paris 1982); Sarah Dillon, *The Palimpsest: Literature, Criticism, Theory* (2007); Barthes, 'Death of the Author', 146.

58 Barthes, 'Death of the Author', 146.

59 Hillis Miller, 'Walter Pater', 97.

60 André Topia, 'The Matrix and the Echo: Intertextuality in *Ulysses*', in *Post-Structuralist Joyce*, ed. Derek Attridge and Daniel Ferrer (Cambridge 1984), 103–25 (104).

61 Julia Kristeva, 'Word, Dialogue, and Novel' [1966], in *Desire in Language: A Semiotic Approach to Art and Literature*, trans. Thomas Gora, Alice Jardine, and Leon S. Roudiez, ed. Leon S. Roudiez (New York 1980), 64–89 (66).

62 Inman, 'A Dialogue', 168.

63 See Baron, '*Strandentwining Cable*', 242–75.

64 James Joyce, *Finnegans Wake* (1939), 182–3.

65 James Joyce to George Antheil, in *Letters of James Joyce*, vol. i, ed. Stuart Gilbert (1957), 297.

66 MacFarlane, *Original Copy*, 183.

67 Hillis Miller, 'Walter Pater', 100; 'L'artiste doit être dans son oeuvre comme Dieu dans la création, invisible et tout-puissant' ('The author in his work must be like God in creation, invisible and all-powerful'), writes Flaubert

(Flaubert to Mlle Leroyer de Chantepie, 18 March 1857, *Correspondance*, vol. 2, 691); 'The artist, like the God of creation, remains within or behind or beyond or above his handiwork, invisible, refined out of existence, indifferent, paring his fingernails', says Stephen Dedalus, covertly misquoting Flaubert, in *A Portrait of the Artist as a Young Man*, ed. Jeri Johnson (Oxford 2000), 181.

68 Kristeva, 'Word, Dialogue, and Novel', 66.
69 Barthes, 'Death of the Author', 42.
70 See Baron, *'Strandentwining Cable'*, 255–6.
71 René Descharmes, *Autour de 'Bouvard et Pécuchet'* (Paris 1921), 91. See *James Joyce's The Index Manuscript: 'Finnegans Wake' Holograph Workbook VI.B.46*, ed. Danis Rose (Colchester 1978), xiii.
72 MacFarlane, *Original Copy*, 179; Mikhail Bakhtin, *The Dialogic Imagination: Four Essays*, trans. Caryl Emerson and Michael Holquist, ed. Michael Holquist (Austin, TX 1981), 11.
73 Inman (1981), xxix.
74 Inman (1981), xxix.

Individual Authors: Early Moderns, Romantics, Contemporaries

Introduction to Part II

The second part of this book focusses on Pater's engagement with a number of major English writers. *Appreciations* covers all post-medieval centuries, excluding only the 'Augustan' period about which Pater was rather less than enthusiastic (though he did design, and perhaps complete, an essay on Dr Johnson). Pater is not normally thought of as a leading Shakespearean, but unsurprisingly Shakespeare was central to his idea of English literature, and at one point he may possibly have planned a whole volume on him; he was also at least sympathetic to the idea of undertaking a commentary for schoolboy use on *Romeo and Juliet*, whose 'flawless execution' he commended ('Measure for Measure', *App.*, 170). Typically he did not write about the most celebrated plays (his own favourites also included *Hamlet*), but instead chose for treatment ones less popular in his day: *Love's Labour's Lost* (perhaps because of its reflections on language and style), *Measure for Measure* (arguably the finest of his three essays, centrally concerned with the way a work of art can profitably engage with ethics), and *Richard II* (the main focus of 'Shakespeare's English Kings', where Pater contributed to the idea of Richard as the 'poet-king' and added to the understanding of the deposition scene). Alex Wong examines all three essays in detail, and comments on the overall value and distinctive character of Pater's view of Shakespeare.

Pater was part of a critical movement that gradually brought back into favour seventeenth-century writers of prose, neglected in the previous century. Kathryn Murphy explores Pater's use of the word 'quaint' in 'Sir Thomas Browne' to examine the qualities in Browne's prose that attracted him, despite any reservations he might have felt about a mode of writing that often fell short of classical precision. Through a careful reception history she shows that Pater develops the earlier positive estimates by Coleridge and Lamb, and anticipates the revaluation of the 'metaphysical' writers (so dubbed by Dr Johnson in critical vein) in the Modernist generation.

Pater was committed to stressing the importance across time of the 'romantic' tradition in English literary history, and included in *Appreciations* three essays on writers of the generation now generally described as Romantic. While Blake never became the subject of an essay, Pater refers to Blake on what is, for him, a quite unusual number of occasions, from the essay on Michelangelo (1871) onwards. This is doubtless partly because Blake is both a poet and a painter, and thus relevant to the issue of the relationship between the various arts discussed in 'The School of Giorgione', partly because Blake is a figure in some ways 'out of his time' or particularly relevant to other times (something that always fascinated Pater). Luisa Calè suggests that Pater's interest may have been triggered by exhibitions in 1871 and 1876, at which he encountered Blake's paintings *The Spiritual Form* of Pitt, of Nelson, and of Napoleon. It also seems likely that Pater's interest throughout was fuelled by his still greater interest in the art and poetry of Rossetti, and in Pre-Raphaelitism and Aestheticism generally. Blake's illustrations to Job were highly admired in these circles, especially '*When the Morning Stars Sang Together*', mentioned by Pater more than once. Blake can readily be seen as a forerunner of Romanticism and of the Pre-Raphaelites, for example in his hostile annotations to Reynolds's art theories, from which Pater quotes. Next Charles Mahoney demonstrates the ways in which Pater's accounts of two of the great Romantic poets, Coleridge and Wordsworth, established new terms for their consideration (in Coleridge's case in the context of his relative neglect; in Wordsworth's, as an alternative to an already established pattern of reading his poetry), that in a number of important respects helped to evolve approaches that are still operative in our appraisal of their works. Of course Pater, like his contemporaries, did not use the designation 'English Romantic poets' in the current manner – for him Wordsworth and Coleridge were part of the 'Lake School' – but the word 'romantic' is used throughout the essay on Coleridge to characterise both the man and his work. In the last chapter on this group of writers Stacey McDowell explores Pater's view that the writings of Lamb illustrate 'the value of reserve' in literature and examines what Pater meant by the term. Within the context of the Tractarian doctrine of reserve, Keble and Newman identify its poetic expression with verbal indeterminacy, indirectness, metaphor, and irony. By flaunting such qualities, Lamb's openness becomes a form of deflection, his lightness valued in itself and for what it modestly conceals.

Finally, we come to the Victorians. Lewis R. Farnell, who was inspired by Pater's lectures on Greek sculpture to become an archaeologist, records a dinner-party conversation in Oxford:

> One of our best conversationalists was Walter Pater, who gave charming dinner-parties, where his talk had the delicate aroma of his writings, but with more ease and simplicity. ... we were talking of the comparative merits of contemporary poets, Tennyson, Browning, Swinburne, Matthew Arnold and William Morris, each of whom had his champion, when Pater summed up with a gentle but emphatic decision that each of the others excelled Tennyson in some particular quality, but that generally and all round Tennyson excelled them all and would outlive them. (*An Oxonian Looks Back* (1934), 113)

Characteristically Pater did not write about the acknowledged favourite (though he did review Arthur Symons's book on the more controversial Browning). Instead, consonant with his especial interest in Pre-Raphaelitism and Aestheticism, he published essays on Morris and Rossetti (the latter not included in Farnell's list, presumably because already dead). Marcus Waithe takes Pater's engagement with Morris as a basis for thinking about his contribution to the development of English studies, exploring his evaluative criteria and methodology; what Pater values in Morris also envisions what he values in literature more generally. As a poet-painter, like Michelangelo and Blake, Rossetti was always a special point of reference for Pater; William Sharp recalls Pater describing him in 1880 as 'the greatest man we have among us, in point of influence upon poetry, and perhaps painting' ('Reminiscences of Pater', 1894, in *Walter Pater: A Life Remembered*, ed. R. M. Seiler, 81). Elizabeth Prettejohn argues not only that Pater's densely intertextual essay plays a more important role in Pater's overall critical project than previous scholars have recognised, but also that Pater's treatment had a distinctive impact on the next generation of Modernist critics. Indeed, Pater's essay may be most important for explaining to us a historical fact that may seem difficult to understand: the extraordinary influence of Rossetti on both painters and poets of his own and succeeding generations, an influence out of all proportion, some may think, to his actual achievement in either art form.

CHAPTER 8

Pater's Shakespeare

Alex Wong

Besides the many scattered references that appear throughout his writing, Pater's Shakespearean criticism is contained in three published essays, all finally included in *Appreciations*. At one time, however, they may have been intended for parts in a larger whole.

'A Fragment on *Measure for Measure*' was the earliest, printed in the *Fortnightly Review* in November 1874. Pater may have intimated that it was to be the first of several such pieces: that very month, the 'Notes and News' section of the *Academy* reported that he meant 'to continue his short aesthetic studies of Shakspere's plays', building up a 'series that will some day make a book'. A note in December added: 'we understand that Mr Pater's next Shakespeare "study" for the *Fortnightly Review* will be on *Love's Labour's Lost*'.[1] But the essay 'On *Love's Labours Lost*' did not appear in print until December 1885, almost exactly eleven years later, and not, as promised, in the *Fortnightly*, but in *Macmillan's Magazine*.

A brief letter survives from Pater to the scholar F.J. Furnivall (1825–1910), founder in 1873 of the 'New Shakspere Society'. It is dated only 'May 18'. 'I should like much to edit a play of Shakspere, e.g. Romeo and Juliet, for schoolboys,' Pater writes, ostensibly replying to an invitation from his correspondent, 'but see no prospect of my having time to do so for a long while to come, so must deny myself the pleasure of saying and fancying that I will do so.'[2] He also remarks that he has 'not yet had time to read over again [his] notes on L.L.L.'. Lawrence Evans plausibly dates the letter to 1875, supposing that Furnivall had been prompted to write to Pater by the *Measure* essay and the notes in the *Academy*. If this is correct, then Furnivall was kept waiting three years for the piece on *Love's Labour's Lost*: Society records indicate that a paper of Pater's on that play, probably an early version of the essay, was read (we do not know by whom) at a meeting on 13 April 1878. Six months later, apparently willing to give up the idea of a whole book on Shakespeare, we find Pater listing both of the then completed essays in a list of proposed contents for a book, pitched to

Macmillan, to be called *The School of Giorgione, and Other Studies*.[3] That book never came into being, but neither was any notion of a Shakespeare volume ever practically revived. Pater sat on his study of *Love's Labour's Lost* for seven more years before seeing it into print, and the third of his Shakespeare essays, 'Shakespeare's English Kings', did not appear until April 1889 in *Scribner's Magazine*, not long before its inclusion in *Appreciations* in the following November.[4]

The three plays to which Pater substantially attended were relatively unpopular in his own day, and rarely if ever performed. *Richard II*, the main focus of 'Shakespeare's English Kings', he had seen as a schoolboy, after which it was not performed again in commercial English theatres until after Pater's death. *Measure* he could never have seen professionally performed before writing about it, though a production was mounted at the Haymarket Theatre in April 1876, the sole London production in Pater's adult life. Having missed it, presumably, at Sadler's Wells in 1857, he could not have seen *Love's Labour's Lost* acted either.[5] As Adrian Poole notes, Pater 'fastened on plays that had been caviar to the general'.[6] Not only to the 'general', theatre-going public, however, but also to most critics of his own day and of preceding decades. *Measure* had been branded 'painful' by Coleridge, and Swinburne speaks of 'the relative disfavour' in which the play had 'doubtless been at all times generally held'.[7] *Richard II*, though the Romantic critics brought some new appreciation, had been relatively neglected since the early seventeenth century, save for some periods in which current affairs reactivated its political valency. *Love's Labour's Lost*, meanwhile, had more consistently been regarded as Shakespeare's first and worst play. Pater's appreciations were supplied where they were needed.

Measure for Measure

Of the three essays, the study of *Measure for Measure* has had the least effect on later Shakespearean criticism. It is, however, the most obviously revealing of Pater's own values. His reading of the play is unusual, turning the familiar moral complaints of most other nineteenth-century critics virtually inside out. Coleridge's famous objections to *Measure*, for example, with which many have concurred, are squarely moral. He finds the comedic aspects of the play 'disgusting' and the tragic aspects 'horrible', but really it is the play's ending that makes it so obnoxious to him, for 'the pardon and marriage of Angelo not merely baffles the strong indignant claim of justice' but is furthermore 'degrading to the character of woman'.[8]

Swinburne, writing a little later than Pater's essay, pays more attention to the aesthetic character of the play, but considers its merits essentially tragic, and so returns to an ethical criterion: the 'evasion of a tragic end' is 'ingenious' in its management, but unworthy of Shakespeare 'in a moral sense'.[9] Yet for Pater, *Measure for Measure* is 'an epitome of Shakespeare's moral judgments':

> The action of the play, like the action of life itself for the keener observer, develops in us the conception of this poetical justice, and the yearning to realise it, the true justice of which Angelo knows nothing, because it lies for the most part beyond the limits of any acknowledged law. The idea of justice involves the idea of rights. But at bottom rights are equivalent to that which really is, to facts; and the recognition of his rights therefore, the justice he requires of our hands, or our thoughts, is the recognition of that which the person, in his inmost nature, really is; and as sympathy alone can discover that which really is in matters of feeling and thought, true justice is in its essence a finer knowledge through love. . . . It is for this finer justice, a justice based on a more delicate appreciation of the true conditions of men and things, a true respect of persons in our estimate of actions, that the people in *Measure for Measure* cry out as they pass before us . . . (*App.*, 183)

Poetical justice is 'true justice', truer than the law's inflexible approximations. It has for its objects the facts of human lives and selves, 'that which really is' – the facts that must be found out through sympathy; a knowledge that comes from love, which, to those who can apprehend it, confers 'rights' which are ethically imperative. It has to do with a 'finer' estimate of reality – 'life *itself*' – and not only reality as simulated by a work of poetic creation.

But the ethical appeal of a play like *Measure* is reliant on its being, to sensitive minds, 'like the action of life itself' – more like reality than a simpler or more reductively moralistic play might be. And, as Pater will confirm with his passionate final sentence, it may be that the moral exercise of attending keenly to such works of literature can make us keener observers in the real world too, perhaps not only through the simulation of moral situations, but through the discriminating activities of mind always required and rewarded by poetry, in which intellectual understanding of subtle language is connected naturally to feelings and values:

> It is not always that poetry can be the exponent of morality; but it is this aspect of morals which it represents most naturally, for this true justice is dependent on just those finer appreciations which poetry cultivates in us the power of making, those peculiar valuations of action and its effect which poetry actually requires. (184)

'Actually', the penultimate word in the essay, has the effect here of dissolving the boundary between reading and reality. Poetry and the *actual* world may not be identical, but poetry is part of our *actual* lives and 'actually', really, makes demands upon us, which in turn may modify our habits of mind and conduct. The 'finer appreciations' which the reader or critic of poetry is called upon to make are offered as the basis for true justice beyond the limits of literature. It is fitting that the essay finally found a place in a volume called *Appreciations*. The kind of criticism Pater writes is 'appreciative', and, while the word implies evaluation, and could in one sense be glossed as the setting of prices on things, Pater is particularly in the habit of raising, not lowering, the accepted price. Taking another etymological route, we might think of his appreciations as contributions towards the 'prizing' of things of value, often things undervalued or ignored by others but for which he feels a special affinity or sympathy. In this sense it is a process of 'finer knowledge through love'.

This theme of taking care over what others neglect is obliquely suggested in Pater's striking choice of illustrative quotation:

> 'Tis very pregnant:
> The jewel that we find we stoop and take it,
> Because we see it; but what we do not see
> We tread upon, and never think of it.
> (II.1.23–6, quoted as in *App.*, 183)

Earlier, Pater has said that 'it is Isabella with her grand imaginative diction ... who gives utterance to the equity, the finer judgments of the piece on men and things'; she is one of the women in Shakespeare whose 'intuitions interpret that which is often too hard *or fine* for manlier reason' (179; emphasis added). But these lines on the jewel, the ones he actually quotes, are spoken not by the virtuous Isabella, nor by the philosophical Duke, but by Angelo, the play's chief villain. Inclining to be rigid in exercising legal justice in the case of Claudio (held guilty of pre-nuptial fornication), he has just been advised by Escalus to consider whether he himself, Angelo –

> Had time coher'd with place, or place with wishing,
> Or that the resolute acting of [your] blood
> Could have attain'd th' effect of your own purpose
> (II.1.11–13; *Riverside Shakespeare*, 590)

– might not by some imaginable chance have 'erred' in a like manner. What Escalus puts to Angelo is an ethical urging of the very point Pater stresses in various parts of the essay: his conviction that Shakespeare 'inspires in us the sense of a strong tyranny of nature and circumstance', the tyranny of chance 'over human action' (174, 180). In fact, those lines from Escalus, which he does not otherwise quote, Pater echoes closely in his own elaboration of the point, taking the character of Angelo as his example:

> The bloodless, impassible temperament does but wait for its opportunity, for the almost accidental coherence of time with place, and place with wishing, to annul its long and patient discipline, and become in a moment the very opposite of that which under ordinary conditions it seemed to be, even to itself. (180)

The unusual use of 'coherence' helps to mark the echo. But Angelo's own airing of the jewel metaphor, which Pater does quote – though without reminding us of the context or the speaker – is all the more powerful in Pater's hands for being an ironic reflection on that very 'tyranny' of chance. Angelo replies to Escalus by emphasising the difference between temptation and the actual commission of 'error': no simple distinction in cases such as his own will turn out to be, though he little suspects it at this moment. He acknowledges that the jurors may well be guiltier than Claudio, but sees this as no impediment. 'What's open made to justice, / That justice seizes' (II.1.21–22). The lines about the jewel, almost immediately following this, are meant to convince Escalus that it's no use worrying about the jewels, or the crimes, you can't see: what is *obvious* is what one has to deal with, even if it becomes obvious only by chance. When Pater repurposes the lines, they become – with an ironic edge for those who recall the context – a moving exhortation, without exhorting, to look for the unnoticed jewels trodden underfoot: to 'see' more, and so 'tread' more carefully. Angelo subverts the essential, commonplace meaning of the lines, by making jewels stand for crimes; but in restoring Angelo's chosen maxim (for it is produced as a piece of conventional wisdom) to something closer to its basic sense, Pater has allowed it to retain the dramatic irony it has accrued through Angelo's use of it, and through its applicability to his later actions and experience in the plot. The sentiment is given a renewed humaneness, not only by its having been sullied by Angelo first, but by the breadth of moral meaning which Pater's whole interpretation of the play gives to it.

In its 'finer' details, that interpretation is Pater's; but it has one important forerunner and inspiration in Hazlitt's book, *The Characters of Shakespear's Plays* (1817). In the first place, several critics and surely many readers have been struck by the prominence given by Pater to the character of Claudio, and his claim that 'the main interest in *Measure for Measure* is not ... in the relation of Isabella and Angelo, but rather in the relation of Claudio and Isabella' (177). But this is where Hazlitt also fixed his focus, calling the scene in which Isabella visits her condemned brother in his cell 'one of the most dramatic passages' in the play, and then quoting from it extensively.[10] It is on just that exchange between brother and sister that Pater focuses his own attention. As with Angelo, he is exercised by the way in which, under the stress of unexpected circumstance, each character's nature is revealed in a new way. Isabella, a 'cold, chastened personality', is exposed in the drama to 'two sharp, shameful trials' which 'wring out of her a fiery, revealing eloquence' (177–8) – and this is the second of those trials. She becomes 'the ground of strong, contending passions', undergoing a 'tigerlike changefulness of feeling'; her angry indignation at Claudio's apparent willingness to sacrifice her honour (perhaps her soul) in order to live, leaves her 'stripped in a moment of all convention', revealing her in a new light, or atmosphere – 'clear, detached, columnar' (178). But, as in Hazlitt, it is the offending eloquence wrung out of Claudio in the same scene that strikes Pater most forcefully.

> Called upon suddenly to encounter his fate, looking with keen and resolute profile straight before him, he gives utterance to some of the central truths of human feeling, the sincere, concentrated expression of the recoiling flesh. Thoughts as profound and poetical as Hamlet's arise in him; and but for the accidental arrest of sentence he would descend into the dust, a mere gilded, idle flower of youth indeed, but with what are perhaps the most eloquent of all Shakespeare's words upon his lips. (181)

Adrian Poole has paid tribute to Pater's 'deep feeling', in this essay, 'for the force of words that can take us by surprise, for better or worse, revealing capacities in us we did not know we had and the absence of others we supposed that we did'.[11]

But Pater's closeness to Hazlitt goes further than this. Like Pater, Hazlitt too rises from specific criticisms of *Measure* to broader comments on the moral significance of Shakespeare's work. 'In one sense,' Hazlitt says, 'Shakespear was no moralist at all: in another, he was the greatest of all moralists.' That what he provides to us is 'like the action of life itself for the keener observer', and thus able, as Pater thought, to develop in us a 'finer' sense of justice, is implied by Hazlitt's comment that Shakespeare was 'a moralist in the same sense in which nature is one'. Unlike the 'pedantic moralist', he does not seek out 'the bad in every thing', but the opposite:

his talent, according to Hazlitt, 'consisted in sympathy with human nature, in all its shapes, degrees, depressions, and elevations'.[12] Pater's emphasis on 'sympathy' seems clearly indebted to Hazlitt's memorable chapter on the same play, though it is also highly characteristic of himself. Inman makes a telling comparison when she notes that the argument here about Shakespeare recalls Pater's earlier essay on Botticelli: 'His morality is all sympathy' (*Ren.*, 43).[13]

Strangely enough, before arriving at his formulation of Shakespearean 'sympathy', Hazlitt has already, in the same brief chapter, made the seemingly contradictory point that in this particular play there is 'a general system of cross-purposes between the feelings of the different characters and the sympathy of the reader or the audience'. 'Our sympathies', he says, 'are repulsed and defeated in all directions.'[14] How, then, does a consideration of *this* play, which he seems to find defective in the very quality for which he lauds Shakespeare as a moralist in general, lead Hazlitt shortly into those grand statements about Shakespeare's sympathetic morality? In fact, he arrives there by way of a discussion of the minor 'low' characters – Barnardine, Lucio, Pompey, Master Froth, Abhorson. He thinks Schlegel too 'severe' on such characters in calling them 'wretches'; Shakespeare himself does not look at them with such contempt.[15] Pater will be still more apologetic, and he sympathises with them all the more because they do so with one another:

> The slightest of them is at least not ill-natured: the meanest of them can put forth a plea for existence—*Truly, sir, I am a poor fellow that would live!*— ... they are capable of many friendships and of a true dignity in danger, giving each other a sympathetic, if transitory, regret—one sorry that another 'should be foolishly lost at a game of tick-tack.' (174)

For him too the 'low' characters are important to a moral reading of the play, but he brings them into closer proximity to at least some of the major characters (and their weaknesses), and so for him the Shakespearean sympathy is not limited to the peripheries of the drama but extended to its whole purview. They belong to the 'group of persons' powerfully portrayed by Pater as 'attractive, full of desire, vessels of the genial, seed-bearing powers of nature, a gaudy existence flowering out over the old court and city of Vienna, a spectacle of the fulness and pride of life which to some may seem to touch the verge of wantonness' (173–4). Pater is 'pleasantly unshocked', says Poole, suggestively, 'by the seedier aspects' of the play.[16] Seedy or, as Pater has it, seed-bearing. He places himself on the side of 'life'. It is Claudio's horror of death that seems to move him most.

The 'low-life' characters are united with Claudio in their vitality – not only their 'vivid reality' (174), but their earthiness and alliance with what is generative and vibrant in human experience, even unto the 'verge of wantonness'. They are among 'the children of this world', though not among 'the wisest'.[17]

As Mark Hollingsworth simply puts it, 'Pater has found a moral in Shakespeare's play—but it is not a moral of which certain of his contemporaries would approve'.[18] Largely avoiding the main ethical cruces of the plot – totally neglecting, above all, to make any explicit comment on its ending – Pater's reading relies on an appreciation of Shakespeare's treatment of the material as being true to life in its multiplicity: not only in the moral implications of the action itself, but through the presentation of characters, the sentiments put into their mouths, the seeming gratuitousness of small details. Though, via its source in Whetstone, the play inherits some evolved qualities of the older morality plays, it achieves its moral significance by implicitly denying the validity of that tradition's didactic clarity:

> The old 'moralities' exemplified most often some rough-and-ready lesson. Here the very intricacy and subtlety of the moral world itself, the difficulty of seizing the true relations of so complex a material, the difficulty of just judgment, of judgment that shall not be unjust, are the lessons conveyed. (182)

In the words of Philip Davis, the Victorian period was 'full of commentators anxiously concerned about the work of Shakespeare being no more than (as it were) the world all over again, lacking an extrapolatable morality or an external philosophy that could give extra meaning to the universe'.[19] These are the commentators who might have been less willing to 'approve', as Hollingsworth says, of Pater's interpretation. Arnold is one of the chief critics of the period who are troubled by Shakespeare's putative lack of interest in committing to a distinct governing conception to which details are subservient, and the antagonism between his and Pater's approaches to Shakespeare has been helpfully emphasised by Poole.[20] But Pater was far from alone in adhering to a rather different tradition, reaching back into the prehistory of Romanticism: the vision of Shakespeare as specially endowed to recreate reality itself. He was 'Nature's darling', as Gray had famously called him, to whom 'the mighty Mother did unveil / Her awful face', conferring upon him the pencil to 'paint', like her, the natural world, and the 'golden keys' to open human experience: joy, horror, fears – and 'sympathetic tears'.[21] Hazlitt is invoking the same notion in his notes on *Measure* when he calls Shakespeare 'a moralist in the same sense in which nature is one', adding, in a movement not unlike Gray's: 'He taught what he had learnt from her. He shewed the greatest knowledge of humanity with the greatest fellow-feeling for it.'[22] From this to 'finer knowledge through love' is a small but Paterian step.

For Pater, Shakespeare's moral intelligence is that of an 'observer', a 'spectator', who 'knows how the threads in the design before him hold together under the surface', in hidden complexities or complications. He is also a 'humourist', 'who follows with a half-amused but always pitiful sympathy, the various ways of human disposition, and sees less distance than ordinary men between what are called respectively great and little things' (184). These terms, taken from the final paragraph of the essay, are very similar to those in which he will later describe and celebrate Montaigne, and indeed the connection between the two writers is explicitly made: 'Shakespeare, who represents the free spirit of the Renaissance moulding the drama, hints, by his well-known preoccupation with Montaigne's writings, that just there was the philosophic counterpart to the fulness and impartiality of his own artistic reception of the experience of life' (*Gast.*, 83, ch. 4; *CW*, iv. 80). Again what is stressed is a fullness of receptivity to reality as experienced. Thinking of Montaigne brings Pater close, again and again, to his thoughts on *Measure*. When he speaks of Montaigne's apprehension of 'the variableness, the complexity, the miraculous surprises of man, concurrent with the variety, the complexity, the surprises of nature, making all true knowledge of either wholly relative and provisional', we are reminded of the interplay of nature and circumstance, the tyranny of their chance 'coherence', that he sees in Shakespeare: 'coherent', borrowed from Escalus, becomes 'concurrent' (89; *CW*, iv. 83). A few pages later, another version of the same thought, and two more Latinate words in substitution: here we have the 'collision or coincidence, of the mechanic succession of things with men's volition' (*Gast.*, 101, ch. 5: *CW*, iv. 90). Montaigne, like Shakespeare, has 'many curious moral variations' to show us, unsettling easy judgements on human conduct (94; *CW*, iv. 86).

But for the reader of *Appreciations*, the closing paragraphs on *Measure* are most likely to recall Pater's study of Charles Lamb, placed earlier in the same volume. Shakespeare's 'half-amused but always pitiful sympathy' ('Measure', *App.*, 184) is that of the 'humourist', a type exemplified in Pater's work most obviously by Lamb. In both writers, the 'laughter which blends with tears', humour as distinguished from wit, proceeds from a 'deeply stirred soul of sympathy' ('Charles Lamb', *App.*, 105). The latter phrase is applied to Shakespeare, but 'a sort of boundless sympathy' belongs also to Lamb (110). He too attends closely to life's 'organic wholeness, as extending even to the least things in it' (116). He 'can write of death, almost like Shakespeare' (120). And perhaps Pater is thinking in part of Elia's love for life and 'recoil', like that of Claudio, from death. Both are genial natures who find they must, in Elia's phrase, 'reluct at the inevitable course of destiny'.[23]

Love's Labours Lost

The humour of Lamb finds interest and significance, not mere trivialising or scoffing mirth, in 'fashions', 'tricks', and 'habits', the trappings and ephemera of a time and place – including one's own, which the humourist can see with an uncommon 'understanding', amounting to a 'refined, purged sort of vision'. The humourist sees any instance of such 'outward mode or fashion, always in strict connexion with the spiritual condition which determined it' ('Lamb', *App.*, 114–15). It is in similar terms, and from the same perspective, that Pater was able in his study of *Love's Labours Lost* [sic] to make an important defence of one of Shakespeare's least popular works. 'Shakespeare brings a serious effect', he says, 'out of the trifling of his characters' (*App.*, 161–2). Reminding us of the theoretical distinction with which he had opened his essay on Lamb, Pater tells us that the play contains 'choice illustrations of both wit and humour' (161); but the implication of the essay as a whole, especially in the light of the essays on Lamb and *Measure*, appears to be that the 'wit' is part of the material with which the 'humour' is dealing. Pater asks us to see the wit not, as earlier critics had done, as a youthful author's fashionable vice in an age of witty conceit and modish artificialities, but as an object we are to regard *through* the essential humour of the treatment.

Modern critics and editors of *Love's Labour's Lost*, in contrast with those of *Measure*, have been much readier to recognise Pater's importance in the critical tradition. The play's unmistakable 'foppery' of language, as Pater calls it, had seemed off-putting to most of its earlier critics, as well as to theatre companies. His essay is an early and innovative insistence that a concern with style and 'euphuism', with fashions and modes, was a sophisticated and self-conscious theme in the play; and this is an idea that most later critics have taken for granted. One recent editor comments that Pater, exceptionally before the 1920s, 'does justice' to the play's 'curious foppery of language' and also to Shakespeare's own 'ambivalent attitude towards it'.[24] Most others, in going over the reception of the play, have felt at least the obligation to register in a passing mention Pater's voice in the wilderness.

For Pater it is the humourist's peculiar gift to be able to see the modes of contemporary life, including its small details and fribbling aspects, with something of the vision that hindsight will later give to others ('Lamb', *App.*, 114–16). Shakespeare, in Pater's view, was actively reflecting on current and recent literary styles, including his own. His true subject was 'that old euphuism of the Elizabethan age',[25] –

> that pride of dainty language and curious expression, which it is very easy to ridicule, which often made itself ridiculous, but which had below it a real sense of fitness and nicety; and which, as we see in this very play, and still more clearly in the Sonnets, had some fascination for the young Shakespeare himself. It is this foppery of delicate language, this fashionable plaything of his time, with which Shakespeare is occupied in *Love's Labours Lost.* (165)

'Play is often that about which people are most serious', Pater says, 'and the humourist may observe how, under all love of playthings, there is almost always hidden an appreciation of something really engaging and delightful' (164). Shakespeare can show this, and we ought to be engaged, delighted – to appreciate the appreciation. Pater himself, whether a humourist or not, is certainly a literary aesthete willing to give hints of his own predilection for this 'foppery' of language, which 'satisfies a real instinct in our minds—the fancy so many of us have for an exquisite and curious skill in the use of words' (166).

John Kerrigan is unusual among the more recent editors in his having taken Pater's 'magnificent but flawed essay' seriously enough as to argue with it. In identifying the theme of linguistic foppery and showing how the play displays it to us in various degrees of 'sophistication', Pater was the first 'to unite', in Kerrigan's words, 'the high and low', the courtiers and the commoners, explaining the 'dramatic function' of the latter and bringing into focus an overarching thematic cohesion. 'In one sense', Kerrigan judges, 'Pater did not go far enough, though in another he went too far'. If Pater had focused less exclusively on the language theme, he might have found other things to say. 'He overestimated the unifying power of the language theme, because he was unresponsive to the other integuments which hold the play together. Sex, for instance.' (Unresponsive or not, it is true that Pater has nothing to say on the sexual themes or their structural import.) On the other hand, Kerrigan argues, had he thought further about the language theme, he might have been led to recognise the centrality of another theme: 'fame', the prize at which all the fancified talking is aimed, and a 'more radical and inclusive principle of unity' than the one Pater identified. The vow of studious homosocial retirement from the world (and especially from female company) made by the King and his male companions at the start of the play was not, in Kerrigan's view, acknowledged by Pater as 'both the lynch-pin of the action and a recurring centre of dramatic interest'. To Kerrigan it is clear that the oath belongs with the vulgar or extravagant language of the 'low characters', sharing with them the purpose of attracting admiration.[26] What seems to be suggested here is that Pater's silence on the theme of 'fame' is at least in part the consequence of a lack of interest in the sequence of events and their dramatic handling.

In one of Anne Barton's very early essays, Pater serves as a point of reference in another discussion of the play's 'unity'. His 'beautiful' essay on 'Shakespeare's English Kings' provides her with a useful maxim: 'into the unity of a choric song the perfect drama ever tends to return, its intellectual scope deepened, complicated, enlarged, but still with an unmistakable singleness, or identity, in its impression on the mind' (*App.*, 203–4). In her opinion, such a unity is 'evident throughout' *Love's Labour's Lost*, in spite of Pater's remarks (which she also quotes) about its composition into 'pictorial groups':

> The grouping of the characters into scenes would appear, however, to have been dictated by a purpose far more serious than the mere creation of such patterns; it is one of the ways in which Shakespeare maintains the balance of the play world between the artificial and the real, and indicates the final outcome of the comedy.[27]

She disagrees with Pater's evaluation of the dramatic cohesion of *Love's Labour's Lost* by insisting that his more general comments elsewhere should be held relevant here too. She defends the play as drama by using Pater against himself. But the essay's debts to Pater go far beyond the explicit discussion of him. 'Often, beneath ornament and convention the Elizabethans disguised genuine emotion', she writes, reminding us of Pater's own defence.[28] 'Mannered and artificial, reflecting an Elizabethan delight in patterned and intricate language, Navarre's lines at the beginning of the play are nevertheless curiously urgent and intense': the diction, even the syntax could not be more Pateresque, but these are Barton's words; and it is so again when she talks of the song of the Owl and the Cuckoo from the play's end, 'a song into which the whole of that now-vanished world of *Love's Labour's Lost* seems to have passed, its brilliance, its strange mingling of the artificial and the real, its loveliness and laughter gathered together for the last time to speak to us in the form of a single strain of music'.[29] Slight touches recall some of Pater's most famous passages: the beauty of Leonardo's *Mona Lisa*, 'into which the soul with all its maladies has passed' (*Ren.*, 98); the 'strange dyes, strange colours' and human 'brilliancy' of the 'Conclusion' (*Ren.*, 189). The phrase 'a single strain of music' appears verbatim in 'Shakespeare's English Kings' (*App.*, 203).

It is a Paterian conception of 'Renaissance' that Barton evokes, too, even as she reveals what Pater leaves out of his own discussion of the play. The academic oath springs 'from a recognition of the tragic brevity and imper- manence of life that is peculiarly Renaissance', she says, grazing Pater's own phrase, 'awful brevity', in the 'Conclusion' (*Ren.*, 189). She connects the humanist cult of 'fame' with the fact that, as she puts it (or Pater might have put it himself), 'the thought of Death was acquiring a new poignancy in its contrast with man's increasing sense of the value and loveliness of life in this world'. And if the other primary theme left out in Pater's study is sex, this train of thought leads there as well. The oath, an 'elaborate scheme which intends to enhance life, ... would in reality, if successfully carried out, result in the limitation of life and, ultimately, in its complete denial'.[30] It is partly because Barton's critical idiom is in such close contact with Pater's at this point that she allows us to see what may be behind Pater's tight-lipped comment that the votaries are 'of course soon for- sworn' (164), and how it might connect with his view of the 'genial, seed- bearing' vitality of Claudio and the 'low' characters in *Measure*, ranged on the side of life and worldly experience. The oath and the King's judicial strictures, like Angelo's in *Measure*, represent a misguided attempt to keep life at bay.

Another striking aspect of Pater's reading of this play is his overwhelm- ing preoccupation with the character of Biron (Berowne). He is the 'perfect flower' of that foppery in which Pater would like us, with Shakespeare, to see the 'really delightful side' and hidden depths. In him such a manner, which is merely 'affected' in others, 'refines itself ... into the expression of a nature truly and inwardly bent upon a form of delicate perfection'; the outward fashion 'blends with a true gallantry of nature and an affectionate complaisance and grace' (166). He sees things clearly, is sensitive to the feelings and conduct of social intercourse, and – as the 'Conclusion' to *The Renaissance* seems to persuade us to do – he trusts more in 'actual sensation' than in 'men's affected theories'. He 'delights in his own rapidity of intuition', such as 'could come only from a deep experience and power of observation' (167). The passage in which his qualities are described reads at times like an apologia, and Biron seems to have many of the ideal qualities of the Paterian aesthetic critic.

'Power of observation' is not the endowment only of the critic, but also of the 'humourist', and so of Shakespeare himself – an 'observer' and 'spectator' of life ('Measure', *App.*, 184). Implied there is a quality of detachment. In the final sentence of the *Love's Labours Lost* essay we are presented with a Biron who, though peculiarly sensitive and intelligent, is 'never quite in touch, never quite on a perfect level of understanding, with the other persons of the play' (169). This, together with another brief passage a little earlier, is as close as Pater comes to grappling with the more rebarbative qualities that modern critics have been much readier to see in Biron, a cynical, embittered character taken unawares by his depth of feeling. Yes, 'that gloss of dainty language is a second nature with him: even at his best he is not without a certain artifice' (167); but one might have expected Pater to go further, to show the glossy, defensive, and deflective reliance on tricks of 'wit' as a kind of irony or 'reserve', such as he identifies in Lamb. Shakespeare, 'in whose own genius there is an element of this very quality', is a sympathetic painter of it, and the essay all but overtly invites us to infer that Pater, in his emphasis on Biron, is also displaying a natural sympathy (168). He was known as a defensive, provocative conversationalist himself. Here, as in the essay on Lamb and the Montaigne chapters of *Gaston de Latour*, he takes it for granted that there is 'something of self-portraiture' in Shakespeare's Biron, 'as happens with every true dramatist' (168) – but also, as in the case of Lamb and Montaigne, with the essayist.

Shakespeare's English Kings

Biron is a figure with 'that winning attractiveness which', Pater says, perhaps betraying another aspect of what seems throughout a delicate and speculative identification with him, 'there is no man but would willingly exercise' (168). He has gallantry and grace; he is 'the flower' of the play's precious euphuism (166). Claudio, in the *Measure* essay, was a 'flowerlike young man', 'a mere gilded, idle flower of youth', raised, in his revolt from death, to a height of Shakespearean eloquence (180–1). Both are attractive young men to whom floral imagery is applied. In 'Shakespeare's English Kings' we find Pater again exercised particularly by a winning and flowerlike young man, Richard II, 'that sweet lovely rose' (*App.*, 189, quoting Hotspur's line in *1 Henry 4*, I.3.175). In Richard's case there is more overt and sustained emphasis on his personal beauty, 'that physical charm which all confessed', and on his attractive 'suavity of manners' (197, 194). He is 'graceful', 'amiable' – possessed of 'those real amiabilities that made people forget the darker touches of his character' (195). Richard's 'fatal beauty, of which he was so frankly aware', and which Pater thinks Shakespeare has dwelt upon with particular attentiveness (194), is potent in its effect:

> it was by way of proof that his end had been a natural one that, stifling a real fear of the face, the face of Richard, on men's minds, with the added pleading now of all dead faces, Henry [Bolingbroke] exposed the corpse to general view; and Shakespeare, in bringing it on the stage, in the last scene of his play, does but follow out the motive with which he has emphasised Richard's physical beauty all through it—that 'most beauteous inn,' as the Queen says quaintly, meeting him on the way to death—residence, then soon to be deserted, of that wayward, frenzied, but withal so affectionate soul. (201)

'Affectionate', like Biron. Readings of Richard's character have rarely been so affectionate.

Richard II had been a set text in Pater's school days, forming part of the Sixth Form examination in July 1858.[31] At his school's Speech Day in the same year, the part of Richard in an extract from the play was played by Pater's close friend Henry Dombrain, with whom Pater and a third friend, John Rainier McQueen, had a year earlier at the same event performed a scene from *Henry IV*, Part I – Pater playing Hotspur, and very probably speaking the line about the old King Richard as a 'sweet lovely rose'.[32] Unlike the other plays, moreover, *Richard II* is one Pater had seen professionally performed. It was in the same year, 1858, that he saw Charles Kean's magnificent production at the Princess's Theatre, an experience he recalls evocatively in the essay, three decades later. 'In the hands of Kean the play became like an exquisite performance on the violin' (195).

In Pater's reading, Richard is an aesthete, a poet by nature, who happens to be a king. Shakespeare's English Kings are 'a very eloquent company', Pater says, 'and Richard is the most sweet-tongued of them all' – 'an exquisite poet if he is nothing else, from first to last, in light and gloom alike, able to see all things poetically, to give a poetic turn to his conduct of them' (194). He is the spin-doctor of his own downfall, even if, in the final analysis, the spin is mainly for his own benefit. But, just as Kean's performance could resemble an 'exquisite performance on the violin', so Richard's performance of himself, as he 'throws himself into the part' that

Fate and his enemies have assigned him, and so 'falls gracefully as on the world's stage' (198), is compared with wordless music: 'As in some sweet anthem of Handel, the sufferer, who put finger to the organ under the utmost pressure of mental conflict, extracts a kind of peace at last from the mere skill with which he sets his distress to music' (200). This is not only the comfort of poetry as reinterpretation, poetry as rhetoric; it implies the comfort of the aesthetic more narrowly defined, of aesthetic form in itself as soothing, or perhaps of the capacity of verbal artistry to accommodate one to circumstance by enacting, through a beautified and rhetorically controlled and contrived speech, the nature, as speaker, of a role with which one must identify: the role made acceptable through the fashioning of the speech which delineates it, imaginatively, creatively, in a way to which one can adjust one's own sense of self. In Pater's words, Richard in his ordeal 'experiences something of the royal prerogative of poetry to obscure, or at least to attune and soften men's griefs' (200). Poetry can console by reinterpreting circumstance, by *obscuring* certain facts, which might amount to a *softening* of grief; but it can also soften by *attuning* the feelings. Attunement, as accommodation, may be of self to circumstance, as in Richard's poignantly self-indulgent speech about 'worms and graves and epitaphs' (III.2.144–77). But attunement is more than accommodation; it suggests harmony as judged by aesthetic instinct.

Pater's essay instigated what might be called the 'aesthetic' reading of the play, associated later with C.E. Montague and W.B. Yeats.[33] The aesthetic approach was vigorously repudiated by Edward Dowden and others of a more 'moralistic' persuasion, who 'tended to stress Richard's contemptible weakness and want of virility'.[34] Yeats pleaded for Richard's 'fine temperament' and 'contemplative' nature, calling him 'an unripened Hamlet': 'I cannot believe that Shakespeare looked on his Richard II. with any but sympathetic eyes, understanding indeed how ill-fitted he was to be King, at a certain moment of history, but understanding that he was lovable and full of capricious fancy, "a wild creature" as Pater has called him.'[35] Denis Donoghue frames matters in a more politicised way when he writes that 'Pater started a little fashion of saying that Shakespeare's imagination was ashamed of its duty' – the duty, that is, of legitimising and celebrating the Tudor dynasty and its antecedents – 'and insisted on giving the defeated kings the most touching lines'.[36]

A.C. Bradley, whose influence on twentieth-century Shakespearean criticism and pedagogy was perhaps pre-eminent, offers a middle-ground reading of Richard. In a lecture given in 1904 he classes him among those, like Romeo and Orsino, of an 'imaginative nature', but draws attention also to the 'weakness' inherent in such natures.[37] Like Pater, and Hazlitt before him, Bradley was particularly responsive to, and has sometimes been held accountable for others' overemphasis upon, subtleties of 'character'. In his non-Shakespearean lectures, he speaks of Pater admiringly, even citing him as an 'authority'.[38] The fact that Bradley in his monumental writings on Shakespeare focused mainly on characters and plays that Pater did not (or not substantively) discuss, leaves us to wonder whether Pater's place in the background of mainstream twentieth-century Shakespearean studies might have been easier to see had Bradley chosen any of the same few plays for his prime examples. But Pater directed his appreciative efforts onto jewels that others tended to tread over without stooping, and the refined alterity of his reading of Shakespeare was not Bradley's way.

More modern critics and editors of *Richard II*, though they sometimes recall, as an extreme example, Pater's sympathetic reading of its protagonist, have generally been more mindful of one particular passage in the essay:

> In the Roman Pontifical, of which the order of Coronation is really a part, there is no form for the inverse process, no rite of 'degradation,' such as that by which an offending priest or bishop may be deprived, if not of the essential quality of 'orders', yet, one by one, of its outward dignities. It is as if Shakespeare had had in mind some such inverted rite, like those old ecclesiastical or military ones, by which human hardness, or human justice, adds the last touch of unkindness to the execution of its sentences, in the scene where Richard 'deposes' himself, as in some long, agonising ceremony ... (198)

Pater's phrase 'inverted rite' is still regularly quoted, especially by editors, though few now seem interested in returning to the essay in detail. An editor who *did* was John Dover Wilson in 1939. First declaring that Pater's essay on *Love's Labour's Lost* was 'the only critique with any understanding of that play which appeared during the nineteenth century', Dover Wilson expresses his agreement with Pater's emphasis on the 'simple continuity' of *Richard II*, and his estimation of the style's appropriateness to the matter. Pater is 'the one writer to see' that the play has more in common with the Catholic Mass than with a play by Ibsen or Shaw, and 'ought to be played throughout as a ritual'. Pater's commentary on the deposition scene 'goes to the heart of the play, since it reveals a sacramental quality in the agony and death of the sacrificial victim'.[39] Pater's insight in this regard was also acknowledged by the historian Ernst Kantorowicz in his important study of medieval 'political theology', *The King's Two Bodies* (1957), containing his own brilliant reading of the relevant scene. 'Walter Pater has called it very correctly an inverted rite, a rite of degradation and a long agonizing ceremony in which the order of coronation is reversed.'[40]

'Shakespeare's English Kings' is significant more generally in its emphasis on 'the irony of kingship' as a unifying theme in the history plays, with Richard 'the most touching of all examples' (189). 'The irony of kingship—average human nature, flung with a wonderfully pathetic effect into the vortex of great events': this is the side of kingship Shakespeare has made 'prominent' in his histories, making 'the sad fortunes' of these pre-eminent individuals 'conspicuous examples of the ordinary human condition' (185–6). Pater's is the classic critical expression of this idea: 'No! Shakespeare's kings are not, nor are meant to be, great men: rather, little or quite ordinary humanity, thrust upon greatness, with those pathetic results, the natural self-pity of the weak heightened in them into irresistible appeal to others as the net result of their royal prerogative' (199). 'No! I am not Prince Hamlet, nor was meant to be', says Eliot's Prufrock, remembering, perhaps ironising, Pater, but also using Pater's 'irony of kingship' in his effort to ironise himself. He is no king, no prince, not thrust upon greatness, with no great momentous decisions to make – only ordinary human nature in an ordinary condition, or thrust upon petty banalities which, being the material of a life, have a trick of feeling weighty.[41] As Eliot's echo registers, Pater's focus is again on personal experience, the single nature in contact with circumstance. The sense of this irony, which Pater makes us feel, elicits sympathy with the individual.

Richard oscillates between eloquent meditations on his frailty and precariousness – as of any other person, though with further to fall and stronger enemies – and proud declarations of his divine sanction as anointed monarch. He takes rhetorical hold of the glimpses he has of his own ironic situation. 'And in truth', Pater says, 'but for that adventitious poetic gold, it would be only "plume-plucked Richard"' (199). His is the 'ordinary human condition', heightened by a streak of the poetic that is itself only adventitious. The 'strong tyranny' of chance here becomes, in another variation on the notion Pater raises in all his Shakespeare studies, 'the somewhat ironic preponderance of nature and circumstance over men's artificial arrangements' (188). Arrange a system to choose you a king, and you may well end up the fool of those ironists, Nature and Circumstance, whose unpredictable concurrences and cohesions Pater finds so powerfully portrayed in the works of Shakespeare.

Conclusion

Christopher Ricks is particularly impatient with the preoccupation with *finesse* in the Shakespeare essays. Pater wanted something 'finer than fineness', says Ricks, and was attracted to *Measure* mainly because it showed Shakespeare reworking a rougher source to 'finer issues' – Pater's own phrase, but borrowed, as Ricks reminds us, from the play: 'Spirits are not finely touch'd, / But to fine issues' (I.1.35–36). Shakespeare *refines*. Pater, in a critical response that is itself 'creative' (for Ricks not a term of praise), refines further.[42]

Cognates of 'fine', however, are not the only central or repeated words across these essays. In *Measure* we have, in close connection with them, justice and the just; also 'grace' – but not another word which might have seemed salient, 'mercy'. What would Pater have made of *The Merchant of Venice*? 'Grace', unlike 'mercy', has both moral and aesthetic senses, its spiritual or theological meaning contributing potentially to the aura of both. In an essay so clear about the intertwining of ethics and aesthetics, that slippage or ambivalence is both useful and suggestive. 'Fine' may seem better suited to aesthetics than to ethics, but when allied with 'justice' it again helps to make the essential connection; while 'just', as in the phrase *le mot juste*, can have its aesthetic applications too; and the basically moral idea of justice is not insignificant to Pater's frequent use of 'just' as a modifier implying critical or artistic discrimination: just here, just there, just that, in just this way. In 'Love's Labours Lost', Pater's emphasis on styles of language might seem to tip his vocabulary towards more clearly aesthetic terms or senses – grace, delicacy, daintiness, refinement; but his insistence on the depths underlying ostensibly superficial fashions encourages us to see the moral correlatives of these qualities, and the essay gravitates towards a consideration of the connections between manner and temperament. 'Intuition' is a moral quality; Biron's attractiveness is more than a surface appearance but a matter of conduct and appeal to sympathy. In all three essays, poetry, style, eloquence, and beauty are shown in their relations to the inner life – especially in Biron and Richard – and with the moral faculties, whether in a wide or, as in *Measure*, even in a narrow sense: the matter of justice and judgment.

What, in sum, does Shakespeare seem to have meant to Pater? Large sympathies; a sensitivity to difficulties of 'moral interpretation'; a 'finer justice', in part manifested through a commitment to the many-sidedness of real life and the avoidance of simple lessons. Pater's Shakespeare does not sympathise only with the refined, but also with the coarse 'low' characters in their 'vivid reality' and 'pride of life'. He is a poet of the 'tyranny' of chance, of life's ironies in the junctures of 'nature and circumstance'; but also a humourist who can see the real significance of apparently small or trivial things. And the fineness of his work, as a workman, cultivates in appreciative readers a fineness of judgment which is of a piece with the sympathetic morality he offers. *Love's Labour's Lost*, especially in the person of Biron, offers, in Pater's words, 'a real insight into the laws which determine what is exquisite in language, and their root in the nature of things' (166). Fineness and delicacy in poetry do not exist in a sealed-off world of art: their roots are in reality, where we live as practical, moral agents, however far some may withdraw to the position of spectator or observer.

Notes

1 'Notes and News', *Academy* 6 (7 November 1874), 506; (12 December 1874), 630.
2 *Letters*, 15 (no. 22).
3 Proposed to Macmillan in a letter dated 1 October [1878] (*Letters*, 32 (no. 52)).
4 Pater's library borrowings, however, suggest he had been thinking of this topic since 1884; see Inman (1990), 460–1, 467, 475 (entries 418, 421, 462, 509).
5 See Janice Norwood, 'A Reference Guide to Performances of Shakespeare's Plays in Nineteenth-Century London', in *Shakespeare in the Nineteenth Century*, ed. Gail Marshall (Cambridge 2012), 348–416.
6 Adrian Poole, *Shakespeare and the Victorians* (2004), 212.
7 *The Literary Remains of Samuel Taylor Coleridge*, ed. Henry Nelson Coleridge, 4 vols, ii (1836), 122; Algernon Charles Swinburne, *A Study of Shakespeare* (1880), 202.
8 Coleridge, *Remains*, 122–3.
9 Swinburne, *Study*, 203–4.
10 *Characters of Shakespear's Plays* (1817), in *The Selected Writings of William Hazlitt*, ed. Duncan Wu, 9 vols, i (1998), 83–270 (255ff). Holman Hunt's painting *Claudio and Isabella* (1853), prominently discussed in the first version of Pater's 'Winckelmann', shows this very scene.
11 Poole, *Shakespeare and the Victorians*, 214.
12 Hazlitt, ed. Wu, i. 255.
13 Inman (1990), 93; *Ren.*, 43.
14 Hazlitt, ed. Wu, i. 254.
15 Hazlitt, ed. Wu, i. 254–5.
16 Poole, *Shakespeare and the Victorians*, 214.
17 Cf. 'Conclusion' in *Ren.*, 190.

18 Mark Hollingsworth, 'A Reference Guide to Nineteenth-Century Works About Shakespeare and Play Publication by Year', in Marshall, *Shakespeare in the Nineteenth Century*, 46.

19 Philip Davis, 'Implicit and Explicit Reason: George Eliot and Shakespeare', in *Victorian Shakespeare, Vol. 2: Literature and Culture*, ed. Gail Marshall and Adrian Poole (Basingstoke 2003), 84–99 (94–5).

20 Poole, *Shakespeare and the Victorians*, 210–14.

21 *Complete Poems of Thomas Gray*, ed. H.W. Starr and J.R. Hendrickson (Oxford 1966), 12–17 (15–16).

22 Hazlitt, ed. Wu, i. 255.

23 'New Year's Eve', in *The Works of Charles and Mary Lamb*, ed. E.V. Lucas, vol. ii (1912), 27–32 (29).

24 *Love's Labour's Lost*, ed. G.R. Hibbard (Oxford 1990), 5.

25 Cf. 'Euphuism', *ME*, i. 92–110, and see Lene Østermark-Johansen, 'The Death of Euphues: Euphuism and Decadence in Late-Victorian Literature', *English Literature in Transition* 45 (2002), 4–25.

26 *Love's Labour's Lost*, ed. John Kerrigan (1982), 22–3.

27 Bobbyann Roesen [later Anne Barton], '*Love's Labour's Lost*', *Shakespeare Quarterly* 4 (1953), 411–26 (414). The revised version in Barton's *Essays, Mainly Shakespearean* (Cambridge 1994), 31–50, is much less Pateresque.

28 Roesen, '*LLL*', 417.

29 Roesen, '*LLL*', 411.

30 Roesen, '*LLL*', 412.

31 Inman (1990), 93.

32 See Michael Levey, *The Case of Walter Pater* (1978), 54, 154.

33 For Montague, see *Richard II: Shakespeare, The Critical Tradition*, ed. Charles Forker (2000), 367.

34 *Richard II*, ed. Charles R. Forker (2002), 95–6.

35 'At Stratford-on-Avon' (1901), in *The Collected Works of W.B. Yeats*, ed. George Mills Harper, George Bornstein, et al., 14 vols (New York 1989–2015), iv: *Early Essays*, ed. George Bornstein and Richard J. Finneran (2007), 73–83 (79).

36 Denis Donoghue, *Walter Pater* (New York 1995), 233.

37 A.C. Bradley, *Oxford Lectures on Poetry* (1909), 326.

38 Bradley, *Oxford Lectures*, 19.

39 *Richard II*, ed. John Dover Wilson (Cambridge 1939), xiii–xiv, xvi.

40 Ernst Kantorowicz, *The King's Two Bodies* (Princeton 1957), 36.

41 'The Love Song of J. Alfred Prufrock' (1917), in *The Poems of T.S. Eliot*, ed. Christopher Ricks and Jim McCue, 2 vols, I: *Collected and Uncollected Poems* (2015), 5–9 (9).

42 Ricks, 'Misquotation', 393–4.

CHAPTER 9

Pater and the Quaintness of Seventeenth-Century English Prose

Kathryn Murphy

Pater's 'Sir Thomas Browne' begins by observing the lawlessness and lack of classical balance in early modern English prose. While 'English prose literature towards the end of the seventeenth century', Pater writes, 'was becoming ... a matter of design and skilled practice, highly conscious of itself as an art, and, above all, correct', the earlier literature was 'singularly informal' and 'eminently occasional', marred by 'unevenness, alike in thought and style; lack of design; and caprice'. A few early exceptions, like Hooker, Latimer, and More, instituted a 'reasonable transparency', 'classical clearness'. Otherwise, before Dryden and Locke, English prose was wayward. Of such writers, Browne was, Pater tells us, '[t]he type' (*App.*, 124–5).

And yet. Despite these faults, there are compensations to be found. Pater writes:

> in recompense for that looseness and whim, in Sir Thomas Browne for instance, we have in those 'quaint' writers, as they themselves understood the term (*coint*, adorned, but adorned with all the curious ornaments of their own predilection, provincial or archaic, certainly unfamiliar, and selected without reference to the taste or usages of other people) the charm of an absolute sincerity, with all the ingenuous and racy effect of what is circumstantial and peculiar in their growth. (125–6)

Pater's inverted commas abstract 'quaint' from the flow of his prose and distance him from its use, an effect compounded by the parenthesis stalling the sentence's progress in mimicry of the distractible prose of the seventeenth century, with its habits of self-annotation and erudite display.[1] Reluctantly, Pater finds a charm in quaintness. Something in Browne beguiles.

This chapter aims to expose what 'quaint' means for Pater, and the work it does in his criticism. Despite the inverted commas, it is a word which appears frequently – a tic of Pater's critical prose. Its meaning, however, is never directly addressed: the closest Pater gets to a definition is his parenthesis on '*coint*'. It is nonetheless, as I hope to show, a keyword, marking a simultaneous discomfort with and interest in the lingering appeal of outmoded aesthetic objects which connects it to Pater's broader theoretical statements on style, and on the relationship between classicism and romanticism. Pater's use of 'quaint' is idiosyncratic, but connected to a wider pattern in criticism: on the one hand, the attempt of his predecessors and contemporaries to account for Browne's peculiarity, what Coleridge called his 'Sir-Thomas-Browne-ness'; on the other, a vogue for the word as a critical term which, as we will see, has strong and ambivalent associations. The later part of this chapter shows how Pater's quaintness fits in the longer history of the reception of Browne, a history which traces changing attitudes to difficulty, Latinity, and 'metaphysical' style. These qualities were associated with forms of religion and philosophical education which were rejected in the later seventeenth century, just as 'classical clearness' became the ideal of prose, and they have remained variously embarrassing, threatening, or appealing ever since: a complex of aesthetic effects which 'quaint' works both to name and conceal.

Quaintness of Mind

What does 'quaint' mean? Derived ultimately from Latin '*cognitus*' – a person or thing known, acknowledged, approved – it comes into English in the thirteenth century from the Anglo-Norman *cointe*: astute, clever, fashionable, devious, ingenious. Its earliest appearances in English fall under this rubric; over the centuries, it slips from associations with cunning, craftiness, and ingeniousness to ornament and elaboration, and thence into affectation, daintiness, fastidiousness, whether applied to persons, speech, or style.[2] Of the nine main definitions offered by the *OED*, only three are not now marked as obsolete. The last citation for the sense most relevant to writing – 'carefully or ingeniously elaborated; highly elegant or refined; clever, smart; (in later use also) affected' – is from 1841. What survives is what the dictionary now deems to be the 'usual sense': 'attractively or agreeably unusual in character or appearance; *esp.* pleasingly old-fashioned', first registered in 1762.[3]

The word 'quaint' is thus now itself quaint. That its senses related to ingeniousness, cunning, and ornament should obsolesce, leaving only today's faint residue as a mark of the quirkily old-fashioned, is ironic. In 'Sir Thomas Browne', Pater foregrounds both the obsolescence and the irony. His account is deliberately archaic: the 'quaint' writers are quaint not only in a contemporary sense, but 'as they themselves understood the term'. Pater's gloss supplies not quite a definition of 'quaint', but a characterisation: adorned, but strangely or excessively so, with 'curious ornaments' idiosyncratic to the writer, pursued with a kind of blind determination which ignores the taste of the generality. Pater's italics and inverted commas present the words 'quaint' and '*coint*' as specimens. '*Coint*' offers the Anglo-Norman spelling; it is an archaic fossil in Pater's own prose. Whether Pater knew it or not, it also had an air of the antique for Browne: in the seventeenth century, the French form appears only in editions of Chaucer, etymological notes on Milton, and dictionaries of French or older English. *Coint* was marked as either foreign or archaic. This doubleness, in which 'quaint' and 'coint' at once characterise obsolete styles of language and exemplify them, is typical of the word's ambivalence.

'Quaintness' recurs in the Browne essay particularly in connection with Browne's *Hydriotaphia*, or *Urne-Buriall* (1658): a treatise in five chapters which takes as a prompt the discovery of urns buried in a field near Walsingham, Norfolk. Browne's initial displays of antiquarian erudition on the sepulchral and funereal practices of the ancients transform into arias of ornate prose on the inevitability of oblivion, the futility of monuments, and the necessity of trust in the Resurrection. That the work's subject is the more literal resurrection of the artefacts of antiquity and the relics of long-dead people keys it closely to Pater's double quaintness, and the antiquarian revivification of the obsolete.

It is therefore no surprise that 'quaintness' is important in Pater's discussion of *Hydriotaphia*. It is a composition, he writes, which 'with all its quaintness we may well pronounce classical' (154). Pater expands:

> Out of an atmosphere of all-pervading oddity and quaintness—the quaintness of mind which reflects that this disclosing of the urns of the ancients hath 'left unto our view some parts which they never beheld themselves'—arises a work really ample and grand, nay! classical ... by virtue of the effectiveness with which it fixes a type in literature ... (156)

This is a tonally and rhythmically sympathetic sentence, working out its sense with the echo of Browne in the ear. The period style steals out from the quotation to render Pater's 'hath' archaic; the interjection of 'nay!' has just the touch of simultaneous oddity and amplitude which he diagnoses, poised between quaint and grand. As a review of *Appreciations* claimed, 'Pater really renders [Browne] for us, conveying to us the finest inflexions of his voice as if by some eclectic telephone'.[4] If Pater's essay is a technology which revives Browne's long-dead voice, then his sympathetic and emulative criticism performs its own quaint archaisms.

The passage also registers Browne's mixture of grandeur and bathos: his ability to generate *multum ex parvo*, to take the negligible or minute and derive from it sublimity, to spin from the uncovered urns both reams of erudite lore, and splendid passages of elegant writing on oblivion. Samuel Johnson wrote of Browne that 'it is a perpetual triumph of fancy to expand a scanty theme, to raise glittering ideas from obscure properties, and to produce to the world an object of wonder to which nature had contributed little'.[5] *The Garden of Cyrus*, the companion piece to *Hydriotaphia*, takes the quincunx (a pattern of five dots arrayed as a square with one in the middle), and makes it the leitmotif of God's creative energy discovered in nature. 'Quaintness' here marks the oxymoron of something at once triflingly oblique and monumental.

In the opening of 'Sir Thomas Browne', Pater makes it sound as if 'quaint' is a strange word, a foreign and archaic fossil lodged in the purer classical throat of the language. But this is the only place where he holds 'quaint' gingerly in the prophylactic tweezers of inverted commas; elsewhere, the word is unostentatiously a feature of his own critical vocabulary. Though Browne is the type of the quaint writer, it is a word which peppers *Appreciations*, *The Renaissance*, *Greek Studies*, and *Imaginary Portraits*, as well as the novels. Across Pater's work, it becomes possible to discern contours of the quaint and its siblings. It is collocated with antiquity and antiquarianism, oddity, heterogeneity, curiosity, conceits, the grotesque, remoteness, foreignness, barbarity, and the medieval. It appears differently in different media. In literature, in regard to content, it is antiquarianism, an interest in minute discriminations, and an erudite assembly of disparate material; in style, elaborate, recondite, or archaic vocabulary and syntax. In art, it is attention, or over-attention, to ornament and decoration, varying the texture of fabric or pavement or sward with repetitive patterns or floral motifs. It fetishises archaism. We hear, for example, that Sir Thomas More wrote a life of Pico della Mirandola in 'quaint, antiquated English' ('Pico della Mirandola', *Ren.*, 27). That near-anagram of 'quaint' and 'antiquated' stresses the sense the word always carries, in Pater, of historicity.

'Nothing', writes Grace Lavery in her recent study of *fin-de-siècle japonisme*, 'is quaint from the get-go; an object, text, body, or event acquires the quality of quaintness as it becomes historical—or, more precisely, as it *fails* to become historical'. The oddity of quaintness, for Lavery, is of something which has persisted beyond its time, which comes trailing its history into the present.[6] Pater shares this sense of quaintness as marking a temporal residue, but with a subtle difference. Pater's quaint is not a measure of how far a work differs in its aesthetic protocols and canons from his present, but a detection of a work's internal anachronisms and incongruities. Some things, contra Lavery, are quaint from the get-go, carrying within themselves a temporal differentiation of surplus historicity even before they have retreated into the past. This is obvious in Pater's comments on the archaisms of Coleridge's 'Rhyme of the Ancient Mariner'. It is not just overt pastiche, however, which Pater calls 'quaint'. As Uttara Natarajan remarks of the Lamb essay, 'Pater declares that Lamb endows the present itself with the quality of past-ness'.[7] Pater finds in Lamb an ability to see a future-perfect quaintness – what will have become quaint – in the present. Lamb, as Pater puts it, 'anticipates the enchantment of distance'. He preserves '[t]he quaint remarks of children which another would scarcely have heard' like 'little flies in the priceless amber of his Attic wit' ('Charles Lamb', *App.*, 115, 110). Like the urns of *Hydriotaphia*, Lamb's essays are a medium preserving quaint ephemera.

Modern discussions of quaintness account differently for this fossilised persistence of a previous era in the art of the present. Daniel Harris suggests that quaintness is what happens to the tools of work and forms of labour of prior periods when they have been technologically superseded, and are used aesthetically or ironically in the present: a typewriter deployed as an ornament; artificially distressed furniture; fashions for artisanally produced food and clothing.[8] This is not what Pater registers, however. While the opposite of Harris's quaintness is the modern, the consumerist, the new, the opposite of Pater's is the classical, the regular, the orderly: the timeless. In Pater's quaintness, it is not that the aesthetic object is appealing because obsolete, but that its appeal is troubling because it manifests historical inconcinnity, a persistence of superseded styles.

This is closer to Lavery, for whom '*quaint temporality*' is 'an aesthetic and elliptical feeling of historicalness' which at the same time refuses to conform to the 'more muscular historical explanations' of historicism; 'what finally defines the quaint', she writes, is 'its irretrievability by *any* major history'.[9] It is historical while refusing to be typical, maintaining its minor irrelevance. That Pater, too, is interested in the relation of the quaint to historicism is explicit in 'Two Early French Stories', where he addresses the appeal of the antique, and its relation to aesthetic anachronism. 'To say of an ancient literary composition that it has an antiquarian interest', he writes, 'often means that it has no distinct aesthetic interest for the reader of today'. This is not to say that it does not have its pleasures, but the appeal involves an anachronistic posture: 'Antiquarianism, by a purely historical effort, by putting its subject in perspective, and setting the reader in a certain point of view, from which what gave pleasure to the past is pleasurable for him also, may often add greatly to the charm we receive from ancient literature.' There is no point, however, unless there is 'real, direct, aesthetic charm in the thing itself': 'no merely antiquarian effort can ever give it an aesthetic value, or make it a proper subject of aesthetic criticism'. The critic takes pleasure in the attempt to 'define, and discriminate' this real charm from the 'borrowed interest' of antiquarianism (*Ren.*, 14–15).

'Quaint' then sits for Pater at a point of crisis, in that word's etymological sense. It marks a point of decision, where the critic determines between what is purely antiquarian, and what is of enduring and transcending aesthetic value. Sometimes, 'quaint' names the first pole of that opposition: those things which have historical charm but not beauty, which are merely curious. This critical sifting is clear in the Browne essay, which repeatedly attempts to separate Browne's beauties from 'what is circumstantial and peculiar' (126), the classical from the quaint. But Pater finds them perplexingly inextricable. Peculiarity and strangeness are not burned off in the flame of aesthetic criticism. When Pater writes that, in *Hydriotaphia*, 'a work really ample and grand' arises '[o]ut of an atmosphere of all-pervading oddity and quaintness', or that 'with all its quaintness we may well pronounce [it] classical', the initial sense is surprise and concession (156, 154). But the suspicion that oddity and quaintness are the materials *out of* which the grandeur emerges, that it is classic not despite but *with* quaintness, still lurks.

The essay on Botticelli in the *Renaissance* addresses this problem directly. For Pater, Botticelli's Venus typified his strange combination of 'classical subjects' with realism in depiction of the Italian landscape and its people. Pater is again attuned to stylistic anachronism: in the painting, 'the grotesque emblems of the middle age, and a landscape full of its peculiar feeling, and even its strange draperies, powdered all over in the Gothic manner with a quaint conceit of daisies, frame a figure that reminds you of the faultless nude studies of Ingres'. Pater strikes nearly every adjective in his repertoire of quaint collocations: grotesque, medieval, peculiar, strange, Gothic, conceited. What makes the quaintness remarkable is its anachronism: the jarring effect of its yoking with something classical, something recognisably of a different aesthetic order. Pater harps on the word. 'At first, perhaps', he writes, 'you are attracted only by a quaintness of design, . . . afterwards you may think that this quaintness must be incongruous with the subject'. Quaintness is attractive but inappropriate, and a mature aesthetic sense must surely reject it. But eventually, when 'you come to understand what imaginative colouring really is, ... you will find that quaint design of Botticelli's a more direct inlet into the Greek temper than the works of the Greeks themselves' ('Sandro Botticelli', *Ren.*, 45–6). If 'quaint' registers anachronism, here the usual temporal relation is reversed: rather than the uncanny or unexpected survival of the antique into the present, Botticelli manifests the spirit of Greek style more vividly than it was realised in the place or period for which it was named.

Pater's insistence on Botticelli's quaintness reflects one of the main resonances of the term in the late nineteenth century: its association with the Pre-Raphaelites, for whom Botticelli was a particular model. In David Masson's early critical assessment, published in the *British Quarterly Review* in 1852, a 'studied quaintness of thought, most frequently bearing the character of archaism, or an attempt after the antique' is the 'third peculiarity of the Pre-Raphaelite painters', after their disregard for established aesthetic canons and 'fondness for detail, and careful finish'.[10] The Pre-Raphaelites were thereafter so persistently linked with quaintness that Dante Gabriel Rossetti, in a letter of 2 August 1871 to fellow artist and poet William Bell Scott, bewailed the revival of 'that infernal word "quaint"'. 'I cannot see the faintest trace of this adjective in either of your etchings ... nor in the design of your mantelpiece', Rossetti consoled Scott, 'though I suppose ... it might be described as peculiar, if that is one meaning of the hellish "quaint"'.[11] Rossetti's oxymoron, applying the sulphuric terms 'infernal' and 'hellish' to the belittling 'quaint', indicates both his frustration with a term which does not seem to take its subject seriously, and quaintness's own typical incongruity.

Masson's 'attempt after' suggests that quaintness is an unsuccessful pastiche of the antique – the opposite of what Pater finds in Botticelli. This is not the only distinction in their use of the term. Although Masson introduces it as a 'peculiarity' of painters, he turns to the writing of the Pre-Raphaelites for examples. The desire to be true to nature, he argues, results in 'a kind of baldness of thought and expression, a return to the most primitive style of thinking and speaking; a preference ... for words of one syllable'. Masson's immediate example is Wordsworth – whom Pater only once, and glancingly, designates 'quaint', for his use of 'a certain quaint gaiety of metre' ('Wordsworth', *App.*, 58). Quaintness for Masson leads away from 'artificiality and rhodomontade', towards 'an affected simplicity often offensive to a manly taste'.[12] Neutral description tips into implicit critique: there is something juvenile and artificial about the quaint.

Though Pater frequently uses the phrase 'quaint simplicity', this is not what he finds in Browne, whom no one could accuse of being simple. Browne's quaintness is complexity, overwroughtness, involution. Nonetheless, Masson's discussion of the Pre-Raphaelites links with the roots of the vogue for quaint in nineteenth-century criticism. To object to 'quaint' as infernal and hellish seems an escalation of register. But it fits with what I will argue, later in this chapter, is the apotropaic role that 'quaint' has for some of Pater's contemporaries.

The Quaintness of Sir-Thomas-Browneness

Opening a review of a new edition of Thomas Browne in 1923, Virginia Woolf lamented its limited scope and its high price, despite the editors' claim of 'a great revival of interest in the work of Sir Thomas Browne'. 'But why fly in the face of facts?' she went on: 'Few people love the writings of Sir Thomas Browne, but those who do are of the salt of the earth.'[13] Woolf's suggestion of coterie connoisseurship sits with Pater's remarks on historicism in 'Two Early French Stories'. A passion for Browne, Woolf implies, is at once a minority interest, and a litmus of cultivated taste.

Though feted and fashionable in his lifetime, and much imitated, by Browne's death in 1682 he had already been consigned to an earlier age. As Pater suggests, the emergence of the classical formalities of Dryden, and the plain style of Locke, Hobbes, and the Royal Society, rendered Browne's orotundities characteristic of the religious and political strife of the earlier part of the century, cancelled and made obsolete by the Restoration. During the eighteenth century, with one notable exception, he was neglected.

The first revival of Browne's reputation came with the enthusiasm of Coleridge and Lamb. In William Hazlitt's essay 'Of Persons One Would Wish to have Seen' (1826), Lamb names Browne and Fulke Greville as 'the two worthies whom he should feel the greatest pleasure to encounter on the floor of his apartment in their nightgowns and slippers'. Lamb chose Browne and Greville because, as Hazlitt records, 'their writings are riddles, and they themselves the most mysterious of personages'; reading the 'obscure but gorgeous' *Urne-Buriall* is like looking into 'a deep abyss, at the bottom of which are hid pearls and rich treasure; or it is like a stately labyrinth of doubt and withering speculation'.[14] Coleridge's response to Browne emerges in entertaining marginalia and in a letter written to Sara Hutchinson in a fly-leaf of Browne's *Works* on 10 March 1804, later printed in *Blackwood's Magazine*, which begins 'Sir Thomas Brown is among my first Favorites'. Browne is, Coleridge writes,

> Rich in various knowledge; exuberant in conceptions and conceits, contemplative, imaginative, often truly great and magnificent in his style and diction, tho' doubtless too often big, stiff, and hyperlatinistic .... Fond of the Curious, & a Hunter of Oddities and Strangenesses, while he conceives himself with quaint & humorous Gravity a useful enquirer into physical Truth ...[15]

Both Lamb and Coleridge found in Browne not only anachronistic appeal, but a model for prose which could embrace at once curiosity and metaphysics: an endorsement for the involutions of *Biographia Literaria*, or for the essays of Elia, steeped in the humours of Jacobean and Caroline literature. For Hazlitt, Lamb was 'the only imitator of old English style [he] can read with pleasure', because his 'inward unction, a marrowy vein, both in the thought and feeling ... carries off any quaintness or awkwardness arising from an antiquated style and dress'.[16] If others pastiche the 'old English style', Hazlitt suggests, Lamb revivifies it in his person; like Botticelli's 'inlet' into the 'Greek temper', this is not anachronistic reiteration, but reanimation.

   That the sequence of essays in *Appreciations* runs 'Style', 'Wordsworth', 'Coleridge', 'Charles Lamb', 'Sir Thomas Browne' shows that Pater recognises and pursues this affinity. He depicts Coleridge and Lamb both as interested in the quaint, and as practitioners of it. Pater notes Coleridge's reading in sixteenth- and seventeenth-century literature – 'the old-fashioned literature of the marvellous' – and points to his own 'quaint conceits' ('Coleridge', *App.*, 96, 95; see also 99); similarly, Lamb is described relishing the 'quaint, dimmed' literature of the Jacobean period, while exhibiting his own 'quiet, ... quaintness, ... humour' ('Charles Lamb', *App.*, 115, 121). Pater remarks on Lamb's 'fine mimicry' of Browne's *Pseudodoxia Epidemica* in the late Elia essays on 'Popular Fallacies'. Such imitation, he writes, shows Lamb's 'mastery ... of those elements of [Browne] which were the real source of style in that great, solemn master of old English, who, ready to say what he has to say with fearless homeliness, yet continually overawes one with touches of a strange utterance from worlds afar' (113). The incongruous mingling of the strange and familiar is legible in Hazlitt's image of Browne in his slippers, admitting Lamb to labyrinths and abysses. This is characteristic of the uncanny: the jarring effect of incompatible frames presented simultaneously, 'all ... so oddly mixed' ('Sir Thomas Browne', *App.*, 126).

In 1835–6, Simon Wilkin published a four-volume edition of Browne's works, which laid the foundation for subsequent nineteenth-century encounters with Browne and was reprinted in 1852 and 1884. It was read in America, and influenced Hawthorne, Emerson, and Thoreau, as well as Melville, who called Browne a 'crack'd Archangel' and wrote, in *Mardi*, 'Be Sir Thomas Brown our ensample'.[17] Wilkin's edition – titled *Sir Thomas Browne's Works: Including His Life and Correspondence* – provides compendious supporting material, including Coleridge's remarks on Browne and Johnson's 'Life of Sir Thomas Browne'. The lending records at Brasenose College Library show that Pater borrowed a copy of *Religio Medici* from 27 August to 16 October 1871; and, from 28 February to 20 May 1883, the first volume of Wilkin's *Works*. In the same period, he began reading more widely in criticism on Browne, resulting, in 1886, in the first publication of the Browne essay.[18]

Pater's initial reading of *Religio Medici* in 1871 may have been prompted by the first publication of Leslie Stephen's essay 'Sir Thomas Browne' in that year in the *Cornhill Magazine*. Stephen's long assessment is a cabinet of curiosities, curating the oddest of Browne's many oddities. Stephen takes it upon himself to exhibit 'the strange furniture of [Browne's] mind', providing a guide to his 'queer museum' – a space in which Pater too locates Browne, to whom, he claims, 'the whole world is a museum' (134).[19] Stephen describes Browne compulsively as 'quaint': he remarks his 'quaint pages', 'quaint apologue', 'his usual quaint and eloquent melancholy', his 'quaint train of reflections'. Browne 'asks, not whether a dogma is true, but whether it is imposing or quaint'. In *Pseudodoxia Epidemica*, Browne is interested only in the 'quaintness of the objects unearthed'. His wide-ranging erudition reflects an 'omnivorous appetite for every quaint or significant symbol to be discovered in the whole field of learning'.[20]

Stephen's quaint blizzard – these examples are not exhaustive – makes clear that Pater was not alone. Indeed, it suggests that Pater's inverted commas around 'quaint' might register not unease with the word, but an ironic recognition of its predictability. Certainly 'quaint' was in fashion: the admittedly fallible guide of Google n-grams shows a significant peak in usage around 1900, and the 1890s show a rash of books with the word in the title: to take examples from 1895 and 1896 only, *Quaint Epitaphs*; *Quaint Korea*; *Quick Truths in Quaint Texts*; *Dundee: Its Quaint and Historic Buildings* (all 1895); *Quaint Nantucket*; *Quaint Crippen* (both 1896) – et cetera. 'Quaint' was also used to describe ornamented Arts and Crafts and Art Nouveau objects.[21] But while Stephen's use is an unstudied reaction to Browne's curiosity, there is something more complex at work in Pater: something which sees in 'quaint' not just old-fashionedness, but a register of anachronicity, a residue of historical style out of its time, or temporal differentiation within a work of art.

It may have been the sense that 'quaint' was a period term of the 1890s which led to a rejection of it in twentieth-century discussions of Browne. In *The Seventeenth-Century Background*, Basil Willey claimed that it was 'a romantic falsification to "relish" Browne for his "quaintness"'. Instead, he wrote, '[i]t is more valuable ... to try to recover something of his own inclusiveness, in virtue of which his juxtapositions are *not* quaint, but symbols of his complex vision'.[22] Joan Bennett, meanwhile, taking Stephen and Pater to task, asserted that '[i]n his own time [Browne's] style was not in any sense quaint although it was from the first individual'.[23] But while Willey and Bennett had work to do to recuperate Browne's reputation from the belittling implications of the 'infernal word', their rejection misses Pater's grasp of the power in quaintness. In most other critical usages, 'quaint' attempts to diminish the power with which things come back from the past and to relegate them safely to it. It wards off strangeness and peculiarity, and defangs and belittles what it identifies. Lavery notes that quaintness can be read as 'an emptied out remnant of what once might have been "charm"—quaintness as a low-intensity aesthetic fondness, enabled and finally marred by its reassuring historical irrelevance'.[24] It is striking how frequently Pater uses the word 'charm' in close proximity to 'quaint', since 'charm', too, has undergone a semantic diminution: a slip from bewitchery and enchantment to mere appeal.[25] 'Charm' and 'quaint' work along the same axis from potentially destabilising power to mere fancy. To apply them to a literary work usually suggests they take the frightening power of the uncanny and render it safe. But Pater's sense of quaintness retains the power.

Heterogeneous Composition

One of the works which Wilkin printed alongside Browne was Johnson's 'Life', first published in 1756 as a preface to an edition of *Christian Morals*. Johnson interspersed a chronological account of Browne's life and works with acute criticism of his style, on which he writes: 'it is vigorous, but rugged: it is learned, but pedantick; it is deep, but obscure; it strikes, but does not please; it commands, but does not allure: his tropes are harsh, and his combinations uncouth'.[26] Johnson's rhythmically repetitive phrases of qualification, praising only to retract, are typical of criticism of Browne in its ambivalence and mistrust – the sense that Browne's powers cannot be wholeheartedly assented to. Johnson, predictably, finds Browne 'curious'; 'quaint', however, appears nowhere.

Pater evidently read Johnson's life, possibly in the Wilkin edition, and referred to it repeatedly in 'Sir Thomas Browne'. Pater writes of Browne's Norwich home, which 'must have grown, through long years of acquisition, into an odd cabinet of antiquities'. This is analogous to his books, Pater suggests: 'The very faults of his literary work, its desultoriness, the time it costs his readers, that slow Latinity which Johnson imitated from him, those lengthy leisurely terminations which busy posterity will abbreviate, all breathe of the long quiet of the place' (133–4). It is not only Johnson who is imitative here. Pater's sentence enacts the slumberous dilation of which he convicts Browne's prose: the four parenthetical examples of fault interpose before the verb 'breathe' to suspend the sentence's sense; despite the ostensible lack of patience for the sesquipedal polysyllables that are Browne's medium and forte, Latinity suffuses the subsequent clause in the terminations which posterity will abbreviate. Again, Pater detects a 'fault' in Browne which turns out to give pleasure.

There is another telling Johnsonian influence in Pater's essay. Johnson characterised Browne's style as 'a tissue of many languages; a mixture of heterogeneous words, brought together from distant regions, with terms originally appropriated to one art, and drawn by violence into the service of another'.[27] In his life of Abraham Cowley, Johnson reworked the terms he used for Browne, and made them stand for a whole seventeenth-century mode. Johnson's account of Cowley's style again rests on ambivalence: acknowledging its wit, eloquence, and intellectual power, but also discomfort at oddity and incongruity. This inconcinnity of force of thought and naturalness of expression Johnson took as characteristic of the age. The famous passage begins 'About the beginning of the seventeenth century appeared a race of writers that may be termed the metaphysical poets'. Such writers are characterised by their tendency to

> a kind of *discordia concors*; a combination of dissimilar images, or discovery of occult resemblances in things apparently unlike. ... The most heterogeneous ideas are yoked by violence together; nature and art are ransacked for illustrations, comparisons, and allusions; their learning instructs, and their subtilty surprises; but the reader commonly thinks his improvement dearly bought, and though he sometimes admires is seldom pleased.[28]

Pater almost certainly knew this passage: he knew Johnson well, and wrote an unfinished study on him which has been lost.[29] Its traces are detectable in Pater's remarks that the Walsingham urns, for Browne, 'resuscitated . . .

a whole world of latent observation, from life, from out-of-the-way read-ing, from the natural world, and fused into a composition, which with all its quaintness we may well pronounce classical, all the heterogeneous elements of that singular mind' (154). Cowley's ransacking of nature and art is reiterated in Pater's observation of Browne's disparate sources. That Johnsonian word 'heterogeneous' draws Browne, and quaintness, into the ambit of the metaphysical.

'Quaint' and 'metaphysical' both mark the appeal and discomfort of heterogeneous fusion. Stephen finds in Browne 'a strangely vivid humour that is always detecting the quaintest analogies; and, as it were, striking light from the most unexpected collocations of uncompromising mate-rials' – making 'quaint' the measure of the distance between the terms of an analogy, the width of the hinge of the metaphysical conceit – while his daughter Virginia Woolf, recalling Johnson, notes Browne's 'power of bringing the remote and incongruous astonishingly together'.[30] All of this associates Browne with what has been called the 'metaphysical revival' of the late nineteenth century, and allies his changing reputation to that of John Donne.[31] Like Browne, Donne was much read and imitated in the seventeenth century, until taste turned against him at the Restoration. Dryden chided him in 1693 for 'affect[ing] the Metaphysicks ... in his amorous verses, where nature only shou'd reign; and perplex[ing] the Minds of the Fair Sex with nice Speculations of Philosophy'.[32] The sin is metaphysical incongruity. The rescue of Donne's reputation from eclipse was, like Browne's, begun by Coleridge, and, with his 'metaphys-ical' contemporaries, accelerated between 1880 and 1910.[33] The first anthology of metaphysical poetry, Herbert Grierson's *Metaphysical Lyrics and Poems of the Seventeenth Century*, was published in 1921; a review by T.S. Eliot in the *Times Literary Supplement* canonised the term.

In the Winckelmann essay, Pater suggests, with reluctance, that 'a taste for metaphysics may be one of those things which we must renounce, if we mean to mould our lives to artistic perfection' (*Ren.*, 183). But everywhere the yen for metaphysics persists. Pater recognises it in Coleridge, who encountered a living metaphysical tradition in Germany – 'What an opportunity for one reared on the colourless analytic English philosophies of the last century, but who feels an irresistible attraction towards bold metaphysical synthesis!' ('Coleridge', *App.*, 74). In his review of Grierson, Eliot lamented that 'metaphysical' had for too long been 'the label of a quaint and pleasant taste': that sense of a coterie historicism and antiquar-ianism which Woolf saw typified in lovers of Browne, and Pater criticised as lacking aesthetic value. Eliot's review, and the general 'metaphysical

revival', invites us to consider quaint and metaphysical style under a
different rubric – as the last exemplification of a poetic sensibility which
is 'constantly amalgamating disparate experience', fusing heterogeneity
'into a composition'. 'In the seventeenth century', Eliot famously wrote
in his review, 'a dissociation of sensibility set in, from which we have never
recovered'; an effect produced in poetry by the baleful influence of Milton
and Dryden. Before 1660 it was still possible to fuse sensuousness and
metaphysics. Grierson's anthology offers Eliot the opportunity to rescue
the quaintness of metaphysics from belittling critics, and to make the
metaphysical poets forebears of the difficult poetry he champions – and
writes. They have, he writes, 'been enough praised in terms which are
implicit limitations because they are "metaphysical" or "witty," "quaint" or
"obscure"'; it is time, instead, to take them seriously.[34] Like Willey and
Bennett, Eliot feels the faint praise of 'quaint', and reasserts the style's
intellectual claims.

Metaphysical Browne

Browne's fortunes in the later nineteenth and early twentieth century are
implicated in this 'metaphysical revival': a revaluation of the 'difficult' and
conceited literature of the seventeenth century, 'the Stuart age revenant in
the present'.[35] Browne himself is referred to as 'metaphysical', and associated with the conceits which are the badge of the style – Pater refers to 'the
strange "conceit" of his nature' (130). Though Eliot demotes the period's
prose below his praise for the poetry (from which he would later exempt
the sermons of Lancelot Andrewes), the same claims may be made on its
behalf. Pater's ambivalent quaintness is the prehistory of this recuperation.

I want to suggest that there is more here; that there is a *particular*
uncomfortable anachronism and style which 'quaint', like 'metaphysical',
works to name without summoning it directly, and which is for historical
reasons difficult to assimilate or metabolise within English canons of taste.
The connection is clear in Masson's essay on the Pre-Raphaelite brotherhood. His discussion of the quaint simplicity of Rossetti's poetry slips to
'the same tendency to quaintness and archaism' in those Pre-Raphaelites
who were 'guiltless of the use of the pen', who exhibit quaintness in their
sympathy with 'the peculiarities of mediæval ecclesiastical art'. This
Masson exemplifies by quoting at length from Ruskin, who judges that
if the Pre-Raphaelites paint with 'the earnestness of the men of the
thirteenth and fourteenth centuries', they will succeed; if, however, 'their
sympathies with the early artists lead them into mediævalism or

Romanism, they will of course come to nothing'. 'There may be some weak ones', Ruskin continues, 'whom the Tractarian heresies may touch; but if so, they will drop off like decayed branches from a strong stem'. Masson takes up this worry, noting that 'Mr. Collins' is the only one of the brotherhood 'in whom this tendency takes so pronounced a form as to indicate what would be called a leaning to Puseyism'; worse: 'one or two of the original Pre-Raphaelites have gone farther in this direction than he, and actually fulfilled Mr. Ruskin's prediction, by laying their Pre-Raphaelitism at the feet of the ancient mother-church'.[36] Quaintness, in other words, is a gateway to Rome.

Browne's earliest readers worried about his closeness to Catholicism. *Religio Medici*, published in 1642, was a young man's statement of faith, in which Browne, while asserting his adherence to the English church, also insisted on tolerance, abjuring controversy and expressing his eirenic attraction to various Romanist practices. This instantly raised his contemporaries' suspicions. A Parisian Latin edition, published in 1645, claimed that Browne was a Roman Catholic, only kept from admitting so by repression in England. The cantankerous Scottish scholar and controversialist Alexander Ross joked that Browne's religion 'may be indeed *religio Medici*, the religion of the House of *Medicis*, not of the Church of England'.[37]

What was alarming for some of Browne's contemporaries, however, made him attractive in the late nineteenth century, as debates over English churchmanship were again in spate. This, Tracy Seeley argues, is the basis of the 'metaphysical revival': the topical salience of writers in the thick of Reformation controversy, negotiating inherited styles and their theological implications. W.A. Greenhill, who published a selection of Browne's works in 1881, just before Pater began working on his essay, was a friend of Newman's. Seeley argues that the 'critical language' of *fin-de-siècle* converts 'resonates with the Catholic incarnational world view: the metaphysical conceit conjoins, as the divine incarnation conjoins, spirit and flesh'.[38] The fusion of the heterogeneous so threatening to Johnson becomes, in this light, a reassociation of sensibility through conversion to Roman Catholicism.

Though it is rare to see the connection made so directly, the frequent association of the 'quaint' with the medieval brings the word into the ambit of Catholicism; more precisely, it reiterates a way of characterising difficulty, ornament, and obscurity as either suspiciously or attractively crypto-Catholic which emerged in the seventeenth century. Pater's references to quaintness in *The Renaissance* cluster around traces of superseded medieval religion, liturgy, and architecture. Pater refers to the 'quaint Latin of the middle age' ('Two Early French Stories', *Ren.*, 4). It is 'in the Gothic manner' that Botticelli sprinkles his draperies with 'a quaint conceit of daisies' ('Sandro Botticelli', *Ren.*, 45). The 'character of medieval art' expresses itself 'as a subdued quaintness or grotesque' in Michelangelo's poetry ('The Poetry of Michelangelo', *Ren.*, 57). The essay on 'Joachim du Bellay' sees 'the old Gothic manner' persist even 'when the spirit of the Renaissance was everywhere, and people had begun to look back with distaste on the works of the middle age'; one example is the 'quaint, remote learning' of Ronsard (*Ren.*, 123, 133). *The Renaissance* is especially interested in the persistence of these Gothic, medieval, grotesque energies beyond their own time.

That Browne's style evokes earlier religious institutions is clear in critical metaphor. Reading Browne, Woolf suggests, '[i]t is as if from the street we stepped into a cathedral where the organ goes plunging and soaring and indulging in vast and elephantine gambols of awful yet grotesque sublimity'.[39] This picks up a simile used by her father: for Stephen, 'Sir Thomas's witticisms are like the grotesque carvings in a Gothic cathedral'. He suggests that Browne's 'imagination everywhere diffuses a solemn light such as that which falls through painted windows'; this light 'harmonises the whole quaint assemblage of images. The sacred is made more interesting instead of being degraded by its association with the quaint'. This reconciles Reformation breach: 'painted windows' restore the stained glass smashed by iconoclasts. More: 'a page of Sir Thomas seems to revive the echoes as of ancient chants in college chapels, strangely blended with the sonorous perorations of professors in the neighbouring schools, so that the interferences sometimes produce a note of gentle mockery and sometimes heighten solemnity by quaintness'.[40] Browne, for Stephen, revives the bare ruined choirs where once the sweet birds sang.

Stephen's reference to the schools takes quaintness into the realm of the pedagogy and philosophy with which 'metaphysical' is associated. Metaphysics was identified with scholasticism: with styles of education and philosophy which descended from Aristotle and St Thomas Aquinas, and bolstered the sacramental theology of the Roman Catholic church. Such 'dialectical quaint subtilties', according to Reformers, mired writing in riddling quibbles.[41] But quaint subtlety has its charms, and despite attempts by later English stylists to reject what Milton called 'metaphysical gargarisms', it is for and not despite hyperlatinity and riddling complexities that Browne's style is relished.[42] Pater himself observes his 'difficulty and halting crabbedness of expression' (155). In 'Style', such involutions are suggestively described: great style, he suggests, requires pliancy to 'the inherent perplexities and recusancy of a certain difficult thought' (*App.*, 32). 'Perplex' was Dryden's word for Donne's metaphysical style, and 'recusancy' the technical early modern term for the refusal of Catholics to adhere to the English church.

Browne appears explicitly only once in 'Style', used in the first paragraph as an example, alongside Plato and Michelet, of 'mystical and intimate' style (6). But his influence can be detected elsewhere. Pater famously writes of the 'literary artist': 'Racy Saxon monosyllables, close to us as touch and sight, he will intermix readily with those long, savoursome Latin words, rich in "second intention"' (16). This is, as usual, mimetic, turning from the speedy single-syllable trochaic phrase 'close to us as touch and sight' to the long vowels and languor of 'savoursome' – a word which itself yokes the ultimately Latinate 'savour' with the Germanic ending '-some'. It also recalls the tone of Browne's most recognisably 'metaphysical' passages. In *Religio Medici*, for example, he discusses the nature of God's existence: 'he onely is, all others have an existence with dependency and are something but by a distinction; ... God being all things is contrary unto nothing out of which were made all things, and so nothing became something, and *Omneity* informed *Nullity* into an essence'.[43] Stanley Fish called this passage 'bastard scholasticism'.[44] Though meant as criticism, this gets at something Pater likewise recognises. Browne alternates between articulating the same idea in simple 'Saxon' phrases ('he onely is'), and Latinate metaphysical terms of art ('dependency', 'distinction', '*Omneity*', '*Nullity*'). The monosyllabic phrase 'out of which were made all things' has exactly the stress of Pater's 'close to us as touch and sight', and achieves the same effect of contrast between simple rhythmic alternation and the syncopation of the nearby polysyllabic Latinities.

The term 'second intention', as Angela Leighton has pointed out, is used in logic 'to mean a concept of reason rather than of sense perception' – precisely the kind of metaphysical abstraction from the 'touch and sight' of experience which writers of the later seventeenth century mistrusted, and which led to the obsolescence of the Brownean style. Pater reverses this polarity, as Leighton observes, preferring – or at least relishing – the secondary.[45] The metaphysical concept and style ends up savoured, favoured.

Pater is explicit about this, identifying 'a kind of poetry of scholasticism' in Browne ('Sir Thomas Browne', *App.*, 147). When Willey chides early critics for the 'romantic falsification' of relishing Browne's quaintness, it is in order to appreciate something else: he claimed that Donne and Browne shared a fusion of thought, experience, and sensibility, which they 'owe . . . to the scholastic tradition'.[46] Pater's quaintness, however, recognises precisely this debt; the peculiar qualities of English seventeenth-century writing which are 'scholastic', associated with forms of religion and literary education which would later be rejected, and which have remained embarrassing, threatening, or mysteriously beguiling ever since.

Conclusion

Browne makes a brief incognito appearance in Pater's 'Sebastian van Storck'. The imaginary portrait, set unspecifically in the Dutch Golden Age, describes an incident in which an unusually low tide on the coast reveals 'some remarkable relics': a preserved 'chariot of state'. To 'antiquarians' this is an accident, an ancient chief overwhelmed in a storm; to Sebastian's temperament, however, 'this object was sepulchral . . . the one surviving relic of a grand burial'. Pater then quotes a phrase from Browne, '*Sunt metis metæ!*', not from *Hydriotaphia*, but from a shorter essay-letter 'Of Artificial Hills, Mounts, or Burrows' (*IP*, 93–4; *CW*, iii. 103).[47] Browne's fascination with the uncanny preservation of the artefacts of the past, with antiquarian pleasure and the melancholy contemplation of oblivion it bequeaths, is here deployed to characterise Sebastian.

The ambivalent word 'relics' imports traces of Roman Catholic practice, secularised into a style and mental attitude – just as 'recusancy', 'metaphysical', 'Gothic', or 'quaint' suggest without emphasis associations with modes of religious institution. As Lene Østermark-Johansen remarks, 'Sebastian von Storck' is in part a transposed portrait of Browne. It is therefore significant that Sebastian is described as 'not altogether a Hollander': 'His mother, of Spanish descent and Catholic, had given a richness of tone and form to the healthy freshness of the Dutch physiognomy' (*IP*, 82; *CW*, iii. 97). In Sebastian, as in Browne, the influences of the Catholic south and the Reformed north, of hyperlatinity and racy Saxon monosyllable, mingle, the disparate influences of the 'great theological strife' fusing in a single figure.

It is important, however, that while Sebastian is '[a]live to that theological disturbance in the air all around him', it is not in itself important:

> he refused to be moved by it, as essentially a strife on small matters, anticipating a vagrant regret which may have visited many other minds

since, the regret, namely, that the old, pensive, . . . Catholicism, which had
accompanied the nation's earlier struggle for existence, and consoled it
therein, had been taken from it. (*IP*, 97–8; *CW*, iii. 105)[48]

In associating the 'quaintness' that Pater finds in Browne with
Catholicism, I have not meant to suggest actual confessional allegiance,
either on Browne's part or Pater's. Instead, the taste for the quaint and
metaphysical expresses that vagrant regret, which salvages the relics of
the obsolete, transposed from sacramental efficacy or theological commitment, into style – perplexity and recusancy, the savoursome syllables
of latinity, the charm of the strange, grotesque relic revivified in the
present.

   But it is not only that. If quaintness can subside into nostalgia, the
merely curious or charmingly old-fashioned, for Pater, at its best – in
Lamb, Browne, Botticelli – it marks heterogeneous fusion, successful
composition, unifying the fractured and dissociated inheritances of varied aesthetic impetus, overcoming the anachronisms of periodisation. If
Johnson objected to the 'violence' with which disparate ideas are yoked
together, Pater suggests they can be 'fused into a composition, which
with all its quaintness we may well pronounce classical' – a fusion which
does not dissolve the oddity of quaintness, but instead acknowledges it
part of aesthetic success. In the 'Postscript' to *Appreciations*, Pater turns
to the 'old opposition' between the classical and romantic in European
style, and suggests that the best art couples the curious, peculiar energies
of romanticism with classical beauty. 'If there is a great overbalance of
curiosity', he writes, 'we have the grotesque in art: if the union of
strangeness and beauty, under very difficult and complex conditions, be
a successful one, if the union be entire, then the resultant beauty is very
exquisite, very attractive' (243, 247). The 'Postscript' can seem an
incongruous capstone to *Appreciations*, turning from the largely English
concerns of the earlier essays into critical generalisation, and European
literature. But in the studies of Lamb and Browne, the large question of
the 'union of strangeness and beauty' has a peculiarly English expression.
How to account for the strain of 'quaintness', metaphysicality, oddity of
which Browne is the type, and its persistent recurrence in English
literature? If some critics tend to reject quaintness as a foreign importa-
tion into a clear, unadorned, simple English style, then Pater encourages
us to see it as integral to the literature's history. It is precisely in
ambivalent incongruity, its yoking of the verbally and intellectually
heterogeneous, that its charm lies.

Notes

1 Parenthetical addition is a Paterian habit; Edmund Gosse reported that he wrote on alternate lines of lined paper, to leave room for 'fresh descriptive or parenthetical clauses' (quoted by Angela Leighton, 'Walter Pater's Dream Rhythms', in *Thinking Through Style*, ed. Michael Hurley and Marcus Waithe (Oxford 2018), 218–30 (220)). Parentheses abstracted by lunulae rather than commas or dashes are infrequent, however.

2 The substantive sense of 'quaint' as female genitals is first found in 1330; the *OED* speculates that this is a euphemistic substitution. See *OED s.v.* quaint, *n*.

3 *OED s.v.* quaint, *adj.*, A.III.9a. The two other modern senses are 'characterized or marked by cleverness, ingenuity, or cunning' – now '*rare* and *archaic*' (A.I.2); 'strange, unusual, unfamiliar', a regional sense confined to northern England (A.III.8).

4 William Watson, review of *App.*, *Academy* 36 (21 December 1889), 399–400, repr. in *Critical Heritage*, 205–9 (207).

5 Samuel Johnson, 'The Life of Sir Thomas Browne', in *The Yale Edition of the Works of Samuel Johnson*, ed. Robert DeMaria Jr. et al., 22 vols (New Haven and London) xix, *Biographical Writings*, ed. O.M. Brack Jr. and Robert DeMaria Jr (2016), 306–41 (320).

6 Grace Lavery, *Quaint, Exquisite: Victorian Aesthetics and the Idea of Japan* (Princeton 2019), xii.

7 Uttara Natarajan, 'The Spirit of His Age: Hazlitt and Pater on Lamb', *Nineteenth-Century Literature* 66 (2012), 449–65 (461).

8 Daniel Harris, 'Quaintness', in *Cute, Quaint, Hungry, and Romantic: The Aesthetics of Consumerism* (New York 2000), 23–50. This differs significantly from the nineteenth-century 'craft revival' – on which see Marcus Waithe, *The Work of Words: Literature, Craft, and the Labour of Mind in Britain, 1830–1940* (Edinburgh 2023), 4–5 and *passim*.

9 Lavery, *Quaint, Exquisite*, 22, xii.

10 David Masson, 'Pre-Raphaelitism in Art and Literature', *British Quarterly Review* 16 (1852), 197–22 (205).

11 Dante Gabriel Rossetti to William Bell Scott, 2 August 1871, in *The Correspondence of Dante Gabriel Rossetti*, vol. 5, ed. William E. Fredeman (Cambridge 2005), 94. I am grateful to Elizabeth Prettejohn for alerting me to this letter, and for noting the telling fact that Pater's own essay on Rossetti nowhere uses the word 'quaint'.

12 Masson, 'Pre-Raphaelitism', 206; on quaintness and queerness, see Lavery, *Quaint, Exquisite*, xii, 39.

13 Virginia Woolf, 'Sir Thomas Browne', *Times Literary Supplement* 1119 (28 June 1923), 436.

14 William Hazlitt, 'Of Persons One Would Wish to Have Seen', in *The Complete Works of William Hazlitt*, ed. P.P. Howe, xviii (1933), 122–34 (123–4).

15 Samuel Taylor Coleridge, *Collected Works*, ed. Kathleen Coburn, 16 vols (Princeton), xii. i, *Marginalia I*, ed. George Whalley (1980), 762–3. This is edited from the manuscript, not the printed version; I have not retained the preserved deletions.

16 William Hazlitt, 'On Familiar Style', *The Selected Writings of William Hazlitt*, ed. Duncan Wu, 9 vols, vi, *Table-Talk* (1998), 217–22 (219).

17 See Brian Foley, 'Herman Melville and the Example of Sir Thomas Browne', *Modern Philology* 81 (1984), 265–77, esp. 265, 266. See also David C. Cody, '"Of Oddities and Strangenesses": Hawthorne's Debt to Sir Thomas Browne', *Nathaniel Hawthorne Review* 14 (1988), 10–14.

18 Christian William Willerton, 'A Study of Walter Pater's *Appreciations*', unpublished PhD thesis, University of North Carolina, Chapel Hill, 1979, 141–2.

19 Leslie Stephen, 'Sir Thomas Browne', *Hours in a Library (Second Series)* [1876] (repr. Cambridge 2012), 1–43 (10).

20 Stephen, 'Sir Thomas Browne', 4, 5, 12, 34–5, 5, 21, 6, 40.

21 See *OED s.v.* quaint, *adj., adv., n.*, III.9.b.

22 Basil Willey, *The Seventeenth Century Background* [1934] (reissue 1972), 48.

23 Joan Bennett, 'A Note on *Religio Medici* and Some of Its Critics', *Studies in the Renaissance* 3 (1956), 175–84 (175).

24 Lavery, *Quaint, Exquisite*, 23.

25 On this slippage, see Adrian Poole, 'Henry James and Charm', *Essays in Criticism* 61 (2011), 115–36; Ros Ballaster, 'Heart-Easing Mirth: Charm in the Eighteenth Century', *Essays in Criticism* 63 (2013), 249–74.

26 Johnson, 'Life of Sir Thomas Browne', 337.

27 Johnson, 'Life of Sir Thomas Browne', 338.

28 Samuel Johnson, 'Cowley', in *The Lives of the Poets*, vol. 1, ed. John H. Middendorf (New Haven 2010), 5–84 (23, 25–6).

29 See Samuel Wright, *A Bibliography of the Works of Walter Pater* (Folkestone 1975), 139, 142. I am grateful to Lene Østermark-Johansen for supplying me with this reference and information.

30 Stephen, 'Sir Thomas Browne', 2; Woolf, 'Sir Thomas Browne'.

31 See Tracy Seeley, '"The Sun Shines on a World Re-Arisen to Pleasure": The Fin-de-Siècle Metaphysical Revival', *Literature Compass* 3 (2006), 195–217.

32 John Dryden, 'A Discourse concerning the Original and Progress of Satire', in *The Works of John Dryden*, ed. E.N. Hooker, H.T. Swedenberg Jr., et al., 20 vols (Berkeley, Los Angeles, CA, London) iv, ed. A.B. Chambers and William Frost (1974), 7.

33 See Seeley, 'The Sun Shines', 195–6. Murray Pittock tabulates editions of fourteen seventeenth-century writers from 1800 to 1933; Browne – the only prose writer – received seven editions between 1800 and 1879, thirteen between 1880 and 1910, and thirteen between 1910 and 1933. This outstrips all other tabulated writers except Herbert and Herrick; unaccountably, Donne was excluded. See Pittock, *Spectrum of Decadence: The Literature of the 1890s* (1993), 91.

34 T.S. Eliot, 'The Metaphysical Poets', *Times Literary Supplement* 1031 (20 October 1921), 669–70.
35 Pittock, *Spectrum of Decadence*, 93.
36 Masson, 'Pre-Raphaelitism', 208, 209, quoting Ruskin's *Pre-Raphaelitism*.
37 Alexander Ross, *Medicus medicatus* (1645), 2. On Browne's early reception, see Kathryn Murphy, 'The Best Pillar of the Order of Sir Francis: Thomas Browne, Samuel Hartlib, and Communities of Learning', in *'A man very well studyed': New Contexts for Thomas Browne*, ed. Kathryn Murphy and Richard Todd (Leiden 2008), 273–92.
38 Seeley, 'The Sun Shines', 212.
39 Woolf, 'Sir Thomas Browne'.
40 Stephen, 'Sir Thomas Browne', 27, 30, 41.
41 Quotation from Erasmus, *Praise of Folly*, trans. Challoner (1577), sig. Cvi^v.
42 John Milton, *The Reason of Church-Government* (1642), 62.
43 Thomas Browne, *Religio Medici and Other Works*, ed. L.C. Martin (Oxford 1964), 34–5.
44 Stanley E. Fish, *Self-Consuming Artifacts: The Experience of Seventeenth-Century Literature* (Berkeley 1974), 355.
45 Leighton, 'Walter Pater's Dream Rhythms', 219.
46 Willey, *Seventeenth-Century Background*, 47.
47 'Meta' means a pyramid or obelisk used as a boundary marker. The phrase could be understood as 'there are monuments to monuments', or 'monuments have their own limits'. Shortly afterwards Pater quotes *Religio Medici*, on the 'thriving ... genius' of the Dutch. See Lene Østermark-Johansen's notes *ad loc.*, *CW*, iii. 270–1.
48 Cf. 'The Poetry of Michelangelo', *Ren.*, 70–1.

CHAPTER 10

'Spiritual Form': Walter Pater's Encounters with William Blake

Luisa Calè

The relationship between the arts was central to Walter Pater's literary criticism. In the works of the painter-poets William Blake and Dante Gabriel Rossetti, Pater found an ideal corpus for thinking about form through visual analogies. However, while Rossetti plays a significant role in *Appreciations* (1889), Blake is a subterranean presence. Although Pater never devoted a whole essay to Blake, his name surfaces in discussions about form and style, image and meaning, and soul and mind. Artistic examples and analogies shape a comparative and complementary understanding of literature and art through exercises in appreciation and inter-artistic lines of cultural influence.

Pater made a significant number of references to Blake between 1871 and 1889, at a time when 'this no longer unknown painter-poet . . . became a figure in our life of culture that it was in future impossible to ignore', as Edmund Gosse put it.[1] Blake's Victorian position as a poet-painter was established by Alexander Gilchrist's *Life of William Blake, 'Pictor Ignotus'* (1863), published after Gilchrist's untimely death with a selection of Blake's writings heavily edited by Dante Gabriel Rossetti and a catalogue by his brother William Michael. This was soon followed by Algernon Charles Swinburne's *William Blake: A Critical Essay* (1868), and by two editions of Blake's writings in 1874. Exhibitions in 1871 and 1876 were crucial to Pater's engagement with Blake: in 1871 Blake's tempera *The Spiritual Form of Pitt* featured in the second *Exhibition of the Works of the Old Masters, associated with the Works of Deceased Masters of the British School* at the Royal Academy. In 1876 Blake's visual corpus was crystallised in a retrospective of 333 works at the Burlington Fine Arts Club, which also included *The Spiritual Form of Nelson* and *The Spiritual Form of Napoleon*. It is from these picture titles, rather than from Blake's poetry, that Pater drew the concept of 'spiritual form', which is central to his essay 'A Study of Dionysus: The Spiritual Form of Fire and Dew' (1876).

Tracing Pater's explicit references brings into view Blake's *Illustrations of the Book of Job* (1823–26), and visual modes of appreciation of verbal texts by means of an intermedial reading practice. For instance, Pater associates Sir Thomas Browne with the Soul 'exploring the recesses of the tomb' in Blake's illustration to Robert Blair's *The Grave* (1808) (*App.*, 155). In addition to identifying the sensory work of visual images in shaping Pater's acts of reading, references to Blake shed light on Pater's tendency to turn to visual compositions to exemplify the interfusion of form and matter in literary writing. This chapter reconstructs Pater's engagement with Blake, and examines the role that art appreciation played in developing his writing about literature. Pater's Blake identifies a discipline of literary form that defies the separation of literature as a distinct aesthetic domain, showing how writing and reading are shaped by the multisensorial aesthetic of an inter-art critical practice.

Anachronies

Pater's aesthetic criticism is underpinned by an 'anachronic' apprehension of time in which different historical moments can coexist.[2] In a review of poems by William Morris (1868), Pater distinguishes his engagement with the past from 'vain antiquarianism', arguing for an embodied aesthetic: 'the composite experience of all the ages is part of each one of us'. Looking back 'we may hark back to some choice space of our own individual life', capture a 'more ancient life of the senses', and experience 'a quickened, multiplied consciousness'.[3] In 'The School of Giorgione' (1877) Pater associates this temporal mode with 'the highest sort of dramatic poetry' for its capacity to create an interval, 'a kind of profoundly significant and animated instants ... which seem to absorb past and future in an intense consciousness of the present' (*Ren.*, 118). This composite experience of time paves the ground for Blake's appearances in different historical moments in Pater's writing.

Blake's name first surfaces on the initial page of Pater's essay on 'The Poetry of Michelangelo', published in the *Fortnightly Review* in 1871, where Pater identifies the appeal of Michelangelo's 'sweetness and strength' in terms of 'strangeness', a key element of 'all true works of art' (*Ren.*, 57). 'Strange' is also a recurrent keyword in Swinburne's Blake essay.[4] Instead of a composed classical ideal, Pater appreciates in Michelangelo 'the presence of a convulsive energy', which is 'the whole character of medieval art' (57). Yet the medievalism that Pater finds in

Michelangelo has a nineteenth-century ring, evoking the contortions of
the swan's neck in a poem that Baudelaire dedicated to Hugo,[5] the first
modern poet to be named on the opening page of the essay as a point of
comparison. Then Pater refers to Leonardo and Blake to illuminate a
contrast: 'The world of natural things has almost no existence' for
Michelangelo; 'He has traced . . . nothing like the fretwork of wings and
flames in which Blake frames his most startling conceptions' (58). These
words allude to an engraving from Blake's *Illustrations of the Book of Job*
captioned 'When the morning Stars sang together, & all the Sons of God
shouted for joy', which is a recurring image in Pater's aesthetic thinking.
While Blake's composition might in itself exemplify 'convulsive energy', its
function here is to foreground what is not found in Michelangelo's 'blank
ranges of rock, and dim vegetable forms' (58). However, as Pater locates
these forms in 'a world before the creation of the first five days' (58), his
explanation paradoxically brings Michelangelo closer to the Blake illustration used as a benchmark for thinking about such energy, since in Blake's
'When the morning Stars sang together' 'the fretwork of wings' captures
angels singing at the dawn of creation.

   Pater's appreciation is informed by a physiological aesthetic. Reworking
Winckelmann's classical ideal, he redefines the embodied relationship
between surface and depth:

> Beneath the Platonic calm of the sonnets there is latent a deep delight in
> carnal form and colour . . . The interest of Michelangelo's poems is that
> they make us spectators of . . . the struggle of a desolating passion. (63–4)

'Carnal form' surfaces through glimpses and an indirect play of
allusions:

> That *strange interfusion of sweetness and strength* is not to be found in those
> who claimed to be his followers; but it is found in many of those who
> worked before him, and in many others down to our own time, in William
> Blake, for instance, and Victor Hugo, who, though not of his school, and
> unaware, are his true sons, and help us to understand him, as he in turn
> interprets and justifies them. Perhaps this is the chief use in studying old
> masters. (76; emphasis added)

Pater's choice of words reveals a dialogue with Swinburne's essay about
Blake, celebrated for his 'mixed work' in which 'text and design . . . so
coalesce or overlap as to become *inextricably interfused*'.[6] By echoing
Swinburne's critical account of Blake in his appreciation of

Michelangelo, Pater's writing evokes the intermingling and inextricable twofold nature of the hermaphrodite, and thus translates the concept of carnal form into an emblem for the fusion of the arts. Their 'strange interfusion' functions as a token for a hermaphroditic inter-art community in which Pater's Michelangelo identifies Blake in the company of Swinburne and Rossetti, Gautier and Baudelaire.[7] Perception generates anachronic, reciprocal ways of seeing: 'studying old masters' requires a practice of appreciation in which the reader understands Michelangelo through Blake and Hugo, and interprets and justifies Blake and Hugo through Michelangelo. Their simultaneous coexistence in the act of perception revokes the distance established by historical thinking.

Blake stands out of time in Pater's 'Preface' to *Studies in the History of the Renaissance* (1873). Against the historical impulse to identify the workmen embodying 'the genius, the sentiment of the period', Pater uses Blake to critique periodisation: '"The ages are all equal," says William Blake, "but genius is always above its age"' (*Ren.*, xxi). [8] This aphorism from Blake's marginalia to Sir Joshua Reynolds's Royal Academy Discourses was excerpted in Gilchrist's *Life*:

> With strong reprobation our annotator breaks forth when Sir Joshua quotes Vasari to the effect that Albert Dürer 'would have been one of the finest painters of his age, if,' &c. 'Albert Dürer is not "would have been!" Besides, let them look at Gothic figures and Gothic buildings, and not talk of "Dark Ages," or of any "Ages!" Ages are all equal, but genius is always above its Age'.[9]

Blake's criticism of periodisations that close off the past as past helps Pater to articulate the function of aesthetic criticism: to revitalise the past by identifying 'the *virtue*, the active principle' or 'unique, incommunicable faculty, that strange, mystical sense of a life in natural things' (*Ren.*, xxii). In the 'Conclusion' to *The Renaissance*, reworked from his review of Morris, Pater advocates an enhanced aesthetic practice to capture fleeting impressions, 'exquisite intervals', 'momentary acts of sight and passion and thought' through 'constant and eager observation'. 'Every moment some form grows perfect in hand or face ... for that moment only'; hence the need to 'grasp at any exquisite passion, or any contribution to knowledge that seems by a lifted horizon to set the spirit free for a moment' (186, 187, 188, 189). In what follows I will explore how this poetics of the moment informs Pater's encounter with Blake.

When the Stars Sing Together

Blake's anachronic appearances in 'momentary acts of sight' revitalise glimpses of a utopian past in essays associated with the plan for *Dionysus and Other Studies*, and published posthumously in *Greek Studies* in 1895. In an essay on Demeter and Persephone, published in the *Fortnightly Review* in January 1876, Pater discusses Blake in association with Edward Burne-Jones:

> If some painter of our own time has conceived the image of *The Day* so intensely, that we hardly think of distinguishing between the image, with its girdle of dissolving morning mist, and the meaning of the image; if William Blake, to our so great delight, makes the morning stars literally 'sing together'[10] – these fruits of individual genius are in part also a 'survival' from a different age, with the whole mood of which this mode of expression was more congruous than it is with ours. But there are traces of the old temper in the man of to-day also. (*GS*, 99–100; *CW*, viii. 68)

Pater's visual references flesh out an experience of erotic revelation surfacing in moments of vision that disappear in the rhythm of Pater's syntax, concealed within an accumulation of hypothetical clauses, which move so fast as to limit or pre-empt the translation of words into images. First, a 'girdle of dissolving morning mist' promises to bring into full view not a landscape, but the genitalia of a handsome naked man in Burne-Jones's painting *Day* (1870).[11] His identity as a personification of Day is crystallised in a quatrain composed by William Morris inscribed on a fictive label in the threshold of the doorway, beneath the figure's feet:

> I AM DAY I BRING AGAIN
> LIFE AND GLORY LOVE AND PAIN
> AWAKE ARISE FROM DEATH TO DEATH
> THROUGH ME THE WORLDS TALE QUICKENETH.[12]

The 'dissolving mist' in this painting can be compared to the falling drapery revealing male genitalia in Burne-Jones's *Phyllis and Demophoön*, a picture that he withdrew from the exhibition of the Society of Painters in Water-Colours in 1870. Burne-Jones painted *Day* for his patron Frederick Leyland, who had also bought *Phyllis and Demophoön*. The *Illustrated London News* compared *Phyllis and Demophoön* to 'the amatory poetry of the Swinburne school'.[13]

A Swinburnian way of reading clarifies Pater's juxtaposition of Burne-Jones with Blake. Pater's 'dissolving morning mist' evokes the prophetic imagery that Swinburne associates with Blake, the 'oracular vapour' of work 'made up of mist and fire'.[14] In his essay on Blake Swinburne developed a hermaphroditic myth of origin in his reading of Blake's emblem book *The Gates of Paradise* (1793, 1818), supplementing the 'keys' that Blake had provided 'for the sexes' in later printings. Swinburne could read Blake's key to plate 5 in Gilchrist's *Life*:

> Blind in Fire, with Shield and Spear,
> Two Horrid Reasoning Cloven Fictions,
> In Doubt which is Self Contradiction,
> A dark Hermaphrodite I stood.[15]

In Blake's reasoning and self-doubting Swinburne registers the fall into division, turning Blake's emblems into an expanded myth of origin in which man is: '"a dark hermaphrodite," enlightened by the light within him, which is darkness – the light of reason and morality; evil and good, who was neither good nor evil in the eternal life before this generated existence; male and female, who from of old was neither female nor male, but perfect man without division of flesh, until the setting of sex against sex by the malignity of animal creation. Round the new-created man revolves the flaming sword of Law, burning and dividing in the hand of the angel, servant of the cruelty of God, who drives into exile and debars from paradise the fallen spiritual man upon earth'.[16] Swinburne returned to his hermaphroditic aesthetics to capture the 'double-natured genius' and 'double-gifted nature' of the artist as poet and painter in his review of Rossetti's poetry in 1870.[17] His critical idiom resonates in Pater's writings as a cipher for an intergenerational aesthetic community, opening the door to queer readings of Blake, which help to make sense of Pater's critical juxtaposition of Blake with Burne-Jones.

The second image that Pater evokes is plate 14 from Blake's *Illustrations of the Book of Job*, captioned 'When the morning Stars sang together, & all the Sons of God shouted for joy', a quotation from Job 38:7 (Figure 1). This work had great impact among the Pre-Raphaelites. Rossetti rephrased its caption in his poem 'The Blessed Damozel' (1850): 'and then she spake, as when / The stars sang in their spheres'; in 1870, he added a variation: 'Her voice was like the voice the stars / Had when they sang together.'[18] In the entry on Blake's Job inventions, which Rossetti contributed to Gilchrist's *Life*, the engraving is praised as 'a design which never has been surpassed in the whole range of Christian art' (ii. 286–7). The framing roundels depicting the days of creation in Blake's engraving inspired roundel decorations for the frames that Rossetti designed for his paintings *Beata Beatrix* (1864–70) and *The Blessed Damozel* (1875–79) to mark the threshold of experiences of mystic incarnation.[19]

Figure 1   William Blake (1757–1827), 'When the morning Stars sang together, & all the
Sons of God shouted for joy', *Illustrations of the Book of Job* (1825), plate 14, 40.6 ×
27.3 cm, Yale Center for British Art, Gift of J. T. Johnston Coe in memory of Henry
E. Coe, Yale BA 1878, Henry E. Coe Jr., Yale BA 1917, and Henry E. Coe III, Yale BA
1946 (B2005.16.15).

In Pater's writing, Blake's illustration of Job demonstrates the visionary
potential of aesthetic criticism. Blake's engraving captures the speech with
which 'the Lord answered Job out of the whirlwind' (Job 38:1). The
Biblical text addresses the reader in the second person: 'gird up now thy

loins like a man' (38:3). Although this line is not reproduced in Blake's engraving, it helps us to understand Pater's incongruous association of the scene with the girdle of mist and the erotic promise of frontal revelation in Burne-Jones's painting. While the Lord speaking in the whirlwind harshly questions where Job was at the moment of creation (38:4), suggesting that he was not there when 'all the sons of God shouted for joy' (38:7), this negative element is not featured in Blake's selective quotation of 'When the morning Stars sang together'. Both Blake and Burne-Jones open up that experience through a form of vicarious participation and re-enactment. In Pater's prose the morning stars 'sing together' with Burne-Jones's *Day*, offering a glimpse of utopian promise, perhaps announcing a new day of sexual freedom.

Most readers of the *Fortnightly* would hardly have visualised or remembered Burne-Jones's painting, let alone grasped such a reference to an 'image' that is so intense that 'we hardly think of distinguishing between the image . . . and the meaning of the image' ('The Myth of Demeter and Persephone', *GS*, 99; *CW*, viii. 68). If Pater's reference meant to evoke an experience of erotic incarnation, it was not for all to see. Unlike Blake's Job illustration, which was printed in multiple copies, Burne-Jones's *Day* is a unique art work produced for the dining room of Leyland's home;[20] it was not exhibited until two years after the publication of Pater's essay.[21] Burne-Jones's withdrawal from the Water Colour Society exhibitions after 1870 indicates the boundaries of social decorum: the visual revelation of the male nude could only be shared within a restricted aesthetic community.[22] Can prose evoke what painting cannot show? Pater's later essay 'Style' argues that 'the figure, the accessory form or colour or reference, is rarely content to die to thought precisely at the right moment, but will inevitably linger awhile, stirring a long "brain-wave" behind it of perhaps quite alien associations' (*App.*, 18). What defines the writer is a 'tact of omission', but also a tactic that activates the utopian possibility of images glimpsed in an ecstatic interval, 'singing together' for a moment, before disappearing in the rhythm of Pater's prose.

Pater's anachronic practice draws on an anthropological concept from E. B. Tylor's influential *Primitive Culture* (1871). Like Michelangelo, who 'lingers on; a *revenant*, as the French say, a ghost out of another age' (*Ren.*, 71),[23] Blake and Burne-Jones are a '"survival" from a different age'. Tylor defines 'survivals' as 'processes, customs, opinions . . . carried on by force of habit into a new state of society different from that in which they had their original home, and they thus remain as proofs and examples of an older condition of culture'.[24] Pater applies this concept to the 'spiritual life' of nature in Wordsworth's writing, a '"survival" . . . of that primitive condition, . . . that mood in which the old Greek gods were first begotten, and which had many strange aftergrowths' (*App.*, 46–8). While Pater's Wordsworth reveals the survival of the primitive moods of nature in the present, his classical criticism finds modern counterparts in the past.

Spiritual Form

The most striking use of Blake occurs in 'A Study of Dionysus: The Spiritual Form of Fire and Dew', first published in the *Fortnightly Review* in December 1876, subsequently collected in *Greek Studies* in 1895. In this essay, Pater tracks the emergence of Dionysus as 'the *spiritual form* of the vine, . . . of the highest human type', 'the reflexion, in sacred image or ideal' of 'the mystical body of the earth', 'the vine-growers' god' (*GS*, 15, 25, 28; *CW*, viii. 94, 99, 100). Religion emerges as a process of knowing by making, 'shadowing forth, in each pause of the process, an intervening person—what is to us but the secret chemistry of nature being to them the mediation of living spirits', a 'fantastic system of tree-worship' (*GS*, 13, 14; *CW*, viii. 93). For Pater the 'office of the imagination' (*GS*, 32; *CW*, viii. 102) is to capture this evanescent form refracted through different arts: remnants of 'primitive tree-worship . . . found almost every-where in the earlier stages of civilisation, enshrined in legend or custom' show that the ancient 'fancy of the worshipper' persists in modern 'poetical reverie'. For instance, in Percy Shelley's *Sensitive Plant* the spiritual meta-morphosis of plants 'may still float about a mind full of modern lights, the feeling we too have of a life in the green world, always ready to assert its claim over our sympathetic fancies' (*GS*, 11; *CW*, viii. 92). Sculpture can 'condense the impressions of natural things into human form; . . . retain that early mystical sense of water, or wind, or light, in the moulding of eye and brow; . . . arrest it, or rather. . . set it free' (*GS*, 32–3; *CW*, viii. 102). Human form offers a mould for 'the spiritual flesh allying itself happily to mystical meanings', but this human limitation is precarious, always in 'danger of an escape from them of the free spirit of air, and light, and sky' (*GS*, 34; *CW*, viii. 103). Pater's search for the primitive mystical union of the spirit with nature, working against the divided condition of the modern mind, is close to Blake's embodied enthusiasm.

The notion of 'spiritual form' derives from Emanuel Swedenborg's account of human perfection seen from an angelic point of view and underpinned by a dualist distinction between the human body's earthly and spiritual form.[25] Emblematic of this 'divided imperfect life' is the 'spiritual philosophy' of Samuel Taylor Coleridge (*App.*, 71, 82), whose poetry Pater compares to Blake's visionary ability to see spirits in the everyday, 'that whole episode of the re-inspiriting of the ship's crew in *The Ancient Mariner* being comparable to Blake's well-known design of the "Morning Stars singing together"' (*App.*, 97). The difference between the painter-poet and the philosopher-poet indicates 'a change of temper in regard to the supernatural which has passed over the whole modern mind, and of which the true measure is the influence of the writings of Swedenborg' (98). Access to a supernatural sense requires an altered state, or a visionary work of art that exhibits a moment of revelation and 're-inspirits' the reach of words through a complementary appeal to the senses, which can heal the division between spirit and matter, subject and form.

In Pater's writing, the concept of 'spiritual form' signals a paradox; so too does its attribution to Blake two-thirds of the way into the Dionysus essay:

> Well,— the mythical conception, projected at last, in drama or sculpture, is the *name*, the instrument of the identification, of the given matter, — of its unity in variety, its outline or definition in mystery; its *spiritual form*, to use again the expression I have borrowed from William Blake—form, with hands, and lips, and opened eyelids—spiritual, as conveying to us, in that, the soul of rain, or of a Greek river, or of swiftness, or purity. (*GS*, 37; *CW*, viii. 104)

The term 'spiritual form' appears only once in Blake's poetical corpus. While Blake uses the expression 'spiritual body' in the Swedenborgian sense in an illustration for 'To Tirzah ('It is raised a spiritual body') and in Night VIII of *Vala or the Four Zoas*, [26] in *Jerusalem*, the 'spiritual forms' in Luvah's sepulchre will 'wither' without a veil. An apocalyptic weaving of bodies is required to protect humanity from its state of splitting and separation in order to restore the original unity of the eternals. [27] In other words, Blake uses the word 'spiritual' to describe a fallen state of separation that emphasises the paradoxical contradiction inherent in the concept of 'spiritual form'. The tension between ideal, dystopian, and parodic is active in William Michael Rossetti's 'Prefatory Memoir' to the Aldine edition of Blake's works in 1874. After discussing Blake's 'spiritual sense' and 'spiritual eye', he alludes to the 'spiritual visitants' that Blake captured in his visionary heads, and wonders whether Blake will approve of 'the present re-issue of the *Poetical Sketches*', a 'portrait' that is 'a reflex of his "spiritual form"'. [28] Will the edition capture Blake's corpus or a divided image, a caricatural distortion like his visionary heads? The ambiguous possibilities of this statement register Blake's own ambivalent relationship with Swedenborg.

The Blakean source for Pater's concept of 'spiritual form' is a pictorial title: *The Spiritual Form of Pitt* is the only Blake painting entered in the Royal Academy's Old Masters exhibition in 1871, but the English politician is joined by the 'Spiritual Forms' of Nelson and Napoleon in the

Burlington Fine Arts Club Blake retrospective in 1876.[29] In the
'Introductory Remarks' to the catalogue, William Bell Scott argues that
'the Spiritual Form of Pitt' is a puzzle, 'among the most difficult to
decipher'.[30] A review of the 1876 exhibition recalls the public's reaction
to the painting at the Old Masters exhibition in 1871: 'a stout segment of
Respectability who looked at the picture, solemnly read to his companion
the title, *The spiritual form of William Pitt guiding Behemoth*, looked again,
shook his head'.[31] Yet what the review cites is the title as it appears in the
catalogue of 1876.[32] The catalogue entry in 1871 reads:

> **William Pitt**
> 'The spiritual form of Pitt guiding Behemoth. He is that angel who, pleased
> to perform the Almighty's orders, rides in the whirlwind, directing the
> storms of war. He is *commanding the Reaper to reap the vine of the earth*, and
> the ploughman to plough up the cities and towers.' —. (*Blake's Title, as it
> appeared in his Catalogue*)[33]

In 1871 comparing the catalogue entry with the tempera hanging on the
wall produced an experience of double vision. The title, 'William Pitt',
raised the expectation for a historical portrait, but it was subverted by the
grotesque revelation of a nude and a demonic Dionysian counterpart.
Blake's visionary portraiture exploits the possibilities of allegory as a
satirical yoking of opposites, which is closer to Samuel Johnson's denunciation of metaphysical wit, than to an ideal of style in which form and
meaning coalesce in ways that cannot be separated.

The dialectical tension between visionary allegory and historical portraiture in *The Spiritual Form of Pitt* undermines the Swedenborgian framing
of Blake in the Burlington Fine Arts Club catalogue of 1876. In his
'Introductory Remarks', Scott quotes from the Swedenborgian John
Garth Wilkinson's preface to *Songs of Innocence and of Experience* (1839):
'if it leads one reader to think that all Reality for him, in the long run, lies
out of the limits of Space and Time; and that Spirits, and not bodies, and
still less garments, are men . . . it will have done its work in its little day'.[34]
Still drawing on Wilkinson, Scott goes on to detail Blake's objection to
nature – 'natural objects did and do weaken, deaden, and obliterate
imagination in me' – to articulate an alternative form of 'determinate
vision', which does not mean that 'the object is visible to the eye, but that
it is apparent to the mental vision, by interior light'.[35] Scott cites
Wilkinson announcing that *Songs of Innocence* represent 'the New
Spiritualism which is *now*', in 1839, 'dawning on the world' (9). This
Swedenborgian reception of Blake can find some corroboration in Blake's

ambivalent return to Swedenborg in the late 1800s, probably under the influence of Charles Augustus Tulk, whose copy of *Songs* provided the basis of Wilkinson's edition.[36] However, Scott's claim that Blake was 'sympathetic' to Swedenborg (10) goes against the evidence of Blake's 'objurgatory' marginalia to a copy of Swedenborg's *Angelic Wisdom*, which was brought to the Burlington Fine Arts Club at the time of the exhibition. W. M. Rossetti's review of Scott's catalogue reminds the reader of Blake's critical denunciation of Swedenborg in *The Marriage of Heaven and Hell*, where he claimed that 'any man of mechanical talents may, from the writings of Paracelsus or Jacob Behmen, produce ten thousand volumes of equal value with Swedenborg's'.[37] In the context of the exhibition Pater's incongruous association between Dionysus as a celebration of nature and Blake's dystopian pictorial title is puzzling. The strong language that shapes Pater's attribution of 'spiritual form' to Blake as an example of 'unity in variety' suggests something more than meets the eye.

Both Blake and Pater think about form through a relationship with Greek sculpture and Greek gods. Blake first exhibited his spiritual form paintings in 1809 and discussed them in *A Descriptive Catalogue of Pictures, Poetical and Historical Inventions*, reprinted in Gilchrist's *Life*: 'The two Pictures of Nelson and Pitt are compositions of a mythological cast, similar to those Apotheoses of Persian, Hindoo, and Egyptian Antiquity ... wonderful originals ... from which the Greeks and Hetrurians copied Hercules Farnese, Venus of Medici, Apollo Belvidere, and all the grand works of ancient art.'[38] In the next catalogue entry on *Chaucer's Canterbury Pilgrims*, also exhibited in 1876, Blake uses classical sculptural prototypes to capture 'characters repeated again and again, in animals, vegetables, minerals, and in men ... physiognomies or lineaments of universal human life'.[39] Such were, for Blake, the 'Grecian gods', 'visions of eternal attributes, or divine names, which, when erected into gods, become destructive to humanity'.[40] Blake develops his negative account of the effects of apotheosis in his entry about *The Spiritual Preceptor, an experiment Picture*, a subject

> taken from the Visions of Emanuel Swedenborg. Universal Theology, No. 623 ... corporeal demons have gained a predominance; who the leaders of these are, will be shown below. Unworthy Men, who gain fame among Men, continue to govern mankind after death, and, in their spiritual bodies, oppose the spirits of those who worthily are famous.[41]

Here 'spiritual' stands for an antithetical destructive power of division.

Pater repurposes Blake's dystopian image through an intermedial act of criticism that exemplifies the practice of misquotation, misrepresentation, or deliberate appropriation discussed by Christopher Ricks.[42] Pater's intervention discards the negative associations of 'spiritual form' as an instrument of political imposition. It is Blakean in spirit, if not in the letter, because to repurpose the concept of 'spiritual form' means to release the utopian potential of the 'human form divine' and restore the eternal body that Blake sought to heal in his prophetic writings.

Style: 'Soul and Body Reunited'

Blake's visual inventions come to Pater's mind when he explores forms that cannot be captured through logical processes of reasoning structured around distinctions or boundaries between the arts. In 'The School of Giorgione' Pater argues for the incommunicable, 'untranslatable sensuous charm' peculiar to each art (*Ren.*, 102). Building on Lessing's *Laocoon*, Pater argues that '[o]ne of the functions of aesthetic criticism is to define these limitations; to estimate the degree in which a given work of art fulfils its responsibilities to its special material' (102). Yet as the artist produces form out of matter, 'in its special mode of handling its given material, each art may be observed to pass into the condition of some other art, by what German critics term an *Anders-streben* —a partial alienation from its own limitations' (105). This does not mean that they can replace each other or turn into music, following the progression from more material to more spiritual forms set out in Hegel's *Aesthetics*, but that they 'reciprocally ... lend each other new forces' in the 'constant effort ... to obliterate' the distinction between matter and form (105, 106). Since Pater argues that poetry needs to find 'guidance from the other arts' (105), what 'guidance' do Blake's visual compositions provide in Pater's search for literary form?

At the level of composition, in Blake's *Chaucer's Pilgrims* and the *Spiritual Form of Pitt* Pater finds visual approaches to the revelation of eternal characters resurfacing in different times, a type of recognition that Pater explored in different writing genres, from classical criticism to the *Imaginary Portraits*. The 'Grecian gods' that Blake sees in *Chaucer's Pilgrims* may well have prompted Pater's association of Chaucer with the Marbles of Aegina, discussed in Chapter 2, while Blake's Dionysian Pitt offers a model for developing literary character in his 'quaint legend' 'Denis L'Auxerrois' (*IP*, 47; *CW*, iii. 81).

Blake's art helps define form in literary writing by means of analogy, through visionary moments of aesthetic plenitude. While 'poetry ... works with words addressed in the first instance to the pure intelligence' (*Ren.*, 107), in Blake Pater finds art informed by artistic spirit that can heal the modern dissociation of mind and soul: 'meaning reaches us through ways not distinctly traceable by the understanding, as in some of the most imaginative compositions of William Blake' (*Ren.*, 108). Visual associations complement words, enhancing their reach by appealing to the senses and supplementing the limitations of the understanding.

In 'Style', after defining the pleasure of 'conscious artistic structure', Pater turns to the literary artist's mode of communication by means of soul as opposed to mind and finds in Blake 'an instance of preponderating soul, embarrassed, at a loss, in an era of preponderating mind' (*App.*, 24, 25). Consider Pater's wording against J. Comyns Carr's introduction to Blake for T. H. Ward's *English Poets* (1880), which sums up a nineteenth-century tradition around Blake's insanity:

> he possessed only in the most imperfect and rudimentary form the faculty which distinguishes the functions of art and literature; and when his imagination was exercised upon any but the simplest material, his logical powers became altogether unequal to the labour of logical and consequent expression. ... If Blake had never committed himself to literature we should scarcely be aware of the morbid tendency of his mind. It is only in turning from his design to his verse that we are forced to recognize the imperfect balance of his faculties.[43]

Blake's appeal to Pater is in stark contrast to Comyns Carr's indictment of his 'imperfect balance' of faculties. On the contrary, Pater reaches out to Blake to rebalance the division of the faculties; against Comyns Carr's separation of the artist from the poet, Pater seeks in the artist the complement of sense that is needed to 'inspirit' poetry.

Blake's visionary art articulates an aesthetic politics for modern literature, which is neither objective, nor 'legible to all; by soul, he reaches us, somewhat capriciously perhaps, one and not another, through vagrant sympathy and a kind of immediate contact' ('Style', *App.*, 25). This formula activates an experience of aesthetic embodiment that traverses Pater's critical idiom, from the early formulation of 'carnal form' to 'spiritual form'. Pater goes on to discuss 'soul' operating through 'unconscious literary tact' and 'immediate sympathetic contact' (26) in terms of religious literature and the 'plenary substance' of 'what can never be uttered' (27), then shifts to the 'martyr of literary style', Gustave Flaubert, and returns to Blake to illustrate his 'adaptation' between thought and language, 'meeting each other with the readiness of "soul and body reunited," in Blake's rapturous design' (27, 30, Figure 2). This reference to Blake ironically recentres the passion for style that Flaubert advocates in a passage from his correspondence with Madame X quoted in

Figure 2   Louis Schiavonetti (1765–1810), after William Blake (1757–1827), 'The Reunion of the Soul & the Body', illustration to *The Grave, A Poem. By Robert Blair. Illustrated By Twelve Etchings Executed From Original Designs. To Which Is Added A Life Of The Author*, London, Published Mar. 1st 1813, by R. Ackermann, 101 Strand, sheet 38.1 × 28.9 cm, plate 29.8 × 22.9 cm, Yale Center for British Art, Paul Mellon Collection (B1974.8.6).

the essay. As a tangible image of what is left unsaid, Blake's illustration to Robert Blair's *The Grave* becomes an emblem of the complementarity of text and image, showing how visual allusion integrates writing by addressing the senses and pointing to an experience of embodiment in which thought and language coalesce in ways that words alone fail to express.

Notes

1 Edmund Gosse, 'William Blake', *Examiner* (14 November 1874), 1243; for the 'painter-poet' formula, see Alexander Gilchrist, *Life of William Blake, 'Pictor Ignotus'*, 2 vols (1863), i. 47.

2 On the concept of 'anachronic' time to 'liberate historical thinking from linear temporality' and anachronism, see Alexander Nagel and Christopher S. Wood, *Anachronic Renaissance* (New York 2010), 13–14, and 370, footnote 18.

3 Walter Pater, 'Poems by William Morris', *Westminster Review*, n.s. 34 (October 1868), 307, 312.

4 For instance, 'if elsewhere the artist's strange strength of thought and hand is more visible, nowhere is there such pure sweetness and singleness in his work' (Algernon Charles Swinburne, *William Blake: A Critical Essay* (1868), 113); 'the achieved divinity of man' in *The Marriage of Heaven and Hell* is a 'strange faith' (217).

5 'Le Cygne: À Victor Hugo', line 27, in Charles Baudelaire, *Les fleurs du mal et autres poèmes*, ed. Henri Lemaître (Paris 1964), 108.

6 Swinburne, *Blake*, 108 (emphasis added); see also: 'allegory, here as always, is interfused with myth in a manner at once violent and intricate', 241.

7 Lene Østermark-Johansen, 'Between the Medusan and the Pygmalian: Swinburne and Sculpture', *Victorian Literature and Culture* 38 (2010), 25, 29, 30. On allusions identifying the 'group identity' of an inter-art community and discussion of 'shared motifs as badges of participation in Aestheticism', see Elizabeth Prettejohn, 'Walter Pater and Aesthetic Painting', in *After the Pre-Raphaelites: Art and Aestheticism in Victorian England*, ed. Elizabeth Prettejohn (Manchester 1999), 37.

8 Pater must have found Blake's manuscript annotation to Reynolds in Gilchrist, *Life*, i. 263; 'Ages Are All Equal. But Genius is Always Above the Age', *The Complete Poetry and Prose of William Blake*, ed. David Erdman (Berkeley 1982), 649.

9 Gilchrist, *Life*, i. 263.

10 A reference to Job 38:7 quoted by William Blake in *Illustrations of the Book of Job*, Plate 14. This plate was on display at the Burlington Fine Arts Club exhibition, 22, no. 39: 'From the Book of Job. | "When the morning stars sang together". Lent by John Linnell.'

11 On Burne-Jones's *Day* (1870), see Sarah Herring's entries for *Day* and *Night* in *A Private Passion: 19th-Century Paintings and Drawings from the Grenville*

L. Winthrop Collection, Harvard University, ed. Stephan Wolohojian (New Haven 2003), 361–3 (nos. 155–6).

12 For the text's transcription, see https://harvardartmuseums.org/collections/object/298118.

13 'Fine Arts. The Society of Painters in Water Colours', *Illustrated London News* 56 (30 April 1870), 459.

14 Swinburne, *Blake*, 3–4.

15 Gilchrist, *Life*, i. 103; two other copies read 'we stood' (Blake, *Complete Poetry and Prose*, 268).

16 Swinburne, *Blake*, 21–2.

17 Algernon Charles Swinburne, 'The Poems of Dante Gabriel Rossetti', *Fortnightly Review* 7 (1870), 551–79 (551).

18 D. G. Rossetti, 'The Blessed Damozel', *The Germ*, no. 2 (February 1850), 80–3 (80), lines 59–60; *Poems* (1870), 3–4, lines 53–54, 59–60.

19 Alastair Grieve, 'The Applied Art of D. G. Rossetti-I. His Picture-Frames', *Burlington Magazine* 115 (1973), 16, 18–24. Pater compares Rossetti's 'really new kind of poetic utterance' to 'Blake's design of the Singing of the Morning Stars', Jacob's Dream in Genesis, and Addison's Nineteenth Psalm ('Dante Gabriel Rossetti', *App.*, 210). See Chapter 14 in this volume.

20 Herring, in *A Private Passion*, 361.

21 Photographic reproduction of *Day* is documented in Frederick Hollyer, *Catalogue of platinotype reproductions of pictures &c. photographed and sold by Mr. Hollyer No 9 Pembroke Sqe. London W.* (1902), 6, no. 10. In the mid-1870s, Frederick Hollyer was engaged in photographic reproductions of Burne-Jones's paintings. For evidence of the erotic appreciation of nude paintings in photographic reproduction, see John Addington Symonds on receiving photographs of Simeon Solomon's drawings of classical subjects from London in 1869 (*The Letters of John Addington Symonds*, ed. Herbert M. Schueller and Robert L. Peter, 3 vols (Detroit 1967–69), ii. 27). I am grateful to Elizabeth Prettejohn for these references.

22 Billie Andrew Inman, 'Estrangement and Connection: Walter Pater, Benjamin Jowett, and William M. Hardinge', in *Pater in the 1990s*, ed. Laurel Brake and Ian Small (Greensboro, NC 1991), 1–20; Laurel Brake, 'After *Studies*: Walter Pater's Cancelled Book, or Dionysus and Gay Discourse in the 1870s', in *Beauty and the Beast: Christina Rossetti, Walter Pater, R.L. Stevenson and their Contemporaries*, ed. Peter Liebregts and Wim Tigges (Amsterdam and Atlanta 1996), 115–26.

23 Lene Østermark-Johansen, *Michelangelo and the Language of Sculpture* (Aldershot 2011), 35.

24 Edward B. Tylor, *Primitive Culture*, 2 vols (1871), i. 14–15.

25 Emanuel Swedenborg, *A Treatise Concerning Heaven and Hell*, 2nd edn (1784), 75; *The Wisdom of Angels, Concerning Divine Love and Divine Wisdom* (1788), 386. Blake owned and annotated both works. See also *Circular letter addressed to all the Readers of the Theological Writings of the Honourable Emanuel Swedenborg*, transcribed in minutes signed by Blake, quoted in Robert Rix, *William Blake and the Cultures of Radical Christianity*

(Aldershot 2007), 55: 'Immediately on the death of the material body, man rises again, as to his spiritual or substantial body, in the spiritual world, wherein he existeth in a perfect human form'; this text is also reproduced in Robert Hindmarsh, *Rise and Progress of the New Jerusalem Church in England, America, and other Parts* (1862), 92.

26 Blake, *Complete Poetry and Prose*, 30, 378.

27 Blake, *Complete Poetry and Prose*, 166.

28 'Prefatory Memoir', *The Poetical Works of William Blake: Lyrical and Miscellaneous* (1874), lx, lxii–iii, xlix, cxxxiii.

29 'William Pitt | "The Spiritual form of Pitt guiding Behemoth..."', Royal Academy of Arts, Burlington House, *Exhibition of the Works of the Old Masters, associated with the Works of Deceased Masters of the British School* (1871), 26 (no. 285); listed as *The Spiritual Form of W. Pitt guiding Behemoth* in Burlington Fine Arts Club, *Exhibition of the Works of William Blake* (1876), 53 (no. 201), and 32 (no. 90) for *The Spiritual Form of Napoleon*, and 38 (no. 126) for *The Spiritual Form of Nelson guiding Leviathan, in whose wreathings are enfolded the Nations of the earth*.

30 William Bell Scott, 'Introductory Remarks', *Exhibition of the Works of William Blake* (1876), 4.

31 H.H. Statham, 'The Blake Drawings at the Burlington Fine Arts Club', *Macmillan's Magazine* (May 1876), 55.

32 *Exhibition of the Works of William Blake*, 53 (no. 201), where the reader is referred to the companion piece *The Spiritual Form of Nelson* for further reference to Blake's *Descriptive Catalogue* reprinted in Gilchrist's *Life*.

33 *Exhibition of the Works of the Old Masters*, 26, no. 285 (emphasis added to the quotation); punctuation and capitalisation differ from the relevant entry in Gilchrist, *Life*, ii. 120.

34 *Songs of Innocence and of Experience, shewing the Two Contrary States of the Human Soul by William Blake* (1839), xxi; Wilkinson's edition is discussed in Colin Trodd, *Visions of Blake: William Blake in the Art World 1830–1930* (Liverpool 2012), 101–14.

35 Scott, 'Introductory Remarks', 4–5. Further references are given parenthetically in the text.

36 On the influence of the Swedenborgian Charles Augustus Tulk, see Morton Paley, '"A New Heaven Is Begun": William Blake and Swedenborgianism', *Blake: An Illustrated Quarterly* 13 (1979), 64–90 (78–83).

37 W.M. Rossetti, 'The Blake Catalogue', *Academy* (15 April 1876), 364–5.

38 Blake, *Complete Poetry and Prose*, 530–1; Gilchrist, *Life*, ii. 120.

39 Blake, *Complete Poetry and Prose*, 532–3; Gilchrist, *Life*, ii. 123.

40 Blake, *Complete Poetry and Prose*, 536; Gilchrist, *Life*, ii. 127.

41 Blake, *Complete Poetry and Prose*, 546; Gilchrist, *Life*, ii. 138–9.

42 Ricks, 'Misquotation', esp. 395 on misquotation as resurrection and 405 on mistranscription.

43 *The English Poets: Selections: With Critical Introductions by Various Writers and a General Introduction by Matthew Arnold*, ed. Thomas Humphry Ward, 4 vols (1880), iii: *Addison to Blake*, 597.

Pater on Coleridge and Wordsworth

Charles W. Mahoney

When Walter Pater's *Appreciations* was first published in 1889, the chapters on Wordsworth and Coleridge were prominently afforded pride of place, uniformly praised, and generally considered the finest in the volume. In reviewing it for the *Athenaeum*, Arthur Symons astutely connected *Appreciations* with the critical principles outlined in the 'Preface' to *The Renaissance* (1873). Reminding readers of Pater's language there regarding the role of the 'aesthetic critic' in distinguishing the special 'virtue' of a work of art in order to 'disengage' them from the undistinguished aspects, he inflected 'appreciation' as precisely that sort of critical weighing and valuing.[1] Symons cited the Wordsworth essay as 'certainly the very best example of this, for it has fallen to the lot of Wordsworth to suffer more than most at the hands of interpreters'. The writing on Wordsworth was 'perhaps the finest of Mr Pater's critical essays', because in 'Disengaging the better from the baser elements, he seizes thus upon what is fundamental, getting at the true root of the matter'. Symons was not alone in lavishing praise on the Wordsworth essay: in the *Spectator*, C. L. Graves thought it 'excellent, and full of acute remarks', while Oscar Wilde, in the *Speaker*, singled it out as 'the finest' in the book, because 'It appeals, not to the ordinary Wordsworthian with his uncritical temper, and his gross confusion of ethical with aesthetical problems, but rather to those who desire to separate the gold from the dross'.

Although not noticed in as much detail, the Coleridge essay was considered 'difficult to overpraise' and 'one of the most delightful of all', according to Clement Shorter in the *Star*. Graves thought that 'Mr Pater is at his best in what he says of Coleridge's superlative skill in handling the supernatural' in 'The Rhyme of the Ancient Mariner', while W. J. Courthope, in the *Nineteenth Century*, noted that 'Mr Pater's appreciation of Coleridge is more severe, and therefore more just'. Although Pater had previously published versions of both essays (on Coleridge in 1866 and on Wordsworth in 1874, with additional commentary on Coleridge's poetry in 1880), the essays in *Appreciations* are the most frequently cited. In order responsibly to assess Pater's 'appreciations' of both writers – and to understand the importance of these writings for Pater's critical achievements as well as for the late nineteenth-century reputations of Wordsworth and Coleridge – it will be valuable to contextualise these essays within the longer arc of Pater's career.

***

Pater commenced his career as a critic with 'Coleridge's Writings', published anonymously in the *Westminster Review* in January 1866. Nominally a review of the third edition of Thomas Allsop's *Letters, Conversations and Recollections of S. T. Coleridge*, it evaluates the competing priorities in Coleridge's prose writings between his 'religious philosophy' and his 'theory of art-criticism' ('CW', 114, 117). It marks Pater's first attempt to delineate the functions of criticism and culture in relation to religion (Christianity) and philosophy (both Greek and German Idealist) and, in doing so, offers a preview of the 'religious aestheticism' later developed in *The Renaissance*. It is an ambitious first foray into criticism: tackling the contested matter of Coleridge's posthumous reputation, Pater examines both the prose writings and the man (with whom he clearly sympathises, even as he outlines what he considers to be Coleridge's shortcomings) in the course of setting forth his own priorities as a critic. When he later revised much of 'Coleridge's Writings' for the chapter on Coleridge in *Appreciations*, Pater reworked material from the opening sixteen pages and final two paragraphs of the article (excising most of the material in which he criticised prevalent Christian dogmatics) to bookend that study around the consideration of Coleridge's poetry that he contributed to T. H. Ward's *The English Poets* (1880).

In order to arrive at a proper assessment of both Pater's aspirations and his achievements in the early essay, it will be useful to consider the book allegedly under review: the *Letters, Conversations and Recollections of S. T. Coleridge*. First published in 1836 (then republished in 1858 and 1864), Allsop's volume had played a significant role in the shaping of Coleridge's posthumous reputation for thirty years.[2] Noting in the preface to the third edition that 'the name of Samuel Taylor Coleridge [is] a puzzle to this later generation' (np), Allsop sought to resolve the 'puzzle' through presenting Coleridge as first and foremost a religious thinker, one who systematically attempted to 'reconcile religion with philosophy' and 'truth with Christianity' (np). This is not the (now) better-known Coleridge of the

early poetry or the *Biographia Literaria* (1817), but the Coleridge of the
Aids to Reflection (1825) and *On the Constitution of the Church and State*
(1829), whose readers were imagined as young men who were 'becoming
conscious of the difficulty of holding Christian beliefs within the new
intellectual climate' of the early nineteenth century.[3] *Aids to Reflection* had
been a popular, influential book since its first publication, and (after
Coleridge's death in 1834) was instrumental for the public perception of
Coleridge and his writings.[4] Coleridge was admired by many mid-century
critics for his recognition of the need for a 'spiritual' religion and his
attempt to define Christianity in philosophical terms, apart from questions
of historical evidence. In undertaking a review of the third edition of
Allsop's collection (and taking various of his bearings from Allsop's preface
to the same), Pater in his first publication was plunging into a contentious
public debate, not merely about Coleridge's posthumous reputation but
also about the authority of religion for English culture in the 1860s.[5]

'Coleridge's Writings' may be considered Pater's attempt to solve the
'puzzle' of Coleridge. He touches on numerous points from Allsop's
preface to the third edition (for example, the importance of German
Idealist thinkers such as Kant for effecting the reconciliation Coleridge
sought between religion and philosophy), and focuses on *Aids to Reflection*
as the central text of what he ultimately denigrates as Coleridge's reliance
on 'inferior theological literature' ('CW', 111–12), when compared with
his theory of poetry, or 'art-criticism', in which, according to Pater,
Coleridge 'comes nearest to true and important principles' (117). As
John Beer has noted, 'Pater was singularly well equipped to attempt a
critical re-evaluation of Coleridge, being temperamentally attuned to his
poetic sensibility yet aware of the growth of evolutionary and relativist
thinking'.[6]

Pater frames his approach to Coleridge in terms of the tension
between the 'relative' (or modern) spirit and the 'absolute' (or ancient)
spirit: whereas ancient philosophy 'sought to arrest every object in
an eternal outline, to fix thought in a necessary formula', for the modern
spirit 'nothing is or can be rightly known except relatively under
conditions' (107):

> The literary life of Coleridge was a disinterested struggle against the
> application of the relative spirit to moral and religious questions.
> Everywhere he is restlessly scheming to apprehend the absolute; to affirm
> it effectively; to get it acknowledged. Coleridge failed in that attempt,
> happily even for him, for it was a struggle against the increasing life of
> the mind itself. (108)

Coleridge's pursuit of an absolute was both his greatest ambition and his greatest shortcoming – his signature failure. In light of Pater's conviction that only the relative can make a difference in contemporary thought, Coleridge's insistence throughout his prose writings on fixed principles, in concert with his refusal 'to see the parts as parts only' (132), brings into view his 'chief offence' – namely, an 'excess of seriousness, a seriousness that arises not from any moral principle, but from a misconception of the perfect manner' (111). In other words, Coleridge's insistence on thinking in terms of an absolute marred what Pater would later denominate his 'style' as a critic, and compromised both his appeal and his reputation as a humanist. Despite this, there is for Pater a 'peculiar charm' about Coleridge, the 'charm of what is chastened' in Coleridge's lifelong contention against the relative and 'the new order of things' (107).

Pater's critical re-evaluation of Coleridge operates under two antagonistic yet complementary headings, as he disparages Coleridge's 'religious philosophy' in order to celebrate his 'theory of art-criticism'. Allsop's volume is representative of the degree to which Coleridge's posthumous reputation was tied to his status as a religious thinker, and Pater is pointedly taking aim at Allsop's veneration of Coleridge when he castigates *Aids to Reflection* (the central text in the Victorian valorisation of Coleridge as one of the greatest philosophers of his age) as '*ennuyant*, depressing', little more than 'Archbishop Leighton's vague pieties all twisted into the jargon of a spiritualistic philosophy' (112). He repeatedly dismisses Coleridge's attempt to fashion 'an intellectual novelty in the shape of a religious philosophy' that could reconcile the conflict between reason and faith (114):

> The peculiar temper of Coleridge's intellect made the idea of reconciling this conflict very seductive. With a true speculative talent he united a false kind of subtlety and the full share of vanity. A dexterous intellectual *tour de force* has always an independent charm … A method so forced as that of Coleridge's religious philosophy is from the first doomed to be insipid. (115)

Pater seems more interested in *Aids to Reflection* for its 'dexterity' as an 'intellectual *tour de force*' (a signature mark of Coleridge's 'literary egotism' (112)) than as a sustained argument about the possible relation between rational thought and spiritual devotion.

Beyond the specific engagement with *Aids to Reflection*, Pater's re-evaluation of Coleridge's religious thinking provides him with the opportunity for a wholesale disparagement of Christianity. Maintaining that 'what chains men to a religion is not its claim on their reason, their hopes or fears, but the glow it affords to the world, its "beau ideal"', Pater argues at some length that, for those who no longer believe in traditional Christianity, its most compelling features are to be replaced by 'culture', understood as our 'intellectual life' (126). Characterising this new 'spiritual element' as 'a chastened temper', with its 'passion for inward perfection with its sorrows, its aspirations, its joy', Pater declares that 'These mental states are the delicacies of the higher morality of the few' and that 'like culture itself they are remote, refined, intense, existing only by the triumph of a few over a dead world of routine in which there is no lifting of the soul at all' (126). It is an uncompromising substitution of culture for religion, which Pater sums up thus:

> Our culture, then, is not supreme, our intellectual life is incomplete, we fail of the intellectual throne, if we have no inward longing, inward chastening, inward joy. Religious belief, the craving for objects of belief, may be refined out of our hearts, but they must leave their sacred perfume, their spiritual sweetness, behind. This law of the highest intellectual life has sometimes seemed hard to understand .... How often do we have to look for some feature of the ancient religious life, not in a modern saint, but in a modern artist or philosopher! (126–7)

David DeLaura has written of Pater's 'remarkable argument' here that it not only 'breathes a total and almost contemptuous detachment from Christianity and Christian belief', but that it furthermore provides 'the most explicit rationale for what may be called a "religious aestheticism", not only in Pater but perhaps in the English language', which 'Pater himself, even in the years of the Renaissance studies, never again revealed so uncompromisingly'.[7] It is one of the most memorable passages in 'Coleridge's Writings', and (as is also the case with the criticism of *Aids to Reflection*) it was removed when Pater revised the article for *Appreciations*.[8] Under the heading of 'the higher morality of the few', Pater is attempting here to preserve a spiritual element in life 'For those who have passed out of Christianity' (127) – or, as T. S. Eliot put it, 'to get all the emotional kick out of Christianity one can, without the bother of believing it'.[9]

In between the critique of Coleridge's theological writings and the celebration of a new religious aestheticism (both excised in 1889), Pater offers a sustained and sympathetic account of Coleridge's art criticism (most of which was retained in *Appreciations*), claiming that it is here that Coleridge 'comes nearest to true and important principles' (117). Integral to Pater's assessment of Coleridge's non-religious criticism is his emphasis on the importance of German Idealist philosophy (what Pater goes so far as to claim was his 'one singular intellectual happiness'), which Coleridge applied 'with an eager, unwearied subtlety', in an 'attempt to reclaim the world of art as a world of fixed laws' (117, 118). This is most evident in the *Biographia*, in which Coleridge 'refine[d] Schelling's "Philosophy of Nature" into a theory of art' (118). Pater is unusual among nineteenth-century readers in that he shares Coleridge's interest in transcendental philosophy (certainly not the case with the first reviewers of the *Biographia*), and neglects the long chapters on Wordsworth (the usual centre of attention) in order to explain Coleridge's critical philosophy, tracing the 'Philosophy of Nature' all the way back to evidences of pantheism in Greek philosophy ('the suspicion of a mind latent in nature', which he valorises as the 'Greek spirit' or 'Greek mind' (119, 132)). He even detects 'that faint glamour of the philosophy of nature' in Coleridge's famous definitions of the imagination in the *Biographia*, setting forth the Coleridgean imagination as that faculty which 'attains a strange power of modifying and centralizing what it receives from without according to an inward ideal': in Pater's interpretation, 'in imaginative genius, ideas become effective; the intelligence of nature, with all its elements connected and justified, is clearly reflected; and the interpretation of its latent purposes is fixed in works of art' (121, 120).

Pater singles out Coleridge's Shakespeare criticism (at the time available in the *Literary Remains* (1836–39) and Sara Coleridge's *Notes and Lectures upon Shakespeare* (1849)) to explain Coleridge's theory of organic unity, the 'law of gravitation from within' that finds 'the most constraining unity in the most abundant variety' (121). In Coleridge's terms, 'The organic form is innate; it shapes, as it developes [*sic*], itself from within, and the fulness of its development is one and the same with the perfection of its outward form' (quoted, 122).[10] Under the Coleridgean heading of organic unity, '"the absolute" has been affirmed in the sphere of art' (Coleridge again 'straining' after the absolute), yet Coleridge ultimately 'overstrained the elasticity of his hypothesis', rendering the artist 'almost mechanical' as a result: while a theory of organic form may explain the 'impression of a self-delighting, independent life which a finished work of art gives us', it 'does not express the process by which that work was produced' (122). Such an achievement, and such a limitation, are characteristic of Coleridge's work as a critic: while he excels in determining the 'metaphysical definition of the universal element in an artistic effort' – the 'absolute formula' – he is less adept in explaining the 'subtle gradation of the shades

of difference between one artistic gift and another' (123). His comments
on individual works of art are therefore of less interest and value than his
abstract pronouncements on the rules of art: Pater's Coleridge is ultimately
not a practical but a philosophical critic.

When Pater revised 'Coleridge's Writings' for inclusion in *Appreciations*,
he retained much of his account of Coleridge the critic (rather than
Coleridge the theologian) as a way to preface the 'critical introduction'
to Coleridge's poetry that he had initially contributed in 1880 to T. H.
Ward's multi-volume anthology *The English Poets*, which he then inserted
fundamentally unabridged (collated with several pages on Wordsworth
from 'Coleridge's Writings') as the second half of the Coleridge chapter.[11]
Pater continues to emphasise Coleridge's dissemination of German metaphysics and transcendental philosophy (presented here as a manifestation
of 'the *a priori*, or absolute, or spiritual, or Platonic, view of things') as 'the
one thread of continuity in a life otherwise singularly wanting in unity of
purpose, and in which he was certainly far from uniformly at his best'
(*App.*, 81, 82). 'Fragmentary and obscure' as he may have been, Coleridge
was 'often eloquent, and always at once earnest and ingenious', classified
by Pater 'as a student of words, and as a psychologist, that is, as a more
minute observer or student than other men of the phenomena of mind'
(82). The latter designation is particularly important for Pater's subsequent
analysis, providing as it does a way to explain both Coleridge's 'imaginative
philosophical expression' in so much of his meditative blank verse and his
'presentation of the marvellous' in the supernatural poems 'The Rhyme of
the Ancient Mariner' and 'Christabel' (93, 97).

Pater sympathetically describes Coleridge in terms of his 'morbid want
of balance ... [mixed with] a kind of languid visionariness', a poet who
claimed he wrote poetry 'after the more violent emotions of sorrow, to
give him pleasure, when perhaps nothing else could', which poetry was
then characterised by 'a certain languidly soothing grace or cadence' (83).[12]
The languid Coleridgean combination of sorrow and pleasure is central to
Pater's estimation of the poetry: as he remarks of several youthful lines
pertaining to the mode in which 'even saddest thoughts / Mix with some
sweet sensations', the 'expression of two opposed, yet allied, elements of
sensibility in these lines, is very true to Coleridge:—the grievous agitation,
the grievous listlessness, almost never entirely relieved, together with a
certain physical voluptuousness' (84). A related register is that of 'stifled,
drowsy, unimpassioned grief' (the source of which was closely allied with
the source of those pleasures), as Coleridge puts it in 'Dejection: An Ode',
a poem critical for Pater's understanding of Coleridge's temperament,

'with its faintness, its grieved dejection', such as when he laments, 'I may not hope from outward forms to win / The passion and the life whose fountains are within' (86; ll. 22, 45–6).[13]

Pater initially contrasts Coleridge's dejection with Wordsworth's joy, his 'joyful and penetrative conviction of the existence of certain latent affinities between nature and the human mind, which reciprocally gild the mind and nature with a kind of "heavenly alchemy"' (85). But whereas Wordsworth instinctively believed in the reciprocal and 'exquisite' fit of the mind of man and the external world (such as in the 'Prospectus' to *The Recluse*, which Pater quotes), for Coleridge this was not a belief so much as an idea (and one that failed him in moments such as those recorded in 'Dejection'): 'In Coleridge's sadder, more purely intellectual, cast of genius, what with Wordsworth was sentiment or instinct became a philosophical idea' (87). He is also compared and contrasted with the prolix Wordsworth in terms of the 'limited quantity of Coleridge's poetical performance', memorably described as 'like some exotic plant, just managing to blossom a little in the somewhat un-english air of Coleridge's own south-western birthplace, but never quite well there' (84–5). As astute as Pater can be in managing the comparison of the two poets, he somewhat reductively confines much of Coleridge's poetic output to the *annus mirabilis* of 1797–98 with Wordsworth (to which Pater assigns the composition of 'Kubla Khan', 'The Rhyme of the Ancient Mariner', and the first part of 'Christabel'), lamenting 'the sudden blossoming, through one short season, of such a gift already perfect in its kind, which thereafter deteriorates as suddenly, with something like premature old age' (87).

Of much greater value, and lasting insight into Coleridge's poetics, is Pater's sustained and nuanced explication 'of what Coleridge meant by Imagination' across a wide range of poems (88). Pater demonstrates an uncannily Coleridgean sense of the 'infusion ... of the figure into the thought', of the ways in which Coleridge manages the 'identification of the poet's thought ... with the image or figure which serves him', such as when he writes in 'To a Gentleman [William Wordsworth]', 'Amid the howl of more than wintry storms, / The halcyon hears the voice of vernal hours / Already on the wing' (88–9; ll. 89–91). In Coleridge's compressed figure here, in the collision of the winter tumult and the summer calm, the halcyon (already on the wing itself) 'hears' the voice of the (halcyon) vernal hours as if in anticipation of the peace that is nigh, the peace that Coleridge found so elusive. This sort of imaginative identification is in turn integral to the 'impassioned contemplation' (similar to Wordsworth's) 'on the permanent and elementary conditions of nature and humanity' that Pater celebrates throughout Coleridge's writing, nowhere perhaps as prominently as in 'To [William Wordsworth]', when Coleridge's celebration of Wordsworth's *Prelude* – 'high and passionate thoughts / To their own music chanted' (ll. 46–7) – may be said to apply equally to his own blank verse, such as in the infrequently cited 'Lines Written in the Album at Elbingerode', in Coleridge's declaration to have found 'That outward forms, the loftiest, still receive / Their finer influence from the world within' (89–91).[14] A crucial manifestation of the Coleridgean imagination is to be read in his 'imaginative treatment of landscape', such as in his foregrounding in 'Fears in Solitude' of 'A green and silent spot amid the hills, / A small and silent dell!' (ll. 1–2), against which silence his fears of a French invasion reverberate. In this pointedly political poem, 'written in April 1798, during the alarm of an invasion', the 'silent dell is the background against which the tumultuous fears of the poet are in strong relief, while the quiet sense of the place, maintained all through them, gives a true poetic unity to the piece' (92). Coleridge's 'singular watchfulness for the minute fact and expression of natural scenery' (here, the dwelling of the poet's mind on a particular spot, green and small and silent, and 'bathed by the mist'), in concert with his 'minute realism', is integral to his imaginative and 'highly sensitive apprehension of the aspects of external nature' and, in the end, 'pervad[es] all he wrote' (90–1).

Pater reserves his most sustained attention for 'The Rhyme of the Ancient Mariner' (the 1817 text, with gloss) and the first part of 'Christabel'. These are Coleridge's 'greatest' poems, for 'In poetic quality ... they are quite out of proportion to all his other compositions' (95). They are both 'romantic' poems, notable for their 'bold invention, and appealing to that taste for the supernatural, that longing for *le frisson*, a shudder', Coleridge's taste for which had been 'encouraged by his odd and out-of-the-way reading in the old-fashioned literature of the marvellous' (96). Pater is particularly interested in Coleridge's handling of this aspect of the poem: 'it is the delicacy, the dreamy grace in his presentation of the marvellous, which makes Coleridge's work so remarkable' (96–7). Whereas intruders from the spiritual world are typically too palpable (even in Shakespeare and Walter Scott), Coleridge writes with a plausibility which Pater finds it hard to pin down: his power 'is in the very fineness with which, as by some really ghostly finger, he brings home to our inmost sense his inventions, daring as they are—the skeleton ship, the polar spirit, the inspiriting of the dead corpses of the ship's crew', resulting in a 'finer, more delicately marvellous supernaturalism' (97, 98). Ever attentive to the fragmentary nature of Coleridge's oeuvre, Pater celebrates 'The Ancient

Mariner' for being a finished poem: 'It is Coleridge's one great complete work, the one really finished thing, in a life of many beginnings' (99). 'Christabel', despite its length (and Coleridge's repeated promises to complete it), 'remained a fragment', albeit one also representative of the tendencies of the 'old romantic ballad, with a spirit made subtle and fine by modern reflection', and notable for Coleridge's innovative experiments in metre (Pater being regularly attentive to Coleridge's 'cadence' (100, 102)).

In citing the passage on the friendship of Sir Roland and Sir Leoline (from the second part of 'Christabel') as an illustration of Coleridge's 'gift of handling the finer passages of human feeling', Pater revisits the question of Coleridge's 'grieved dejection' in order to invert it, in his conclusion, into something radically different (100, 86). What is the predominant quality in Coleridge's poetry? Joy is the unexpected answer:

> [I]t is the sense of such richness and beauty which, in spite of his 'dejection,' in spite of that burden of his morbid lassitude, accompanies Coleridge himself through life. A warm poetic joy in everything beautiful, whether it be a moral sentiment, like the friendship of Roland and Leoline, or only the flakes of falling light from the water-snakes [in 'The Ancient Mariner']— this joy, visiting him, now and again, after sickly dreams, in sleep or waking, as a relief not to be forgotten, and with such a power of felicitous expression that the infection of it passes irresistibly to the reader—such is the pre- dominant element in the matter of his poetry . . . (101–2)

That 'joy' should emerge as the signature component of the matter of Coleridge's poetry (as 'cadence is the predominant quality of its form' (102)) comes as something of a surprise so near the conclusion of a long chapter that has attended throughout to Coleridge's manifold failures, his characteristic dejection, his morbid languor, and his 'diseased or valetudi- narian temperament' (84). Making this claim sets Pater up for a long excerpt from the late poem 'A Tombless Epitaph'. In it, Coleridge describes someone who, though 'besieged' by sickness, 'maintained / The citadel unconquered, and in joy / Was strong to follow the delightful Muse'. Equally familiar with the hidden paths of Parnassus and the 'long- neglected holy cave' of 'old Philosophy', he bears an uncanny resemblance to Coleridge the 'Poet-philosopher' (as fondly designated by Humphry Davy), and is finally eulogised for the same: 'O studious Poet, eloquent for truth! / Philosopher! contemning wealth and death, / Yet docile, childlike, full of Life and Love!' (102–3; ll. 18–20, 29–30, 35–7). Standing at the end of Pater's long and sympathetic engagement with Coleridge's poetry in

Ward's *English Poets*, these lines serve as Coleridge's own epitaph – as postulated in the poem's final lines (which Pater does not include), 'Here, rather than on monumental stone, / This record of thy worth thy Friend inscribes, / Thoughtful, with quiet tears upon his cheek' (ll. 38–40). It is with this sympathetic tribute that Pater concludes his commentary in 1880.

Attending simultaneously to both Coleridge the poet and Coleridge the philosopher allows Pater deftly to link the early writing for the *Westminster Review* with the later commentary for Ward's *English Poets*, and prepare the way for the valedictory conclusion, in which Pater reminds us of the abiding tension in Coleridge's life and work: everywhere 'We see him trying to "apprehend the absolute"', to attain 'fixed principles', ever 'refusing to see the parts as parts only' (103). And it is in this quest that Coleridge's signature failure is most legible:

> 'From his childhood he hungered for eternity'. There, after all, is the incontestable claim of Coleridge. The perfect flower of any elementary type of life must always be precious to humanity, and Coleridge is a true flower of the *ennuyé*, of the type of René. More than Childe Harold, more than Werther, more than René himself, Coleridge, by what he did, what he was, and what he failed to do, represents that inexhaustible discontent, languor, and home-sickness, that endless regret, the chords of which ring all through our modern literature. (104)[15]

Through his summoning of the sensitive, restless, and melancholy heroes of Goethe's *The Sorrows of Young Werther*, Chateaubriand's *René*, and Byron's *Childe Harold's Pilgrimage* (three immensely popular and influential examples of a certain type of Romantic *malheur*), Pater enshrines Coleridge too as a discontented outsider ('the perfect flower of the *romantic* type', as he put it in 'Coleridge's Writings' ('CW', 132; emphasis added). Coleridge furthermore epitomises what Pater repeatedly celebrates as the 'simple, chastened, debonair' essence of the 'Greek spirit': 'with his passion for the absolute, for something fixed where all is moving, his faintness, his broken memory, his intellectual disquiet, [Coleridge] may still be ranked among the interpreters of one of the constituent elements of our life' (*App.*, 104). Coleridge matters for Pater because he failed, because he provided an example of heroic, romantic failure that resonated for Pater himself. Pater clearly identifies with Coleridge, not least in terms of the languor and dejection he attributes to the older writer (with Coleridge's ode on the same arguably the critical poem for Pater's evaluation), and sympathises with the irony of his successful and abiding failure.[16]

Had Coleridge achieved the absolute after which he hungered, he would not have mattered nearly as much to Pater.

***

If Pater's Coleridge is principally distinguished by his languor and his abiding dejection, Pater's Wordsworth is, among other things, a poet of joy and optimism. Pater compares the two in 'Coleridge's Writings', confidently pronouncing that, as early as their collaboration on *Lyrical Ballads* (1798), 'What Wordsworth then wrote is already vibrant with that blithe *élan* which carried him to final happiness and self-possession', whereas in Coleridge 'we feel already that faintness and obscure dejection which cling like some contagious damp to all his writings' ('CW', 108).[17] In support of this stark contrast, Pater cites the important lines from the 'Prospectus' to *The Recluse* in which Wordsworth jubilantly proclaims, 'How exquisitely the individual Mind / / ... to the external World / Is fitted: —and how exquisitely, too, / The external World is fitted to the Mind' (ll. 63–7).[18] This is Wordsworth's grounding belief, his 'dream', made possible by 'that flawless temperament ... which keeps his conviction of a latent intelligence in nature' ('CW', 109). Coleridge, on the other hand, 'could never have abandoned himself' to this dream of the abiding affinity between the natural world and the mind of the poet. His temperament, 'with its faintness, its grieved dejection, could never have been like that' (109), Pater explains, going on to cite Coleridge's despair in 'Dejection'. What for Wordsworth was a fundamental conviction and a permanent consolation was for Coleridge a source of doubt, a 'vain endeavour' (l. 42). For Coleridge's sadder, more purely intellectual, cast of genius, according to Pater, 'What in Wordsworth is a sentiment or instinct, is in [him] a philosophical idea', subject to intellectual assent (110). Wordsworth's 'instinct' was central to his genius: it was his belief in the 'exquisite' alliance between the natural world and the human mind that made possible his 'sense of a life in natural objects' and his depiction of nature as 'ennobled by a semblance of passion and thought' (*App.*, 46, 48).

Wordsworth's optimism (by which Pater means his sense of 'the proportion of man to his place in nature' ('CW', 109–10)), his sense of the sentience of apparently little or familiar things, his deeply reflective bent of mind, and the startling intensity of his best poetry – these qualities provide the basis for Pater's sustained analysis in his essay 'On Wordsworth', first published in the *Fortnightly Review* in April 1874, and reprinted (largely unchanged) in *Appreciations*. Pater's Wordsworth is an heroic example of 'impassioned contemplation' (*App.*, 60), a poet whose work is to be celebrated less for the triumph there of imagination over fancy (a distinction which Pater immediately discounts) than for the 'intensity in the poet's perception of his subject, and in his concentration of himself upon his work' (39). It is for this intensity, and for the 'bold thought' and 'strange speculations' (54, 53) that it made possible, that Wordsworth is to be read and studied. The challenge in reading Wordsworth, however, is that this 'special power' is not always on display, due to the perplexed mixture of the 'higher and lower moods' in his poetry (40, 41).

'On Wordsworth' was Pater's first publication following *The Renaissance*, and it has been argued that it was originally intended for publication in that volume.[19] DeLaura describes the essay not only as a landmark in Wordsworth criticism (appearing five years before Arnold's influential 'Preface' to his anthology of Wordsworth's poetry) but also as 'one of the most crucial statements of his career', a 'distillation of the first decade of Pater's critical career, his most precise attempt up to this time to define the nature of art and the nature of the perfected life'.[20] As a definition of the nature of art, the essay is arguably 'Pater's most consistent performance as an aesthetic critic', a sustained exercise in 'aesthetic criticism', written according to the tenets set forth in the 'Preface' to *The Renaissance*.[21] Indeed, Pater's comments on Wordsworth in the 'Preface' provide the template and the critical lexicon for understanding the analysis of the poetry in 'On Wordsworth', for it is in the 'Preface' that Pater initially tries to explain the role of the critic in untangling the 'absolute duality between higher and lower moods', between the poetic and the prosaic, in the work of even the greatest artists (41).

Pater is concerned in the 'Preface' to define the role and function of the aesthetic critic in identifying and analysing the 'elements' and 'virtues' of a work of art, whose 'end is reached when he has disengaged that virtue, and noted it, as a chemist notes some natural element' (*Ren.*, xxi). Once the critic has identified the particular virtue of a work of art – the power or 'property' it has 'of affecting one with a special, a unique, impression of pleasure' (xx) – it becomes his responsibility to 'disengage' that virtue from 'the commoner elements with which it may be found in combination' (xxi), since the virtue does not necessarily appear in isolation or everywhere in an artist's work. Noting that few artists (not even Goethe or Byron) 'work quite cleanly, casting off all *débris*, and leaving us only what the heat of their imagination has wholly fused and transformed' (xxi), Pater suddenly presents Wordsworth as an example of a great artist whose work is far from free of *débris*: 'The heat of his genius, entering into the substance of his work, has crystallised a part, but only a part, of it; and in that great mass of verse there is much which might well be forgotten' (xxi–xxii). Pater will repeat these points in 'On Wordsworth', characterising the 'heat' of his imaginative genius as his 'intensity', and noting that 'Of all poets equally great, he would gain most by a skilfully made anthology', for 'nowhere is there so perplexed a mixture as in Wordsworth's own poetry, of work touched with intense and individual power, with work of almost no character at all' (*App.*, 40).

The function of the critic, then, is to read for the parts of an artist's work that have been 'crystallised' by the 'heat of his genius', in the knowledge that it will be rare to find an entire composition so characterised (Pater cites 'Resolution and Independence' and the Intimations Ode as two isolated Wordsworthian examples). Instead, the critic must vigilantly comb the work, ever on the lookout for 'a fine crystal here or there' (part of what Pater has in mind in citing the Arnoldian dictum that the aim of criticism must be 'To see the object as in itself it really is' (*Ren.*, xix)), in which he can 'trace the action of [Wordsworth's] unique, incommunicable faculty' (*Ren.*, xxii). This is no small task, but rather one that 'will require great nicety' (xxi): as Pater explains when developing this point, 'the mixture in his work, as it actually stands, is so perplexed, that one fears to miss the least promising composition even, lest some precious morsel should be lying hidden within—the few perfect lines, the phrase, the single word perhaps, to which he often works up mechanically through a poem' (*App.*, 41). Once he has identified the embedded lines which reveal Wordsworth's 'unique, incommunicable faculty, that strange, mystical sense of a life in natural things, and of man's life as a part of nature, drawing strength and colour and character from local influences' (*Ren.*, xxii), the critic must proceed to disentangle them from the surrounding brush and make them legible for other readers. As Pater exclaims in concluding this Wordsworthian preview, 'Well! that is the *virtue*, the active principle in Wordsworth's poetry; and then the function of the critic of Wordsworth is to follow up that active principle, to disengage it, to mark the degree in which it penetrates his verse' (xxii). In his later writing on Wordsworth, Pater proceeds to do precisely this.

What Pater here denominates Wordsworth's 'unique, incommunicable faculty' he later inflects as the 'special power' of Wordsworth's poetry, that which produces 'precious morsels' (akin to the earlier 'fine crystals') to be unearthed here and there, 'the golden pieces, great and small, lying apart together' that reward the attentive reader (*App.*, 40, 42–3). Pater consistently emphasises the difficulty of reading Wordsworth in this regard, and the 'peculiar savour' available to the vigilant reader who persists (40). Pater's Wordsworth is a challenging poet, and can be unsettling; to read him successfully requires an unusual degree of discipline and concentration. The constant tension and unpredictable alternation between the poet's higher and lower moods 'makes the reading of Wordsworth an excellent sort of training towards the things of art and poetry':

> It begets in those, who, coming across him in youth, can bear him at all, a habit of reading between the lines, a faith in the effect of concentration and collectedness of mind in the right appreciation of poetry, . . . coming to one by means of a right discipline of the temper as well as of the intellect. He meets us with the promise that he has much, and something very peculiar, to give us, if we will follow a certain difficult way, and seems to have the secret of a special and privileged state of mind. (41–2)

The key term here may be 'difficult': reading Wordsworth is for Pater a sort of training, a *disciplina arcani* which he characterises as an 'initiation' (42). Pater's own essay is itself an initiation in the ways of reading this 'strange' and 'peculiar' poet, one designed to assist its readers in locating Wordsworth's 'secret' and distinguishing 'that which is organic, animated, expressive' in Wordsworth (the bolder, higher mood) from 'that which is only conventional, derivative, inexpressive' (the tedious and prosaic lower mood (42)).[22]

Wordsworth's virtue – the 'active principle' that produces a particularly Wordsworthian 'impression of beauty or pleasure' – may be said to be twofold, consisting in both his heightened 'sense of a life in natural objects' (a new possibility of poetical thought, according to Pater) and the strange, 'bold speculative ideas' that Pater attributes to his peculiarly philosophical imagination (46, 56). This is what Pater is on the lookout for in Wordsworth's poetry, what he tries to 'disengage' from the perplexed mixture of intense and tepid in the poet's vast oeuvre. Proposing a 'just criticism and true estimate' of Wordsworth's poetry (42), Pater sets forth several questions as the criteria for his assessment:

> What are the peculiarities of this residue [the 'golden pieces']? What special sense does Wordsworth exercise, and what instincts does he satisfy? What are the subjects and the motives which in him excite the imaginative faculty? What are the qualities in things and persons which he values, the impression and sense of which he can convey to others, in an extraordinary way? (43)

First and foremost there is Wordsworth's 'intimate consciousness of the expression of natural things, which weighs, listens, penetrates', a product of the poet's 'quiet, habitual observation of inanimate, or imperfectly animate, existence' in concert with his 'quite unusual sensibility, really innate in him, to the sights and sounds of the natural world' (43, 44). Here Pater cites 'Resolution and Independence' (as also in the 'Preface' to *The Renaissance*) as a storehouse of such images, one of Wordsworth's few poems that is entirely characterised by the higher mood and the heat of genius.

Pater turns to *The Prelude* to demonstrate the precision of Wordsworth's imagery, such as the desolation of 'The single sheep, and the one blasted tree, / And the bleak music of that old stone wall' that anchor the second of the 'spots of time',[23] and quotes extensively from 'Home at Grasmere' (published for the first time in 1888) as evidence of 'the leading characteristics of Wordsworth's genius', most prominently perhaps his delineation of the 'close connexion of man with natural objects, [and] the habitual association of his thoughts and feelings with a particular spot of earth' (46 n.1, 48). And he emphasises Wordsworth's belief that 'every natural object seemed to possess more or less of a moral or spiritual life, to be capable of a companionship with man, full of expression, of inexplicable affinities and delicacies of intercourse' (46–7). Although Pater doesn't quote Wordsworth's poetry in support of his 'power of seeing life ... in inanimate things' (48), he might have turned to 'Lines Written a Few Miles Above Tintern Abbey' to do so, specifically the climactic exclamation regarding 'that serene and blessed mood' in which we 'see into the life of things' (ll. 42, 50). Pater's Wordsworth has the 'power to open out the soul of apparently little or familiar things' and, in doing so, to 'rais[e] nature to the level of human thought' (49). The intense correlation of man and nature, with its integration of daily life and permanent natural objects, allows Wordsworth in turn to 'appreciate passion in the lowly' (51). Wordsworth 'chooses to depict people from humble life', Pater reminds us, 'because, being nearer to nature than others, they are on the whole more impassioned, certainly more direct in their expression of passion, than other men' (51). And it was because of this 'direct expression of passion', this 'passionate sincerity', that Wordsworth 'chose incidents and situations from common life, "related in a selection of language really used by men"', as he claims in the 'Preface' to *Lyrical Ballads* (51).[24]

With this emphasis on passion (what Wordsworth 'values most is the almost elementary expression of elementary feelings' (52)), Pater clinches his argument regarding 'this strange, new, passionate, pastoral world, of which [Wordsworth] first raised the image' (think of the haunting pastoral

'Michael', a frequent point of reference for Pater), and shifts his attention to what he calls the 'philosophy' of Wordsworth's poetry, the 'strangeness' of which is for Pater Wordsworth's other great and distinguishing virtue (53). It is here that the real discernment of Pater's reading of Wordsworth emerges. Noting the high value that Wordsworth placed on customariness, 'upon all that is habitual, local, rooted in the ground', and that, as such, one might 'regard him as one tethered down to a world ... with no broad outlook, a world protected, but somewhat narrowed, by the influence of received ideas', Pater abruptly pivots to claim that Wordsworth 'is at times also something very different from this, and something much bolder' and 'seems at times to have passed the borders of a world of strange speculations' (54, 53). This is the essence of the 'higher mood' that Pater so values in Wordsworth, when the poet moves away from the humble and the local 'on bold trains of speculative thought, and comes, from point to point, into strange contact with thoughts which have visited, from time to time, far more venturesome, perhaps errant, spirits' (54). Pater is thinking here of Wordsworth's preoccupation (most notably in the 'Ode (Intimations of Immortality)') with 'those strange reminiscences and forebodings, which seem to make our lives stretch before and behind us' and his 'sense of man's dim, potential powers' (54). More pointedly, Pater is trying to account for moments of intense imaginative power (although Pater doesn't mention them, the 'spots of time' in *The Prelude* again provide an important example), when 'the actual world would, as it were, dissolve and detach itself, flake by flake, and he himself seemed to be the creator, and when he would the destroyer, of the world in which he lived', or 'periods of intense susceptibility, in which he appeared to himself as but the passive recipient of external influences' (55, 56). It was in the grip of such susceptibilities that 'a new, bold thought lifted [Wordsworth] above the furrow, above the green turf of the Westmoreland churchyard, to a world altogether different in its vagueness and vastness, and the narrow glen was full of the brooding power of one universal spirit' (56).

It is at such times that Wordsworth achieved the 'conditions of poetical thought', a rarefied atmosphere in which 'philosophical imaginings' find a place in 'true poetry', being deployed there for 'poetical purposes' (56). Pater admires Wordsworth's avoidance of technical diction in writing about philosophical concerns in his poetry (he emphasises books 12 and 13 of the 1850 *Prelude*, regarding the decay then subsequent restoration of the imagination), his ability to keep them 'within certain ethical bounds' (57). Nevertheless, it is

> the contact of these thoughts, the speculative boldness in them, which constitutes, at least for some minds, the secret attraction of much of his best poetry—the sudden passage from lowly thoughts and places to the majestic forms of philosophical imagination, the play of these forms over a world so different, enlarging so strangely the bounds of its humble churchyards, and breaking such a wild light on the graves of christened children. (57)

The 'speculative boldness' of Wordsworth's philosophical imaginings constitutes for Pater the highest register of his higher mood, that 'virtue' which any critic of Wordsworth must 'disengage' from the mass of the more prosaic writing in the lower mood. It is a mood characterised by 'faultless expression', a seemingly effortless unification of 'the word and the idea; each, in the imaginative flame, becoming inseparably one with the other, by that fusion of matter and form, which is the characteristic of the highest poetical expression' (57, 58). Pater's 'strange' Wordsworth is most legible at these moments, such as the stolen boat episode in *The Prelude*.

Pater's argument regarding Wordsworth's arresting strangeness and speculative boldness effectively ends here – but the chapter does not.[25] In what remains, Pater moves from 'aesthetic criticism' of the poetry to his assessment of the more comprehensive significance of Wordsworth as an example of 'impassioned contemplation' ('*being* as distinct from *doing*'), which in turn is 'the end-in-itself, the perfect end' and the fundamental principle of what Pater proceeds to formulate as 'the higher morality' (60, 62).[26] Pater doesn't present Wordsworth as a moralist per se (his work is 'not to teach lessons, or enforce rules, or even to stimulate us to noble ends' (62)) but, like other great poets, as a 'master' in the 'art of impassioned contemplation' who manifests what it is 'to withdraw the thoughts for a little while from the mere machinery of life, to fix them, with appropriate emotions, on the spectacle of those great facts in man's existence which no machinery affects' (62–3). What are these great facts? Pater turns to Wordsworth for clarification, quoting two important passages from the 'Preface' to *Lyrical Ballads* regarding 'the great and universal passions of men' and 'the operations of the elements, and the appearances of the visible universe' (63).[27] Wordsworth's poetry serves as an effective stimulant for the 'appropriate emotions' with which to contemplate the great facts of life, for 'he sees men and women as parts of nature, passionate, excited, in strange grouping and connexion with the grandeur and beauty of the natural world', 'suffering, amid awful forms and powers' (63; quoting from *Prelude* 8.165). This is Pater's final rationale for persisting with the *disciplina arcani* necessary to learn how to read the difficult Wordsworth, to access 'the more powerful and original

poet, hidden away, in part, under those weaker elements ..., a poet
somewhat bolder and more passionate than might at first sight be
supposed' (63).

Pater's Wordsworth is not the soothing Wordsworth of John Stuart
Mill, who characterised the poetry in his *Autobiography* as 'a medicine for
my state of mind', or Leslie Stephen, who wrote that Wordsworth 'seems
to me to be the only consoler', or John Morley, who remarked that 'What
Wordsworth does is to assuage, to reconcile, to fortify', leading his readers
'into inner moods of settled peace'.[28] Such writers represent the 'fervent
Wordsworthian[s]' against whom Arnold says one must be on guard, given
their propensity to praise Wordsworth for the wrong things.[29] Although
Arnold too had earlier praised Wordsworth in 'Memorial Verses' for his
'healing power',[30] by the time of his influential 'Preface' to his anthology
of Wordsworth's poetry (1879), he sounded much more like Pater, whose
essay of 1874 resonates throughout the later 'Preface'.[31] Arnold shares
Pater's conviction that Wordsworth's oeuvre is radically uneven, that there
is a 'mass of inferior work ... imbedding the first-rate work and clogging
it', as a consequence of which 'Wordsworth needs to be relieved of a great
deal of the poetical baggage which now encumbers him'.[32] Arnold's
understanding of the work of the anthologiser is precisely what Pater
advocated in the 'Preface' to *The Renaissance*, namely 'To *disengage* the
poems which show his power'.[33] Arnold also joins Pater in presenting
Wordsworth as a poet 'Of joy in widest commonalty spread' (citing the
'Prospectus' to *The Recluse*) and develops Pater's insight into the unification of word and idea in the poetry of his higher mood when he writes of
'the successful balance' in Wordsworth's best poems 'of profound truth of
subject with profound truth of execution'.[34] Arnold departs from Pater,
however, in discounting the quality of Wordsworth's thinking in the
poetry: where Pater champions Wordsworth's 'bold trains of speculative
thought', Arnold dismisses any 'formal philosophy' in Wordsworth:
'Poetry is the reality, philosophy the illusion.'[35]

Pater's influence extends beyond the reception of Wordsworth in the
1870s and 1880s. In his *Oxford Lectures on Poetry* (1909), A. C. Bradley
contrasts Arnold's and Pater's essays, criticising Arnold for portraying
Wordsworth's poetry as 'more easily apprehended than it ever can be'
(far from Pater's difficult Wordsworth) and for downplaying anything
resembling a 'Wordsworthian philosophy'.[36] Pater is praised for not being
so one-sided, and for having written 'an extremely fine piece of criticism',
but Bradley nevertheless takes issue with Pater for what he perceives to be
an excessive emphasis on 'the peculiar function of Wordsworth's genius'

as a poet of nature.[37] Bradley's objective is to bring into greater critical focus the '"mystic", "visionary", "sublime" aspect of Wordsworth's poetry',[38] but that seems to be precisely what Pater had already done in concentrating on the ways in which Wordsworth crosses 'the borders of a world of strange speculations' with his 'speculative boldness'. Indeed, it is the strangeness and difficulty of Pater's Wordsworth that distinguishes his interpretation from the more conventional emphases on the poet of consolation or the poet of nature. Therein remains Pater's insight and influence as a critic of Wordsworth.

***

Pater initially wrote about both Coleridge and Wordsworth at times when their posthumous reputations were still unsettled. While certainly viewed as integral parts of what was coming to be called the 'Romantic' canon, it was unclear for what writings they would be remembered. After his death, Coleridge was thought of first as a religious 'philosopher' and second as a poet. Pater's essay of 1866 marks an important re-evaluation of his prose writings, with its unabashed criticism of his recycling of 'inferior theological literature' (particularly in the *Aids to Reflection*) and its detailed praise for his 'theory of art-criticism' in both the *Biographia* and the lectures on Shakespeare. Later, in his commentary on the poetry in 1880, Pater was instrumental in redefining Coleridge's relationship to the 'Lake School' and explaining the significance of the poems he considered to be Coleridge's finest achievements, notably 'Dejection: An Ode' and 'The Rhyme of the Ancient Mariner'. In revising and combining these writings for the chapter on Coleridge in *Appreciations*, Pater effectively codified the Coleridge that mattered for the final decades of the nineteenth century. In his essay on Wordsworth of 1874, Pater simultaneously completed the work that he proposed in the 'Preface' to *The Renaissance* and anticipated many of the criteria for the evaluation of Wordsworth that Arnold would popularise five years later in his 'Preface'. He wrote at a time when the textual authority of various editions of the poet's work was unclear, and for readers who were often confused or put off by Wordsworth's strange, unwieldy classifications of his own poems. Pater presented Wordsworth as a poet who required effort to read, but rewarded this *disciplina arcani* with 'an excellent sort of training towards the things of art and poetry' (41–2). As is the case with his writing on Coleridge, Pater's essay on Wordsworth was instrumental in shaping the poet's reputation and reception from the 1870s onwards.

These writings are significant not only for shaping the posthumous reputations of two Romantic poets, but also for what they reveal about

Pater's development as a critic. The precocious (if not always internally coherent) Coleridge essay reveals Pater assimilating Arnold's writings, even as he moves away from the older critic in the development of what would become his 'higher morality' or 'religious aestheticism'. And the Wordsworth essay shows Pater completing, as it were, the work he began in *The Renaissance* in what is arguably his most sustained piece of aesthetic criticism. When revised and republished in *Appreciations*, they provided telling examples of the combination of critical acumen, admiration, and sympathy that Pater implies in the modest term 'appreciation'. A remark of Pater's on Charles Lamb is noteworthy for what it reveals about Pater's own critical sensibility: 'To feel strongly the charm of an old poet . . . and then to interpret that charm, to convey it to others . . . this is the way of his criticism' (*App.*, 112). 'Charm', of course, is the note on which Pater began the essay on Coleridge in 1866. The 'disengagement' and interpretation of that charm (or 'special power', in the case of Wordsworth) is integral both to Pater's aesthetic practice and to his enduring value as a critic.

Notes

1 All quotations from reviews of *Appreciations* will be found in *Critical Heritage*: 201–3 (Symons); 212–13 (Graves); 235–6 (Wilde); 196 (Shorter); 240 (Courthope).

2 [Thomas Allsop, ed.], *Letters, Conversations and Recollections of S. T. Coleridge* (1836; 2nd edn 1858, 3rd edn 1864). The title is given slightly erroneously in the heading to Pater's article in the *Westminster*.

3 Samuel Taylor Coleridge, *Aids to Reflection*, ed. John Beer; vol. ix in *The Collected Works of Samuel Taylor Coleridge* (Princeton 1993), cxiii.

4 The same is true of the posthumously published *Confessions of an Inquiring Spirit* (1840), on the inspiration of the Scriptures, which according to Pater entirely 'discredit[ed] his name with the orthodox' ('CW', 129).

5 David DeLaura has persuasively argued that Pater takes many of his initial bearings in 'Coleridge's Writings' from Matthew Arnold, specifically the *Essays in Criticism* (*Hebrew and Hellene in Victorian England: Newman, Arnold, and Pater* (Austin, TX 1969), 193).

6 Coleridge, *Aids to Reflection*, cxlvii.

7 DeLaura, *Hebrew and Hellene*, 195–6. 'The experience of the residuary perfume and sweetness of older erroneous beliefs in this new higher morality or broader spirituality will be evoked by a wide acquaintance with the best art or philosophy or theology, and will no longer be claimed exclusively by the older narrow and untenable forms of religious life' (196).

8 Pater remarked of the essay in 1882 that 'both as to matter and manner, I should now be greatly dissatisfied' (Lawrence G. Evans, 'Some Letters of

Walter Pater', unpublished PhD thesis, Harvard University, 1961, 53; quoted in DeLaura, *Hebrew and Hellene*, 198 n.6). The theological passages from 'Coleridge's Writings' were republished in Walter Pater, *Sketches and Reviews*, ed. Albert Mordell (1919); see DeLaura, *Hebrew and Hellene*, 195 n.3.

9 T. S. Eliot, 'Arnold and Pater', in *Selected Essays 1917–1932* (New York 1932), 349.

10 Samuel Taylor Coleridge, 'Shakespeare's Judgment equal to his Genius', in *The Literary Remains of Samuel Taylor Coleridge*, ed. Henry Nelson Coleridge (1836), ii. 67–8.

11 T. H. Ward, ed., *The English Poets: Selections: With Critical Introductions by Various Writers*, 4 vols (1880); Pater's introduction to Coleridge, and the selections from the poetry (made by Pater or Ward, or the two of them in consultation), are to be found in iv. 102–54. The following poems were included, in this order: 'Time, Real and Imaginary'; 'Love'; 'Sonnet' ('La Fayette', from 'Sonnets on Eminent Characters'); 'The Eolian Harp'; 'Frost at Midnight'; 'Dejection. An Ode'; 'Sonnet. Composed on a Journey Homewards'; the first part of 'Christabel'; 'The Rhyme of the Ancient Mariner' (1817 text).

12 Pater here paraphrases Coleridge's preface to *Poems on Various Subjects* (1796).

13 Unless otherwise noted, all quotations from Coleridge's poetry may be found in *Coleridge's Poetry and Prose*, ed. Nicholas Halmi, Paul Magnuson, and Raimonda Modiano (New York 2004).

14 Coleridge, 'Lines Written in the Album at Elbingerode', ll. 16–17, in *Sibylline Leaves* (1817).

15 Pater quotes Charles Lamb regarding Coleridge's 'hunger' for eternity; see also *App.*, 73. Charles Lamb, 'The Death of Coleridge', *The Works of Charles Lamb*, 2 vols, ed. Thomas Hutchinson (Oxford 1910), i. 454.

16 As Seamus Perry has observed, 'in the later part of [the] nineteenth century, that sense of tragic failure starts to transform itself into a paradoxical sort of success, as it does in Pater's essay, a special kind of Romanticism' ('Coleridge's English Afterlife', in *The Reception of S. T. Coleridge in Europe*, ed. Elinor Shaffer and Edoardo Zuccato (2007), 21).

17 Pater later adapted this comparison for inclusion in the Wordsworth chapter in *Appreciations*.

18 Unless otherwise noted, all quotations from Wordsworth's poetry may be found in *Wordsworth's Poetry and Prose*, ed. Nicholas Halmi (New York 2014).

19 Billie Andrew Inman maintains that 'On Wordsworth' 'might have been the unnamed essay in manuscript sent to Macmillan in June 1872 for inclusion in *The Renaissance* to illustrate the survival of a Greek sense of God in nature in the mind of a nineteenth-century poet' (Inman (1990), 42).

20 David J. DeLaura, 'The "Wordsworth" of Pater and Arnold: "The Supreme, Artistic View of Life"', *Studies in English Literature* 6 (1966), 651, 652. Adam Lee has further argued that Pater's 'professional intent' in the essay was 'to establish Wordsworth's literary legacy in Britain' (*The Platonism of Walter Pater: Embodied Equity* (Oxford 2020), 58).

21 Inman (1990), 42. See also Kenneth Daley, *The Rescue of Romanticism: Walter Pater and John Ruskin* (Athens, OH 2001), 33–4.

22 In the *Biographia*, Coleridge too noted the radical disparity of a higher and a lower mood in Wordsworth's poetry, identifying the first 'defect' of Wordsworth's poetry as the 'INCONSTANCY of the *style*', by which he means 'the sudden and unprepared transitions from lines or sentences of peculiar felicity (at all events striking and original) to a style, not only unimpassioned but undistinguished' (*Coleridge's Poetry and Prose*, 525).

23 William Wordsworth, *The Prelude: 1799, 1805, 1850*, ed. Jonathan Wordsworth, M. H. Abrams, Stephen Gill (New York 1979), Book 12 (1850), ll. 319–20. All citations from *The Prelude* are taken from the 1850 text.

24 William Wordsworth, *The Prose Works of William Wordsworth*, 3 vols, ed. W. J. B. Owen and Jane Worthington Smyser (Oxford 1974), i. 123. All citations from the 'Preface' are taken from the 1850 text.

25 For a more sustained consideration of 'Pater's strange Wordsworth', see Daley, *Rescue of Romanticism*, 30ff.

26 Inman suggests that Pater 'added the five paragraphs of the essay preceding the last paragraph, which are defensive in tone, after he had become aware of unfavorable responses to *The Renaissance*' (Inman (1990), 42). DeLaura has argued that Pater's central terms and assumptions in these paragraphs 'are derived from Arnold, especially from his farewell lecture at Oxford in 1867, now known to us in *Culture and Anarchy* as "Sweetness and Light"' ('"Wordsworth" of Pater and Arnold', 652).

27 Wordsworth, *Prose Works*, i. 145, 142.

28 John Stuart Mill, *Autobiography of John Stuart Mill* (New York 1924), 104; Leslie Stephen to Charles Eliot Norton, 5 March 1876, quoted in Stephen Gill, *Wordsworth and the Victorians* (Oxford 1998), 215; John Morley, Introduction, in *New Edition of Wordsworth's Complete Poetical Works* (1888), 48.

29 Arnold, *Prose*, ix. 48.

30 Matthew Arnold, *The Poetical Works of Matthew Arnold*, ed. C. B. Tinker and H. F. Lowry (1950), 272 (l. 63).

31 See DeLaura, '"Wordsworth" of Pater and Arnold', 663 n.11.

32 Arnold, *Prose*, ix. 42. Pater acknowledged Arnold for his 'excellent' selections when he republished his own essay on Wordsworth (*App.*, 43 n.1).

33 Arnold, *Prose*, ix. 54; emphasis added.

34 Arnold, *Prose*, ix. 54.

35 Arnold, *Prose*, ix. 48.

36 A. C. Bradley, *Oxford Lectures on Poetry* (1909), 127.

37 Bradley, *Oxford Lectures*, 128. Bradley is quoting a passage added for the republication of the Wordsworth essay in 1889; *App.*, 49.

38 Bradley, *Oxford Lectures*, 129.

CHAPTER 12

Walter Pater, Charles Lamb, and 'the value of reserve'

Stacey McDowell

A sense of humour might not be one of the first qualities that readers associate with Pater. Frequently described as shy, reticent, and reserved in his personal manner, in his writings he maintains a degree of reserve through the careful measure and polish of his style. 'Yet he was instinct with veritable *fun*, and wrote with quiet mirth', Lionel Johnson insists. Reviewing his *Essays from 'The Guardian'*, Johnson urges us to 'have done with the fabled Mr Pater of a strict and strait solemnity' and to recognise instead 'the wise laughter rippling so pleasantly beneath the studied phrases'.[1] If there is fun beneath Pater's reserve, then his essay on Charles Lamb in *Appreciations* asks us to see the reserve beneath the fun, or rather to see Lamb's fun as its own form of reserve. First published in the *Fortnightly Review* in October 1878, the essay begins by praising Lamb's humour, yet concludes: 'The writings of Charles Lamb are an excellent illustration of the value of reserve in literature' (*App.*, 121). The remark is surprising. Lamb is said to be so well loved precisely because of his lack of reserve, his easy familiarity, and open and laughing gregariousness. But Pater sees that Lamb's humour is concealing something, and that it does so through a kind of stylistic flourish, rather than the buttoned-up withholding normally associated with reserve.

Lamb's way of seeming so familiar while keeping something back raises questions about the place of the critic's self within critical prose. His essays have an unassuming quality, Pater notes; more suggestive than assertive, they seem merely casual, accidental, and slight, while holding a deeper knowledge in reserve. In the background of Pater's remarks is the new meaning that reserve had taken on within the context of Tractarian doctrine, which placed an emphasis on indirectness and a certain degree of withholding in matters of religious exegesis. When reserve is thought of as a principle of critical exegesis and as an element of essayistic style, then it begins to seem like something Lamb and Pater might have in common. The two writers can otherwise seem an unlikely pair. 'A more charming essay on Lamb could hardly be written by a completely un-Lamb-like man', writes Edward Thomas. A review of *Appreciations* from December 1889 notes that 'Mr Pater's habitual pensiveness as a critic, and the autumnal tone of his work, make this tribute to Charles Lamb all the more remarkable'.[2] Pater's essay shows a side of Lamb's humour in keeping with reserve, while also bringing out a side of Pater, which, if not exactly laugh-a-minute funny, answers to his description of the critic as humourist. By bringing together two seemingly contradictory qualities in Lamb, the essay helps us to understand what seems so paradoxical about Pater: his famed reserve versus the flair and personal distinctiveness of his style.

Robert Southey was dismayed by Lamb's attempt to laugh off his heartbreak after he found out that the woman he had loved unrequitedly and penned devoted sonnets to had married someone else. 'There is something quite unnatural in Lamb's levity', Southey wrote:

> If he never loved her why did he publish those sonnets? If he did why talk of it with bravado laughter, or why talk of it at all? My opinions are for the world but my feelings are to myself. I would proclaim the one under the gallows, but shrink from the indulgence of the other in the presence of my nearest friends.[3]

All Lamb's talk and bravado shocks Southey's guarded sense of privacy. Yet what Southey does not see is how such bravado works as a form of reserve, its flaunting display concealing the true nature of Lamb's feelings. If a manner of talk that seems so exposing could keep Southey guessing, then the side of Lamb that is so open and laughing need not be seen as at odds with the quality of reserve. What Pater sees is that in the defences and feints of Lamb's humour lies a trick of style that reveals as much as it conceals.

It has become common in Lamb criticism to suspect something darker is lurking beneath the humour, but Pater was the first to identify this as a characteristic undertone: 'Below his quiet, his quaintness, his humour, and what may seem the slightness, the occasional or accidental character of his work, there lies ... a genuinely tragic element' (121).[4] When Lamb was twenty-one, his sister Mary killed their mother in a fit of madness and Lamb, to save her from being shut up in an asylum, devoted the rest of his life to looking after her. This was the tragedy lying always beneath the 'blithe surface' (107). Then there were the lower-pitched miseries of Lamb's life: an early disappointment in love, the drudgery of his job as a clerk at the East India Company, the ever-present threat of returning madness – not just for Mary but for Lamb, too, after his own past spell in an asylum. His humour in the face of all this Pater saw not as incongruous but of a piece. If your understanding of comedy appreciated how closely bound it is with tragedy, then Lamb's humour could be understood not simply as a form of denial or defiance but as an abreactive form of release. In Lamb, Pater identified the 'union of grave, of terrible even, with gay' (106).

Lamb's humour has otherwise been regarded as merely charming, quaint or whimsical, with a fondness that might be dismissive or else working hard to keep something at bay. 'What is so unsettling about Lamb', asks David Russell, 'that he has been so often quarantined by means of an aggressive sentimentality?'[5] Pater draws out the edgier side of Lamb's humour by focusing not only on the pseudonymous *Essays of Elia* for which he is most famous and best loved, but also on his letters and criticism, and on the grave facts of his life. 'In estimating the humour of *Elia*', Pater says, 'we must no more forget the strong undercurrent of this great misfortune and pity, than one could forget it in his actual story. So he becomes the best critic, almost the discoverer, of Webster' (108). This reflects Pater's principle of viewing a writer within the context of his or her life, while the causal link signalled by that 'so' recognises the autobio-graphical element also involved in writing literary criticism. Lamb's first-hand knowledge of tragedy is what makes him so responsive to it in the works of others. His *Specimens of English Dramatic Poets Who Lived about the Time of Shakespeare* (1808) helped to rescue Webster, and early modern drama more generally, from neglect. These works, with their dark morality and violence, had fallen out of fashion in the period surrounding the French Revolution. But they held a fascination for Lamb, whose own life story was, in Pater's words, 'dark and insane as in old Greek tragedy' (122). The insights that appear scattered in the footnotes of his *Specimens of English Dramatic Poets* are for Pater 'the very quintessence of criticism' (111). Lamb's note on the *Duchess of Malfi*, for example, begins, 'She has lived among horrors till she is become "native and endowed unto that element"', which seems to be echoed faintly in Pater's description of Leonardo's *Mona Lisa*.[6]

What Pater observes of the function of humour in Lamb, Lamb had similarly noted in his own critical writings. Discussing John Kemble's performances of Shakespeare, Lamb praises the actor for being particularly alive to 'the relaxing levities of tragedy' and for 'the sportive relief which he threw into the darker shades of Richard'.[7] This coincides with Pater's view that Lamb's humour works both to relieve and set in relief the tragedy of his life. Pater similarly invokes Shakespeare when drawing a distinction between 'Wit and Humour', between 'that unreal and transitory mirth' and 'the laughter which blends with tears and even with the sublimities of the imagination, and which, in its most exquisite motives, is one with pity—the laughter of the comedies of Shakespeare' (105). Although the essay begins with this conceptual differentiation, the terms 'wit', 'humour', 'comedy', and 'mirth' are often so variously used by both writers that it is difficult to keep hold of any firm distinctions. Still, Lamb, like Pater, is keen to elevate a particular kind of humour, one bound up with tragedy and feelings of sympathy or pity. Defending William Hogarth from the imputation that he is a 'mere comic painter' preoccupied solely with 'shaking the sides', Lamb identifies a 'tragic cast of expression and incident, blended in some instances with a greater alloy of comedy' (i. 82, 95, 89–90). His essay 'On the Genius and Character of Hogarth' involves an extended discussion of humour as a blended alloy, and Pater singles out Lamb's criticism of Hogarth when noting that his talent as a critic of art is rarely discussed (which continues to be the case). Shakespeare again pro-vides a touchstone. Comparing the final madhouse scene in *The Rake's Progress* to *King Lear*, Lamb discerns 'a medley of mirth checked by misery, and misery rebuked by mirth' (i. 83). Alliteration and chiasmus suggest connection while also asking us to notice that 'checked' and 'rebuked' are not quite the same thing.

That mirth is not to be rebuked in the face of the misery it can help to assuage is something Lamb firmly believed, even if it occasionally got him into trouble. 'Any thing awful makes me laugh', he reports in a letter, 'I misbehaved once at a funeral. Yet I can read about these ceremonies with pious & proper feelings—. The realities of life only seem the mockeries'.[8] He had misbehaved by making a pun. Clowning, cracking jokes, nervous laughter: humour is a common, if precarious, form of defence. 'Charles who like an undermined river bank leans carlessly [*sic*] over his jollity', was John Clare's impression on first meeting Lamb.[9] His famed gregariousness and drinking and fooling in company sometimes seem like the forced sociability of the constitutionally shy man. Writing as Elia, he boasts of his 'foolish talent', in moments of awkwardness or 'in any emergency, of thinking and giving vent to all manner of strange nonsense' (ii. 275). Making a pun at a funeral is part of this, while doing so also bears out Lamb's conviction in 'the compatibility of the *serious pun* with the expres-sion of the profoundest sorrows'.[10] Lamb knows the pun's best defence is to have none: 'a man might blur ten sides of paper in attempting a defence of it against a critic who should be laughter-proof' (ii. 293). Pater, allegedly, did not like puns (although as Lene Østermark-Johansen notes, he employs them often enough in his own writings, and anyone with such a keen interest in words and their shifting usage might be expected to particularly appreciate a pun).[11] Pater is not the po-faced, 'laughter-proof' kind of critic. His liking for Lamb suggests as much – at least according to the commonly held belief that liking Lamb is proof of the reader's own good humour.

'People have come to talk as if a sense of humour were one of the cardinal virtues', Leslie Stephen gruffly complained in his 1881 article on 'The Essayists'. He was objecting more to an insiders' club superiority that he perceived among Lamb 'worshippers' than to anything about humour itself.[12] The tendency to valorise Lamb is epitomised by the 'Saint Charles' epithet, coined by William Makepeace Thackeray, that gained currency in the Victorian period.[13] Although Pater does not go this far, his essay on Lamb forms part of a broader claim about the moral value of that particular type of humour that for him defines the humourist. The essay on Lamb, when initially published in the *Fortnightly Review*, carried the subtitle: 'The Character of the Humourist'. In his essay on Thomas Browne, Pater makes a case for 'the literary purpose of the humourist, in the old-fashioned sense of the term', defined as one 'who has hardly a sense of the distinction between great and little among things that are at all, and whose half-pitying, half-amused sympathy is called out especially by the seemingly small interests and traits of character in the things or the people around him' (*App.*, 128). Lamb answers to this description. The words 'little' and 'small' crop up again and again as Pater notes Lamb's sympathy for children and animals and sundry things (tatty books, old sundials, china teacups). '[H]e could throw the gleam of poetry or humour on what seemed common or threadbare; has a care for the sighs, and the weary, humdrum preoccupations of very weak people, down to their little pathetic "gentilities"', Pater writes, his finicky adjectives suggesting some-thing of the weary and wearying manner that Lamb observes in such people (he is very good on how annoying ill people can be, for example, or on the gentilities and vain affectations with which individuals attempt to mask insecurity) (119–20). Throwing a gleam of humour over things does not just gloss over them, since what is also acknowledged here is the generosity or fond indulgence such care requires. What makes for the 'boundless sympathy' of the humourist is Lamb's way of being 'in imme-diate contact with what is real, especially in its caressing littleness, that littleness in which there is much of the whole woeful heart of things' (110).

'What sudden, unexpected touches of pathos in him!' Pater adds, and
there are occasionally such touches in his own writing, too (110). Towards
the end of *Marius the Epicurean*, Marius seems likewise struck:

> Men's fortunes touch us! The little children of one of those institutions for
> the support of orphans, now become fashionable among us by way of
> memorial of eminent persons deceased, are going, in long file, along the
> street, on their way to a holiday in the country. They halt, and count
> themselves with an air of triumph, to show that they are all there. Their gay
> chatter has disturbed a little group of peasants; a young woman and her
> husband, who have brought the old mother, now past work and witless, to
> place her in a house provided for such afflicted people. They are fairly
> affectionate, but anxious how the thing they have to do may go—hope
> only she may permit them to leave her there behind quietly. And the
> poor old soul is excited by the noise made by the children, and partly
> aware of what is going to happen with her. She too begins to count—one,
> two, three, five—on her trembling fingers, misshapen by a life of toil. 'Yes!
> yes! and twice five make ten'—they say, to pacify her. It is her last
> appeal to be taken home again; her proof that all is not yet up with
> her; that she is, at all events, still as capable as those joyous children.
> (*ME*, ii. 175–6, ch. 25)

The opening exclamation seems as much surprised as reassured by this
readiness to be touched, before there comes a scene which, in all its
humdrum, caressing littleness, cuts to the woeful heart of things and offers
an instance of that 'half-pitying, half-amused sympathy' by which Pater
defines the humourist. It might as easily come from Victorian England as
Marius's Rome. The jibe about fashionable philanthropy serving as a
personal tribute gives way to a worldly perspective. The need to outsource
care to institutions is not cause for outrage but accepted as a sad matter of
fact. Pater does not judge the couple for sending the old woman away. The
situation demands kindness but also a degree of detachment, as he says
plainly: 'They are fairly affectionate, but anxious how the thing they have
to do may go.' There is humour in the way the children triumphantly go
about their counting, before the old woman's mimicry and the couple's
playing along bring home the pathos of the scene. The incidents, if not
precisely the treatment, are such as might be found in Lamb. Pater may
even have had Lamb in mind, since in the preceding paragraph Marius's
pity for an old horse is like the pity for animals Pater associated with Lamb,
and the horse is then worked up into a symbol of the 'imperfect sympathies' between men, which is the title of Lamb's essay on that same topic
(*ME*, ii. 175, ch. 25).

If a sense of humour has been raised to a cardinal virtue, as Stephen complained, then taking things, or oneself, too seriously has come to be seen as one of the cardinal sins in literary criticism. It is a sin Lamb sometimes seems too fearful of committing in his quickness to puncture anything in his writing where he might come across as too worthy, too full of himself or highfalutin. In a letter full of brilliant insights about a performance he had just seen of *Richard III*, Lamb, after running on for several pages, suddenly pulls himself up short: 'Are you not tired with this *ingenious* criticism? I am.'[14] The bathetic jolt threatens to rebound on the reader ('have you really been swallowing all this?'). Pater, by contrast, might be accused of taking himself too seriously. A contemporary reviewer of *Appreciations* owned that 'one feels now and then an impish longing to play some practical joke on this bland imperturbability, in the hope of extorting from it either a smile or a frown'.[15] But Pater's keen enjoyment of Lamb's humour rescues him from this caricature.

In outlining 'the value of reserve' Pater does not argue for a sense of humility or neutrality regarding the status of criticism; instead he raises questions about where to locate the critic's self, how obtrusive or personal to be. Lionel Johnson's review of *Appreciations* picks up on the title of Pater's volume, noting its French provenance and suggesting the new twist that Pater gives to the term: 'we may fancy in it a meaning something more delicate and subtile [*sic*]; it would seem to promise a quality of reserve, a judgment very personal, a fine tolerance towards the reader'.[16] Reserved even about its quality of reserve (here only the conditional hint of a promise), such critical appreciation is of an unassuming, unobtrusive type. For as Lamb complained on being urged to admire some poems: 'one does not like to have 'em ramm'd down one's throat— "Pray take it—its very good—let me help you—eat faster"'.[17] Pater's criticism does not assert the self, and yet at the same time still manages to feel like 'a judgment very personal'.

His comments on the critical writings of others provide a useful guide to what he values in his own. In discussing Lamb's 'exquisite appreciations', he identifies a comparable mix of self-effacement and self-assertion: 'It was as loyal, self-forgetful work for others, for Shakespeare's self first, for instance, and then for Shakespeare's readers, that that too was done: he has the true scholar's way of forgetting himself in his subject' (111). That self-forgetfulness, a badge of scholarly distinction, comes to seem like an excessive modesty that does not fully recognise one's own hand in the process. Lamb's skill lies first in his ability to 'feel strongly' the charm of a given writer, 'and then to interpret that charm, to convey it to others—he seeming to himself but to hand on to others, in mere humble ministration, that of which for them he is really the creator' (112). This is the remark that so bothered Christopher Ricks, who complains that 'the wistful note—"he seeming to himself but to hand on to others, in mere humble ministration"—is a consequence of Pater's proud, self-conscious longing for Lamb's humble unselfconsciousness'.[18] There is a kind of self-forgetfulness here that equates to a lack of self-awareness, a blind spot when it comes to the critic's own sense of what they are about: on Lamb's part, a failure to be conscious of the shaping influence he actually exerts; on Pater's, a pride that wants to win for himself the quality he extols in another (on Ricks's too, perhaps, about whatever is driving such indignation in this essay).

The impression Lamb gives of downplaying his criticism also has to do with the form in which it appears. Aside from some review essays published in periodicals, Lamb wrote little formal criticism. Thrown out as a passing remark in a letter or scattered through the footnotes of his *Specimens of English Dramatic Poets*, his critical insights accordingly strike Pater as 'casual', 'slight', 'accidental' (121). His subjects were the literature and art that happened to please him best: the more obscure works of out-of-fashion seventeenth-century dramatists, or the poetry of George Wither. Pater also wrote according to personal preference, and on a yet more varied and cosmopolitan range of literature and art. Similarly, some of Pater's sharpest criticism does not announce itself as such, but is woven in with anecdote, disguised autobiography, fiction, and historical study.

Pater saw the 'slight', 'accidental' quality of Lamb's writings as an intrinsic feature of the essay. He compares this to Montaigne's habit of never judging 'system-wise of things' but proceeding 'glimpse-wise' (116). 'A casual writer for dreamy readers, yet always giving the reader so much more than he seemed to propose' (116). Where art comes 'proposing frankly', promising 'to give nothing but the highest quality to your moments' (*Ren.*, 190), Lamb's writings keep in reserve more than they seem to propose, giving nothing but 'glimpses, suggestions, delightful half-apprehensions, profound thoughts of old philosophers, hints of the inner-most reason in things, the full knowledge of which is held in reserve; all the varied stuff, that is, of which genuine essays are made' (*App.*, 117). The list echoes Lamb's own description, in his essay 'Imperfect Sympathies', of individuals who have an unassuming sort of style: 'hints and glimpses, germs and crude essays at a system, is the utmost they pretend to' (ii. 68). The essay reels off stereotypes of different kinds of people (in an ironic example of the systematising Lamb derides). The Caledonian is said to have an unyielding need for certainty: 'surmises, guesses, misgivings, half-intuitions, semi-consciousnesses, partial illuminations, dim instincts, embryo conceptions, have no place in his brain, or vocabulary' (ii. 69). Pater reads the remark as a self-appraisal of Lamb's own style, which delights in all that the Caledonian will not brook, but it could also stand as a comment on Pater's own. Though scrupulously exacting in his vocabulary, Pater's brain is one that readily admits of half-intuitions and partial illuminations, of misgivings and second thoughts. 'Half' often forms a qualifying compound in his writings: 'half-apprehensions', 'half-developed imaginings', 'half-conscious intuitions', 'a sort of half-playful mysticism', 'regrets for a half-ideal', 'half-known' (117, 173, 112, 58, 55, 71). He frequently employs the formulation, 'sort of', 'kind of', 'a kind of x y', or refers only to what 'may be' or 'may seem'.[19] All this could look like tentativeness or vagueness; but by working thus 'glimpse-wise', through hint and gesture, Pater allows for the kind of intuitiveness and suggestiveness that he admires in Lamb.

Given that Pater discerned 'something of the follower of George Fox about him' (116), what Lamb has to say about Quakers in 'Imperfect Sympathies' is also worth noting:

> The indirect answers which Quakers are often found to return to a question put to them may be explained, I think, without the vulgar assumption, that they are more given to evasion and equivocating than other people. They naturally look to their words more carefully, and are more cautious of committing themselves. (ii. 72)

Though more famous for their silence, the Quakers follow a set of rules about the need to speak with truthfulness and simplicity handed down in the teachings of Fox and the early Friends.[20] Lamb explains that what looks like evasiveness may be down to a carefulness about words and their significance. Indirection paradoxically arises from a concern for directness, a respect for the committed word. Pater's carefulness about words may be a cause, rather than a symptom, of the evasiveness or vagueness critics have often detected in him. Edward Thomas notes the impression of 'detachment' or remoteness this evasiveness could nonetheless produce: 'Pater cannot wind into our confidence. He is a shy man, full of "it may be" and "we may think".'[21] This studied manner may be like that of the Quaker who, Lamb says, 'knows that his syllables are weighed' and so comes to speak with a sense of 'imposed self-watchfulness' (ii. 73). But it is also a mark of care – of the kind that Flavian in *Marius the Epicurean* describes in setting out his plans for an ambitious study of literary art that will consist in 'weighing the precise power of every phrase and word' (*ME*, i. 96, ch. 6). So a style of hints, suggestions, and glimpses that in Lamb can look like casualness and in Pater like studiedness may be a sign of just how much weight each ascribes to their words.

That Pater associates reserve with Quakerism is telling, because the more immediate religious context that the term was associated with at the time was the Tractarian doctrine of reserve. It might be an easy assumption to make, that Lamb should be aligned with the demotic Quakers and Pater the rarefied Oxford Movement. The particular meaning the term had taken on in Tractarian thought offers insight into what Pater means by reserve and what kind of alternative model he might have found in Lamb. Pater writes that Lamb shared 'the Quaker's belief in the inward light coming to one passive, to the mere wayfarer', one who is quick to recognise in the slightest glimpse or suggestion 'hints of the innermost reason in things, the full knowledge of which is held in reserve' (116–17). For the Tractarians, reserve was similarly a means of veiling full knowledge in hints, but as a way of preserving the mystery of God and making it accessible only to the initiated believer. In matters of religious exegesis, God's word should not be made too explicit but discussed only indirectly. The principle was also linked to poetry, since the figurative mode of poetic expression was able to render religious truth in subtle ways. '[O]ne most essential feature of all poetry is a due reserve, which always shrinks from pouring forth everything', John Keble argued in his *Lectures on Poetry* (*Praelectiones Academicae*), delivered in Oxford between 1832 and 1841. Part of the appeal for Pater may have been this extension of reserve from a form of exegesis that preserved the mystery of its subject to a mode of self-expression that, while shying away from spilling all, still allows for veiled disclosure. As Keble went on to say: poetry gives vent to feeling only by hints, granting 'healing relief to secret mental emotion, yet without detriment to modest reserve'.[22] Pater's insight in the Lamb essay is to apply this principle to prose, and, more unexpectedly, to humour, which gave vent and brought healing relief to the tragedy it also concealed.

Just as Tractarian reserve sought to restrict understanding to only the initiated, Lamb's humour may have the equivalent exclusivity of the 'in joke'. The fake obituary Lamb wrote for Elia recalls how 'he would interrupt the gravest discussion with some light jest; and yet, perhaps, not quite irrelevant in ears that could understand it' (ii. 172). In the Bible, only 'those that hath ears to hear' receive the prophecy about the coming of Elijah.[23] Incidentally, Isaac Williams later cited this passage in his essay, 'On Reserve in Communicating Religious Knowledge'.[24] As Emma

Mason notes, 'the reserve which Keble and his supporters pushed towards was as marked by elitism as it was by modesty'.[25] The aspect which Lamb helped to draw out was not just about withholding knowledge or concealing the self, but also about a quality of fine discernment that could appreciate, even see through, the reserve in people as well as art. In a letter thanking a friend for a gift of roast brawn, Lamb parodies the way that such discernment risks tipping over into an elitist principle of knowledge restricted only to those in the know:

> Brawn was a noble thought. It is not every common Gullet-fancier tha[t] can properly esteem of it. It is like a picture of one of the choice old Italian masters. It's [sic] gusto is of that hidden sort. As Wordsworth sings of a modest poet: you must love him ere he will seem worth of your love: so Brawn, you must taste it ere to you it will seem to have any taste at all. But tis nuts to the adept: those that will send out their tongue and feelers to find it out.[26]

Hiddenness, modesty, a taste of the kind only the true adept can feel out: Lamb applies to critical appreciation the same principle of reserve that the Tractarians would apply to religious interpretation. While mimicking the diction of the rarefied gourmand, he upends the standards of aesthetic taste by celebrating brawn, that coarser kind of meat – unlike 'ham-essence, lobsters, turtle' which 'lay themselves out to strike you at first smack, like one of David's pictures (they call him Darveed), compared with the plain russet-coated wealth of a Titian or a Corregio [sic]'.[27] Lamb wants to distinguish between an affected connoisseurship and a genuinely refined sensitivity, able to appreciate what is plain or vulgar, undervalued or obscure. His relish for a meal whose gusto is 'of that hidden sort' offers an equivalent to what Pater sees as his ability to discover in mere 'glimpses, suggestions, delightful half-apprehensions' those hints of a deeper knowledge held in reserve.

It seems like a surprising turn in Pater's essay when, having just outlined Lamb's manner of writing by glimpses and holding things in reserve, he goes on to claim that 'the desire of self-portraiture is, below all more superficial tendencies, the real motive in writing at all' (117). This desire 'is closely connected with that intimacy, that modern subjectivity, which may be called the *Montaignesque* element in literature' (117). Such intimacy would seem to rely on a willingness to offer up the revelations of self-portraiture. But Pater suggests that rather than relinquishing reserve, Lamb's essayistic intimacy is made possible only through a degree of withholding: 'What he designs is to give you himself, to acquaint you with his likeness; but must do this, if at all, indirectly, being indeed always more or less reserved, for himself and his friends' (117). The qualifying phrase, 'if at all', whenever it appears in Pater's writings, seems just on the point of whisking away whatever it is barely conceding. Virginia Woolf similarly linked the essays of Montaigne and Lamb, observing in both 'the reticence which springs from composure, for with all their familiarity they never tell us what they wish to keep hidden'.[28] Lamb's famed familiarity represents a warmer kind of reserve than the chilling effect such withholding might otherwise produce. What Woolf calls composure Pater sees as a kind of suspension, whereby Lamb balances between the competing impulse to 'give you himself' and to remain 'reserved, for himself'. 'This lover of stage plays significantly welcoming a little touch of the artificiality of play', Pater adds, in a seemingly offhand comment that offers a hint about how to pull off this balance (117).

The remark implies that Lamb is able to bring to his writings something of the same element of performance that he outlined in his Elia essays on 'Stage Illusion' and 'The Artificial Comedy of the Last Century'. Lamb describes a 'perpetual sub-insinuation', 'a sort of sub-reference' by which an audience can at once see the performance of character, and see through it (ii. 185, 186). To those who object that 'there is something not natural in this everlasting *acting*; we want the real man', Lamb replies: 'what if it is the nature of some men to be highly artificial?' (ii. 192). A similar account of his own writing persona appears in his fake obituary for Elia, where he says of the essays:

> crude they are, I grant you—a sort of unlicked, incondite things—villain-
> ously pranked in an affected array of antique modes and phrases. They had
> not been *his*, if they had been other than such; and better it is, that a writer
> should be natural in a self-pleasing quaintness, than to affect a naturalness
> (so called) that should be strange to him. (ii. 171)

This offers a gloss on the maxim, 'the style is the man', cited in Pater's essay on 'Style' (*App.*, 35). Both Lamb and Pater highlight the paradoxical way in which style can seem so impersonal in its assumed manner, and at the same time so distinctive a mark of the individual.

'In no critic perhaps—not even in Mr Pater—does style count for so much as in Lamb', George Saintsbury writes in his *History of English Criticism* (1911).[29] For Thomas De Quincey, the secret of Lamb's style also reveals, in its 'coyest and most wayward features', the secret of his character: 'the syllables lurk up and down the writings of Lamb which decipher his eccentric nature'.[30] Pater does not suggest anything quite so cryptic, or at least he does not go in for any syllable-by-syllable deciphering (in fact he quotes directly from Lamb's writings only rarely, and is more interested in drawing attention to the stylistic effect of reserve than in exposing what is lying behind it). By contrast, De Quincey's unshrinking exposure of self in his *Confessions of an English Opium-Eater* (1821) begins with an apology (really a boast) for the necessity of 'breaking through that delicate and honourable reserve, which, for the most part, restrains us'.[31] In a later autobiographical sketch he links such freedom from restraint with freedom of motion:

> vast numbers of people, though liberated from all reasonable motives to self-restraint, cannot be confidential – have it not in their power to lay aside reserve; and many, again, cannot be so with particular people. I have witnessed more than once the case, that a young female dancer, at a certain turn of a peculiar dance, could not – though she had died for it – sustain a free, fluent motion.[32]

Reserve here is like the feeling of self-consciousness that causes the dancer to stumble. With Lamb and Pater, however, it seems that reserve is kept up by, and inheres within, the maintained fluency of their prose. It is just when their writing is at its most nimble that the writers manage to elude with a flourish. James Eli Adams describes 'a peculiarly theatrical reticence and ostentatious reserve' operating in Pater's prose as a conspicuous mask.[33] This helps to account for the apparent incongruity between the distinctiveness of his style, so unmistakeably 'Pateresque', and the famed elusiveness summed up by Henry James's description of him as 'the mask without the face'.[34]

An idea of reserve as an achieved performance of style also places it in a different relationship to the forms of shyness and self-effacement with which the term is normally associated. A. C. Benson suggested that, in social settings, keeping up a steady flow of speech was a way for Pater to uphold reserve: 'he was shy in large mixed assemblies, but his shyness did not make him silent', writes Benson; rather 'he was apt to talk, gently and persistently, of trivial topics, using his conversation rather as a shield against undue intimacy'.[35] Reserve can be a form of defence, and various critics and biographers have sought to uncover what Pater's written and public persona may have been shielding: his sexuality, the trauma of childhood bereavement and displacement, an inner turmoil over religion, thwarted ambition, sensitivity to hostile reviews after the backlash against *The Renaissance*. When the word reserve is used in a military or financial context, it refers to a system of defence that operates by holding back certain powers or resources. Personal reserve, rather than marking a desire for concealment and self-effacement, may convey a self-possession or composure that comes from a quiet confidence in one's inner resource.

Denis Donoghue suggests that James 'regarded Pater as one of those who take undue pride in their reserve'.[36] Shyness can often be mistaken for haughtiness, its aloofness taken as a sign not of low self-worth but superiority. Pater is alert to this in *Marius* when describing a stoical composure, which, he is careful to stipulate, is 'very far from being pride—nay, a sort of humility rather' (*ME*, i. 192, ch. 12). Lamb draws a similar distinction when, recalling his schooldays at Christ's Hospital, he describes the distinctive character of the pupils: 'there is *pride* in it . . . and there is a *restraining modesty*'. The Christ's Hospital boy displays 'silence and a reserve before strangers, yet not that cowardly shyness', Lamb writes: 'within his bounds he is all fire and play' (i. 164). The security of being within one's own bounds brings a paradoxical sense of release, so Lamb finds release by upholding the reserve of a humour that is all fire and play.

Pater's recollection of his schooldays at the King's School in Canterbury, given in the short fictional work 'Emerald Uthwart', explores how the bounded refuge of an academic institution instils a self-restraining modesty that is also the basis for scholarly pride. 'Submissiveness!—It had the force of genius with Emerald Uthwart' (*MS*, 217; *CW*, iii. 185). Pater reiterates: 'His submissiveness, you see, *was* a kind of genius; made him therefore, of course, unlike those around him' (*MS*, 219; *CW*, iii. 185). He approaches scholarship with a reverential awe, 'would scarcely have proposed to "enter into" such matters; was constitutionally shy of them' (*MS*, 218–19; *CW*, iii. 185). Emerald's earnest scholarliness is questioned, and at times seems not far from parody. 'He holds his book in a peculiar way', one of his tutors remarks, 'holds on to it with both hands; clings as if from below' (*MS*, 227; *CW*, iii. 189). Yet Pater wants to take seriously the sense of awe whereby, 'just at those points, scholarship attains something of a religious colour' (*MS*, 218; *CW*, iii. 185). This idea of scholarship as religion is one of the touching points with the essay on Lamb, whom Pater describes as 'one of the last votaries of that old-world sentiment, based on the feelings of hope and awe, which may be described as the religion of men of letters' (120). Lamb, who for Pater epitomises the value of reserve, also presents a model of scholarship in which reserve is not just a mark of disciplined self-restraint but amounts also to a readiness to be awed.

Pater concludes the essay on Lamb with one of his most personal responses, which suggests the sense of affinity he felt with him. This was partly to do with place: Enfield is where Lamb had moved with his sister in search of quiet refuge, and it is where Pater and his family moved in his infancy following his father's death. Pater rounds off with a fond recollection of the fields of Enfield, 'in one of which the present writer remembers, on a brooding early summer's day, to have heard the cuckoo for the first time' (122). It is hardly the most revealing disclosure, and yet in another sense it is surprisingly revealing, given that Pater so rarely introduces into his writings any first-person reflections. He might be at his least 'Pateresque' just when he is owning to be the 'present writer'. The cuckoo story has the whimsical, occasional, or accidental character Pater associated with the essayistic style, Lamb's especially. Having spent the essay explaining how Lamb employs that style as a means of disguise, Pater ends by just briefly dropping his own habitual reserve.

Notes

1 *Critical Heritage*, 387, 386. Charles Martindale gives an account of the presence of humour in Pater's works, which is rarely noted by other critics, in *Pater the Classicist*, ed. Charles Martindale, Stefano Evangelista, and Elizabeth Prettejohn (Oxford 2017), 8–11.

2 Edward Thomas, *Critical Studies: Swinburne and Pater*, in *Prose Writings: A Selected Edition*, ed. Guy Cuthbertson and Lucy Newlyn, 6 vols (Oxford), v, ed. Francis O'Gorman (2017), 275; *Critical Heritage*, 213.

3 Quoted in Winifred Courtney, *Young Charles Lamb* (1982), 77.

4 See Joseph Riehl, *That Dangerous Figure: Charles Lamb and the Critics* (Rochester 1998), 64. For discussions of Lamb's humour see Seamus Perry, 'Charles Lamb and the Cost of Seriousness', *Charles Lamb Bulletin* 83 (1993), 78–89 and Matthew Bevis, 'Charles Lamb . . . Seriously', in *Thinking Through Style: Non-Fiction Prose of the Long Nineteenth Century*, ed. Michael Hurley and Marcus Waithe (Oxford 2018), 35–54.

5 David Russell, '"Our Debt to Lamb": The Romantic Essay and the Emergence of Tact', *English Literary History* 79 (2012), 179–209 (179).

6 *Specimens of English Dramatic Poets*, in *The Works of Charles and Mary Lamb*, ed. E. V. Lucas, 7 vols (1903–05), iv. 179.

7 *The Works of Charles and Mary Lamb*, ed. E. V. Lucas, 6 vols (1912), ii. 168. Subsequent references to this edition are given in the text.

8 *The Letters of Charles and Mary Lamb*, ed. Edwin Marrs, 3 vols (1975), iii. 181.

9 *John Clare: By Himself*, ed. Eric Robinson and David Powell (Ashington and Manchester 1996), 143.

10 *Specimens*, 398.

11 Lene Østermark-Johansen, *Walter Pater and the Language of Sculpture* (Farnham 2011), 284–5.

12 Quoted in Riehl, *That Dangerous Figure*, 60.

13 Riehl, *That Dangerous Figure*, 52.

14 *Letters of Charles and Mary Lamb*, ii. 9.

15 Unsigned Review, *Pall Mall Gazette* (10 December 1889), 3, repr. in *Critical Heritage*, 198–200 (199).

16 Lionel Johnson, signed review, *Century Guild Hobby Horse* 6 (January 1890), 36–40, repr. in *Critical Heritage*, 220–4 (220).

17 *Letters of Charles and Mary Lamb*, i. 274.

18 Ricks, 'Misquotation', 402.

19 Ricks notes the 'kind of x y' formulation in 'Misquotation', 397.

20 See Richard Bauman, *Let Your Words be Few: Symbolism of Speaking and Silence Among Seventeenth-Century Quakers* (Cambridge 1983).

21 Thomas, *Critical Studies*, 256–7.

22 *Keble's Lectures on Poetry 1832–41*, trans. Edward Kershaw Francis, 2 vols (Oxford 1912), i. 257, 22.

23 Matthew 11:14.

24 Isaac Williams, 'On Reserve in Communicating Religious Knowledge', *Tracts for the Times*, 5 vols (1840), iv. 7.

25 Emma Mason, 'Christina Rossetti and the Doctrine of Reserve', *Journal of Victorian Culture* 7 (2002), 196–219 (199).

26 *Letters of Charles and Mary Lamb*, ii. 155–6.

27 *Letters of Charles and Mary Lamb*, ii. 156.

28 Virginia Woolf, *The Common Reader*, 2 vols (2003), ii. 177.

29 George Saintsbury, *A History of English Criticism* (1911), 354.

30 *The Works of Thomas De Quincey*, ed. Grevel Lindop, 21 vols, xvi, ed. Robert Morrison (2003), 369.

31 *The Works of Thomas De Quincey*, ii, ed. Grevel Lindop (2000), 9.

32 *The Works of Thomas De Quincey*, xx, ed. Frederick Burwick et al. (2003), 12–13.

33 James Eli Adams, *Dandies and Desert Saints: Styles of Victorian Masculinity* (1995), 185.

34 *Henry James Letters*, ed. Leon Edel (Cambridge, MA 1974–84), iii, 492. Stephen Cheeke discusses this matter in '"Pateresque": The Person, the Prose Style', *Cambridge Quarterly* 46 (2017), 251–69.

35 A. C. Benson, *Walter Pater* (1906), 180.

36 Denis Donoghue, *Walter Pater: Lover of Strange Souls* (New York 1995), 13.

CHAPTER 13

Poetry in Dilution: Pater, Morris, and the Future of English

Marcus Waithe

Walter Pater's answer to the *Pall Mall Gazette*'s question about a School of English at Oxford confirms the primacy of his affiliation to Classics, as well as his sense of its civilisational priority.[1] But equally that response need not imply indifference to the fortunes of literature in English, nor to its critical import as a focus for 'study'. On the contrary, Pater presents the literatures of ancient civilisation as a beneficent well-spring, a resource 'effective for the maintenance of what is excellent in our own'. This sense of a radiant, rather than exclusive, good justifies a turn towards a less familiar Pater: a vernacular version of the great critic who lives alongside the Classics don mindful of how the old literary languages could achieve 'infusion' with the new. While this rules out thinking of Pater as an architect of modern subject categories – invested, as they tend to be, in distinguishing English literature from other modern literatures – there remains scope for considering him in relation to what English would become, and in particular to its status as a repository of disciplinary thinking. My focus in this respect is his unsigned review of 'Poems by William Morris'.[2] Published in the *Westminster Review* as far back as 1868, it more often receives attention as a quarry of passages destined for better-known titles. Considered in its own right, however, it offers one of the most concerted, and revealingly counterfactual, accounts of critical method in Pater's canon of works.

What might we understand by 'disciplinary thinking'? While the words 'subject' and 'discipline' are often used interchangeably, the distinction between them has a crucial bearing on this discussion. Literary subjects may differ in their linguistic content but share much of the same disciplinary apparatus; equally, they may coincide in content while differing in discipline, or differ with respect both to content and discipline. Anecdotal reflection is not out of place here because it reveals the staggered, experiential path that disciplinary understanding travels. The last two scenarios dawned on me as an undergraduate when I moved from studying English at a British university to taking courses in French literature at a Belgian university, and also in taking courses there in English literature. Even where the literary content was the same, the methods of commentary, and the judgements at stake, could be radically different. And while the basis for these differences is often a matter of national intellectual tradition, it is not exclusively so, as revealed by the different textual approaches taken in the same university by departments, say, of English, French, History, and Theology. This is one reason why the 'efficiencies' delivered when university literature departments merge can be so brutal. Even when separate subject streams are maintained, the result can be annihilation of the disciplines subtly imbricated with them. At stake, then, is not the general understanding of 'discipline' as derived from the Latin *disciplīna*, or 'branch of study' (*OED*). Rather, I am concerned with the rules and laws that become associated with an area. Put differently, this is the regime that transforms a mere pupil (*discipulus*) into a disciple: one, that is, who upholds an intellectual 'order' as derived from the originally monastic form of Western educational norms.

Of course the 'discipline' associated with individual subjects is rarely stable, and in the case of 'English' notably contested. Only I am thinking here less of changing critical fashions – which may aspire to revolutionise critical methods – than of assumptions and methods embedded more deeply. This distinction is often missed. As Helen Thaventhiran observes, we tend to approach 'critical history as a pattern of ideas and influences rather than as a . . . set of practices'.[3] Typically, such practices are reproduced institutionally, and expressed across generations, ensuring that new approaches are often more modified by the classroom than modifying. Another way of conceiving this effect arises from Carolyn Levine's commentary on the studied repetitions of institutional life, and the 'path dependency' – or prohibitive cost of change – that reflects and reinforces them.[4] Because English is a relatively young subject, it is still possible to identify this disciplinary subconscious with its roots. These are apparent in the Victorian historicism of a subject whose independent status remained uncertain, and then in the philological and 'practical' curricula pioneered at Oxford and Cambridge respectively in the early twentieth century.[5] The success in particular of the Cambridge School – and of the American New Criticism – in establishing English as reputable, independent, and no longer confined to 'extension' teaching, is a familiar story. By attending to 'the words on the page', the 'practical' method evolved a set of core skills and interpretative priorities that countered Frederic W.H. Myers's foundational concern about the subject's uncertain 'difficulty', and guided teaching in secondary schools for generations.[6]

Not accidentally, the interpretative toolkit that English inherited was adapted to parsing modernist literary forms. As many critics note, this circumstance exercised a crucial influence on canon formation.[7] A discipline emerged that knew how to talk about verbal concision and compression, about formal integrity, about writing (as opposed to orality), and about austerity (whether linguistic, religious, or political). And it outlined the forms of apprenticeship that authors required to achieve these qualities. When I first encountered Pater as an undergraduate in the 1990s, my critical faculties were still channelled through these precepts, honed as they had been by my Cambridge-trained A-Level teacher. Reading Pater entailed a related sense that he was an accidental Victorian, precisely because he wrote in ways one knew how to explain. His prose seemed not so far removed from the cerebral impressionism of Virginia Woolf, or the early modern preferences of T. S. Eliot. A more historically situated 'Victorian Pater' had long since been established in the specialist literature. But my point is that this state of 'research' – a scientistic principle domesticated only slowly by the liberal arts – tells us surprisingly little about the practical persistence of disciplines.

Of course there are several reasons for resisting this view of Pater as a precedent for modernist critical orthodoxies. Like the Woolfian impressionism he inspires, his approach feeds more obviously into the poet's essay – a learned, but not academic, genre revived by the likes of Seamus Heaney, Geoffrey Hill, and Denise Riley – than into the hygienic precincts of academic English.[8] Equally, the fundamental aspects of Pater's convergence of fact and fiction are derived from a range of European progenitors – from authors such as Sainte-Beuve, Lamb, Carlyle, and Ruskin – in a way that confounds the idea of a late Victorian critical 'big bang'. Rather than seeing Pater as a precursor to the impressionistic strand in Modernism, or indeed the 'modernist paradigm' as explored by Francis McGrath, this chapter proposes an alternative way of understanding Pater's freshness.[9] More particularly, it strikes me that Pater's version of English is less anticipatory than counterfactual, and that its unrealised lineaments might be reconstructed. This possibility is appreciated more readily if, instead of tracing the afterlife of Pater's prose style, we attend to his status as a disciplinary thinker, and to the origins of his own critical discipline. The essay on 'Style' has a great deal to say about discipline in the straining Flaubertian sense (*App.*, 26) – a sense that seems indirectly to channel Carlylean versions of literature as strife and struggle. Pater's most notorious statement of critical procedure, as set out in his 'Conclusion' to *The Renaissance* (1873), is not exempt from this unification of stylistic discretion with values. It, too, invites us to think forward to Bloomsbury, and if not that, then from the 'hard, gem-like flame' (*Ren.*, 189) to Poundian imagism and lapidary poetry.[10] Certainly, the work's broader neoclassicism rejects Gothicist Victoriana in favour of lighter habiliments.

But here we must reconfigure our sense both of origins and of destination. Pater's 'Conclusion' saw its first incarnation as the closing phase of his Morris review. The early part experienced a different second life: in its case, as the essay on 'Aesthetic Poetry' in the first edition of *Appreciations* (1889).[11] Indeed, the bare fact that Pater's most notorious critical statement derives from a reading of modern poetry suggests a view of English literary criticism as generative rather than secondary. Through its subsequent, partial republication, it also represents an unusual instance of a press notice – originally sandwiched between articles on 'Landed Tenure in the Highlands' and 'Reform of Our Civil Procedure' – attaining the status and primacy of an artwork. Equally pertinent is the author in question. While Pater's connection to Morris is not much discussed outside Morris studies, its disciplinary import seems not to have been considered at all. The review addresses Morris's early – and until then neglected – collection of Arthurian and Froissartian lyrics, *The Defence of Guenevere and Other Poems* (1858), alongside two more recent narrative poems: *The Life and Death of Jason* (1867) and *The Earthly Paradise* (1868–70).[12] All three apply the referred dreamwork of late Pre-Raphaelitism to familiar mythic subject matter. But while the first work is determinedly Gothic, the last two develop a kind of mythic cosmopolitanism. *The Earthly Paradise*, most notably, unfolds a story cycle whose frame narrative recalls that of *The Canterbury Tales* (*c.*1345–1400) and *The Decameron* (*c.*1348–53), and as such facilitates a mixing of Greek, Norse, and Persian legend. Such mixing posits the artful as the artificial: an anticipation of aestheticist ideology according to which roots and realities weaken, and 'the forms of things are transfigured' (300). While the combinations are pleasing, things are not found in their usual places.

Pater alters not just the location and use of his review, but redeploys its limited scope to serve a creative art history ranging from the late Middle Ages right up to Winckelmann's eighteenth-century classicism. That move alone assumes considerable flexibility of purpose, a kind of contextual amplitude. As a critical manoeuvre, however, it is not isolated or accidental: rather, it reflects the breadth of analysis implicit in Pater's biographical imagination, a method of thinking *through* texts that not only reimagines them through recycled uses – as the history of the review itself reveals – but addresses wide, unanticipated fields from an initially narrowed point.

As Denis Donoghue puts it, 'Such thinking as Pater did, he did by commenting on the work of other writers'.[13] The whiff of condescension in 'such thinking' should not distract from the more interesting point that Pater's critical thinking is also a sympathetic thinking, which is as interested in creating a chain as manifesting a source. The effect, crucially, is not to downgrade his thought but to uplift the status of criticism, so as to spurn the idea of a parasitical or secondary endeavour in favour of a co-creative impulse. As with its heterodox equivalent in theology – which understands artistic creation less as praise or prayer than as occupying a continuum with divine creation – there is a danger of profaning the original word, of overlaying rather than reading.[14] Even when that applies, though, an inviting space opens for interpretative work that is not simply exegetical.

Pater's appreciation of these poems also implies specific critical values. On first publication, *The Defence of Guenevere and Other Poems* was attacked either for being evasive of modern life, or an inauthentic rendering of the medieval past; by contrast, it now stands alongside *Sigurd the Volsung* (1876) as the most admired of Morris's poetical works, largely on account of its Browningesque concision.[15] By contrast, *The Life and Death of Jason* and *The Earthly Paradise* were popular in their time, as well as admired by, among others, George Eliot and Henry James.[16] They have been found unpalatably prolix by modern readers – despite scholarly attempts to rehabilitate them dating back to the 1970s.[17] Pater registers the differences between these works, but presents them as a single achievement unrelated to the virtues or the faults detected by later generations. Moreover, he dwells on characteristics that are not just stylistic but suggestive of how we might account for the shape and value of literature as critics. In short, they elaborate a counterfactual formalism – one that points beyond a familiar association of form with fixed or tangible shape, and imagines a poetry whose qualities are keenly felt yet curiously amorphous. If Pater is the inadvertent founder of a subject of which he disapproved – that is, of a vernacular competitor to Classics – he is also the founder of a parallel discipline, a version of English whose tenets were never enacted. The evaluative criteria and methodology of Pater's review are both germane in this regard: what he values in Morris envisions what he values in literature more generally. Whereas modernist form typically privileges classical aesthetics, clean shapes, and marked boundaries, Pater's review discloses four alternative formal values.

The most prominent of these is fluidity: a quality that Pater detects and describes before recuperating it as an artistic principle applicable elsewhere.

Betokening an aversion to walls and other fixed points, it prepares the
ground for the account of 'flux' and perceptualism elaborated in *The
Renaissance*. Though not formlessness exactly, it removes Pater's aesthetics
from Poundian values of concretion, or 'boundary stones'.[18] Indeed, he
reads 'The Defence of Guenevere' as a commentary on sealed 'outlets' that
beget the 'tension of nerve' and 'convulsed sensuousness' of medieval
poetry (303). But Pater is more precisely concerned with a related set of
analogies with water, often expressed through a preference for immersive
experience. Morris's later poems are seen as expressing a Golden Age
innocence whose ongoing 'impression of surprise' recalls 'the touch of
water as one swims' (306). Far from being a complete resignation to flow,
or a dissolution, the experience is intimate, indeed imputed to the agency
of 'touch'. Escape from the self-confining ego dawns in a suggestion that
physical selves – '[o]ur physical life' (310) – might operate across a broader
spectrum than the mind knows. We are invited to consider the 'delicious
recoil from the flood of water in summer heat' (310), in whose moment
one learns that 'those elements, phosphorus and lime, and delicate fibres,
are present not in the human body alone', but extend 'beyond us' (310).
The bodily imagination of the review thus understands contact with water
as a point of interface, an opportunity to connect with a world of related
chemical traces. Pater is sensitised, likewise, to physical and architectural
symbols of this interrelation, quoting as he does Morris's lines in which
Medea 'came down to a gilded watergate, / Which with a golden key she
opened straight, / And swiftly stept into a little boat' (308). Medea moves
between elements in this way, migrating through a portal – the watergate –
that symbolises the kinds of passage that Pater's prose strives to enact.

The aestheticist watchword 'exquisite' recurs here (307, 308, 309, 310,
311), its mobility along the pain–pleasure axis activated by related perme-
abilities. As the rush of the 'whirlpool' (310) and the 'race of the mid-
stream' (310) intensify, we approach the perceptual flow better known to
readers of *The Renaissance*, and relatedly the Heraclitan 'PANTA RHEI'
('everything flows') that animates *Marius the Epicurean* (1885). Crucially,
though, Pater's attention to water also offers a way of thinking about
qualities of story. Claiming that 'in perfect story-telling like this the
manner rises and falls with the story itself' (309), he imputes a natural
swell that turns the painterly category of 'manner' into a buoy inseparable
from the height of the flood. In the Paterian universe, stories are never far
away from histories. In this case, a quotation from *The Life and Death of
Jason*, concerning an encounter with the Sirens, heightens their watery
interrelation. Medea invokes 'lovely things once sung / Beside the sea,

while yet the world was young' (307), and Pater finishes the image: 'Then literally like an echo from the Greek world, heard across so great a distance only as through some miraculous calm, subdued in colour and cadence, the ghosts of passionate song, come those matchless lyrics' (307). Once again, his commentary assumes a primary quality, based in textual, generic, and historic permeability – and, more conspicuously, these qualities are staged syntactically by the collapse of a sonorous linguistic wave at the suspended verb, 'come'.

From these fluid affinities, Pater moves to perverse affinities, between styles, forms, and times. In *The Renaissance*, he enlarges on the internal conflict between 'Christian asceticism' and its provocation 'of the artistic life, with its inevitable sensuousness' ('Winckelmann', *Ren.*, 177). The abrupt shifts and passionate interjections of *The Defence of Guenevere* help develop this idea of the unlikely pairing: here, Pater finds 'the mood of the cloister taking a new direction' ('Poems by William Morris', 302), so that 'religion shades into sensuous love, and sensuous love into religion' (301). It is not always clear whether this reading of the Middle Ages is an accessory to a reading of Morris, or whether Morris is an accessory to reading the Middle Ages; but a broader conception of the perverse affinity helps Pater knit together discrete textual bodies. The change of manner from Guenevere to Jason is 'almost a revolt' (305), he claims, but a revolt that discloses unsuspected links between opposites. In *The Life and Death of Jason* and *The Earthly Paradise*, no such damming up applies. Instead, connections are intensified. And the affinities here are not perverse, but a marker of enlarged consciousness: an anti-purism expressed through Pater's observation that 'the choice life of the human spirit is always under mixed lights, and in mixed situations' (307). The 'mediævalisms' of 'a Greek poem' – Morris's *Life and Death of Jason* – become 'delicate inconsistencies' (308). As the review proceeds, such 'mixed lights' increasingly resemble an active literary-critical procedure, one that favours a set of alternative structuring mechanisms governing relations between different pasts and different texts. Though heavily invested in periodisation, Pater repeatedly licenses redemptive anachronism. The effect is to recast history as a formal property. By 'an exquisite dexterity the two threads of sentiment' – medievalism and Hellenism – 'are here interwoven and contrasted' (308). Historical character becomes sentiment, and sentiments are threaded with dexterous hands in a process at once amenable to splicing, and susceptible to cut and paste.

The idea that Morris might inspire this historical amplitude pulls against the way that critics commonly situate Pater. According to

Jonathan Freedman, such 'historical shuttling' redefines the Renaissance 'not as a historical phenomenon but rather as an ideal criterion of value, an abstract standard'.[19] Certainly, periods become plastic in Pater's hands. In medieval history and literature, he discovers transitions 'of which what we call the Renaissance is only a supreme instance' (305). Losing its singularity, it becomes a vivid example of something that can happen to all cultures. But Freedman also claims that 'this move ... explicitly prohibits the escape into nostalgic reverie that Ruskin and Morris's critical methodology permitted'.[20] One might argue here with 'nostalgic'. In his criticism, at least, Pater tends to resist fall narratives. But he agrees with Ruskin and Morris – and, indeed, T. S. Eliot – in seeing that 'anything in the way of an actual revival must always be impossible' (307). Morris's opposition to restorative architecture, for instance – his understanding that buildings cannot be returned to an authentic moment – finds a point of origin in the kind of 'shuttling' between contexts enacted in *The Earthly Paradise*.[21] This work imagines a haunting down the ages that influences Pater in the 'real time' of his review. Recognising this habit of transferred sensibility, Pater speaks of 'the Hellenism of Chaucer' (307); and he refers to Morris as 'this Hellenist of the middle age' (305).

Apart from redescribing historical periods as repeatable forms to be recycled and spliced, Pater's interpretative methodology psychologises our relationship with the past. Rather as Freud describes Rome as an analogue for the unconscious, this model of culture posits a place where 'everything past is preserved'.[22] That realm is never wholly alien, Pater explains, because 'The composite experience of all the ages is part of each one of us' (307), and equally it is 'not possible to repress a single phase of that humanity' (307). Such psychologising leads to the next major structuring mechanism that Pater privileges over concrete form, that of dream. The emphasis here is less on sleep than on the cargo transferred when we move 'from dreamlight to daylight' (305). Equally, Pater notices the forms of connection and scene-making that dreams can model for the waking mind: 'as in a dream the scene shifts', he remarks on noting the Argus's embarkation in *The Life and Death of Jason*, 'and we go down ... to the sea through a pageant of the fourteenth century in some French or Italian town' (308). If 'the strangest creations of sleep seem here' (303), this strangeness is figured as a resource for art, indeed for human civilisation. These dreams are not excluded from the sphere of history – rather, the formal bounds of history and historicity are vastly expanded to accommodate them, so that 'Reverie, illusion, delirium' (302) figure less as mind-states than as lapses from medieval civilisation. Importantly, though, it is the *structure* of the dream, rather than analysis of its content, that preoccupies Pater. This sets in train an associative method of composition that reveals affinities in a 'strange perpetual weaving and unweaving of ourselves' (311). Pater takes dreams seriously, then: seriously enough to categorise and distinguish their types. But he does not present them as a content to be read diagnostically, whether in search of coherence or conflict (311). They escape that burden on account of their unconscious artistry, and their tendency to slip between the personal, the collective, and the mythic. Instead, we contemplate a psychologised version of that proto-Arts and Crafts Penelope whom Morris depicts 'weaving a web within the hall' that she 'undid' at night.[23]

Pater's last alternative structure relates back to fluidity, but is expressed in terms of the poem rather than bodily experience. This initially takes the form of an apology for the length of *The Earthly Paradise*. As if addressing the author's self-doubt about spawning such 'flabby' poems, Pater makes a case for larger units of analysis, a stretching out that is not necessarily a harmful thinning:[24]

> We have become so used to austerity and concentration in some noble types of modern poetry, that it is easy to mislike the lengthiness of this new poem. Yet here mere mass is itself the first condition of an art which deals with broad atmospheric effects. (309)

This 'lengthiness' suggests something happening in space, as well as on the folded page: a poem whose sheer mass is hard to see around. But as the idea of atmosphere is introduced, the sense of an environment rather than an obstruction emerges. Pater mentions 'desolate' thoughts as if they were coagulating: 'at times', he writes, 'all the bitterness of life seems concentrated in them' (311). Here he commends a 'mass' or volume that rejects 'austerity' and 'concentration' as critical virtues. Pater's confidence, here, depends on the notion that something dormant or inert can harbour unexpected rewards in large quantities. Speaking of the fourteenth book of *The Life and Death of Jason*, he remarks that 'The power of an artist will sometimes remain inactive over us . . . till on a sudden we are *found* by one revealing example of it which makes all he did precious' (306). Indeed, we are missing something if we mistake tranquillity for a lack of effect in large volumes. In this way, he musters the beginnings of an apology for literature administered in high degrees of dilution. 'The water is not less medicinal', he writes, 'not less gifted with virtues, because a few drops of it are without effect; it is water to bathe and swim in' (309). There are hints here of the culture of public bathing and spa visits. Pater and his sisters spent several summers by the sea at Sidmouth. Morris, for his part, took the waters at Bad Ems in Germany while he was completing *The Earthly Paradise*, a trip whose poetic import Dante Gabriel Rossetti lampooned in the form of 'The M's at Ems', a sketch that shows Morris reading the *Earthly Paradise* to Jane Morris as she lies in the bath, severally drowning her sorrows.[25]

More seriously, Pater reconfigures Morris's poetic 'mass' – and the narcotic copiousness elsewhere imputed by Edward Burne-Jones[26] – as a homeopathic cure: a method, in other words, that recovers strength from the dynamisation of extreme dilution. Pater's reading of German literature would have exposed him to the debates surrounding this controversial school of alternative medicine. Indeed, the 'curative' foot-stomping scene in Goethe's *Faust* (1808) explicitly sends up the central claims of its founder, Samuel Hahnemann (1755–1843), that *similia similibus currentur* ('like can cure like', known as the Law of Similars).[27] It was in any case a familiar preoccupation of intellectual life in the late nineteenth century: while Oscar Wilde has his hero dress up neat poison as 'homeopathic medicine' in *Lord Arthur Savile's Crime* (1887), the broader concepts of dose and efficacy arise in *The Picture of Dorian Gray* (1890) (whose famous allusion to a 'poisonous book' could be reread as an aestheticist reclamation of toxicology along homeopathic lines) and in Robert Louis Stevenson's *Strange Case of Dr Jekyll and Mr Hyde* (1886).[28] Closer to home, the Epps family – who were closely integrated into the social circle surrounding the Rossettis and Ford Madox Brown – were known for their advocacy of Hahnemann. As such, his name would have been familiar to Morris (and probably also to Pater) through personal channels as well.[29]

Drawing on Paracelsus's notion that 'in all good things poison also resides',[30] Hahnemann developed the related Law of the Minimum Dose, applicable to poisons that resemble or simulate the symptoms of a disease. This posits the counterintuitive principle that 'curative power will be wonderfully increased in proportion to the reduction of the dose'.[31] Pater's figurative attraction to homeopathic methods has been noted only in passing by critics: Jay Fellows observes that 'To be in a curative position and to be acting from it are not, with Pater, the same thing. Pater's medicine would only be homeopathic',[32] while Matthew Beaumont compares his focus on the 'instant itself' to 'some homeopathic solution'.[33] But the principle of dilution also applies to the critical and poetic values that inform Pater's high valuation of Morris, and his suspicion of those poetic concentrations later upheld by modernist critics. Had Jacques Benveniste's more recent conception of 'water memory' – according to which water recollects substances previously and undetectably dissolved in it – been a part of the original homeopathic regime, it too might present as a source for Pater's proto-Jungian notion of 'composite experience'. But Hahnemann's equally outlandish notion of succussion, or shaking to activate 'vital force', does inflect Pater's confidence in the principle of mixing, whether of time, cultures, or literature.[34] Equally, it recalls that broader aestheticist 'agitation' more usually understood as nervous or perceptual. Principles of miscellaneity, flood, and copiousness also resolve back into the immersive principle of the review, where the body is cathartically engulfed in recollection of the fashionable transfer of curative bathing from the eighteenth-century spa to the Victorian coast, and related treatises on medical hydrology.[35]

The closing phase of this chapter addresses the meaning of these alternative structures at the level of English's disciplinary fabric. Though inspired by Morris's poetry, Pater's review increasingly resists the contingency of that narrowed attention. By the time we reach the last section, on 'modern thought' (310), the connection is almost amusingly weak. Pater delights in a gratuitous movement from the particular to the general: he likewise observes of the Sirens episode in *The Life and Death of Jason* that it prompts the unnerving feeling that literary sources are immaterial – a suspicion strengthened by the ease with which the review's philosophical conclusion becomes the conclusion to an altogether different work. But of course this vaunting sense of disproportion is part of the appeal, and perhaps a necessary evil which can be accepted in favour of greater gains. It is possible, of course, that the structuring mechanisms I have surveyed are a dead-end: that they are self-confining, in as much as they reflect the limits of a single personality, a single set of associations, a Paterian critical encounter. A 'discipline', as such, cannot rely on the vagaries of one personality. But it seems to me that more is at stake in Pater's refusal to prioritise concision over copiousness, and shape over flow. These are not Victorian critical values. And while T. S. Eliot mounts an apology for Swinburne's 'diffuseness' as 'one of his glories', such values are not readily assimilable to modernist aesthetics, hinting as they do at an English organised around radically different principles.[36] In this parallel universe, the dilution rendered by length is understood not as a threat to formal integrity or authorial control, but as a cathartic method, and a dispersed source of atmosphere. As Pater intimates in the 'Conclusion' to *The Renaissance*, the means to expand consciousness are not supplied by limitation or refinement. This is not monitory reading – or reading as

'scrutiny' – but a ritual dunking that rejects the baptismal divide between
new life and old. It is a full-blown immersion that makes everything
present and available at once. One might think of Eliot's 'Tradition and
the Individual Talent' (1919) – only, here, the new work is not entering
'an existing order', but a constant wash of art, experience, fantasy, and
dream.[37] At the opposite pole from harmful concentration, Pater glimpses
'the image of one washed out beyond the bar in a sea at ebb, losing even
his personality' (311). Unlike the 'mixed lights' of Paterian physical
communion, the threat here is of complete dissolution. And it is a threat
that he actively resists. His critical method relies on identities, after all, on
patterns of association. A discipline based on this might be regarded as an
'anti-discipline', in as much as it resists hygienic procedures, but it must
retain enough integrity to ensure flow from one position to the next.

   This paradoxically amorphous formalism can be parsed in ways that
address the four pillars of modern literary criticism: namely, the work, the
text, the author, and the reader. Where 'the work' is concerned, the link
between concentration and significance – understood both as meaning and
as artistic value – is broken. Indeed, the word 'text' may be more appropriate, albeit without the connotation of more modern 'textualities' where
a boundless system of signs transgresses the arbitrary limits upheld by title
pages. Pater, as we have seen, secures identities, but privileges signs of flow.
Contrary to his modernist successors, he avoids analogies that present
literature as a fixed shape in the world. Equally, an incipient Arts and
Crafts materiality conditions a blended understanding of the work in
relation to the text. Pater turns abstractions like history or dream into a
physically worked substance, a material form in effect; meanwhile, the
hard edges of literature dissolve into an immersive experience that values
dilution over concentration, and prolixity over concision. As the names
studded through *The Renaissance* indicate, 'the author' remains a mean-
ingful entity in this vision, the proviso being that the work of life is also the
work of art. It is not so much that all writing occupies a levelled plain of
discourse, but that Paterian criticism undertakes enough biographical
thinking to activate the perceptualism upon which his impressionism
depends. Walt Whitman manages a similar balancing act in 'Song of
Myself', where authorial and lyric voices meld in ways offensive to New
Critical precepts: 'To me the converging objects of the universe perpetually
flow', the speaker declares, secure that 'My foothold is tenon'd and
mortis'd in granite'.[38] Adding that 'I laugh at what you call dissolution',
he implies that force of will maintains the distinction between solvent flow
and self-annihilation.[39] This example acquires an ironic valence in the light

of Havelock Ellis's dismissive description (later recanted) of Edward Carpenter's *Towards Democracy* (1st edn, 1883) as 'Whitman and water', which by implication imagines the great American poet not as submerged, but as ordinarily having dry feet.[40]

The Paterian reader follows the author in resisting rigid historicisms and concentrations of focus, preferring to absorb matters even of periodicity into the ambit of manipulable form. A resolution to use the 'interval', to get 'as many pulsations as possible into the given time' (312), applies here too: it is, in some senses, a theory of reading based on mortal awareness, a version of *The Arabian Nights* predicament, where stories must be told (or read) to ward off the arrival of death in the morning. This is not reading as 'research' or edification, but an existential strategy, far removed from the ideas of scientificity that I. A. Richards instilled through readings unburdened by 'presuppositions' and 'preconceptions'.[41] If we are to sum up the fundamental tenet of Pater's counterfactual disciple, we might just as well concentrate on the word 'discipline' itself. It hints at an approach to 'English' that relies not so much on a stated content – whether a canon based on value, language, or nation – than on a set of principles applicable across different literatures and different genres. Pater's version of this – a kind of immersive *habitus* – assumes a flow between the work and the life, between criticism and authorship, between past states and present ones. The resulting interpretative amplitude flourishes in the 'dreamlight' of a fully solvent consciousness, underpinned by the strange affinity of his own Law of Similars.

Notes

1 Walter Pater, 'English at the Universities. – IV.', *Pall Mall Gazette* (27 November 1886), 1–2.

2 [Walter Pater], 'Poems by William Morris', *Westminster Review* n.s. 34 (October 1868), 300–12. Further references are given parenthetically in the text.

3 Helen Thaventhiran, *Radical Empiricists: Five Modernist Close Readers* (Oxford 2005), 2.

4 Caroline Levine, *Forms: Whole, Rhythm, Hierarchy, Network* (Princeton 2017), 59.

5 See Terry Eagleton, *Literary Theory: An Introduction* (Oxford 1983), 15–46; Franklin E. Court, *Institutionalizing English Literature: The Culture and Politics of Literary Study, 1750–1900* (Stanford 1992); H. Momma, *From Philology to English Studies: Language and Culture in the Nineteenth Century* (Oxford 2013).

6 F. W. H. Myers, 'English at the Universities. – IV.', *Pall Mall Gazette* (27 November 1886), 2.

7 See Rebecca Beasley, *Theorists of Modernist Poetry: T. S. Eliot, T. E. Hulme and Ezra Pound* (2007), 122.

8 See Introduction, *On Essays: Montaigne to the Present*, ed. Thomas Karshan and Kathryn Murphy (Oxford 2020), 1–30 (16).

9 Francis Charles McGrath, *Sensible Spirit: Walter Pater and the Modernist Paradigm* (Gainesville, FL 1986).

10 McGrath, *Sensible Spirit*, 210.

11 Walter Pater, *Appreciations: With an Essay on Style* (1889), 213–27.

12 William Morris, *The Defence of Guenevere and Other Poems*, in *The Collected Works of William Morris* [hereafter, *CWWM*], ed. May Morris, 24 vols (1910–15), i. 1–145; *The Life and Death of Jason*, in *CWWM*, ii; *The Earthly Paradise*, in *CWWM*, iii.

13 Denis Donoghue, *Walter Pater: Lover of Strange Souls* (New York 1995), 97.

14 See Jacques Maritain's claim that 'artistic creation does not copy God's creation, but continues it' (*Art and Scholasticism*, trans. J. F. Scanlan (1930), 63.

15 Peter Faulkner, ed., Introduction, in *William Morris: The Critical Heritage* (1973), 1–29 (6).

16 Faulkner, Introduction, 9–10.

17 See Clive Wilmer, 'The Names of the Roses: Modernity and Archaism in William Morris's *The Earthly Paradise*', *Times Literary Supplement* (6 June 2003), 3–4 (3).

18 Alex Houen, 'Anti-Semitism', in *Ezra Pound in Context* (Cambridge 2010), 391–401 (394).

19 Jonathan Freedman, *Professions of Taste: Henry James, British Aestheticism, and Commodity Culture* (Stanford 1990), 64.

20 Freedman, *Professions of Taste*, 64.

21 See Marcus Waithe, *William Morris's Utopia of Strangers: Victorian Medievalism and the Ideal of Hospitality* (Woodbridge 2006), 106–16.

22 Sigmund Freud, *Civilization and Its Discontents*, in *The Standard Edition of the Complete Psychological Works of Sigmund Freud*, ed. James Strachey, Anna Freud, and Carrie Lee Rothgeb, 24 vols (1953), xxi. 71.

23 William Morris, *The Odyssey of Homer Done into English Verse*, in *CWWM*, xxxi. 280.

24 Faulkner, Introduction, 11.

25 Fiona MacCarthy, *William Morris: A Life for Our Time* (1994), 243.

26 MacCarthy, *William Morris*, 200.

27 See Alice A. Kuzniar, *The Birth of Homeopathy Out of the Spirit of Romanticism* (Toronto 2017), 3.

28 Oscar Wilde, *Lord Arthur Savile's Crime*, in *The Complete Works of Oscar Wilde*, ed. Ian Small, 11 vols (Oxford 2017), viii. 49–77 (65); Wilde, *The Picture of Dorian Gray*, ed. Joseph Bristow, in *Complete Works* (Oxford 2005),

iii. 103; Robert Louis Stevenson, *Strange Case of Dr Jekyll and Mr Hyde and Other Tales*, ed. Roger Luckhurst (Oxford 2006), 1–66 (54).

29 I am grateful to Liz Prettejohn for alerting me to this connection.

30 Paracelsus, 'Alchimia', in *Essential Theoretical Writings*, ed. Andrew Weeks (Leiden 2008), 211–57 (247).

31 Samuel Hahnemann, *Organon of the Art of Healing*, trans. C. Wesselhoeft (New York 1879), 181.

32 Jay Fellows, *Tombs, Despoiled and Haunted: 'Under-Textures' and 'After-Thoughts' in Walter Pater* (Stanford 1991), 7.

33 Introduction, in Walter Pater, *Studies in the History of the Renaissance*, ed. Matthew Beaumont (Oxford 2010), xx.

34 Hahnemann, *Organon of the Art of Healing*, 136.

35 See John Horner, *The Philosophy of Bathing* (1859); see also James M. Adams, *Healing with Water* (Manchester 2015). I am grateful to James Grellier for discussing these matters in the light of recent research on 'Blue Health' at the University of Exeter.

36 T. S. Eliot, 'Swinburne as Poet', in *The Sacred Wood* (1997), 122–7 (123).

37 Eliot, 'Tradition and the Individual Talent', in *The Sacred Wood*, 39–49 (41).

38 Walt Whitman, 'Song of Myself', *Leaves of Grass*, in *Complete Poetry and Collected Prose*, ed. Justin Kaplan (New York 1982), 188–250 (206–7).

39 Whitman, 'Song of Myself', 207.

40 *Edward Carpenter: In Appreciation*, ed. Gilbert Beith (1931), 47. I am grateful to Michael Robertson for bringing this passage to my attention.

41 I. A. Richards, *Practical Criticism: A Study of Literary Judgment* (1930), 292–305.

CHAPTER 14

Dante Gabriel Rossetti and His School

Elizabeth Prettejohn

Dante Gabriel Rossetti died on 9 April 1882, aged fifty-three, on the Kent coast at Birchington-on-Sea, where he was buried without pomp or fanfare, the ceremony attended only by family and close friends. This quiet event, out of London, was the very opposite of the grand funerals accorded to the Victorian literary and artistic giants – Tennyson's of 1892 in Westminster Abbey, for example, or Leighton's in St Paul's Cathedral, early in 1896. Yet Rossetti's can be seen as the first of the prominent deaths of the *fin-de-siècle* that spurred reflection on the century's achievements in art and literature. He was the first of the Pre-Raphaelite Brotherhood to die, and thus to close an era – or perhaps to open a new and different one, not only for his own legend but also for the literary and artistic histories in which he played a part. With a precision that does not detract from its poignancy, Pater captures the complexity of this moment of transition in the opening and closing paragraphs of his essay, first published in the aftermath of Rossetti's death and later given a key position in *Appreciations*. 'Mr. Rossetti', the reclusive individual who avoided public art criticism by declining to exhibit and who took great pains to control the critical response to his poems, could now emerge as 'Rossetti', the historical figure and leader of a school.

Pater had made reference to Rossetti before, although not by name, and one is tempted to wonder whether he was avoiding the jarring sound – or sense – of the 'Mr.', required by Victorian critical decorum for living people, when he refers, in 'The School of Giorgione' of 1877, to 'a delightful sonnet by a poet whose own painted work often comes to mind as one ponders over these precious things' (*Ren.*, 114).[1] Pater adheres strictly to the convention in his review-essay of 1868 on the living poet William Morris, but avoids Morris's name by leaving it to the citation, at the head of the essay, of the three volumes under review; in something of a tour de force he manages to do without the name 'Mr. Morris' except on a single occasion late in the essay.[2] As many scholars have noted (sometimes censoriously), it was characteristic for Pater to omit the proper names of those with whose work or ideas he was engaging, particularly when they were still living; the reluctance to use the ugly word 'Mr.' does not fully explain that practice of Pater's, but may have been a contributing factor.[3]

Rossetti's death freed him from the 'Mr.', and also rendered him eligible for inclusion in Thomas Humphry Ward's seminal anthology *The English Poets: Selections*, which had an explicit principle of excluding living poets.[4] Thus the fourth and final volume of its first edition, published in 1880, had the subtitle 'From Wordsworth to Dobell', perhaps bathetic in its effect from the start. The addition of Rossetti at the end of the second edition of 1883 not only solved that problem, but also provided the occasion for an introductory essay by Pater, Ward's Brasenose colleague, his long-time neighbour on Bradmore Road in Oxford, and the close friend also of Ward's wife, Mary Augusta, niece of Matthew Arnold, known to the public as the novelist Mrs Humphry Ward.[5] In the revised edition, then, Rossetti assumes the culminating final position, with Pater's introduction and a generous selection of thirteen sonnets and longer poems. It is hard not to imagine Pater and the Wards planning this together. Two other poets who had died since the publication of the first edition were also added: James Thomson, whose *City of Dreadful Night* was much admired in Rossetti's circle and whose introduction in the anthology is by Rossetti's protégé Philip Bourke Marston, and Arthur O'Shaughnessy, another Rossetti disciple, introduced by the mutual friend of Rossetti and Pater, Edmund Gosse. The new arrangement gives Rossetti and his school a distinctive position in the history of English poetry at the end of a 'romantic' trajectory, 'From Wordsworth to Rossetti'. This literary-historical position would become familiar to the many readers of Ward's influential anthology, rooted in the University of Oxford, with its general introduction by Matthew Arnold, and reprinted fifteen times through to the end of the First World War.[6] Pater's essay marked the transition from 'Mr. Rossetti' of literary criticism to the Rossetti of literary history.

This was also a transition from art criticism to art history, something that Pater finds frequent occasion to remind the reader, beginning in the first paragraph: 'For those poems were the work of a painter, understood to belong to, and to be indeed the leader, of a new school then rising into note' ('Dante Gabriel Rossetti', *App.*, 205). The phrasing seems to echo the earlier reference in 'The School of Giorgione' and perhaps to clarify Rossetti's role in that essay. Rossetti is one of Giorgione's 'school', collaborating across history with his Renaissance forebears, while his sonnet,

'For a Venetian Pastoral by Giorgione', provides the intellectual underpinning for the radical aesthetic theory of Pater's essay.[7]

But which 'school' does Pater mean? Is he referring to Rossetti's leadership of the Pre-Raphaelite Brotherhood, formed in 1848 just after the composition of 'The Blessed Damozel', the poem that initiates the selection in Ward's anthology? The account of 'sincerity', in the next sentence, can be read as an exquisitely succinct summary of the aims of the Brotherhood:

> Common to that school and to him, and in both alike of primary significance, was the quality of sincerity, already felt as one of the charms of that earliest poem – a perfect sincerity, taking effect in the deliberate use of the most direct and unconventional expression, for the conveyance of a poetic sense which recognised no conventional standard of what poetry was called upon to be. (205–6)

That is Pre-Raphaelitism in a nutshell, and the word 'painting' could easily be substituted for 'poetry'. But the precision of chronology, evident throughout the essay, suggests that Pater is referring – primarily or additionally – to a school that was just emerging around 1870, the publication date of Rossetti's *Poems*, and Rossetti's best recent critic, Jerome McGann, takes it for granted that Pater means that new school.[8] Such an interpretation is consistent, too, with the original position of the essay in Ward's *English Poets*, alongside Rossetti's own younger followers, Marston, Gosse, O'Shaughnessy, and – as I shall argue – Pater himself. If that is the case, Pater's claim is a striking one: Rossetti's teenage production, 'The Blessed Damozel', prefigures, or indeed initiates, the aesthetic aims not merely of the Pre-Raphaelite Brotherhood, but also of the next avant-garde, the Aesthetic Movement in poetry and the visual arts. A blurred boundary between those two 'movements' has been characteristic of the historiographies of both art and literature of the later Victorian period, something often remarked and sometimes lamented.[9] Perhaps, at this early point of reckoning, Pater is already adumbrating the possibility that the blurring might be productive. The history is not like a relay race, in which one movement passes the baton to the next in relentless – and competitive – progressivity, a pattern often attributed to the French avant-garde movements of the same decades. Rather it is one where later artworks may turn for inspiration to possibilities latent in earlier ones, whether of their own 'school' or of past ages (as with the 'school of Giorgione').

When Pater came to collect the essay with others in his volume of 1889, *Appreciations*, he placed it immediately after a version of the review-essay of

1868 on Morris, deprived of its final theoretical paragraphs (which in the meantime had become the 'Conclusion' to Pater's previous collection, *The Renaissance* of 1873), and retitled 'Aesthetic Poetry' (see further Chapter 13 in this volume). That sequence predisposes the reader to suppose that the 'school' mentioned at the start of the Rossetti essay is the 'aesthetic' one, just coalescing around the time of the review-essay on Morris, and the supposition is reinforced by the transitional paragraph Pater provides at the end of 'Aesthetic Poetry':

> One characteristic of the pagan spirit the aesthetic poetry has, which is on its surface – the continual suggestion, pensive or passionate, of the shortness of life. This is contrasted with the bloom of the world, and gives new seduction to it – the sense of death and the desire of beauty: the desire of beauty quickened by the sense of death. But that complexion of sentiment is at its height in another 'aesthetic' poet of whom I have to speak next, Dante Gabriel Rossetti.[10]

That paragraph, however, had only the briefest existence: it disappeared, along with the entire essay on Morris, from the second edition of *Appreciations*, published just six months after the first and, in the event, the final version of Pater's lifetime – taken, therefore, as definitive for the Library Edition of *The Works of Walter Pater* (1910) and still the copy-text for the new Oxford *Collected Works* (2019–). For the historian of nineteenth-century art or literature, it is difficult not to regret the loss of the first-edition sequence, with its clear progression from the rugged medievalism of Morris's *Defence of Guenevere* (1858) to the 'aesthetic' (although still medievalising) poetry of his *Life and Death of Jason* (1867) and *Earthly Paradise* (first instalment, 1868), to be followed so closely by Rossetti's *Poems* of 1870. In the second edition, moreover, Pater substitutes a different essay, 'Feuillet's "La Morte"', not in the original position of 'Aesthetic Poetry' but *after* the essay on Rossetti. That eliminates one of the most magical moments of the first edition: the page-turn from the end of the Rossetti essay, where Pater has been emphasising the ways in which Rossetti's poetry is new or novel, to the epigraph of the 'Postscript', from Pindar's 9th Olympian Ode: 'Praise old wine, but the flowers of new hymns' (lines 48–9). With the Rossetti essay fresh in the memory, the quotation from Pindar seems also to recall Charles Dickens's famous attack on the Pre-Raphaelite artists back in 1850, 'Old Lamps for New', and the covert reference to it in the preface to the volume of translations by Rossetti, *The Early Italian Poets*, which plays a conspicuous role in Pater's essay.[11] The discussion of Rossetti's originality, in this sequence, leads directly to the theoretical discussion of romanticism *versus* classicism in the 'Postscript'.

The page-turn also makes vivid another set of connections. Rossetti, in the essay devoted to him, is 'but the "Interpreter"' of his own *House of Life* – his sonnet sequence, which Pater here extends to include 'the whole of Rossetti's work' (214). Rossetti the painter-poet thus becomes an analogue for the 'true aesthetic critic' in the first paragraph of the 'Postscript', and his *House of Life* an analogue for a conception of Pater's own, the 'House Beautiful' introduced earlier in *Appreciations* in the essay on 'Wordsworth' (60):[12]

> But in that *House Beautiful*, which the creative minds of all generations – the artists and those who have treated life in the spirit of art – are always building together, for the refreshment of the human spirit, these opposi-tions [between 'classical' and 'romantic'] cease; and the *Interpreter* of the *House Beautiful*, the true aesthetic critic, uses these divisions, only so far as they enable him to enter into the peculiarities of the objects with which he has to do. (241)

The intertextuality between these passages is not, of course, lost in the second edition, but the intervention of 'Feuillet's "La Morte"' between the Rossetti essay and the 'Postscript' makes it significantly less evident.

The change, then, not only disrupts the elegant transition from Morris to Rossetti in the first edition, but also deprives Rossetti of his penultimate position in the sequence – the position that enables his work to complete the set of critical essays and to herald the theoretical discussion about romanticism and classicism of the 'Postscript'. For the literary or art historian this seems a lost opportunity to create a compelling narrative, although it is some consolation that the essay on the French novelist Octave Feuillet reinforces the cosmopolitan aspect of the collection – its refusal to conform to an exceptionalist history of English literature (or art). Many reasons have been suggested for the change, among them Pater's putative timidity in the face of increasing moral and sexual regulation, as well as xenophobic attitudes among more conservative critics.[13] This explanation, frequent in recent discussion of Pater's work, seems far-fetched in this case (well over a decade after the scandals of the mid-1870s over supposed peccadilloes in Pater's personal life and the apparent irreligion of *The Renaissance*), although it has a certain poetic resonance with the parallel charge against Rossetti, that he refused to exhibit for fear of hostile criticism. A more plausible explanation might be to see the change as a response to certain critics of the first edition, who had reproved the Morris essay for stylistic incongruity with the later writings in the collection.[14] Pater included in *Appreciations* his very first published essay,

'Coleridge' of 1866, but this had been much more heavily revised (and amalgamated with the introduction to the selection from Coleridge in volume IV of Ward's *English Poets* from its first edition of 1880).[15] In a collection framed by 'Style' and the 'Postscript', Pater might reasonably have decided that the more emphatic or florid writing in the Morris essay made it seem dated. One is tempted to wonder whether Pater might have reinstated it, suitably revised, had he lived to design a third edition (as, indeed, he reinstated the 'Conclusion', originally the final paragraphs of the Morris essay, after its deletion from the second edition of *The Renaissance*).

Perhaps it is most likely that Pater weighed a variety of considerations when he changed the sequence for the second edition, and in our sorrow over the disappearance of the Morris essay we may have overlooked something important. The original sequence makes Rossetti follow Morris's lead as an 'aesthetic poet', even though Pater is at great pains, from the start, to demonstrate the complexity of the chronology: 'some of his poems had won a kind of exquisite fame before they were in the full sense published', so that *Poems* of 1870 – Rossetti's first volume of original poetry – 'came at last to satisfy a long-standing curiosity as to the poet, whose pictures also had become an object of the same peculiar kind of interest' (205). This can be read as an oblique acknowledgement of the occasion for the essay: Rossetti's death had enabled his paintings at last to emerge into public view, in memorial exhibitions held in the winter of 1882–83, so that Pater's essay was one of many, that winter, that attempted to size up Rossetti's role in his generation.[16] It also makes the case for Rossetti's priority over Morris, despite the actual dates of their publications.

Pater deftly transforms these events – the belated public revelations of Rossetti's poems (in the volume of 1870) and of his paintings (in the memorial exhibitions) – from mere historical facts to qualities or features of the works themselves: 'archaic' (216), indeed imitative, to an extreme degree, of the artists and poets of the past, Rossetti's works are distinctive nonetheless for their originality. The words 'originality', 'new', and 'novel' appear ten times in the essay, and particularly at the beginning and end; at the same time, Pater dwells on the utter fidelity (or what he calls the 'perfect sincerity') with which Rossetti transcribes or imitates his poetic or visual matter, whether he has found it in nature, in himself, or in his literary and artistic precursors. As always with Pater, the choice of words is precise. In a review of 1887, Pater repeatedly uses the word 'modern' to characterise Browning's poetic project ('Browning', *Essays*, 43–9), its 'obscurity' a necessary counterpart to the 'difficulty of his matter' (41). Rossetti is 'new', 'novel', or 'original' rather than 'modern', and for Pater that is not inconsistent (as it would become for some modernist critics) with a heightened reverence or faithfulness to artistic precedent.

This paradoxical combination of originality and imitation is the hall-mark or leitmotif of Rossetti's achievement, in Pater's account, and he finds for it a striking image:

> That he had this gift of transparency in language – the control of a style which did but obediently shift and shape itself to the mental motion, as a well-trained hand can follow on the tracing-paper the outline of an original drawing below it, was proved afterwards by a volume of typically perfect translations from the delightful but difficult 'early Italian poets': such transparency being indeed the secret of all genuine style, of all such style as can truly belong to one man and not to another. (206–7)[17]

The sentence recalls a passage in the essay on 'Style', which uses precisely the same image apropos translation: 'if the original be first-rate, one's first care should be with its elementary particles, Plato, for instance, being often reproducible by an exact following, with no variation in structure, of word after word, as the pencil follows a drawing under tracing-paper' (14–15) (as we shall shortly see, the reference to Plato is equally apropos). In the context of *Appreciations*, the sentence in the Rossetti essay appears to echo, or to provide a concrete illustration for, the theoretical point made earlier in 'Style'. In point of chronology, however, it is the passage in 'Style' (1888) that imitates the one in the Rossetti essay (1883). The word 'transparency' draws on an even earlier text, 'Diaphaneitè' of 1864, where it describes a kind of ideal character: 'It is just this sort of entire transparency of nature that lets through unconsciously all that is really lifegiving in the established order of things' ('Diaphaneitè', *MS*, 251; in that context the image is a 'clear crystal' (253) rather than the later 'tracing-paper'). In form as well as content, then, the sentence in the Rossetti essay shows how closely related may be those apparent opposites, imitation and originality – two sides of the same coin, or a dialectical pair.

The same sentence also argues implicitly for an equivalence between the verbal ('language') and the visual ('drawing') in Rossetti's work. Translated poems, far from being inferior or subordinate to original creation, are another equivalent, and even come to seem exemplary in their special form of sincerity, fidelity to the source text. Pater here draws on ideas from Rossetti's own preface to *The Early Italian Poets*, first published in 1861, which Pater rightly recognises as a significant artistic manifesto (one which also made its impact on Pound, Yeats, and the Modernist generation).[18] Pater notes the 'definiteness of sensible imagery' in 'The Blessed Damozel' (207) and the 'lovely little sceneries scattered up and down his poems, glimpses of a landscape, not indeed of broad open-air effects, but rather that of a painter concentrated upon the picturesque effect of one or two selected objects at a time' (211); the phrasing recalls Pater's comment on the 'alert sense of outward things' of Botticelli, the 'naturalist' painter of the early Renaissance so closely identified with Rossetti (*Ren.*, 41).[19] Here, however, Pater is not primarily concerned with identifying similarities in imagery or incident between poems and pictures. The equivalence between them is to do, instead, with the 'fundamental brainwork' that underpins their creation.[20] It is important that this is not a matter of establishing an intellectual content that can then be 'translated' into the different media of poetry or painting; the first paragraph of 'The School of Giorgione' is sufficient warning against that misconception (*Ren.*, 102–3). Instead, it is a matter of the intellectual work the artist must do to ensure 'perfect sincerity', and here Pater (the Classics don who taught the philosophical elements in the Greats curriculum) is able to draw out the deep theoretical or philosophical consistency in Rossetti's way of going about artmaking, in either visual or verbal form.

In part, Pater is arguing against the critics (of our day as well as his and Rossetti's) who see only the sensuous and sensual in Rossetti's work, those for whom the paintings of female figures are mere objects of male desire, and the poems immoral or indecent. It may be interesting that, while the latter charge no longer carries conviction in our sexually liberated days, the former remains persistent for current critics who cannot (or will not) see beyond the representational content of the paintings of female figures. McGann digs deeper when he notes that the female figure in Rossetti's paintings 'means more and other than we have grown to think' and he attributes the insight to Pater: 'This was Pater's argument when he interpreted the Rossettian woman under her earlier incarnation as the *Mona Lisa*.'[21]

If McGann is right, this dates Rossetti's influence on Pater's critical project much earlier than his first explicit reference to the painter-poet (in 'The School of Giorgione' of 1877), and relates it to Pater's crucial experiment, also the most enduringly famous passage in his writing: the ecphrasis on the *Mona Lisa* in Pater's essay of 1869 on Leonardo da Vinci. Rossetti's haunting sonnet on Leonardo's *Virgin of the Rocks* was not 'in the full sense published' until the volume *Poems* of 1870 – that is, after the publication of Pater's essay on Leonardo. However, it was circulating in privately printed form among Rossetti's friends in the late summer and early autumn of 1869, when Pater was at work on the Leonardo essay;[22] this was also the period of his closest association with the artistic circle around Rossetti, including Swinburne (who might have had the sonnet by heart) and Gosse (who records the intimacy between Pater and Swinburne at this date).[23] In his later essay on Rossetti, Pater evinces considerable familiarity with Rossetti's personal life – his house with its many mirrors, his insomnia, his 'great affections' (213–15), and he also emphasises (as we have already seen) the circulation of his poems, among intimates, before publication (205). Even if he had not seen the Leonardo sonnet, he certainly knew Rossetti's sonnet on his own painting, *Lady Lilith*, which Swinburne had printed in his section of the Royal Academy review he published in collaboration with Rossetti's brother, William Michael Rossetti, in 1868, lines 5–7 from which read compellingly as intertexts for Pater's ecphrasis on the *Mona Lisa*:

> And still she sits, young while the earth is old,
>   And, subtly of herself contemplative,
>   Draws men to watch the bright net she can weave,[24]

More generally, Rossetti's sonnets for pictures (six of which had been published as early as 1850, in the Pre-Raphaelite 'little magazine', *The Germ*) set a kind of precedent for 'aesthetic criticism' in Pater's sense – description not simply of the art object under review but of what it is 'to me' (*Ren.*, xx).

Perhaps, then, Pater himself can be seen as one of Rossetti's 'school', of those who learn to write (or paint) under his inspiration. If Pater writes in prose rather than verse, that too is theorised in the essay 'Style', and in developing his own critical practice partly by writing about visual art he is following the example of French critics, among them those favourites of Pater, Swinburne, and the Rossetti circle: Gautier and Baudelaire. At the same time, Pater is saying something important about Rossetti's practice as a painter, when he likens his paintings of women to the *Mona Lisa*, even though he makes the point in imaginative rather than logical or discursive form.

To borrow McGann's terms, Pater is prepared to see 'more and other' than a sensual woman, a mere object of heterosexual desire, in Rossetti's paintings. Moreover, he is able to offer a cogent philosophical rationale for his view, one that draws together the disparate points of literary and artistic reference – the objects, one might say, of intellectual or aesthetic desire – that he shares with Rossetti. The reasoning is intricate, and Pater's craftsmanship leaves it up to the reader whether to follow the argument closely or simply to enjoy the unfolding of the prose. Let us try, however, to follow the argument, beginning with Pater's deconstruction of the opposition between 'spirit' and 'matter', so central to negative criticisms of Rossetti's art as 'fleshly' or immoral.[25] Pater enlists Dante, Rossetti's namesake and the focus of his early self-education as a translator, whose Thomist philosophy (or theology) rejected any Manichean division of body and soul: 'To [Dante], in the vehement and impassioned heat of his conceptions, the material and the spiritual are fused and blent: if the spiritual attains the definite visibility of a crystal, what is material loses its earthiness and impurity' (212). The image of the crystal harks back all the way to 'Diaphaneitè' of 1864 (*MS*, 253). Perhaps more surprisingly, the sentence recurs, almost verbatim, in the chapter on 'The Genius of Plato' in *Plato and Platonism* of 1893, Pater's most extended meditation on basic problems of philosophy (*PP*, 135). There the comparison is between Plato and Dante, but this is just one of a sequence of correspondences between *Plato and Platonism* and Pater's essay on Rossetti that set up a sustained comparison between the ancient philosopher and the modern painter-poet, with Dante, perhaps, as mediator. Poetry is a *mania* in Plato's thought ('The Doctrine of Plato', *PP*, 172) and in Rossetti's practice (209). The personifications in Rossetti's sonnets ('his hold upon them, or rather their hold upon him', 208) are like the philosophical Ideas that Plato knows as intimately as one knows a person (his 'hold on persons, that of persons on him', 'The Genius of Plato', *PP*, 130). The images and objects in Rossetti's 'dwelling-place' (his poems or paintings, as well as his literal house in Cheyne Walk) have been handed down, each with 'its associations' (214); thus they are like the 'thoughts of Plato', which 'have had their earlier proprietors' ('The Doctrine of Motion', *PP*, 7–8). The phrase 'fundamental brainwork' is Rossetti's, but Pater quotes it not in his essay on Rossetti, but rather in chapter 3, 'Plato and the Sophists', of *Plato and Platonism*, where it is attributed to 'an intensely personal, deeply stirred, poet and artist of our own generation' (*PP*, 118–19).[26] In perhaps his boldest move, Pater associates Plato – and, by implication, Rossetti and Dante, since the phrasing in the Rossetti essay is so close to that in 'The Genius of Plato' – with Théophile Gautier, unnamed but clearly referenced (by way of an entry in the diary of the Goncourt brothers): 'one, for whom, as was said of a very different French writer, "the *visible* world really existed"' (*PP*, 126).[27]

There is more, however, to the dialectic of spirit and matter: 'In our actual concrete experience, the two trains of phenomena which the words *matter* and *spirit* do but roughly distinguish, play inextricably into each other' (212). Rossetti (as interpreted by Pater) has fully grasped a basic point of Kant's *Critique of Pure Reason*, which haunts the essay although (characteristically) it remains unnamed. Humans do not have knowledge of things as they are in themselves, but only of phenomena as we experience them; thus there is no fundamental difference (as there is, for example, in Descartes) between our knowledge of external nature and that of our inward feelings – both are things of our experience, not things-in-themselves.[28] Rossetti's artistic project is devoted to the most sincere or faithful attention to things of either kind, and he makes no difference between them. Pater takes as examples poems by Rossetti that envision, respectively, external nature ('The Stream's Secret') and inward experience ('Love's Nocturn'): 'In the one, what a delight in all the natural beauty of water, all its details for the eye of a painter; in the other, how subtle and fine the imaginative hold upon all the secret ways of sleep and dreams!' (210).[29]

In the final paragraph of the essay, Pater generalises the point to describe 'two distinct functions' of poetry: one, to reveal 'the ideal aspects of common things' and the other, 'the imaginative creation of things that are ideal from their very birth' (218). The distinction recalls that between the phenomena of external nature and those of inward experience. It also seems uncannily to prefigure the French Symbolist manifestoes, not published until 1886. Pater's first function corresponds to realism or impressionism – 'nature seen through the eyes of a temperament', or the subjective representation of the external object. The second function corresponds to the theoretical definition of Symbolism as objectifying the subjective, or giving concrete (artistic or poetic) form to the Idea.[30] Pater believes Rossetti to have been an originator in both functions, but above all in the second, and he concludes the essay: 'Rossetti did something, something excellent, of the former kind; but his characteristic, his really revealing work, lay in the adding to poetry of fresh poetic material, of a new order of phenomena, in the creation of a new ideal' (218). This final sentence also reads as a parallel to what Hegel says about Winckelmann, as Pater had translated it in the essay of 1867 that established his critical project in crucial respects:

> 'Winckelmann, by contemplation of the ideal works of the ancients, received a sort of inspiration, through which he opened a new sense for the study of art. He is to be regarded as one of those who, in the sphere of art, have known how to initiate a new organ for the human spirit.' (*Ren.*, 141)

If, as suggested above, the ecphrasis on the *Mona Lisa* is intellectually indebted to Rossetti's sonnets on pictures, then the implied comparison to Winckelmann – whose ecphrases on ancient sculptures are surely another prime inspiration for Pater – is entirely appropriate.

Pater enrols Rossetti among his special pantheon – Winckelmann, Hegel, and Kant; Dante, Gautier, and Plato; Leonardo and Botticelli. As poet-painter, Rossetti is also comparable to other favourites, Michelangelo and Blake. Pater's reference to Blake's design from *The Book of Job*, 'When the Morning Stars Sang Together', also acknowledges Rossetti's fascination with that image, and perhaps credits Rossetti for drawing his own attention to it (210).[31] The intertextual network in this essay is particularly dense even for Pater; like Wagner's *Ring* cycle from the third act of *Siegfried* onwards, it seems to multiply and overlap its characteristic leitmotifs with greater complexity than ever before. Thus the essay, although prompted by the specific occasion of Rossetti's death in 1882, provides the clues by which the literary or art historian may trace the presence of Rossetti and his works throughout Pater's criticism, at least from 'The School of Giorgione' (1877) through to *Plato and Platonism* (1893). Perhaps, as suggested above, it even reveals the importance of Rossetti in the formation of Pater's aesthetic criticism from its beginnings in the seminal essays 'Winckelmann' (1867), 'Notes on Lionardo da Vinci' (1869), and 'A Fragment on Sandro Botticelli' (1870).[32]

The web of allusions can therefore be seen as one way to acknowledge and document the place of Rossetti in Pater's criticism – or, in the words of the 'Preface' to the Renaissance, what Rossetti is 'to *me*' (*Ren.*, xx). But – *pace* those who find only solipsism in Pater (or Rossetti) – that is just the 'first step' in aesthetic criticism (xix), and the critic must proceed to account, rigorously and precisely, for how the artist or work of art has made its impression on her or him, 'to distinguish, to analyse, and separate from its adjuncts, the virtue' of the work or artist, 'as a chemist notes some natural element, for himself and others' (xx–xxi).[33] The analysis may be surprising to those who still cling to received ideas about Rossetti's art as merely sensual or salacious, self-indulgent or autobiographical, but Pater is clear about the 'reflective force, the dry reason, always at work behind his imaginative creations, which at no time dispensed with a genuine intellectual structure' (215). The phraseology recalls, again, the surprising correspondence between Rossetti and Plato that can now be seen as a continuous thread in Pater's writing, brought together in the final sentences of *Plato and Platonism* with other recurring points of theoretical, or philosophical, reference: 'Heraclitus had preferred the "dry soul," or the "dry light" in it, as Bacon after him the *siccum lumen*. And the dry beauty, — let Plato teach us, to love that also, duly' ('Plato's Aesthetics', *PP*, 283). However, the words also look forward to the famous phrase 'all dry and hard', used to describe 'a properly classical poem' of any age in T.E. Hulme's essay, 'Romanticism and Classicism', written shortly before the First World War. Hulme's essay, published after his death in action in a collection entitled *Speculations*, might be described as a modernist reworking of the essay by Pater, originally entitled 'Romanticism', that became the 'Postscript' to *Appreciations*.[34]

Pater could not, of course, foresee the importance of Rossetti (or indeed of his own writing) to the next, Modernist generation, and in volume IV of Ward's *English Poets* Rossetti takes his place among the more limited 'school' of his immediate followers: here he is the 'last romantic'. Aesthetic criticism, as Pater had theorised it from the start, had always included an aspiration to locate its objects within a movement or a history, which is itself distinguished or analysed in the process, as in the case of the Renaissance in Pater's early essays; such aspiration is also a conspicuous element in the Pre-Raphaelite movement, its insistent historical orientation implied in its very name. The range of allusion in the Rossetti essay expands, in both chronological and cosmopolitan scope, beyond the more limited, Hegelian historicism of the review-essay on Morris. That permits Pater not merely to situate Rossetti as an 'aesthetic poet' in his own, late Victorian generation, but also to link him to longer and wider histories, including those not yet written and still unknown, from the Pre-Socratic philosophers to the Modernist poets whose careers had not yet begun. Now that we are at some distance from the first Modernist generation, Pater's essay can give us what we may call 'the place of Rossetti' for a twenty-first century readership.

Notes

1 Pater added a footnote identifying this painter-poet as 'Dante Gabriel Rossetti' only in the fourth edition of 1893, well after Rossetti's death.

2 [Published anonymously], 'Poems by William Morris', *Westminster Review*, n. s. 34 (October 1868), 300–12 (308).

3 Billie Andrew Inman finds Pater's 'errors and omissions in regard to proper names ... baffling' (Inman (1981), xxii), and in Chapter 7 of this volume Scarlett Baron discusses Pater's refusal to name Guy de Maupassant in 'Style'. However, Pater's practice of not-naming cannot easily be explained away as timidity or avoidance of controversy; often, as in his references to Rossetti, there is clearly no attempt to hide the identity of the not-named person.

4 'Preface', in *The English Poets: Selections: With Critical Introductions by Various Writers and a General Introduction by Matthew Arnold*, ed. Thomas Humphry Ward, 4 vols (1880), i. *Chaucer to Donne*, vi.

5 See Pater's thoughtful review of her novel *Robert Elsmere*, reprinted from *The Guardian* (28 March 1888), *Essays*, 53–70.

6 Browning, Arnold, and Tennyson were added as an Appendix to the reprint of 1894, and integrated into the volume in subsequent reprints, until they were moved to a new Volume 5, 'Browning to Rupert Brooke', first published in 1918, which also included a selection of eleven poems by Christina Rossetti (d. 1894), introduced by Percy Lubbock, and large selections from Morris (d. 1896, intro. J.W. Mackail) and Swinburne (d. 1909, intro. Edmund Gosse). The contents and history of this anthology, and its impact on the study of English literature, deserve further study.

7 I have argued this more fully in *Modern Painters, Old Masters: The Art of Imitation from the Pre-Raphaelites to the First World War* (New Haven and London 2017), ch. 5 ('On Beauty and Aesthetic Painting').

8 Jerome McGann, *Dante Gabriel Rossetti and the Game That Must Be Lost* (New Haven and London 2000), 145.

9 See Elizabeth Prettejohn, *Art for Art's Sake: Aestheticism in Victorian Painting* (New Haven and London 2007), 1–2, 11–35.

10 Walter Pater, *Appreciations: With an Essay on Style* (1889), 227.

11 See Prettejohn, *Modern Painters*, 35–6.

12 In fact the phrase 'House Beautiful' first occurs in Pater's review of a book by Sidney Colvin, *Children in Italian and English Design*, first published in the *Academy* 3 (15 July 1872), 267–8, repr. in Donald Hill's edition of Pater's *Renaissance* (*Ren.*, 191–5 (194)).

13 See for example Laurel Brake, *Print in Transition, 1850–1910: Studies in Media and Book History* (Houndmills, Basingstoke 2001), 225–47; ibid., 'The Entangling Dance: Pater after *Marius*, 1885–1891', in *Walter Pater: Transparencies of Desire*, ed. Laurel Brake, Lesley Higgins, and Carolyn Williams (Greensboro, NC 2002), 24–36. For a different account, which emphasises the benefits of including the essay on Feuillet, see Kenneth Daley, 'Pater's *Appreciations* and the Problem of "Feuillet's *La Morte*"', *English Literature in Transition 1880–1920*, 60 (2017), 471–89.

14 See the reviews by William Watson and Charles Larcom Graves, in *Critical Heritage*, 206, 209.

15 Pater avows this history, succinctly and precisely, by including both dates at the end of the essay: '1865, 1880' ('Coleridge', *App.*, 104).

16 An interesting example is the essay by the classicist and psychical theorist F.W.H. Myers, 'Rossetti and the Religion of Beauty', in *Essays Modern* (vol. 2 of Myers's *Essays Classical and Modern*, 1883), 312–34. Myers touches on many of the ideas that also appear in Pater's essay: Rossetti's originality (313), his leadership of a 'movement' (314), his 'Platonism' (317–18), and even the word 'interpreter' (which Myers derives from Plato's Greek, 334). Unlike Pater (or McGann), however, Myers fails – or refuses – to see these ideas as

fully intellectually integrated or programmatic; he sees the affinities to Platonic philosophy as 'probably unconscious' (317), and takes the Rossettian female figure as examplifying both personal romantic love and the changing social role of women in contemporary society (319–21).

17 The word 'afterwards' (in the very careful chronology of this essay) strengthens the hypothesis that the 'school' under discussion is (or at least includes) the original Pre-Raphaelite Brotherhood, since the volume of translations was first published by Smith, Elder in 1861, as *The Early Italian Poets: From Ciullo d'Alcamo to Dante Alighieri: (1100—1200—1300): In the Original Metres: Together with Dante's Vita Nuova: Translated by D.G. Rossetti.*

18 Rossetti, *Early Italian Poets*, vii–xii; repr. in *The Works of Dante Gabriel Rossetti*, ed. William M. Rossetti (1911), 282–4. In McGann's view, T.S. Eliot 'took Rossetti's translations as a point of departure, a useful antithesis, whereas Yeats and Pound turned to the translations as useful guides and models' (McGann, *Dante Gabriel Rossetti*, 59).

19 For Rossetti's role in the revival of interest in Botticelli (which predates, and must have influenced, Pater's better recognised contribution), see Elizabeth Prettejohn, 'Botticelli and the Pre-Raphaelites', in *Botticelli Reimagined*, ed. Mark Evans and Stefan Weppelmann (2016), 76–81.

20 'Conception, my boy, FUNDAMENTAL BRAINWORK, that is what makes the difference in all art', quoted from Rossetti in T. Hall Caine, *Recollections of Dante Gabriel Rossetti* (1882), 249. McGann also emphasises the phrase (McGann, *Dante Gabriel Rossetti*, 6 and *passim*), which Pater quotes in *Plato and Platonism* ('Plato and the Sophists', *PP*, 119); Pater also paraphrases the passage from Hall Caine in a letter of 1888 to Arthur Symons (*Letters*, 79).

21 McGann, *Dante Gabriel Rossetti*, 17.

22 I am indebted to Hilary Fraser for this train of thought about how Pater might have encountered Rossetti's sonnet.

23 Edmund Gosse, 'Walter Pater: A Portrait', *Contemporary Review* 66 (December 1894), 801–2.

24 William Michael Rossetti and Algernon C. Swinburne, *Notes on the Royal Academy Exhibition, 1868* (1868), 47. The sonnet was later incorporated into *The House of Life* under the title 'Body's Beauty', and the word 'net' in line 7 changed to 'web', a word conspicuous in Pater's passage on the *Mona Lisa* (Rossetti, *Works*, 100). When he made this change, was Rossetti alluding, consciously or subconsciously, to the relationship between his own sonnet and Pater's ecphrasis on Leonardo's painting?

25 The most notorious of these was 'The Fleshly School of Poetry: Mr. D.G. Rossetti', *Contemporary Review* 18 (October 1871), 334–50, published under the pseudonym 'Thomas Maitland' by the poet Robert Buchanan. See John A. Cassidy, 'Robert Buchanan and the Fleshly Controversy', *PMLA* 67 (1952), 65–93.

26 See note 20 above.

27 The internal quotation derives from the entry for 1 May 1857, *Journal des Goncourt: Mémoires de la vie littéraire: premier volume 1851–1861* (Paris 1887), 182. See Prettejohn, *Art for Art's Sake*, 85.

28 The two kinds of experience also appear in the paragraphs from the essay on Morris that became the first two paragraphs of the 'Conclusion' (*Ren.*, 186–8; thanks to Lene Østermark-Johansen for this point).

29 Cf. the values of 'fluidity' and dream proposed by Marcus Waithe in Chapter 13 of this volume.

30 See Jean Moréas, 'Symbolism – a Manifesto' (translated from *Supplément littéraire du Figaro*, 18 September 1886) and Gustave Kahn, 'Response of the Symbolists' (translated from *L'Événement*, 28 September 1886), in *Art in Theory 1815–1900: An Anthology of Changing Ideas*, ed. Charles Harrison and Paul Wood with Jason Gaiger (Oxford and Malden, MA 1998), 1014–17.

31 Rossetti contributed the section on 'The Inventions to the Book of Job' to *Life of William Blake, 'Pictor Ignotus'*, completed after the untimely death of its author, Alexander Gilchrist, by his widow Anne Gilchrist with the assistance of both Rossetti brothers, and first published in 1863; D.G. Rossetti's contributions are reprinted in Rossetti, *Works*, 600–3. See further Chapter 10 in this volume.

32 These are the titles of first publication in (respectively) *Westminster Review*, n.s. 31 (January 1867), 80–110 (anonymously published); *Fortnightly Review*, n.s. 6 (November 1869), 494–508; *Fortnightly Review*, n.s. 8 (August 1870), 155–60.

33 The terms are those of Kant's *Critique of Judgement*, §8: one must see the object with one's own eyes but speak about it with a universal voice. See the Introduction to this volume.

34 T.E. Hulme, 'Romanticism and Classicism' (*c.*1911–12), in *Speculations: Essays on Humanism and the Philosophy of Art*, ed. Herbert Read (1936, first printed 1924), 113–40 (126). The choice of title for this posthumous collection was presumably Read's, but it nonetheless places Hulme's volume within the sequence initiated by Pater's *Appreciations* (1889); cf. Wilde's *Intentions* (1891), George Moore's *Avowals* (1924), Roger Fry's *Transformations* (1927), and C.S. Lewis's *Rehabilitations* (1939).

Postscript

Stephen Bann

Who was reading Pater's critical works over the century that followed his death? How did his readers place his ideas in the context of their other literary pursuits? And what might a study of Pater's readership tell us about the development of English studies over the period? These questions may appear to be impossibly ambitious. But there is one crucial element that could suggest that they are not entirely meaningless. The writings of Pater's great rival Ruskin were immured in the Library Edition of Cook and Wedderburn, which was completed in 1912, though individual pocket editions continued to circulate in the 'Popular Ruskin' series. By contrast, Pater's works were still being reedited and reprinted in much the same distinctive format as he had agreed with Macmillan in 1872. To choose one example, my personal copy of *Appreciations*, bought in the 1970s, derives from the fourth reprint of the Library Edition of 1910, which succeeded four preceding editions dating back to 1889 and their five intercalated reprints.

One may assume that these repeated publications testify to a continuing demand for Pater's work. The individual books must have circulated widely over the period, and subsequently many of them entered the second-hand market. Moreover, and in common with the other volumes of the period, they offer the bonus of not infrequently giving us the names and the written comments of their successive owners. This Postscript provides me with the opportunity to review a small selection of these inscribed copies. Though this will inevitably be a random selection, I suggest that it offers some glimpses into the reception of Pater over a period when he maintained his place in the canon, though his work was still far from gaining institutional assent in the universities. My review will end with a brief record of the early stages of this process.

The first copy to be considered here has to be the 1925 reprint of the First Pocket Edition of *The Renaissance*, inscribed by my father with his name and dated 'Christmas 1927'. In later life, Harry Bann (1902–98)

286

wrote in a brief unpublished memoir about the readings in poetry and
criticism which he cultivated while preparing to qualify as a solicitor in
Stockport in the 1920s. During his schooldays, he readily admitted, poetry
had been treated in a 'dull, unimaginative way . . . represented chiefly by
pieces suitable or considered suitable for recitation'.[1] Yet he made up for
this deficiency by becoming familiar nonetheless with the poetry of Keats,
Shelley, and Wordsworth. In 1920 he was indebted to his friendship with
an Anglo-Catholic schoolmaster for the gift of the *Poems of Christina
Rossetti*, and he received from the same source the anthology of extracts
from English and French literature, *The Spirit of Man*, compiled by the
poet laureate, Robert Bridges. It is worth noting that Bridges took great
care to underline the support that he had received in this undertaking from
W.B. Yeats, who was a major contributor. But he did not select any work
at all from Morris, Swinburne, or either of the Rossettis, let alone any
passages from Ruskin or Pater.[2]

Over the 1920s, my father's reading became more wide-ranging, as
indicated by the red leather-bound edition of the poems of Lamartine,
which he purchased in Le Havre as a present for my mother, and the
pocket edition of Byron's *Childe Harold's Pilgrimage*, which he annotated
with verses that cheekily parodied Byron's stanzas, the outcome of an
overnight train journey to the North of Scotland in 1928. His interest in
acquiring a copy of Pater's *Renaissance* around this period could well have
been stimulated by another early present of Julia Cartwright's *Raphael* in
Duckworth's 'Popular Library of Art'. But it was another volume from the
same series, G.K. Chesterton's study of the painter G.F. Watts, that
elicited many more marks of assent beside particular passages in the text.
In marking his *Renaissance*, he confined himself to underlining two passages: Pater's intimation in 'Early French Stories' that this medieval
account of a historic friendship appears 'to have been written by a monk'
(*Ren.*, 21), and the mention of Pico della Mirandola as having anticipated
'a later age' which would find 'the true method of effecting a scientific
reconciliation of Christian sentiment with the imagery, the legends, the
theories about the world, of pagan poetry and philosophy' (36). In effect, it
was undoubtedly Chesterton rather than Pater who became my father's
literary mentor. As he later acknowledged: 'In so far as I imbibed a
philosophy of life in my early days it was, I feel sure, inspired largely by
Chesterton's ideas and writings.'[3]

Side by side with this peripheral instance, I can place a figure born in the
previous decade whose interest in Pater undoubtedly began in early youth,
and whose annotated copies of works by Pater turn out to be especially

informative. Bonamy Dobrée (1891–1974) was a Channel-Islander whose Huguenot predecessors had acquired considerable wealth and status in the City of London. He was educated at the public school of Haileybury, which had merged with Kipling's alma mater, the 'Imperial Service College'. It was through his success in the school's 'Mason Prize' in the Summer of 1908 that he acquired his copy of the Second Edition (1907 reprint) of Pater's *Miscellaneous Studies*. As this information is provided together with his signature in a handwritten inscription on the fly leaf, it would appear that the choice of this particular book by Pater was probably a personal one.[4] Maybe it is not coincidental that this posthumously published collection of essays concludes with 'Emerald Uthwart', Pater's affecting account of the schooldays and early death of a young British officer.

Dobrée would move on from Haileybury to the Royal Military Academy at Woolwich. After being commissioned in the Royal Field Artillery in 1910, he resigned as a subaltern in 1913, but rejoined the army in 1914 and emerged as a Major at the end of the First World War. He was later enabled by his private income to embark on a career as a man of letters. He would become a close friend of T.S. Eliot, who commissioned him to write an article on Kipling for the *Criterion*. Moreover the annotation 'T.S.E' that he pencils in the margin of Pater's essay on 'Style' (glossing the use of the term 'correlative') suggests that his intensive reading of *Appreciations* might date back to the 1920s. Among the many underlinings and comments with which he embellishes his copy of the Library Edition (1911 reprint), there is a brief note in the original French that identifies one of Pater's sources for the opening essay on 'Style'. Pater's comment, apropos of Flaubert, that 'the idea only exists by virtue of the form' (*App.*, 30) is glossed with the quote: 'de la forme naît l'idée Gautier'. The essays on 'Coleridge' and 'Wordsworth' are also replete with Dobrée's perceptive annotations.

After beginning his career as an independent critic with a special interest in drama, Dobrée became a lecturer in English at Queen Mary College, London. From 1936 to 1955 he later served as the first Professor of English at the University of Leeds, where he set up a thriving department. It would be unnecessary in this context to summarise his highly productive career as a scholarly author, whose range of subjects ranged from Restoration dramatists to eighteenth-century figures as far apart as John Wesley and Horace Walpole, and extended to Rudyard Kipling. But Pater's abiding influence can be detected in a late essay on the art of prose. Dobrée comments: 'what you can do, what you must do, is to import your own "sense of fact", to use Pater's still seminal phrase, give something of the ethos that surrounds an idea'.[5] He disagrees with Pater's depreciation of the prose of Dryden (here mentioned in Chapters 1 and 6). But he elevates both into his chosen list of prose stylists: 'Very few writers cherish prose, really think about their instrument, as, say, Dryden, Berkeley, Landor, and Pater did.'[6]

After his death in 1974, Dobrée's working library, which included the copies of the works of Pater already discussed here, was donated to the newly founded University of Kent at Canterbury. Mention has been made in this volume of the movement towards the 'institutionalisation of English in British universities' that took place in Pater's own century. Yet the issue of how English studies continued to develop in the following century is equally significant. Marcus Waithe's chapter in this volume refers to the writer's first encounter with Pater as an undergraduate in the 1990s. But the curriculum development of the 'new universities' of the 1960s was surely a material factor in his reception. Dobrée's working library, with its much-thumbed Pater volumes, was a helpful resource for my own students when I introduced Pater's work in a graduate course at Kent in the early 1970s, a development that will be further discussed in this Postscript.

As a prelude, however, I offer two further examples of books by Pater bearing contemporary inscriptions that belong to the mid-twentieth century. It is worth mentioning that the only selection of extracts from Pater's writings that was readily available at this time was the collection by Richard Aldington, which had been compiled during the Second World War although it was only published in 1948. Accordingly, Aldington opens with an apology: 'for a war-weary generation, scrambling on somehow from day to day, Pater's work may seem as remote as Pater's epoch'. He concludes his introduction with a modest plea in favour of what he terms Pater's 'civilising influence, particularly over sensitive and studious youth'.[7]

Some incentive to read Pater was thus being communicated to the postwar generation. My own copy of the second reprint of the 'Caravan Library' edition of *Appreciations* bears the firm signature of 'Mary Wilkinson / Reigate August 1951' on the fly-leaf. Her pencilled annotation to the essay on 'Style' reads: 'With Pater, criticism is quickened meditation, worship of form.' But what is worth bringing out in this case is the commentary added by her fellow students (or maybe her teachers?) from the 'Sizewell Hall, Suffolk, Course for Continuing Students', who have scrawled their sentiments on the inside back cover: 'Best wishes for Oxford 1951'; 'Good Luck, Mary!'; 'Shall think of you in November. Bon chance.' Seemingly, this young woman was then preparing for an Oxford

Entrance exam, and had forearmed herself with a Paterian precept that was probably not in tune with the English course to which she aspired.

Another gift originally proffered in the mid-century period is my edition of *Gaston de Latour* (1928 reprint of the Library Edition) which is dedicated in a graceful hand with the phrase 'Love from the Plowdens of Mayfield'. There is no problem in identifying this Anglo-Indian branch of an ancient Catholic family (one of them a patron of the young Kipling) who had returned to England before the outbreak of the Second World War. The subject matter of Pater's unfinished *Gaston*, and the sender's informal dedication, might suggest that this present was destined for a young family friend, perhaps indeed a 'sensitive and studious youth'.

My own personal interest in Pater's writings (other than his *Renaissance*) can be dated precisely to November 1970, when I returned from visiting the Scottish poet Ian Hamilton Finlay with a sheet of paper on which he had written a set of instructions, the first being: 'Read Pater's Imaginary Portraits.'[8] The injunction was fulfilled in July 1971, and Finlay congratulated me on reading the work which he ranked as his 'Favourite Book of All', adding the suggestion that I 'might well write a kind of contemporary sequel'.[9] When I subsequently wrote a catalogue essay for Finlay's first major exhibition outside Scotland in 1977, I took the advice of this embattled gardener and neoclassicist, and entitled it: 'Ian Hamilton Finlay: An Imaginary Portrait.' My epigraph derived from the essay on 'Duke Carl of Rosenmold': 'To Apollo, praying that he would come to us from Italy, bringing his lyre with him.'[10]

However it was the stimulus offered by the teaching programme of the new University of Kent at Canterbury that encouraged me to pursue my interest in Pater's work more broadly. Kent was established as a collegiate university, with a Faculty of Humanities that placed a high premium on interdisciplinary contact. Though I was appointed as an Assistant Lecturer in History, I was willingly recruited for a Master's degree by coursework set up by the English Board of Studies, and assisted in planning a seminar course devoted to 'The Modern Movement'. With my colleague Ian Gregor, I designed a course for the first of two terms which began with Flaubert's *Madame Bovary* and continued with sessions involving the major English critics of the later nineteenth century. Pater's focus on Flaubert in the essay on 'Style' provided a running thread in a sequence that continued by way of Arnold, Ruskin, and Morris to Pater and Wilde. Over the following two decades, this pattern persisted, though Rossetti was added to Morris, and Wilde was ultimately replaced by Swinburne.

There was initially some difficulty in advising the students on secondary reading. Of the available collections of extracts from Pater's critical writings, Aldington's summons to 'sensitive and studious youth' did not strike the right note, and Jenny Uglow's collection of 1973 hardly galvanised the class, while concluding that Pater 'does not provide us with authoritative judgements, but with suggestive, personal interpretations'.[11] Thus it was timely that Harold Bloom brought out his *Selected Writings of Walter Pater* in 1974. Bloom had been scrupulous in mentioning earlier work on Pater, commending the work of Ian Fletcher as 'a necessary starting point for all future study'.[12] He did not overvalue Pater's contribution, arguing that Coleridge and Ruskin were of greater eminence as critics, though Pater was 'superior to his older rival, Arnold, and to his disciple, Wilde'.[13] But his insistence on Pater's unique role as a harbinger of Modernism (and his relegation of Arnold) proved forceful enough to generate a vigorous altercation. When I met Bloom at New Haven in the spring of 1978, he was still smarting from an editorial in the *Times Literary Supplement* in which Christopher Ricks had professed himself to be 'someone who believes that Arnold's little finger is worth Pater's whole hand'. Arnold had never doubted, as Ricks argued, that 'the critical faculty is lower than the inventive . . .. But a recent critic of the school of Harold Bloom would accept no such thing'.[14]

The launch of this polemic against Bloom, and the 'Yale School', is a reminder that Pater's works had also circulated widely on the other side of the Atlantic. Many graduate students who took the Kent course on 'The Modern Movement' came from outside Britain, and were not deterred by the equivocal reputation that he still held within the local context of English studies. Although there is no room here to investigate his reputation in the United States over the foregoing period, my conclusion will rest with the curious history of the two volumes of *Marius the Epicurean* (Library Edition, 1921 reprint), which were recently presented to me. These were acquired in the 1970s by a Kent colleague who was studying Comparative Literature at the State University of New York at Buffalo. His elegant bookplate adorns the first volume, and the neat pencil marks indicate his attentive reading. But the second volume exhibits the personal book-plates of two remarkable women: Miss Frank E. Buttolph (1850–1924) and Gretta Brooker (1905–53). Miss Buttolph served as a volunteer at the Astor Library in New York, and her contribution to culinary history derives from the fact that she donated her unrivalled collection of over 25,000 menus to the New York Public Library. The handsome bookplate enshrines her surname between two heavily stacked rows of shelves.

Gretta Brooker, born in St Louis, served as a War Correspondent in Indonesia after graduating from Vassar College in 1925. Her last years were taken up with a vigorous campaign against the persecution of the Christian church in Asia, and she was also well known as a committed feminist. Her bookplate once again shows a well-stocked bookcase, with a female figure absorbed in reading while perched on the topmost stand of a ladder. In my previous 'Afterword' to *Pater the Classicist*, I drew attention to the interest in *Marius the Epicurean* shown by the forgotten English nineteenth-century novelist Florence Montgomery, who covered the opening pages of my two volumes with her copious annotations. Pater's readers have often embellished the printed text with their adornments and their inscriptions. They will surely not cease to engage us as we navigate the perimeter of English Studies.

Notes

1 Harry Bann, 'Miscellany', unpublished memoir (typescript), 4.
2 Robert Bridges, *The Spirit of Man: An Anthology in English & French from the Philosophers & Poets made by the Poet Laureate in 1915* (1919).
3 Bann, 'Miscellany', 19.
4 My cousin's husband, Michael Higginbottom, who was at Haileybury in the 1950s, confirms that the choice of books for such prizes was left to the recipient.
5 Bonamy Dobrée, 'Some Remarks on Prose in England Today', *Sewanee Review* 63 (1955), 631–46 (634–5).
6 Dobrée, 'Some Remarks on Prose', 646.
7 See *Walter Pater: Selected Works*, ed. Richard Aldington (1948), 15.
8 See *Stonypath Days: Letters between Ian Hamilton Finlay and Stephen Bann 1970–72*, ed. Stephen Bann (2016), 99.
9 Bann, *Stonypath Days*, 142.
10 See *Ian Hamilton Finlay*, exh. cat., Serpentine Gallery, London (1977), 7–28.
11 *Walter Pater: Essays on Literature and Art*, ed. Jennifer Uglow (1973), xxii.
12 *Selected Writings of Walter Pater*, ed. Harold Bloom (New York 1974), bibliography, xxxvi.
13 Bloom, *Selected Writings*, xxiv.
14 Christopher Ricks, 'Pater, Arnold and Misquotation', *Times Literary Supplement* (25 November 1977), 1383. The further consequence of this disagreement between Ricks and Bloom was a symposium on Plagiarism published by the *Times Literary Supplement* on 9 April 1982, in which Bloom asserted: 'Great critics like Hazlitt and Pater tended to quote from memory in their essays, and their inevitable misquotations are considerably more enlightening than invariable accuracy could have been' (413).

Walter Pater and English Studies:
A Select Bibliography

COMPILED BY CHARLES MARTINDALE

NB: where London is the place of publication only the publication date is given. *Studies in Walter Pater and Aestheticism* (formerly *The Pater Newsletter*) provides short notices of relevant publications.

General

Buckler, William E., *Walter Pater: The Critic as Artist of Ideas* (New York 1987)

Cheeke, Stephen, *Transfiguration: The Religion of Art in Nineteenth-Century Literature before Aestheticism* (Oxford 2016), especially chapter 7, 'Walter Pater's Indifference', 186–215

Coates, John, *The Rhetorical Use of Provocation as a Means of Persuasion in the Writings of Walter Pater (1839–1894), English Essayist and Cultural Critic: Pater as Controversialist* (New York 2011) – on Pater's engagement with leading writers and thinkers of the day, including Ruskin, Arnold, Swinburne, and Newman

Coste, Bénédicte, *Walter Pater critique littéraire: 'The Excitement of the Literary Sense'* (Grenoble 2010)

Dale, Peter Allan, *The Victorian Critic and the Idea of History: Carlyle, Arnold, Pater* (Cambridge, MA 1977), especially 171–256

Daley, Kenneth, *The Rescue of Romanticism: Walter Pater and John Ruskin* (Athens, OH 2001)

Dean, Paul, 'Pater in Arcadia', *The New Criterion* 37 (2018), 18–22 – review of *Pater the Classicist: Classical Scholarship, Reception, and Aestheticism*, ed. Charles Martindale, Stefano Evangelista, and Elizabeth Prettejohn (Oxford 2017)

Eliot, T. S., 'The Place of Pater', in *The Eighteen-Eighties: Essays by Fellows of the Royal Society of Literature*, ed. Walter de la Mare (Cambridge 1930), 93–106 – otherwise printed as 'Arnold and Pater'

Evangelista, Stefano, 'Rome and the Romantic Heritage in Walter Pater's *Marius the Epicurean*', in *Romans and Romantics*, ed. Timothy Saunders, Charles Martindale, Ralph Pite, and Mathilde Skoie (Oxford 2012), 305–26

Literary Cosmopolitanism in the English Fin de Siècle: Citizens of Nowhere (Oxford 2021), especially 'Introduction: The Small World of the Fin de Siècle', 1–31

Farmer, Albert J., *Walter Pater as a Critic of English Literature: A Study of 'Appreciations'* (Grenoble 1931) – interesting chiefly as the first, and still the only, published monograph on *Appreciations*

Hough, Graham, *The Last Romantics* (1947), chapter 4 on Pater, 134–74 – interesting as an early attempt to give a more sympathetic account of Pater and Aestheticism after the Leavisite opposition to 'belletrism' and the critical dominance of T. S. Eliot

Inman, Billie Andrew, *Walter Pater's Reading: A Bibliography of His Library Borrowings and Literary References, 1858–1873* (New York and London 1981)
Walter Pater and His Reading: 1874–1877: With a Bibliography of His Library Borrowings, 1878–1894 (New York and London 1990)

Kermode, Frank, *Romantic Image* (New York 1957) – Pater is a significant presence throughout

Lee, Adam, *The Platonism of Walter Pater: Embodied Equity* (Oxford 2020) – on the importance of Plato for Pater's aesthetic project and views on education

Loesberg, Jonathan, *Aestheticism and Deconstruction: Pater, Derrida, and De Man* (Princeton, NJ 1991)

McGrath, F. C., *The Sensible Spirit: Walter Pater and the Modernist Paradigm* (Tampa, FL 1986)

Ricks, Christopher, 'Walter Pater, Matthew Arnold and Misquotation', in *The Force of Poetry* (Oxford 1984), 392–416

Saunders, Max, *Self Impression: Life-Writing, Autobiografiction, and the Forms of Modern Literature* (Oxford 2012), especially chapter 1, 'Im/personality: The Imaginary Portraits of Walter Pater', 29–70

Seiler, R. M., ed., *Walter Pater: The Critical Heritage* (1980), 29–33, 194–241 on reviews and early responses to *Appreciations*

Shuter, William F., *Rereading Walter Pater* (Cambridge 2013) – on Pater's habits of self-revision

Wellek, René, 'Walter Pater's Literary Theory and Criticism', *Victorian Studies* 1 (1957), 29–46

Willerton, Christian, 'A Study of Walter Pater's *Appreciations*', PhD dissertation, (University of North Carolina at Chapel Hill 1979)

Williams, Carolyn, *Transfigured World: Walter Pater's Aesthetic Historicism* (Ithaca, NY 1989)

Wong, Alex, ed., *Walter Pater: Selected Essays* (Manchester 2018) – the introduction, 9–39, is probably the best brief account currently available of Pater's critical project

The Development of English Studies as a University Discipline

Atherton, Carol, *Defining Literary Criticism: Scholarship, Authority and the Possession of Literary Knowledge, 1880–2002* (Houndmills 2005), especially chapter 3, 59–95

Collini, Stefan, *Public Moralists: Political Thought and Intellectual Life in Britain 1850–1930* (Oxford and New York 1991)

'Cambridge and the Study of English', in *Cambridge Contributions*, ed. Sarah J. Ormrod (Cambridge 2008), 42–64

Court, Franklin E., *Institutionalizing English Literature: The Culture and Politics of Literary Study, 1750–1900* (Stanford 1992)

Hilliard, Christopher, *English as a Vocation: The 'Scrutiny' Movement* (Oxford 2012)

Lawrie, Alexandra, *The Beginnings of University English: Extramural Study, 1885–1910* (2014) – on the importance of the University Extension Movement, with useful bibliography

Palmer, D. J., *The Rise of English Studies: An Account of the Study of English Language and Literature from Its Origin to the Making of the Oxford English School* (1965) – mainly about the early days of the Oxford English Faculty

Small, Ian, *Conditions for Criticism: Authority, Knowledge, and Literature in the Late Nineteenth Century* (Oxford 1991), especially 'Walter Pater', 91–111 – on the response of Pater and Wilde to the increasing professionalisation of literary study

Tillyard, E. M. W., *The Muse Unchained: An Intimate Account of the Revolution in English Studies at Cambridge* (1958)

Wood, Alison, 'Secularity and the Uses of Literature: English at Cambridge, 1890–1920', *Modern Language Quarterly* 75 (2014), 260–77

The Essay Tradition

Evangelista, Stefano, 'Things Said by the Way: Walter Pater and the Essay', in *On Essays: Montaigne to the Present*, ed. Thomas Karshan and Kathryn Murphy (Oxford 2020), 241–57

Himmelfarb, Gertrude, ed., *The Spirit of the Age: Victorian Essays* (New Haven 2007) – useful introduction on the essay genre in the period (especially 18–27 on the essay as genre), though the selection does not include Pater

Levine, George, and William Madden, 'Introduction', in *The Art of Victorian Prose*, ed. George Levine and William Madden (New York 1968), vii–xxi

Russell, David, *Tact: Aesthetic Liberalism and the Essay Form in Nineteenth-Century Britain* (Princeton, NJ 2017), especially chapter 5, 'Relief-Work: Walter Pater's Tact', 111–41

Pater and Individual English Authors

Browne

Daley, Kenneth, 'Pater's Misrepresentations: The Case of "Sir Thomas Browne"', *Studies in Walter Pater and Aestheticism* 4 (2019), 19–34

Ishikawa, Daichi, 'A Great Chain of Curiosity: Pater's "Sir Thomas Browne" and Its Nineteenth-Century British Context', in *Testing New Opinions and*

Courting New Impressions: New Perspectives on Walter Pater, ed. Anne-Florence Gillard-Estrada, Martine Lambert-Charbonnier, and Charlotte Ribeyrol (New York 2018), 109–24

Coleridge

Andrews, Kit, 'Walter Pater's Lives of Philosophers: Inversions of the Aesthetic Life in "Coleridge's Writings" and "Sebastian van Storck"', in *Testing New Opinions and Courting New Impressions: New Perspectives on Walter Pater*, ed. Anne-Florence Gillard-Estrada, Martine Lambert-Charbonnier, and Charlotte Ribeyrol (New York 2018), 200–17

DeLaura, David J., *Hebrew and Hellene in Victorian England: Newman, Arnold, and Pater* (Austin, TX 1969), chapter 13, '"Coleridge" and the Higher Morality'

Wendling, Ronald C., 'Pater, Coleridge, and the Return of the Platonic', *The Wordsworth Circle* 30 (1999), 94–9

Lamb

Coates, John, 'In Defence of Appreciation: Pater's "Charles Lamb"', *The Charles Lamb Bulletin* 137 (2007) 1–15

Rossetti

McGann, Jerome, 'The Poetry of Dante Gabriel Rossetti (1828–1882)', in *The Cambridge Companion to the Pre-Raphaelites*, ed. Elizabeth Prettejohn (Cambridge 2012), 89–102 – reads Rossetti very much through Pater's essay

Shakespeare

Bate, Jonathan, 'Shakespeare in the Twilight of Romanticism: Wagner, Swinburne, Pater', *Shakespeare Jahrbuch* 146 (2010), 11–25

Martindale, Charles, 'Shakespeare Philosophus', in *Thinking with Shakespeare: Comparative and Interdisciplinary Essays*, ed. William Poole and Richard Scholar (2007), 33–50

Poole, Adrian, *Shakespeare and the Victorians* (2004) – use index

Wordsworth

Bassett, Sharon, 'Wordsworth, Pater, and the "Anima Mundi": Towards a Critique of Romanticism', *Criticism* 17 (1975), 262–75

Becker-Lekrone, Megan, 'Wilde and Pater's Strange Appreciations', *Victoriographies* 1 (2011), 93–126

DeLaura, David J., 'The "Wordsworth" of Pater and Arnold: "The Supreme, Artistic View of Life"', *Studies in English Literature 1500–1900* 6 (1966), 651–67

Gill, Stephen, *Wordsworth and the Victorians* (Oxford 1998) – use index

Jackson, Noel B., 'Rethinking the Cultural Divide: Walter Pater, Wilkie Collins, and the Legacies of Wordsworthian Aesthetics, *Modern Philology* 102 (2004), 207–34

Lee, Adam, *The Platonism of Walter Pater: Embodied Equity* (Oxford 2020), chapter 2, 'The Ethics of Contemplation in Wordsworth', 56–86

Østermark-Johansen, Lene, *Walter Pater and the Language of Sculpture* (Farnham and Burlington, VT 2011), 280–90 and use index

Ward, J. P., 'An Anxiety of No Influence: Walter Pater on William Wordsworth', in *Pater in the 1990s*, ed. Laurel Brake and Ian Small (Greensboro, NC 1991), 63–76

Pater and European Literature

Bann, Stephen, ed., *The Reception of Walter Pater in Europe* (2004)

Clements, Patricia, '"Strange Flowers": Some Notes on the Baudelaire of Swinburne and Pater', *Modern Language Review* 76 (1981), 20–30

Baudelaire and the English Tradition (Princeton, NJ 1985)

Coates, John, 'Pater as Polemicist in "Prosper Mérimée"', *Modern Language Review* 99 (2004), 1–16

Conlon, John J., *Walter Pater and the French Tradition* (Lewisburg, PA 1982)

Daley, Kenneth, 'Pater's *Appreciations* and the Problem of "Feuillet's *La Morte*"', *English Literature in Transition, 1880–1920* 60 (2017), 471–89

Østermark-Johansen, Lene, *Walter Pater's European Imagination* (Oxford 2022)

Spirit, Jane, 'Nineteenth-Century Responses to Montaigne and Bruno', in *Pater in the 1990s*, ed. Laurel Brake and Ian Small (Greensboro, NC 1991), 217–27

Form and Style

Chandler, Edmund, *Pater on Style: An Examination of the Essay on 'Style' and the Textual History of Marius the Epicurean* (Copenhagen 1958)

Cheeke, Stephen, '"Pateresque": The Person, the Prose Style', *Cambridge Quarterly* 46 (2017), 251–69

Coates, John, 'Controversial Aspects of Pater's "Style"', *Papers on Language and Literature* 40 (2004), 384–411

Dowling, Linda, *Language and Decadence in the Victorian Fin de Siècle* (Princeton, NJ 1986), especially chapter 3, 104–74

Hurley, Michael D., and Marcus Waithe, eds, *Thinking Through Style: Non-Fiction Prose of the Long Nineteenth Century* (Oxford 2012), chapter 13 on Pater: Angela Leighton, 'Walter Pater's Dream Rhythms', 217–31

Inman, Billie Andrew, 'Reaction to Saintsbury in Pater's Formulation of Ideas of Prose Style', *Nineteenth-Century Prose* 24 (1997), 108–26

Leighton, Angela, *On Form: Poetry, Aestheticism, and the Legacy of a Word* (Oxford 2007), especially chapter 4, 'Aesthetic Conditions: Pater's Reforming Style', 74–98

Merritt, Travis R., 'Taste, Opinion, and Theory in the Rise of Victorian Prose Stylism', in *The Art of Victorian Prose*, ed. George Levine and William Madden (New York 1968), 3–38

Østermark-Johansen, Lene, 'The Death of Euphues: Euphuism and Decadence in Late-Victorian Literature', *English Literature in Transition, 1880–1920* 45 (2002), 4–25

Prettejohn, Elizabeth, 'The Future of Winckelmann's Classical Form: Walter Pater and Frederic Leighton', *Journal of Latin Cosmopolitanism and European Literature* 6 (2021), 33–56

Waithe, Marcus, '"Strenuous Minds": Walter Pater and the Labour of Aestheticism', in *The Labour of Literature in Britain and France, 1830–1910: Authorial Work Ethics*, ed. Marcus Waithe and Claire White (2018), 147–165 – a fresh take on 'Style'

Index

Note: Page numbers in italics refer to figures. Page numbers followed by "n" refer to notes.

CAMBRIDGE STUDIES IN NINETEENTH-CENTURY
LITERATURE AND CULTURE

GENERAL EDITORS
Kate Flint, *University of Southern California*
Clare Pettitt, *King's College London*

Titles published